ELGAR AND CHIVALRY

ROBERT ANDERSON

Other books on Elgar by Robert Anderson

Elgar in Manuscript
Elgar (Dent Master Musicians series)

Also published by Elgar Editions

The Music of Elgar series:
The Best of Me - A Gerontius Centenary Companion
ed Geoffrey Hodgkins
Oh, My Horses! - Elgar and the Great War ed Lewis Foreman

Other titles:
In the Bavarian Highlands by Peter Greaves
Half-Century: The Elgar Society 1951-2001 ed Michael Trott

ELGAR
AND CHIVALRY

ROBERT ANDERSON

𝄴𝄴 Elgar Editions

Published in Great Britain by

Elgar Editions

the publishing imprint of

Elgar Enterprises
20 High Street, Rickmansworth, Herts WD3 1ER
(e-mail : editions@elgar.org)

© Robert Anderson, 2002

First Published : November 2002

British Library Cataloguing in Publication Data
A Catalogue record for this book
is available from the British Library

ISBN 0 9537082 5 X (Elgar Editions)

Printed and bound in Great Britain by Antony Rowe Ltd,
Bumper's Farm, Chippenham, Wiltshire

*Frontispiece: 'poor B.K!' - a sketch by Elgar in a letter to A.J.Jaeger
postmarked 6 December 1897.*

Contents

To

Anthony Payne

for his achievement and inspiration

Foreword

Having written two books on Elgar, I had no intention of embarking on a third. *Elgar in Manuscript* (1990) had examined his working methods; the Master Musicians *Elgar* (1993) covered within tight compass his life and attempted brief analyses of his compositions. What else remained? The complete correspondence, instigated by the riches that Percy Young, Wulstan Atkins, and above all Jerrold Northrop Moore had already placed before us; or deconstruction of the music towards the doubtful entertainment of Schenkerian graphs. Neither course appealed. While idly passing a pleasant life, I was persuaded to attend the Festival Hall concert of 17 February 1998. I went under protest, aware of Elgar's deathbed injunction concerning the Third Symphony, and as familiar as any with the jumble of a jigsaw his sketches presented. Nor even a jigsaw, indeed, where, at the mercy of manifold frustrations, an ultimate design exists. The first movement offered an exposition draft and some scoring. But where was a development in the thematic bits and bobs that was all Elgar vouchsafed? The 'Scherzo' movement seemed to offer most, but thereafter hope must surely be abandoned, if only because Elgar seemed touchingly uncertain where the Symphony was heading and how it might end. I therefore entered the Festival Hall a reluctant sceptic. I came out a grateful convert, astonished at the splendour of Anthony Payne's achievement, result of an intuitive understanding and indomitable persistence that were above praise. If there was also the germ of a book at the back of my mind, any outcome must be dedicated, to the plaudits of most Elgarians, with affectionate gratitude to Anthony Payne.

The Elgar works I am prepared to hold up before any world tribunal remain those championed in the Master Musicians volume : *The Dream of Gerontius, The Kingdom*, the 'Enigma' Variations, the Introduction and Allegro, *Falstaff*, Cello Concerto and String Quartet. Symphony no.2 clamours for admission, but both symphonies and the violin concerto depend so crucially on sympathetic performance that I reserve them for my own mental rehearsal. Having been deprived for the best part of ten years by the baleful result of take-overs and the devious workings of our Byzantine European Union of study access to Elgar sketches, drafts and MS scores towards a Complete Edition, I have actually heard more of his music. It remains a wonder to me, not always in matter, but in manner. Not all his thematic ideas are up to his best standard, but their presentation and scoring is impeccable. If sometimes an excess of tromboning makes me laugh, it is with pleasure that such brave noises could once come out of this country; but more often the subtle dovetailing and doubling of instruments fills me with humble admiration at the fineness of ear that could capture such wonders from the air.

While listening in the Third Symphony to the 'Arthur' music that Elgar intended should feature in two of its movements, prominently and with all its chivalric associations, I thought back to *Froissart*, that first utterance of a confident young genius, and wondered whether there were links to bind them. With '*nobilmente*' as characteristic rallying cry, Elgar's music seems so often a tribute to the chivalry his generation espoused and has become more and more acceptable as its embodiment. Fifteen chapters of the book attach themselves to fifteen of Elgar's works. Not all are masterpieces, far from it; but each has a background that went towards the formation of Elgar's character and hence his music. If some chapters almost avoid his name, at least they hint at his wide-ranging interests and the delight he took in exploring the rich culture of late-Victorian and Edwardian England. I note with a certain wry pleasure that few names occurring in the book began life in the last century; it is none the poorer for that. It might be argued that the chivalry instilling so much vitality into Elgar's music was the same force that drove Europe towards hideous warfare. Arthur as once and future king had been a powerful symbol throughout the 19th century and remained so until 1914. Had he then been spirited finally across the lonely mere by the black-robed queens to Avalon never to return? Had his rediscovered 'tomb' at Glastonbury with those mighty bones been only empty legend? Had he rather been mangled to extinction in the bloody trenches of France? Elgar was out of love with the post-war world, but he was stirred to heal the personal wound of his wife's death with an attempt at 1923 music that might be worthy of the Round Table and its ideals.

Much can be made of the sicknesses, neuroses, depressions, and morbid imaginings that afflicted Elgar the man; more should be made of the wondrous virility and strength that infects so much of the music, and of the wayward sensitivity that is its shy and dreamlike complement. I have no means of gauging how significant to Elgar was the material I have marshalled towards the understanding of each work. Music has a capricious and indeed enviable knack of detaching itself from its surroundings. At best I may have hit upon some points fundamental to Elgar's inspiration; at worst I have produced an anthology that Elgar might well have enjoyed, that has given me enormous pleasure in the browsing, and may inspire others to investigate byways of English culture that were also Elgarian haunts. If I have hinted also at the characters of people Elgar leaned on as man and musician, friends not 'pictured within', but friends who received the gratitude of a dedication perhaps, his personal context is the more enriched.

At the instigation of Bernard Shaw, the BBC commissioned Symphony no.3 towards the end of 1932. Early in the following year Elgar was writing in agonised astonishment at what was happening in Germany. The vulgarity and frivolity of the 1920s had been painful to him, and it is not difficult to imagine how he would have reacted to the Second World War and its aftermath. The nonsensical jingoism at the end of *Caractacus* presupposed an empire on which the sun would never set, and probably not even Bernard Shaw, dying in 1950 to the extinction from deep sorrow and regret of all the lights in Delhi, imagined the empire would collapse within a decade. To the advantage of the world? Perhaps not. The BBC had to wait sixty-six years for its Symphony, by which time the streets of London were paved less with gold than chewing gum.

Near the end of Shaw's *Man and Superman*, John Tanner is allowed a 'Stray Saying' that contains the nub of the matter : 'In moments of progress the noble succeed, because things are going their way : in moments of decadence the base succeed for the same reasons : hence the world is never without the exhilaration of contemporary success.' So it has been entirely natural for *The Times* to increase its circulation by redefining 'music' in a way many younger than Elgar find unacceptable and to decide there is no limit to the depths of popularity reviews might sound with advantage. The Worshipful Company of Musicians, for which Elgar wrote his string *Elegy*, has found jazz evenings a rewarding experiment. The *Newest Grove* plays the Beach Boys off against Beethoven, and Mozart neighbours 'Madonna', when unoccupied with uttering expletives at the award of the Turner prize. Lady Elgar's 'Demos' has not only demanded his due but triumphed unreservedly.

John Ruskin, unaware of television and much else, passionately recommended books to 'Demos'. A small library, he said. Elgar's was large, but no man's library represents exactly his reading list. My complete Scott, for instance, has a number of uncut pages, magical secrets kept for more than a hundred years. The scattering of Elgar's library means we lack an essential index to his thinking, the more so since he would often underline or make marginal jotting for derision or approval.[1] The chivalric aspirations Elgar grew up with and which his music so nobly

[1] The range and extent of Elgar's books on chivalry must remain unknown; but there exist in the collection of Arthur Reynolds four handsome volumes on heraldry once owned by Elgar; three were published under the auspices of the 'De Walden Library': *Some Feudal Lords and their Seals, 1301* (London, n.d.), *Banners, Standards and Badges from a Tudor Manuscript in the College of Arms* (London, 1904) and Joseph Foster, *Two Tudor Books of Arms, being Harleian Manuscrips 2169 and 6163* (London, 1904); *British Heraldic Art to the end of the Tudor Period* was published for the Burlington Fine Arts Club (London, 1916). All have Elgar's Severn House 'sticker' on the inside front cover.

enshrines trickled even into my own childhood. At six, my first school prize for 'general progress' was *King Arthur's Knights* by Henry Gilbert, with illustrations by Walter Crane and an introduction dating to 1911. Longfellow poetry came three years later for 'perfect attendance'; the volume included *Hiawatha* and *Tales of a Wayside Inn* with 'The Saga of King Olaf'. *Ivanhoe* was awarded at my prep. school and then, for 'Latin grammar', Scott's poetry. I read none of the books at the time.

In his *Intelligent Person's Guide to Modern Culture* (London, 1998), p.63, Roger Scruton makes for Wagner claims that Elgar for the most part acknowledged :

> In the mature operas of Wagner our civilisation gave voice for the last time to its idea of the heroic, through music which strives to endorse that idea to the full extent of its power. And because Wagner was a composer of supreme genius, perhaps the only one to have taken forward the intense inner language forged by Beethoven and to have used it to conquer the psychic spaces that Beethoven shunned, everything he wrote in his mature idiom has the ring of truth, and every note is both absolutely right and profoundly surprising.

No such claim could be made for Elgar, who would accept commissions to produce work below his best, turn out commercial winners on the ground that symphonies would not pay. No composer has ever had Wagner's fierce conviction, single mindedness or ruthlessness, call it what you will; nor it must be said, has any other composer managed to create a Ludwig II of Bavaria. Elgar, however, remained true to the early teaching of his mother, to the ideals his wife so generously espoused in her own writings, to his own inheritance as one of 'nature's gentlemen', and above all to a musical language forged from the essence of his being that could indeed attempt the heroic and achieve it.

Elgar's inspiration came largely from places, people and books. The books led naturally to pictures and to the architecture he admired. The people I have concentrated on at the outset are his mother Ann Elgar, and his future wife Alice Roberts, with her Indian, cultural and social heritage. The remarkable gallery of the Elgars' friends is touched on the more as they impinge on individual works; but their support and encouragement were crucial, and many received a dedication in return for it. The places begin with Broadheath as an almost chance extension of the Worcester that, with its grand Cathedral, remained as central to Elgar all his life as the Malvern Hills. Rome is the only great foreign city that retained the Elgars for any length of time. How far the grandeur of its antiquities and the artistic wealth within such a range of magnificent churches influenced the transformation of a 1907 string quartet into the magisterial Symphony no.1 we cannot know. All we know is Elgar's sensitivity to his surroundings, as made clear in countless letters. Tintagel, too, summed up by association his gratitude to Alice Stuart Wortley and his debt to Wagner in its final bars.

Elgar's composer successors caused him little pleasure. He was not to know that in the fullness of time they would discover the broad and enticing highway of serial music; regrettably it turned out to be a *cul-de-sac*, and there seemed no alternative to retreat into a series of ivory towers of increasing rarity and isolation. It was against such a scene of cultural emptiness that the Elgar-Payne Third Symphony suddenly showed for a moment that music might be music again. The Symphony's astonishing progress since the première indicated not that Arthur was king once more but that still, *nobilmente*, sounds might come out of Avalon to stir the spirit.

The chronological framework of the book owes everything to the labours of Jerrold Northrop Moore, in transcription of the Elgar diaries and publication of correspondence. When I have needed to consult holdings at the Elgar Birthplace Museum, Chris Bennett has proved a mine of information and resourceful helpmeet. Arthur Reynolds has whetted my appetite with the riches of his collection and supplied books and pictures to enhance my knowledge. Copyright owners have been approached where possible, and I am particularly grateful to the Superior of the Edgbaston Oratory for his gracious permission to quote whatever I wished from Cardinal Newman's works. The Bavarian State Museums at Munich have permitted reproduction of *The Happy Warrior* by Watts, and the executors of the Herbert Reed estate have allowed the printing of his poem on the subject.

The Executive of the Elgar Society, in their guise as Directors of Elgar Editions, decided on publication of the book before most of it had been perused, and I am touched by such an act of faith. Above all, I am indebted, more than I can say, to the patience, skill and encouragement of John Norris, who has overseen every aspect of the book's production.

October 2002 Robert Anderson

1 - Whence is thy learning?

Chivalry is only a name for that general spirit or state of mind which disposes men to heroic and generous actions and keeps them conversant with all that is beautiful and sublime in the intellectual and moral world.[1]

Edward Dent (1876-1957) was rightly questioned about his article on modern English music in Guido Adler's *Handbuch der Musikgeschichte* of 1924 and 1930. At the time it was written, the proportions were wrong, with Elgar much reduced in comparison with Parry and Stanford; whether the latest *Grove* has been justified in so totally reversing the position is another matter. Shrewd critic that he was, Dent was not altogether inaccurate in his Elgar paragraphs. There was no doubt about 'the unusual glamour of his orchestration' or the 'glowing expression of his music'. Liszt may well have been 'abhorrent to conservative academic musicians'; his worst works make a strong case. Yet Elgar had never directed his appeal at such a body, any more than Wagner had. The Catholicism was a disadvantage, but Elgar wasted no time in hitching his muse to the Anglican bandwagon. For many post-war English ears Elgar may well have seemed 'too emotional', and few Elgarians would claim that the music is 'quite free from vulgarity'. Dent selected *Falstaff* as the finest orchestral work, even if Elgar's essay remained required reading for all its intricacies to be understood. The rest, symphonies, concertos and overtures were dismissed as 'pompous' and aiming at 'too chivalrous a mode of expression'. 'Ritterlich' is the German; 'knightly' or 'gentlemanly' might do as translations.

The First World War, inspiring Britain's young to hurl themselves into the trenches and be mown down by the myriad in France and Flanders gave pause to the exaltation of chivalry and knighthood. It became the War to end War, but proved to be only the first phase of another Thirty Years' War that wasted Europe even more thoroughly than its 17th-century counterpart. It may well be that the Kaiser could have achieved his essential aims without war;[2] but in 1924 the devastating alternative had run its course and the spirit that launched the war was largely discredited. By the end of the 20th century nobility of expression and notions of chivalry were at a premium. This accounts to some extent for the rapid increase in Elgar's popularity from the fiftieth anniversary of his death in 1984 and

[1] Digby, Kenelm: *The Broad Stone of Honour*, Godefridus

[2] Davies, Norman: *Europe* (Oxford, 1996), p.854

above all for the rapturous reception of the Elgar-Payne Third Symphony.

As Dent remarked, Elgar 'first attracted attention in 1890', with the *Froissart* overture. He had in fact conceived most of the music before he gave the work its title. But he owned his copy of Froissart (c.1337-c.1410) and had marked the odd passage that delighted him. The piece is redolent of the tumultuous spirit that Walter Scott (1771-1832) describes in his *Encyclopaedia Britannica* article on chivalry (1818), with Froissart as exultant 'at the encounter of a body of men-at-arms' as the Lord's war-horse, delineated in the book of *Job*: 'He saith among the trumpets, Ha ha; and he smelleth the battle afar off, the thunder of the captains, and the shouting.' At such a moment, writes Scott, 'Froissart's heart never fails to overflow'. He goes on to describe Froissart's attendant circumstances, not shirking the bloodshed: 'The waving of banners and pennons, the dashing of spurs into the side of chargers, and their springing forward to battle; the glittering of armour, the glancing of plumes, the headlong shock and splintering of the lances, the swords flashing through the dust over the heads of the combatants, the thunder of the horses' feet and the clash of armour, mingled with the war-cry of the combatants and the groans of the dying, form the mingled scene of tumult, strife, and death, which the Canon has so frequently transferred to his chivalrous pages.'

Of course Froissart mentions King Arthur (? 6th cent.); Sir Walter is also one of the first to reopen the pages of Malory (d.1471) to 19th-century literature. Arthur and the Round Table knights feature in some Scott poetry and in many textual notes of explanation. Elgar's love of Scott is a leitmotif throughout his career. On 7 January 1887 Elgar writes to Dr. Buck (1851-1932): 'These holidays have been dull; as they are nearly past I look back and find a miserable record of wasted time. I have read three of Scott's Novels - written 3 Ballet airs & partly scored 'em - & coloured a clay pipe.' Which novels were they? Perhaps *Old Mortality* was among them, where Grahame of Claverhouse (?1649-89) urges the young hero to read Froissart. *Redgauntlet* may also have been added at that time, which later gave Elgar disreputable command of the 'Jumpynge Jennye' (the spelling is Elgar's refinement on Scott) from which as Nanty Ewart he 'hiccougheth acknowledgement' of instructions from the three Cavalier sons of 'WMB' in the 'Enigma' Variations (1899). Elgar's *Times Literary Supplement* letter of 21 July 1921 makes reference to a further quintet of novels in connection with Shakespeare (1564-1616): *Waverley, The Antiquary, Ivanhoe, Kenilworth* and *St.Ronan's Well.*

The Arthurian world first impinged on Elgar the composer in connection with opera suggestions. Among them in 1909 was Binyon's *The Madness of Merlin*, a tale based on a northern Merlin rich in prophecy appearing in Geoffrey of Monmouth's *Historia regum Britanniae* (c.1136). Elgar rejected the proposed libretto, and Binyon

Scott's home at Abbotsford

decided to make of it a three-act poetic drama. He died in 1943 with only one act of fourteen scenes complete. But with his *Arthur* play based on Malory he was more successful in stirring Elgar's interest, having also written his *Tintagel* and *The Death of Tristram*. Elgar's contribution in 1923 became the first original music he had written since the death of Lady Elgar (1848-1920) almost three years before. Fragments of the music went towards Elgar's unfinished opera, *The Spanish Lady*; but more significant was the decision to recycle much of the music for the second and fourth movements in Symphony no 3. Elgar covered his traces by allowing no mention of the *Arthur* project in Basil Maine's (1893-1972) two-volume book of 1933.

Elgar's interest in literature may not have been systematic, but it was curious and wide. Elgar's trade, as Bernard Shaw (1856-1950) was to say, was the composition of music: the wonder is that he amassed as impressive a collection of books as he did. There is a delightful letter to Edward Speyer (1837-1934) of 20 January 1912 expressing gratitude for the offer of bookshelves to grace Severn House: 'I have told my books & they are in a state of great glorification - although most of them are on the floor, which attitude, after all has been known to express high exaltation - or the after effects! Anyhow they learn to behave and to seat themselves on your shelves.' An inventory of January 1913, taken for insurance purposes when the books were properly exalted in more seemly fashion, mentions shelves of them in seven rooms. Reference works are legion, including fifteen volumes of the *Catholic Encyclopaedia*, the *Cambridge History of English Literature* in nine volumes, and *Klassiker der Kunst* in eighteen. Poets such as Chaucer, Scott, Keats, Shelley, Tennyson, Matthew Arnold, Rossetti, Morris, to name only those apt to my present purpose, are enumerated with some show of completeness; soon enough the task of complete listing becomes the shorthand of 'Novels, &c. Small - 41', 'Racine Corneille etc. - 39', 'Goethe, Schiller, Grimm - 36'. The *disjecta membra* at the Elgar Birthplace give little impression of Elgar's holding before the death of Lady Elgar ensured its dispersal; but it was not for nothing that Sir Sidney Colvin (1845-1927) had Elgar elected a member of the Literary Society earlier in 1920.

It would be difficult to overemphasise the influence of Sir Walter Scott on those Elgar turned to during his working life. To name only authors closely associated with Elgar, Longfellow (1807-82) has many echoes of the Scott poetry he read when young, and was stimulated to investigate the European world of mediaeval chivalry through Scott novels. Cardinal Newman (1801-90) rated Scott among the finest of writers, and was twice a house guest at Abbotsford, Scott's baronial mansion near the ruined abbey of Melrose; by that time the Scott descendants were Catholic. Ruskin (1819-1900) was a devoted admirer, with *Redgauntlet* a favourite novel and his last rowing-boat on Coniston Water in the Lake District anticipating Elgar with the name of 'Jumping Jenny', the craft of Nanty Ewart. William Morris (1834-96) is supposed to have devoured the Waverley novels by the age of seven; certainly he rode through Epping Forest in a miniature suit of armour as a lad in search of chivalrous adventure.

Froissart's early maturity was spent at the English court of Edward III (1327-77) in the service of Queen Philippa (c.1314-69) of Hainault. This gave him firsthand knowledge of plans to found the Order of the Garter, of jousts and tournaments associated with the event, and the establishment of St.George as patron saint of England. It was natural that when Elgar celebrated the Diamond Jubilee of Queen Victoria in 1897, St. George should be the subject of a festal offering. Froissart followed Edward III to France. The wanderers launched by William Morris on their vain quest for the 'Earthly Paradise' (1868-70) in a book well known to Elgar, encounter the king in mid-Channel. He tried in vain to divert them to the wars in France. They continue over the western ocean until, disillusioned, they settle at 'a nameless city in a distant sea' and begin, in company with the local elders, a series of monthly tales in imitation of Chaucer (c.1343-1400). After the victory of Crécy (1346), Edward III had his last stand before Calais. There took place the episode of the Calais burghers, celebrated by Shakespeare, if it be he, in the uncanonical play of *Edward III* and in impish fashion, with dramatic twist towards the undoing of Queen Philippa, by Bernard Shaw. *The Six of Calais* was the first play Shaw wrote after Elgar's death. The mini-preface is dated 'On the High Seas, 28th May 1935', and Shaw's programme note declares his aim: 'Nothing remained for me but to correct Froissart's follies and translate Rodin into words.'

Various places in the Elgars' journeyings reminded them of chivalrous matters. In 1893 their Bavarian tour took them to the Bethell establishment in Garmisch. This was an obvious and favourite place for them because Henry Slingsby Bethell was a Catholic and had grown up under the watchful eye of John Henry Newman. He and his brother Augustus had their initial education before the founding of the Oratory School in Newman's Edgbaston (1859); but both were in Newman's house at the Catholic University in Dublin. A further pair of Bethell boys went to the Oratory School. By this time Elgar knew well the *Dream of Gerontius* poem (1865); it is unthinkable that Newman was not discussed at Garmisch. Their Wagner experiences in Munich are well documented. *Tristan* plunged them once more into Wagner's heady interpretation of the Arthurian world; with the *Ring* they were immersed in the heroic world of the *Nibelungenlied* and Norse saga; while in *Tannhäuser* it was the singing-knights of mediaeval Germany and the hero's sins at the court of Venus that detained them. It was also the year of an art exhibition at the Munich Glaspalast with important works by G F Watts (1817-1904) and Böcklin (1827-1901). In April 1891 the Elgars had visited the Watts studio in Holland Park Road, and Alice was to extol his work in her essay 'The Ideal in the Present'. Among the paintings they saw was *The Happy Warrior*, bought by the government of Bavaria (1893).

Bavaria was again the main base for the Elgars' 1894 holiday; but this time they continued to Austria and Innsbruck. They were following Paul Flemming, hero of Longfellow's *Hyperion* (1839), in visiting the Hofkirche. They were amazed and moved by the more than life-size statues surrounding the cenotaph of the Holy Roman Emperor, Maximilian I (1508-19). One figure particularly struck Elgar: 'saw monument to *King Arthur*'. The Elgars were so impressed by this solemn array, among whom Arthur was an improbable Count of Habsburg, that they revisited the church on the following two days. Nor was that all. They returned to Innsbruck in August 1895, when they 'attended Mass by Maximilian tomb'. Such was their fascination that they were in Innsbruck twice more, returning from Italy in 1909. It was 'beautiful nearing the mountains', and on 8 June they went 'to the Church, quite as impressive as ever'. Elgar and Carice were back the next day before the family went on to visit Richard Strauss (1864-1949) in Garmisch. In Innsbruck yet again to arrange the journey home, they paid final respects to Maximilian and his astonishing entourage.

Heidelberg was where Longfellow was planning to spend his winter even before his wife Mary died at Rotterdam in November 1835, and it was there he sent his *alter ego* Paul Flemming in *Hyperion*. Longfellow disconsolate had paced the castle terrace and wandered the banks of the Neckar. He had made Paul Flemming take part in literary and philosophical debate, witnessing also the height of student arrogance and riotous behaviour. The Elgars came to Heidelberg at the end of their first Bavarian holiday. Their arrival and progress to the hotel above the castle on 11 August 1892 was delayed by a student procession. Elgar wrote to his mother about it the next day:

> Then when driving up here we suddenly had to stop and make way for a great procession of students - torchlight. The three duelling guilds with a brass band and marching - all their faces wounded (silly fools) & many with bandages on, gay uniforms & no end of torches: it did remind me of Hyperion & the beer scandal etc. etc.

That day the Elgars visited the castle, perhaps lingering before the Elizabeth Tower, named after a daughter of James I (1603-25) married to the count palatine Frederick V (1610-32), and gazing with incredulity at the great barrel with reputed capacity in one of the cellars of 300,000

Maximilian with his entourage

bottles. In the evening there were 'Moonlight views of Schloss & Neckar'.

Ten days in February 1907 encompassed the Elgars' first exploration of Rome. They had been with the Gortons on Capri and arrived in Rome without a hotel reservation. The Bethells happened to have a house there and took them in. There was preliminary investigation of the Capitol and the Vatican. Within two days there was a significant diary entry: 'Rome beginning to impress us deeply.' Elgar met Lorenzo Perosi (1872-1956), director of music at the Sistine Chapel, who showed him the Borgia rooms in the Vatican and his own apartment. The Elgars' decision for a winter in Rome was therefore no surprise. Elgar brought with him an incomplete string quartet when they arrived on 7 November. Within a month the quartet music had been requisitioned for the First Symphony and Elgar had decided not to proceed with his 'Apostles' project for the Birmingham Festival of 1909. In the four and a half Roman months the city was thoroughly scoured. The terse entries of Lady Elgar's diaries were supplemented by the fuller account of Carice, now seventeen and accompanying her father on many jaunts. Elgar's fascination with Rome lingered long after his faith waned, in poring over Piranesi (1720-78) prints and purchasing some. As he explained to Lady Elgar, they prevented his being bothered with small or trivial things: 'looking at these made one think *great* again'.

A main aim of Elgar's west-country tour with Frank Schuster (1852-1927) was to call on the Stuart Wortleys at Tintagel, a visit often urged on Elgar. Initially the April 1910 weather was against them, as reported by Clare, the Stuart Wortley daughter: 'The afternoon of their arrival, we all walked down to the sea in the 'Cove', below the Castle ruins; and saw it all in very bad weather, at its most stern and forbidding.' Indeed Elgar thought back to 1901, and considered the Welsh coast at Llangranog finer. What was it about Tintagel that made him append its name to the short score, MS full score and printed full score of Symphony no.2 (1911)? Careggi, The Hut, Venice and Plas Gwyn are well documented as sources of inspiration or concentrated work on the symphony; yet their names make spasmodic appearance on the material. Only Tintagel persists throughout. Elgar may have known or not about Tintagel as landing stage for early amphorae and wines from the eastern Mediterranean. Undoubtedly he had read of Arthur's supposed conception at the site. Perhaps he had investigated the fascinating history of Richard of Cornwall (1209-72), whose ruined castle still clings to the formidable rocky outcrop. The answer, though, lies on the symphony's last page, at the *crescendo* and *forte-piano* bars, where the conclusion of Wagner's *Tristan und Isolde* is suggested for a moment. Legend has it that King Mark's castle was at Tintagel.

Arthur in the
Hofkirche

Worcester was not Elgar's birthplace. It was true enough, as his sister Lucy's memoir (1912) makes abundantly clear, that their mother's heart was in the country, and the move to Broadheath could only have delighted her. Of equal importance is the fact that the Cathedral was being thoroughly restored from 1857 to 1874, first by A.E.Perkins, a local architect under the patronage of the Earl of Dudley, then by George Gilbert Scott (1811-78). This involved Perkins in rebuilding the Cathedral's east end, changing a large Perpendicular window into five 'Early English' lancets. The Elgars, as Lucy wrote, lived 'within the shadow of our dear, dear Cathedral' and such works would have been a major disturbance. But from boyhood Elgar haunted the Cathedral. The choir stalls are by Gilbert Scott, but lurking below are misericords of 1379, with such spurs to chivalry (Edward III was only two years dead) as knights at the tilt, the loser being encouraged with a kick from behind by his lady; two griffins opposed by a knight; a dragon fighting a lion; a knight hawking. There are also such heraldic beasts as a sphinx and a cockatrice. Look to the spandrels of the Lady Chapel, where a knight fights a centaur, and in the south-east transept is a knight with a lion. The tower of the Cathedral was as important in its way as the Malvern Hills. His dislocated thoughts wandered there soon after the outbreak of the First World War; he would visit it as often as he could before finally settling at Worcester in 1929. The Cathedral was the site of many Elgar triumphs, but it was not till he scored the *Severn Suite* for full orchestra in 1932 that the Cathedral had a direct celebration in music. This was the third fugal movement originally written for piano in 1923.

In his speech when receiving the Freedom of Worcester in 1905, Elgar ascribed his position 'to the influence of my mother'. He continued: 'I was brought up in a knowledge of literature and English and many of the things which my mother said to me I have tried to carry out in my music.' The previous March, his inaugural lecture at Birmingham University had spoken of a music growing 'out of our own soil, something broad, noble, chivalrous', and it is only necessary to consult Ann Elgar's scrapbooks at the Elgar Birthplace to sense her presence in her son's music. Interspersed, for instance, with an illustration of the Glastonbury Thorn and reproduction of Holman Hunt's (1827-1910) *The Light of the World* are a couple of extracts on General Gordon of Khartoum (1833-85). The first recounts his skill as draftsman: 'It has even been said that to it he was largely indebted for the extraordinary successes which he achieved over the Taipings, having before his appointment by the Chinese Government devoted a considerable time to a survey of the region in which the rebellion broke out.' The second quotes Frank Power's diary:

the Mahdi has gone down before him, and to-day sent him a 'salam' or message of welcome. It is wonderful that one man could have such an influence on 200,000 people. Numbers of women flock here every day to ask him to touch their children to cure them; they call him the 'Father and the Saviour of the Soudan.' He has found me badly up in Thomas a Kempis, which he reads every day, and has given me an 'Imitation of Christ.' He is indeed, I believe, the greatest and best man of this century.

It was Frank Power who received General Gordon's copy of *The Dream of Gerontius*, with passages marked that particularly interested him. Newman was concerned as much as any with the fate of Gordon, since old boys from the Oratory School were in the force despatched too late to rescue him, and some did not survive. He was the more moved, therefore, when the sister of the dead Power sent him Gordon's marked copy of the *Dream*. Father Neville at the Oratory made copies of the markings, and Elgar gave such a marked copy to Alice Roberts after the death of her mother in May 1887, receiving another at the time of his marriage two years later. So much for inspiration towards *The Dream of Gerontius*. The death of Gordon in January 1885 was stimulus enough for some commemorative work, but as yet Elgar was no more ready for a 'Gordon' symphony than for a setting of *Gerontius*.

More timely stimulus for a 'Gordon' symphony came in September 1898. There had been widespread feeling in Britain that Gordon must be avenged. The Sirdar of the Egyptian army was Sir Herbert Kitchener (1850-1916). Initially British policy oscillated between building the Aswan Dam or reconquering the Sudan. The Sudan took precedence and Kitchener, responsible to the Foreign Office rather than the War Office, undertook the task. Meticulous in his planning, Kitchener kept every detail of the campaign under his personal control, leaving little to chance. Supplies for the relief expedition to Gordon had gone by the Nile; Kitchener preferred a railway. Freak storms impeded work on the track, but the line was built. On 1 January 1898 Kitchener requested four more battalions; further reinforcements came later, and on 2 September Kitchener won the murderous battle of Omdurman, near Khartoum. Two days later the British and Egyptian flags were flying from the wreckage of Gordon's palace.

The naval aide-de-camp to the Gordon relief force of 1884 was Lord Charles Beresford (1846-1919), recommended by the Prince of Wales. Many years later he received the dedication of Elgar's *The Fringes of the Fleet*. Beresford's memoirs give a graphic account of his narrow escape from beneath casualties inflicted by a Dervish charge. At ease in the highest social circles, it was he who bestowed the name of 'Souls' on an exclusive coterie of beautiful people, among whom Arthur Balfour (1848-

1930) was the main intellect. Beresford resigned from the Board of Admiralty in January 1888 to criticise naval unpreparedness, and a major conflict developed subsequently with John Fisher (1841-1920). In May 1905 he took command of the Mediterranean Fleet, and that September Elgar received an invitation from Lady Charlie (d.1922) through Frank Schuster that he should join the fleet for a Mediterranean cruise. It would involve visits to mainland Greece, Greek islands, Constantinople and Smyrna (the modern Izmir), which produced the only musical reminiscence of the trip. Friendship with the Beresfords remained cordial till their deaths.

Elgar had further connection with the senior service. The baronet Sir George Warrender (1860-1917) also had a command in the Mediterranean fleet. In 1894 he married Lady Ethel Maud Ashley, a daughter of the Earl of Shaftesbury. It was she who first met the Elgars, at a dinner after Steinbach (1855-1916) had conducted the 'Enigma' Variations with his Meiningen orchestra on 20 November 1902. Singer enough to perform publicly with success, she was the most sympathetic of the naval quartet. Elgar dedicated to her the song *Pleading*, and referred to her as 'that rare creature' after she sang the alto solo in *The Music Makers* for Nicholas Kilburn (1843-1923). Sir George became involved with the implications of increasing gun power and the new menace of the torpedo. The main concern till 1914 was the build-up of German naval power. As late as May 1914 Warrender was at Kiel for the Kaiser's (1888-1941) birthday celebrations, when he was both tactful and observant. Later in 1914 he was aiming to intercept German cruisers which had bombarded Scarborough, Whitby and Hartlepool. Because of mist and fog the Germans escaped. On the other side Admiral Tirpitz (1849-1930) felt the commander of the High Seas Fleet controlled the fate of Germany at that moment.

The last of the Elgars' important naval contacts was Sir Julian Corbett (1864-1922). The Elgars were at Brinkwells in Sussex for much of 1918, and the Corbetts were nearby if more grandly at Stopham Manor. The Colvins were mutual friends. He had practised at the bar, written novels, and travelled widely. As correspondent of the *Pall Mall Gazette*, he reported on the initial stages of Kitchener's Sudan campaign, but his lasting reputation was as a naval historian. On 26 September 1918 Elgar regretted in a letter to Colvin that the Corbetts were leaving so soon. As Lady Elgar remarked, Sir Julian's presence meant 'E's flood of talk let loose'. On 16 August of the following year, while fishing Elgar stepped on a wasps' nest as the Corbetts were passing in a boat. Elgar's reaction was commendably restrained: 'Sir Julian sd. he only heard words that sounded like 'dear me'!!!' Corbett's first major contribution to naval history was *Drake and the Tudor Navy* (1898). His Drake interest continued with *Papers relating to the Navy during the Spanish War, 1585-1587,* produced the same year. His final task was to write the three volumes of *Naval Operations*, the official history of the First World War at sea. Much, and notably his account of the battle of Jutland (1916) was inevitably controversial. The last volume was published posthumously in 1923. Like Colvin, Corbett was a member of the Literary Society Elgar was to join.

Elgar's moustache and bearing, however, were military rather than naval, doubtless owing something to his wife's family tradition. He was proud during the Boer War to produce *Pomp and Circumstance* Marches as a troubadour of old at the head of a fighting force; he would beat the imperial drum even for a Caractacus in chains; and the award of the Order of Merit in 1911 (Kitchener had been the first recipient) put him, he felt, far ahead of Sir Henry Gee Roberts (1800-1860) and his KCMG. Yet Sir Henry had seen distinguished action in India, not least during the 1857 mutiny, the year of Elgar's birth. He was called on to relieve a very difficult situation at Kota in Rajasthan. The British agent and his sons had been murdered, and the Maharao was under rebel threat within his palace inside the great fortress. The ferry across the Chambal had been commandeered by the rebels, but the Maharao was able to cross with a small force and invoke British aid. General Roberts and 600 men came over by night on 27 March 1858, and by the end of the month the ancient city had been cleared of rebels. At Hazeldine House Alice Roberts inherited some of her father's military equipment and trophies and was surrounded by the Indian furniture brought back for Sir Henry's retirement. Indian furniture remained with the Elgars until the 1913 inventory of Severn House contents. By then Elgar had paid his own compliment to their Indian heritage in the 1912 *Crown of India* masque.

It was an aspect of chivalry that the knight must aspire to be worthy of his lady. Often enough a man of inferior birth might be seen to deserve the lady through the splendour of his deeds. This was Elgar's case. More than once the young man had let his eye roam towards social spheres higher than his own: the Catholic shopkeeper's son would be confined neither by his religion nor his class. Alice Roberts, geologist, poetess, novelist, chatelaine of a notable house, marked the final achievement. At a bound Elgar was a freeman within Worcestershire county society, with new status as Alice Roberts's husband. She then exacted the mighty works from a composer so diffident he seemed willing to set down hardly a note without her aid and approval. Yet the ancient method worked, and the lady's inspiration produced the music that opened doors intellectual, aristocratic and indeed royal to the emergent couple. It was some time before they had a home worthy of the luminaries surrounding them. Lady Mary Lygon (1869-1927) was too local to be barred from Craeg Lea; but Lady Maud Warrender, Alice Stuart Wortley (1862-1936) and even Frank Schuster had to wait for the acquisition of Plas Gwyn in Hereford.

It was characteristic, perhaps, that the splendour of the Elgarian phenomenon should first be recognised in monied Jewish circles. Frank Schuster, Edward and Edgar Speyer, the Derenburgs (she was Ilona Eibenschütz (1873-1967), a late pupil of Clara Schumann (1819-96)), to be followed by Marie Joshua (d.1918), were ardent admirers. *Gerontius* and the première of the *Coronation Ode* in Sheffield on 2 October 1902 produced the Stuart Wortleys and a number of very distinguished Catholics, while the visit of the Meiningen orchestra was supported not only by Lady Maud Warrender but by John Singer Sargent (1856-1925), the most notable artist Elgar was to meet. The *annus mirabilis*, though, was 1904. Elgar had returned from Alassio to accept an invitation from Edward VII (1901-10) for 3 February and to meet the Prince of Wales; the Covent Garden Festival of 14-16 March introduced him to the Queen (1844-1925), who came to all three concerts; at Lord Northampton's (1851-1913) later in the month the Elgars met Arthur Balfour, now prime minister; at the end of the year, on returning with Frank Schuster from a continental excursion, he was a fellow dinner guest with Sidney Colvin, equally distinguished in the world of art and letters. Based at the British Museum, he was a colleague of Laurence Binyon (1869-1943), spur not only to Arthurian music but to the *Spirit of England*. Colvin nearly secured Thomas Hardy (1840-1928) as operatic collaborator for Elgar; it was no hardship that he had to make do with Henry James (1843-1916), another Colvin connection, as a main literary lion among his acquaintance.

It is remarkable how close-knit were the various strands of society during Elgar's lifetime, at any rate till 1914. Marlborough House might be pitted against the 'Souls' (Victoria (1837-1901) felt 'they ought to be told *not* to be so silly'); Protestant grandees might wonder at the renewed confidence of Catholic families since the Roman hierarchy was re-established in 1850; Whiggish followers of the Grand Old Man (1809-98) (or Murderer of Gordon, as some preferred to reverse the traditional 'GOM') might look askance at a bookish Disraeli (1804-81) in charge of the Tories; composers in the academic world such as Parry (1848-1918), Stanford (1852-1924) and Mackenzie (1847-1935) might despise those without the pale, if Bernard Shaw could be trusted. That said, Carlyle (1795-1881), Ruskin, William Morris and Shaw make a natural progression of artistic achievement and social concern; the Pre-Raphaelites, launched in 1848, the year of Alice Roberts' birth, are only briefly a 'fellowship'; but Ruskin gives them critical acclaim (the collapse of his marriage through Millais became an inevitable stumbling-block); Morris remains a bosom friend of Burne-Jones (1833-98); Rossetti is as devoted to Morris's wife as Morris himself. Then there are those three sisters, the Macdonalds of Birmingham, one of whom mothered Kipling, another married Burne-Jones, and the third was the mother of Stanley

Baldwin (1867-1947), future prime minister. Such lists could be readily extended, if only because the numbers involved were comparatively few, and social gathering was hardly inhibited by the telephone, and not at all by radio or television.

It was Sir Thomas Malory who showed the way to Walter Scott and the Victorian interpreters of Arthurian legend. Like Shakespeare, he came from Warwickshire and represented the county in parliament. His own life was as colourful as his hero's. He seems to have been imprisoned eight times. The alleged crimes include an ambush for the Duke of Buckingham's murder; a break-in at Combe Abbey, where he stole money and valuables from the abbot; later insults to the abbot; an assault on the virtue of Hugh Smyth's wife and theft of her property; raids on cattle; and extortion with menaces. Twice he escaped from jail, swimming a moat and using a nice selection of contemporary weapons. He was among the knightly followers of the Earl of Warwick (1428-71) in 1462 on a campaign into Northumberland. He may later have joined the Lancastrians with Warwick. He seems not to have been pardoned by Edward IV (1461-83) by 1470, when the last of the Yorkist pardons was issued. His last imprisonment saw the completion of 'the hoole book of kyng Arthur and of his noble knyghtes of the Rounde Table'. The chivalry of Arthur's court was a matter of real moment to Malory, at a time when the high-tide of chivalry was already past. Arthur's Round Table was symbol of a great cause and glowing example of former English heroism. He ransacked French sources to recount the bold and fantastic adventures of the knights, and with 'The Most Piteous Tale of the Morte Arthur' he brought his labours to an end, still a prisoner of the king.

Tennyson's (1809-92) first Arthurian poem was *The Lady of Shalott* (1833). The nine-line stanzas usually divide centrally with some mention of Camelot; but as the drama quickens, the city's place is taken by 'bold Sir Lancelot' until finally she 'look'd down to Camelot' and floated there in view of 'All the knights of Camelot'. *Morte d'Arthur*, published in 1842, was cunningly framed within the jollifications of a Christmas Eve party. One of the group had written a twelve-book epic on the subject of Arthur but was said to have burnt it because 'nothing new was said' and now truth looks freshest 'in the fashion of the day'. But Tennyson's spirit haunted the past, and the preamble leads to what was to become the last of his own twelve poems devoted to Arthur and the Round Table in the *Idylls of the King* that came out between 1859 and 1885. He started composition of the poem in the year Arthur Hallam (1811-33) died, and for him too it was a case that 'the old order changeth, yielding place to new'. The desolation of the end is far from the complacency of some Tennyson, with lamentation like

> a wind that shrills
> All night in a waste land, where no one comes,
> Or hath come, since the making of the world.

In the same volume appeared also Tennyson's first brief treatment of Galahad's quest for the Grail, and a quiet moment 'in the boyhood of the year' when Lancelot and Guenevere rode together 'thro' the coverts of the deer' until she sped into the distance, while the 'happy winds upon her play'd'. Tennyson's plan in the *Idylls* was not to divorce them entirely from contemporary events. The shift in the values of society from optimistic aspiration and belief in progress to a materialistic self-satisfaction and sometimes vulgar imperialism might be mirrored in the rise and fall of Camelot. Yet such was the potency of Arthurian legend that Camelot seemed more than an illusion. It was

> built to music, therefore never built at all,
> And therefore built for ever.

It was not for nothing that Tennyson was twice at Tintagel.

Matthew Arnold (1822-88) drew inspiration from Tintagel too. The poem that most engaged Elgar, however, was one that Arnold omitted, except for fragments, from most subsequent editions of the volume because in it the suffering of Empedocles found 'no vent in action'. He considered there was something morbid in a work such as *Empedocles on Etna* where 'a continuous state of mental stress is prolonged, unrelieved by incident, hope or resistance; in which there is everything to be endured, nothing to be done'. *Tristram and Iseult* begins in Brittany at the same point as Wagner's (1813-83) Act 3, with an agonised Tristram waiting only for the ship. Wagner's orchestra is here in the hands of a narrator, who begins with questions: 'What knight is this so weak and pale?' Backward and forward moves the tale between the stricken Tristram and this anonymous chorus. With the arrival of Iseult of Ireland, the drama moves to its Wagnerian climax, and both lovers lie dead. It was a December night, and the chill air stirs 'the ghostlike tapestry' on the wall, where appears a 'stately Huntsman, clad in Green'. It is he who now surveys the hall, assuming Tristram sleeps and Iseult kneels by his side in prayer; so his bugle must not be blown. Not so, directs the narrator, 'For thou wilt rouse no sleepers here'. He goes on to deplore obsessive passion of any kind, 'Call it ambition, or remorse, or love'. As for Iseult of Brittany, 'it is lonely for her in the hall', with only her servants, the children, and 'Tristram's agèd hound'. She tells the children the story of how Vivien beguiled Merlin and rooted him, also the slave of passion, by the 'blossom'd thorn-tree'. Arnold considered sanity 'the great virtue of the

Tennyson by Millais

ancient literature', and so it is that Tristram and Iseult have as background to their hothouse love the court of the castle, the drawbridge leading to the world beyond, the beach that bounds the nearby ocean, and far away the surge of the Atlantic.

Algernon Swinburne (1837-1909) also had his poetry swirl round the cliffs of Tintagel. He met Burne-Jones, Morris and Rossetti at Oxford in 1857, the year they painted the Arthurian murals at the Union. Like Shelley (1792-1822), he left Oxford without a degree. 'Now we are four and not three', Burne-Jones had exclaimed as they became better acquainted. Except in the case of Rossetti, the link was not lasting. Steeped in the Classics, Swinburne had a notable success with *Atalanta in Calydon* (1865). His *Tristram of Lyonesse* (1882) moves slowly and sensuously in heroic couplets softened by subtle assonance. A childhood by the sea on the Isle of Wight greatly influenced his poetry. After a prelude, the poem begins with the sailing of the *Swallow* that brings Iseult from Ireland to King Mark at 'the wind-hollowed heights and gusty bays' of Tintagel. On the journey they encountered foul weather; it blackened 'till its might had marred the skies', while the sea 'thrilled with heart-sundering sighs', and 'the green hardened into iron blue'. When the love-tragedy has run its course, and they are returned dead from Brittany to Cornwall, Swinburne has the chapel where they lay, 'a chapel bright like spring', submerged beneath the changeful tides so that over them remains only the 'light and sound and darkness of the sea'.

Elgar works a quotation from Carlyle's *Sartor Resartus* (1833-34) into his Birmingham lecture on 'English Executants' (29 November 1905). But more important was a letter he wrote to Troyte Griffith from Brinkwells on 16 July 1918. In it he said he had been reading Carlyle's *Past and Present* (1843) again; or rather he had read only 'Past', preferring to avoid the 'indomitable Plugson', 'of the respected Firm of Plugson, Hunks and Company, in St.Dolly Undershot', avoiding not only Carlyle's excoriation of the ignoble industrialist, but his paean to the chivalry of labour and the chivalry of work, culminating in his visionary conviction that 'noble fruitful Labour, growing ever nobler, will come forth, - the grand sole miracle of Man'. 'P'raps' might have been Elgar's justifiable comment if he had got that far. But now, as he told Troyte, he 'longed to see Bury St Edmunds. If you go over there - and you will do so one day - send me any 1d book about it - I haven't a notion if anything tangible is left of the Abbey & Jocelyn de Brakelonde is endeared to me'. Perhaps Troyte went and sent a guidebook; but it has not survived among Elgar collections. Nor, it seems, did Elgar ever see the proud Norman gate leading into the gaunt ruins of the abbey, with 17th-century houses built into the pitiful skeleton of a façade that once outdid many Cathedrals, the vast outline of a church just perceptible, and a shattered column marking a point in the

crossing. But the formidable Abbot Samson (1135-1211), as chronicled by
Jocelyn (fl.1200), had fired Elgar's imagination as much as Carlyle's.
Samson rebuilt the abbey church after a disastrous fire in 1182 and so
magnified its endowment that the royal exchequer was convinced the
abbey could contribute generously to the ransom of Richard Coeur de
Lion (1189-99), then a prisoner on the Rhine. Abbot Samson had visited
the king in Germany but had no wish to see St.Edmund's funds diverted.
As a gesture, he offered the embellishments of the saint's shrine to any
who would take them. The shrine was untouched. Samson's boldest move
was to check the bodily condition of the saint.[3] He and fourteen monks
opened the coffin by night, and the body was in perfect condition, so that
the abbot even touched it. A talking point was the size of the saint's large
nose.

It so happens that my copy of *Past and Present* once belonged to John
Ruskin, and was inscribed by him to Alfred Macfee in January 1887: 'I
have sent you a book which I read no more, because it has become a part
of myself - and my old marks in it are now useless because in my heart I
mark it all.' The marks have survived, and in this he was Carlyle's disciple
and successor. It was not Elgar's primary concern that Ruskin
foreshadowed in his later writings ideas for social security, the public
ownership of key industries, state funding of culture, the planning of new
towns and full employment. The one quotation Elgar makes from Ruskin,
at the end of the MS full score of *The Dream of Gerontius* (1900), is about
books. *Sesame and Lilies* was made up of two lectures given in Manchester
(1864) and one at Dublin (1868). Elgar quotes from the first lecture, the
aim of which Ruskin outlines in his preface: 'life being very short, and the
quiet hours of it few, we ought to waste none of them in reading valueless
books; and that valuable books should, in a civilized country, be within the
reach of every one, printed in excellent form, for a just price'. Ruskin went
on to say that he 'would urge upon any young man' to obtain by severe
economy as soon as possible 'a restricted, serviceable, and steadily -
however slowly - increasing, series of books for use through life; making
his little library, of all the furniture in his room, the most studied and
decorative piece'. These are indeed the 'Kings' treasuries' of Ruskin's
lecture title. He goes on to describe the essential individuality of the
author with a unique message: 'This is the best of me...'. But he has a stern
warning for contemporary England: it cannot 'go on despising literature,
despising science, despising art, despising nature, despising compassion,
and concentrating its soul on Pence'. As a nation, he claims we spend

[3] Gem, Richard: 'A Scientific Examination of the Relics of St Edmund at Arundel
Castle', *Bury St Edmunds: Medieval Art, Architecture, Archaeology and
Economy*, ed. Gransden, Antonia (London, 1998), p.45

more on horses than on books, less on books than on wine cellars.

Elgar was a keen fisherman, notably on the streams, rivers and lakes round Hereford and Brinkwells. Often he was successful, but on 27 August 1907, though he 'fissed all day', he caught nothing. The reason is explained by Lady Elgar: 'E. read Euphranor & missed fish in consequence'. At the time Elgar was working on the *Wand of Youth*, but he was already immersed in music that would take shape in Symphony no.1. Two months previously he had 'Played great beautiful tune' that was to start the symphony, and on 2 August he wrote the *'lovely* river piece' for the second movement. What was the book that so distracted him? *Euphranor* was by Edward FitzGerald (1809-83), known now mainly for his *Rubáiyát of Omar Khayyám* (1859). *Euphranor* (1851) was very different, a Platonic dialogue set in Cambridge on the education and training of youth. There are such characters as the plodding undergraduate Lexilogus; Phidippus was based on William Kenworthy-Browne, who had not been to university but was much admired by FitzGerald as hunter, angler, squire and militia captain; Euphranor himself is an idealistic graduate sensitive to literature and art, reading the first volume of Kenelm Digby's (1800-80) *Broad Stone of Honour* (1822); to guide the discussion is a doctor narrator who contributes the fruits of age and experience while emphasising the importance of physical training to make the body 'a spacious, airy and wholesome tenement' for the soul. Eton must 'sublime their Beefsteak into Chivalry in that famous Cricketfield of theirs by the side of old Father Thames murmuring of so many Generations of chivalric Ancestors'. Euphranor is sceptical and finds it difficult to imagine them 'turning out the young Knight from Cricket on the World'. The doctor perseveres and claims such training can produce youth worthy of the Round Table.

For an epigraph to *The Apostles* (1903), Elgar turned to William Morris and the *Earthly Paradise* (1868-70). Morris divided his Chaucerian scheme into twelve months, with two tales to each. The *Apostles* tale belongs to the Elgarian month of June, and Morris's introduction recalls a trip he and his wife made with the Burne-Joneses on the Upper Thames:

> What better place than this then could we find
> By this sweet stream that knows not of the sea,
> That guesses not the city's misery,
> This little stream whose hamlets scarce have names,
> This far-off lonely mother of the Thames?

The story told by an elder of the city concerns the love of Alcestis, and Morris's argument can be summarised as follows. The god Apollo is constrained to work for Admetus, king of Pherae in Thessaly, and one of the Argonauts who had sailed in search of the golden fleece. Apollo's son Aesculapius (or 'Scap' as Elgar was later to abbreviate him in canine form) had been medical expert to the expedition but had excited the wrath of Zeus by raising many from the dead. Aesculapius was therefore slain, and in revenge Apollo killed the Cyclopes who had made the thunderbolts for Zeus. Hence Apollo's nine-year servitude to Admetus as a shepherd, and the mutual respect between them. He was able to grant Admetus exemption from death if someone should die in his stead. Only his wife Alcestis was willing to do so. The words Elgar used come from Apollo's song before Admetus tells him of his desire for Alcestis and the impossible conditions her father has imposed on any suitor. Apollo urges man to cease his vain striving and remember 'How fair a world to you is given'. His second stanza reminds Zeus 'To what a heaven the earth might grow...'. The *Earthly Paradise* had a decade of extraordinary popularity, to the extent that Morris was considered as a possible successor to Tennyson for the laureateship. Yet his very attitude to poetry undermined its strength: 'if a chap can't compose an epic poem while he's weaving tapestry, he had better shut up'. Georgiana Burne-Jones (1840-1920), wife of the artist, makes a telling witness: 'I remember with shame often falling asleep to the steady rhythm of the reading voice, or biting my fingers and stabbing myself with pins in order to keep awake.'

While at Oxford, Morris and Burne-Jones planned 'A Crusade and Holy Warfare against this age'. In the case of Morris, the crusade took him to the Socialist League, the Social Democratic Federation, the Hammersmith Socialist Society and the police courts. In his review of J.W. Mackail's (1859-1945) biography, Bernard Shaw claims that the author 'knows little more about this part of Morris's life than might be gathered by any stranger from the available documents'. Elgar undoubtedly knew less; and his gradual acceptance of Shaw as valued friend and latter-day inspiration did not include his socialism. His first criticism of Shaw was in a letter of 14 July 1904 to Troyte Griffith (1864-1942) on *Man and Superman*, recently published (1903), and of which he owned a copy:

> Bernard Shaw is hopelessly wrong, as all these fellows are, on fundamental things:- amongst others they punch Xtianity & try to make it fit their civilization instead of making their civilization fit it. He is an amusing liar, but not much more & it is a somewhat curious pt. that in the Don Juan scene he makes his character "live in the remembrance" (in figure, age &c.) just, or not just but very like - Newman in Gerontius: Extremes meet sometimes.

Elgar's copy of the play has a few markings by him. Perhaps he persevered to the end and read Jack Tanner's 'Maxims for Revolutionists'. He might even have agreed that 'A fool's brain digests philosophy into folly, science into superstition, and art into pedantry. Hence University education'. In his own Birmingham lecture on 'Critics' (6 December 1905) Elgar referred to the 'lively and unstable pen of Bernard Shaw' coruscating 'to our great amusement' on music of the 1890s. There was another letter to Troyte about Shaw on 4 November 1907. This concerned *The Devil's Disciple* (1897), which the Elgars had seen because Troyte designed the sets. Elgar was lukewarm: 'its a poor play, with moments of power'; and 'Shaw is very *amateurish* in many ways'. Lady Elgar tended to be brusquely dismissive of most Shaw plays. At the end of May 1911 they saw *Fanny's First Play* (1911): 'Both hated it. & came home instead of going to reception after it to meet author.' Only *John Bull's Other Island* (1904) gave pleasure: 'Most delightful. The noble & ideal left in instead of the poison of other B.Shaw.' The approval doubtless centred on Father Keegan, a 'man with the face of a young saint' in Shaw's description 'yet with white hair and perhaps 50 years on his back', who ends his dream of heaven with a meditation on the Trinity summed up as 'a godhead in which all life is human and all humanity divine: three in one and one in three. It is, in short, the dream of a madman'. On 15 February 1918 Elgar was taken to a first lunch with Shaw by Lalla Vandervelde, daughter of Edward Speyer, who had frequently recited Elgar's *Carillon* and played the year before in *Augustus does his Bit* (1917) by Shaw. The Elgar-Shaw friendship flourished, and Lady Elgar lived to approve the extended appreciation of her 'EDU' that Shaw wrote for the first number of *Music & Letters* in January 1920.

   Man and Superman begins with Roebuck Ramsden 'in his study, opening the morning's letters'. Shaw describes the room, of which the windows open on to Portland Place, with meticulous care. Among busts, portraits and enlarged photographs of significant thinkers and authors are 'autotypes of allegories by Mr G.F.Watts' (for Roebuck believes in the fine arts with all the earnestness of a man who does not understand them). Alice Elgar was a Watts devotee. After the Munich exhibition of 1893, she went to see Watts pictures on 3 February 1897, while Elgar was orchestrating the *Imperial March* (1897). Many years later, at a time when Elgar was engrossed in *The Music Makers* (1912), Alice was taken a 'lovely motor drive' on 22 June 1912. She went 120 miles in all: 'First to Compton, wonderful old Church, then to Memorial Chapel, not at all impressive - The great Watts' grave   touching pan for birds at the foot. Lovely spot & his recumbent figure in marble very beautiful - Then saw his Studio, lovely spot, & Gallery.' The interior of the chapel, with its extraordinary profusion of gesso angels and cherubs' heads, was designed by Mary Watts (1850-1938), the painter's second wife; Pevsner (1902-83) considered it 'one of the most soporific rooms in England'. Watts claimed that 'his only teachers were the Elgin Marbles'. In 1843 he submitted a design for the new Palace of Westminster. The cartoon was entitled 'Caractacus led in Triumph through the Streets of Rome', a subject Elgar was to twist with the help of his librettist to the greater glory of Victoria's England. For the Parliament scheme the Prince Consort (1819-61) preferred an Arthurian cycle eventually entrusted to William Dyce (1806-64). Shaw and Alice Elgar were again at one, when he wrote on 13 March 1897 about the Watts Exhibition at the New Gallery: 'turn to Mr Watts, and you are instantly in a visionary world, in which life fades into mist, and the imaginings of nobility and beauty with which we invest life become embodied and visible ... It is to lose the whole world and gain one's own soul'. No one elucidates Watts's vision more cogently than the artist himself: 'Profoundly deep in the human mind exists a spiritual yearning dependent on no special creed, questions by nature left without response, yearnings the most perfect knowledge of material things will never stifle. The true prophet, be his language prose or poem, art or music, can transport to regions where earth takes its place among the stars and something beyond of heaven's infinity seems borne upon the air.'

Arthurian murals on a smaller scale were painted on the walls of the old debating chamber of the Oxford Union. The architect Benjamin Woodward (1815-61) had tried to interest Rossetti in a mural for the new Oxford Museum; the subject was to be 'Newton gathering Pebbles on the shores of the Ocean of Truth'. Rossetti preferred Arthur at the Union, and assembled a high-spirited team of young artists. The undertaking was known as the 'Jovial Campaign'. A contemporary undergraduate was working in the library nearby: '[I] heard their laughter, and songs and jokes, and the volleys of their soda-water corks, for this innutrient fluid was furnished to them without stint at the Society's expense.' William Morris, one of the team and a devotee of Malory, may have suggested the decorative scheme. Five of the nine scenes concerned Arthur himself: his education by Merlin; obtaining the sword Excalibur; his first victory with the sword; his wedding; his departure to Avalon and return of the sword. The rest dealt with his entourage. Gawaine meets the three ladies at the well; Lancelot is prevented from entering the Grail chapel; Palomides expresses his jealousy of Tristram; and Merlin is imprisoned by the damsel of the lake. Morris painted Palomides; Rossetti the Lancelot scene; and Burne-Jones dealt with Merlin. Coventry Patmore (1823-96) saw the newly completed work: '[it glowed] with a voluptuous radiance of variegated tints, the colour coming from points instead of masses and positively radiant, at the same time they are wholly the reverse of glaring... colouring so brilliant as to make the walls look like the margin of a highly-illuminated manuscript'. Unfortunately the walls had been ill prepared, and the splendour of the paintings fast disappeared. By day they are now hardly visible because of the strong light from the many large windows.

At Oxford Burne-Jones and Morris were both passionate admirers of John Henry Newman. The former said of him: 'In an age of sofas and cushions he taught me to be indifferent to comfort; and in an age of materialism he taught me to venture all on the unseen.' Both began Oxford intending to go into the Church; both left knowing they wouldn't. Burne-Jones would write home from Oxford as Edouard Cardinal de Birmingham and was as dedicated to Malory as was Morris: 'Nothing was ever like Morte d'Arthur - I don't mean any book or any one poem -something that can never be written, I mean, and can never go out of the heart.' In a letter of May 1853 to Cormell Price, Burne-Jones announces plans involving a poem by Tennyson: 'I have set my heart on our founding a Brotherhood. Learn Sir Galahad by heart; he is to be the patron of our Order.' They heard about another Brotherhod, the Pre-Raphaelites, from the publication of Ruskin's 1854 Edinburgh lectures. Burne-Jones explains: 'I was working in my room when Morris ran in one morning bringing the newly published book with him: so everything was put aside until he read it all through to me. And there we first saw about the Pre-Raphaelites, and there I first saw the name of Rossetti. So for many a day after that we talked of little else but paintings we had never seen.' In time Ruskin was to give Burne-Jones highest praise, writing on 12 August 1862 from Geneva in a letter of rebuke to his father:

> You try all you can to withdraw me from the company of a man like Jones, whose life is as pure as an archangels, whose genius is as strange & high as that of Albert Durer or Hans Memling - who loves me with a love as of a brother - and far more - of a devoted friend - whose knowledge of history and poetry is as rich and varied, nay - far more rich and varied, and incomparably more *scholarly*, than Walter Scott was at his age.

Alice Elgar was similarly generous in her account of *The Golden Stair*: 'The maidens are rapt and content in their own existence, fulfilling some law absolutely unknown to us - we know not whence they come or whither they go.'

Elgar himself had a strong feeling for John Everett Millais. The Pre-Raphaelite Brotherhood was founded at his home in 1848, and Elgar's 'favourite painting' the *Isabella* based on Keats was shown the following year. He was already Britain's most promising artist. A comment in the *Saturday Review* makes the point: 'The Millais of the year so soon becomes everybody's talk that there is no need to describe it.' Ruskin urged young artists to go to Nature: '[they should] walk with her laboriously and trustingly, having no other thoughts but how best to penetrate her meaning'. Millais described his first Pre-Raphaelite background to Holman Hunt: 'To do it as it ought to be would take a month a weed.' Euphemia Ruskin (Effie, 1828-97) was the model for the Highlander's wife in *The Order of Release* (1853). The dog gave Millais problems, as he explained to Thomas Combe (1797-1872), Pre-Raphaelite patron: 'All morning I have been drawing a dog, which in unquietness is only to be surpassed by a child.' That summer he went on holiday to Scotland with the Ruskins. His plan for a Ruskin portrait took shape, and Millais selected a magnificent site, as Ruskin told his father: 'Millais has fixed on his place, a lovely piece of worn rock, with foaming water, and weeds, and moss, and a noble overhanging bank of dark crag - and I am to be standing looking quietly down the stream.' The background is superbly done, but triangular complications between Millais and the Ruskins marred the portrait. Millais wished to abandon it now that he and Effie had declared themselves. In the end Ruskin, a magnificent figure in himself, seems an awkward presence, uneasily poised above the stream. Gladstone felt no one was at fault for the débâcle: 'there was misfortune, even tragedy, but all three were blameless'. Alice Stuart Wortley, a close friend of Elgar's, was a child of the marriage, and Millais caught her admirably in *The Convalescent*, now at Aberdeen Art Gallery. There she is off-colour and a little woebegone; but she may also be the subject of the enchantingly self-possessed *Bright Eyes* in the same gallery. Millais's own favourite portrait was that of Cardinal Newman, who sat for him in 1881. After the Elgar festival of March 1904, Alice Stuart Wortley sent Elgar a print of the portrait, which he greatly treasured and is now at the Birthplace. Millais was less successful with his mediaeval knights. *Sir Isumbras at the Ford* (1857) was mercilessly mocked in the *Athenaeum*: '(a) pudgy and dwarfish knight (on) such an animal as Noah would have shut the door against'. Equally attacked was *The Knight Errant* of 1870 in a *Manchester Guardian* review: 'Having painted a great many other things, Mr.Millais has apparently decided to paint the nude - lashed most methodically to the stem of a silver birch by an arrangement of ropes worthy of a sailor. The knight is cutting the ropes as if he were carving a joint of beef. This is an absurd work.'

The Elgars' meeting with John Singer Sargent in November 1902 followed a performance of the 'Enigma' Variations. The conductor Fritz Steinbach had expressed his admiration for the work to Edward Speyer, who sponsored the Meiningen concerts: 'Here is an unexpected genius and pathfinder in the field of orchestration. Nowadays nearly every composer is content merely to adopt Wagner's innovations, but Elgar, as this work shows, is a real pioneer.' Clearly Elgar and Sargent had discussed the Variations in some detail at the dinner, as Elgar wrote to him six days later on 26 November about a four-hand arrangement a

Isabella *by Millais*

friend of Sargent's had completed. Elgar continued: 'May I say that it was the greatest possible pleasure to meet you at Schuster's: I appreciate *your* art so very much, but I thought you would not want to hear an ignoramus discourse on it, so I was tongue-tied - nervously, in your presence.' The Elgars pursued their interest and went with Schuster to the Royal Academy on 17 May 1904, where they 'saw the wonderful Sargent pictures'. The last mention of Sargent in Lady Elgar's diary is on 17 August 1906, when the Littletons drove them from Plas Gwyn to see the fine collection of a Mr.Pilley. There they 'Saw frame for the Prophets picture'. This was to be a reproduction of Sargent's frieze of prophets at the Boston Public Library in Massachusetts (1890-1919). When bored with 'paughtraits', Sargent used his murals as excuse for declining commissions. Among the prophets Moses is a mighty central figure in relief, holding the tablets of the law; either side of him are Elijah and Joshua, the former adapted from a portrait of Coventry Patmore. It was indeed the portraits that took London by storm and had Sargent dubbed the 'Van Dyck of our times'. The pride and near-arrogance of some such portraits was complemented by the quiet heroism Sargent revealed when at the western front for the British War Memorials Committee (from July 1918) searching for an epic subject. He discovered that 'the more dramatic the situation the more it becomes an empty landscape'. How produce an epic without a cast? One night he found his subject: 'a field full of gassed and blindfolded men'. It is a terrifying vision in which the only chivalry is compassion.

Elgar's long delight in art and infinite capacity for amateur experiment took a new form at the beginning of 1905. On 9 January Talbot Hughes arrived at Plas Gwyn to paint Elgar's portrait. The sittings continued into February, the month Elgar completed the Introduction and Allegro. Lady Elgar wrote to 'Nimrod' about the portrait on 1 March:

> I suppose it will be in the Academy & then I do not know what its fate is to be. We missed it so much - it fired E. with a great desire to paint & he has bought a box of oil colours, & paints strange symbolical pictures à la Bocklin & Segantini & Blake! He certainly has a power of representing a scene from his imagination. & one that he has done of a river with sombre trees & a boat crossing is very suggestive. We will explain the symbolism some day I hope to you.

Böcklin had been in Elgar's mind at least since the 1893 Munich exhibition, and on 18 September 1905 he reverted to the subject when describing his first impression of Corfu: 'Lovely looking fortification - like in Böcklin picture.' Böcklin was well read, a friend of Wagner's Wesendoncks (she was the muse behind *Tristan und Isolde*), and much affected by the horrors of the Franco-Prussian war. *The Ride of Death*, a *Self-portrait with Death playing the Fiddle*, *War* and *The Plague* project sinister visions of extinction. Böcklin manages to be both monumental and imprecise, notably in the most influential of his works, *The Isle of the Dead*. It was his answer to a request for a picture to induce dreams. A small boat nears the rocks of a sepulchred island, later to be a powerful influence on Rachmaninov (1873-1943). Segantini (1858-99) was in contact with Klimt, and had a strong effect on Jugendstil artists and the expressionists of South Germany. *The Punishment of Lustful Women* and *Wicked Mothers* have their characters floating aimless in bleak and snowy landscape, both real and incorporeal.

On 6 October 1916 the Elgars viewed a German war casualty. They went early to Bunhill Fields: 'to see Zepp remains - Great crowd'. Elgar was dissatisfied with the arrangements for spectators. After lunch they saw the first one-man show of C.R.W.Nevinson (1889-1946) : it seemed 'rather vivid but not art - or alive except as pictures of war'. The exhibition included such pictures as *La Mitrailleuse, On the Road to Ypres, Troops Resting, Column on the March*. It was a success, which Nevinson dismissed in a letter to Rothenstein (1872-1945) : 'I am afraid that much of my pecuniary success was more due to the public's adoration of war

French Troops Resting *by C.R.W.Nevinson*

than any artistic value.' In May 1917 Nevinson became an official war artist. He could no more glamourise the war than Sargent had. A painting that caused much controversy showed two dead British soldiers under the title 'The Paths of Glory'. It was a reference to the *Elegy written in a Country Church-yard* by Thomas Gray (1716-71), a favourite poet of Elgar's and mentioned by him in a letter to the *Times Literary Supplement* of 4 September 1919 :

> The boast of heraldry, the pomp of pow'r,
> And all that beauty, all that wealth e'er gave,
> Awaits alike th'inevitable hour.
> The paths of glory lead but to the grave.

2 - All the mother's world and his wife

In 1874 Elgar was 17 and his mother Ann 52. She then confided to her scrapbook doubts about the children's upbringing: 'It is no joke to have five men and women to rule, and keep peace between, and to keep *home* in something order & comfort. With so many dispositions, different ways and wants, each one wrestling for the mastery – or trying to have their own way in defiance of the rest.' She felt she had exerted too little discipline on them: 'yes! I own it at last, I *have* given them too much latitude, I have ruled by love instead of terror and the fetters are too weak for their stronger passions, I failed to see that they could be different to myself'. She, indeed, had been an only child: 'I was *alone*, in my youth for so many years, I had no one to disobey, to quarrel with – or *to play with*, but my parents, to whom I always gave implicit, blind, obedience, I never remember stopping to question their authority, or their wisdom – hence, I suppose I expect too much – but I should be happier if they were a little more like I was.'

Elgar's eldest sister Lucy (1852-1925) described in 1912 the family's early life. She had much to say about her mother:

> Her own young life had been peopled from noble books, and it was in their pages she had met her friends and companions – men, romantically honourable and loyal: women, faithful in love, even unto death, both alike doing nobly with this life because they held it as a gauge of life eternal – and in her simple way of thinking she verily believed these shadowy forms to be portraits of the people whom she would one day meet with in the world – no one told her differently, for her own mother had brought her up in that sweet simplicity which makes a woman charming in good fortune and patient and strong in the days of calamity.

Lucy tells much of her mother's delight in nature: 'she was truly one of Nature's gentlewomen – for if any woman ever loved beauty and reverently turned to the very soul of Nature, it was my Mother'. Lucy emphasises her mother's sturdy background: 'my Mother was the daughter of a Herefordshire farmer who came of a strong healthy long-lived stock – thus perhaps accounting for my Mother's splendid constitution, and sincere love of the country and of all things pastoral'. Ann Elgar had to suffer the loss of two sons, Harry the eldest (1848-64), and Jo (1859-66), musical

Left :
Ann Elgar

Right :
Five Elgar children,
with Edward seated
and Lucy standing left

enough to be called the 'Beethoven' of the family, and perhaps of a daughter Mary, to whom there are only shadowy references. Lucy describes how she coped with lesser troubles: 'she sought *material* joy in her daily pin-pricks by taking long walks, and commune with Nature in its beauty when the air was sweet with the breath of violets and all the tender flowers of the first months of the year'. The children were enjoined to a respect for all manifestations of life, something engrained in the peoples of the further east, but less common among the urban or country children of England: 'We were always taught to adore Him in the smallest flower that grew, as every flower loves its life – and we were told never to *dare* destroy what we could not give, that was, the life over again – there is a humanity in every flower and blade of grass.' Lucy then refers to the words of a poem by J.G.Percival which she chose for the 15-year old Elgar to set. He called this his first song *The Language of Flowers*. Lucy gives reasons for her choice: 'a remembrance of our early teaching of the language of flowers – The poem is called "In Eastern lands they talk in Flowers" – every flower carries a mystery, and all flowers have a message'.

Ann Elgar pursued her manifold interests through cuttings, extracts, jottings and verse set down in her scrapbooks. In a cutting about 'Boating on the Severn' she touches on essential Elgarian sites:

> The red cliffs by Stourport gradually tell the descending oarsman that he is reaching the smoother and the wider reaches of the Severn, and soon the tower of Worcester Cathedral appears before him, and then Tewkesbury, raised among the meadows, and then after a passage through wide pastures, Gloucester and its cathedral are reached. The traveller at Gloucester places his boat on the canal which connects the Severn and the Wye; he passes through more thoroughly English country till he reaches Ledbury, and then the Black Mountains are seen in the distance, he is at Hereford and on the Wye.

Ann Elgar notes also a paper on 'The Age of the Wye'. Far distant but of interest to her was the comment of Eugene Thayer at Niagara: ' "There was no roar at all," says Mr Thayer, "but the same great diapason – the noblest and completest one on earth".'

An early recollection of Lucy's about her mother was 'how beautifully she read and recited poetry'. She described the essence of her character: 'She was romantic by temperament, and poetic by nature: she had the unmistakable air of good breeding, which like the perfect manners of the true gentleman is felt, without being defined – being highly educated with fine literary tastes, and a deep reader all her life, and what is more to the point, in her conversation there was always something well worth remembering.' Lucy sums up her mother's achievement: 'She might have shone in many other walks of life, but in none could she have left such a happy memorial behind as will remain in the hearts and homes of those who have had the estimable benefit of her guidance during those impressionable years when character is formed, and ideals of life are implanted.'

There are many literary references in the scrapbooks. Of course Shakespeare intrigued her. 'Shakespeare and his Relations' was one excerpt:

> If not one single line of the handwriting of this wonderful poet and dramatist has been preserved it appears that his family and name are not yet extinct. Some few autographs, three of them being his signatures to the sheets of paper on which his will was written, are beyond doubt by his hand, and within fifteen miles of Bridgnorth, at Wolverhampton, one is now living who, there is little doubt, is of Shakespeare's family and blood.

As a Catholic convert, a letter on the question 'Was Shakespeare a Catholic?' interested her: 'If the evidence that can be produced on the subject, is, after all, inconclusive, it is nevertheless certain that the style and spirit of his writings are uniformly respectful towards the virtues and offices of the Catholic Church.' A piece on 'Thinkers and Observers' also included Shakespeare: 'Probably the most admirable character is one in which these two types are equally combined and equally energetic. Such men as Shakespeare, Bacon, Newton, Beethoven see everything that goes on around them. They are not caught napping. But at the same time they see below the surface into causes and theories of things. They think and generalise, and see the beauty and poetry that fill the universe.'

Many other poets were investigated. Wordsworth (1770-1850) on his travels was approved:

> In Bruges town is many a street
> Whence busy life hath fled,
> Where, without hurrying, noiseless feet
> The grass-grown pavements tread.

Coleridge (1772-1834) was quoted:

> With finest ministrations, thou, O Nature,
> Healest thy wandering and distempered child.

There was a paragraph on Campbell's poetry (1777-1844): 'The poem by which Campbell first became known was "The Pleasures of Hope", published in 1799. It is, without any exception, the finest didactic poem in the English language. Even those who do not admire didactic poetry are forced to admit its charm. The delicacy of the thoughts, the beauty of the imagery, the occasional power of pathos, the felicity of the language, and the harmony of versification, are all extraordinary.' Walter Scott would have added a caveat: 'Somehow he wants audacity, fears the public, and, what is worse, fears the shadow of his own reputation.' Longfellow always found a ready response:

> A wind came up out of the sea,
> And said, "O mists, make room for me."

And Ann Elgar could turn him to her own purpose:

> Come to me, O ye children,
> For I hear you at your play,
> And the questions that perplexed me
> Have vanished quite away.

Walt Whitman (1819-92) on 'Manliness' might have helped with the training of her sons:

> O the joy of a manly selfhood!
> To be servile to none, not to any tyrant known or unknown;
> To walk with erect carriage, a step springy and elastic;
> To look with calm gaze, or with a flashing eye;
> To speak with a full and sonorous voice out of a broad chest;
> To confront with your personality all the other personalities of the earth.

Longfellow remained central. Ann Elgar cut out a paragraph concerning his 72nd birthday:

> Prof.Longfellow's house is at once an art museum and a cabinet of relics. He writes from Coleridge's own inkstand, which was sent to him by Mrs.S.C.Hall. There are tokens and mementos from every quarter of the globe. Among the gifts presented to him on his recent birthday is one very beautiful in its design, and singularly touching in its history. It is a chair made from the wood of the chestnut tree which overshadowed the old smithy referred to in "The Village Blacksmith".

There is much *Hyperion* at the scrapbook beginnings. Ann Elgar seems to have been reading Longfellow's largely autobiographical romance in the autumn of 1876, when Elgar was 19. 'Beware of dreams!', she begins, 'Beware of the illusions of fancy! Beware of the solemn deceivings of thy best wishes (*recte* vast desires)!' This is a slight misquotation from the 'Homunculus' chapter and comes ultimately from the *Endimion* (1591) of

John Lyly (?1554-1606). She continues near the end of a conversation in Heidelberg between the Baron of Hohenfels and Paul Flemming in chapter 7 of Book I: ' "After all", saith the Baron, "we must pardon much to men of genius. A delicate organization renders them truly susceptible to pain or pleasure. And then they idealise everything; and, in the moonlight of fancy, even the deformity of vice seems beautiful." ' She excerpts at length on Flemming's reverie that opens the 'Literary Fame' chapter: 'Time has a doomesday-Book, upon whose pages he is continually recording illustrious names...These are the high nobility of Nature, - Lords of the Public Domain of Thought. Posterity shall never question their titles.' She ends with Longfellow's peroration: 'And as in the sun's eclipse we can behold the great stars shining in the heavens, so in this life-eclipse have these men beheld the lights of the great eternity, burning solemnly and for ever!'

More surprisingly, Ann Elgar includes a mocking paragraph on Oscar Wilde (1854-1900): 'Mr.Whistler's eclectic breakfasts, which are celebrated on Sundays, in Tite Street, are a sure sign of the commencement of the season. The first was graced by the presence of Mr.Oscar Wilde, who has left behind him in Paris all his esoteric properties, including his luxuriant locks, and now arrays himself in nothing more eccentric than the costume and coiffeur of the Boulevards.

> Our Oscar is with us again but, O
> He is changed who was once so fair!
> Has the iron gone into his soul? O, no;
> It has only gone over his hair.

She has an entertaining extract from the *Cornhill Magazine* on why Rudyard Kipling (1865-1936), who was to provide the words for *Fringes of the Fleet* and *Big Steamers*, was so popular: 'He punctuated his writing as he did his speaking; and used more full-stops than any man before him.' She continues: 'the public want to be mystified. They like references to things of which they have never heard. They read the sporting papers for that reason. So this man wrote Anglo-Indian life, and put very little explanation into it.' The article attends to the higher echelons of power: 'There are people connected with the Government of India who are so high that no one knows anything about them except themselves, and their own knowledge is very superficial. Is our author afraid? Not a bit. He speaks of them with freedom but with vagueness. He says UP Above. And the public admire the freedom, and never notice the vagueness.'

Murray's Magazine provided detail on the family of Adam Lindsay Gordon (1833-70), author of 'The Swimmer' in *Sea Pictures* (1899).

Descended from a Scottish Gordon who had made a fortune and bought the barony of Esslemont, he had a grandfather in Worcester and a military father who had settled in Cheltenham:

> Young Adam Lindsay was then a bright boy of eight, who at that early age had a passion for field-sports and horses. "There are still echoes round the Cotswold hills of those wild days and nights when young Lindsay Gordon had for boon companion on "Black Tom Oliver", a local horse trainer, to whom the curious will find admiring references pervading "Bush Ballads and Galloping Rhymes". On one occasion, without the trainer's leave, he took a steeple-chaser and rode at a country meeting.

Gordon was shipped to Adelaide, joined the mounted police and then became a horse-breaker: 'Though a gentleman by birth and feeling, Adam Lindsay preferred the society of unsophisticated humanity. He loved, too, the indescribable solitude of the Australian wilds.' There he produced his best-known poems and, entering parliament locally on the strength of a legacy from his mother, he later ran an unsuccessful livery stable. He then pinned his hopes on his remote ancestry: 'He learned that he was nearest heir to the barony of Esslemont, and made a claim, meanwhile getting ready a new volume of poetry, which he hoped to publish on the arrival of good news from Scotland. But the news was bad; the Scottish court had decided that entails of a particular form were null and void. Still he was able to publish. On June 23rd, 1870, "Bush Ballads" appeared. Next morning he went out with his gun, and was found shot.'

Art was equally interesting to Elgar's mother. There was a cutting on prehistoric art, an illustration of *Dew-drenched Furze* by Millais (1829-96) at the New Gallery, with comment on the incredible detail shown in the plants, and an extended passage from the *Pall Mall Gazette* of 3 May 1890 on the *Beata Beatrix* of Dante Gabriel Rossetti (1828-82), currently displayed at the National Gallery. The cutting adjudges Rossetti's the most interesting of eleven works recently hung there: 'This new and characteristic specimen of Rossetti's work – presented to the nation by Lady Mount-Temple in memory of her late husband – hangs on a screen in Room XXI., opposite his "Ecce Ancilla Domini!" This arrangement is felicitous, as instructive comparison can thus be made by the student between the two pictures, and the change of style wrought by the fourteen years' interval may be easily perceived.' William Rossetti (1829-1919) records the start of the earlier picture on 25 November 1949: 'Gabriel began making a sketch for *The Annunciation*. The Virgin is to be in bed, but without any bedclothes on, an arrangement which may be justified in consideration of the hot climate, and the Angel Gabriel is to be presenting a lily to her.' *Beata Beatrix* dates from about 1864-70. It commemorates not only Dante's Beatrice but Rossetti's own wife Lizzie Siddal, who had died in February 1862. Ann Elgar's cutting describes the scene in some detail:

> The picture is intended to illustrate symbolically the death of Beatrice as illustrated by Dante in his "Vita Nuova." On the frame is the date of Beatrice's death (June 9, 1290), and the words, "*Quomodo sedet sola civitas!*" (how doth the city sit solitary!), the first words of Jeremiah's Lamentation, quoted by Dante to show the grief of Florence at Beatrice's death. Beatrice herself is seated on a balcony overlooking Florence. The city and the bridged river are seen as from afar, dim and veiled with misty lights as though already "sitting alone, made me a widow." In front of Beatrice is a sundial, which points to the hour of her departure; whilst a crimson bird drops between her hands a white poppy, symbol of sleep and painless death.

The cutting ends as follows:

> Rather does she seem, through closed lids, to be conscious of a New World; for she is "that blessed Beatrice who now gazeth on His countenance who is blessed throughout all ages." Dante and the Angel of Love are depicted watching in the background.

Remote antiquity also intrigued Ann Elgar. She cut out a piece speculating on the age of the oldest remains from Egypt. An article on 'Ancient Structures' dealt with the pyramids of Giza: 'Men who are most familiar with steam-power and modern machinery are puzzled to explain how the grand structures of the ancient world were erected. Builders say that no modern contractor could erect the great pyramid in Egypt, and lift the gigantic stones at the summit to the height of four hundred and fifty feet.' A lengthy extract from *Our Own Fireside* on the cache of royal mummies discovered at Deir el-Bahari in 1881 was copied. It was indeed a remarkable find. The period of civil collapse during the 20th Dynasty (c.1188-1069) had involved much robbery in the Valley of the Kings. Mummies of the pharaohs had been gathered for safety in a remote tomb in the cliffs of Deir el-Bahari. Tuthmosis III (c1479-1425) was there, the great conqueror featured on 'Cleopatra's Needles' by the Thames and in New York's Central Park, as also on the Albert Memorial in Kensington Gardens. Ramesses II (c.1279-1212) was among the rediscovered mummies, mighty builder and probable pharaoh of the Exodus. Ann Elgar summed up her Egyptian interests with an illustration of the hypostyle hall at Karnak, forested with more than a hundred massive columns mainly by Ramesses II and his father.

Lucy was aware of her father's considerable musical gifts. She claimed for him 'a well regulated mind, and undisturbed by that unbalancing element known as genius'. In music Ann Elgar was less gifted: 'My Mother, was not in a way called musical, though her calm, high-thinking mind could fully appreciate the nice little musical evenings we so often had in those early days.' Ann Elgar was nevertheless sensitive to the delights and expressiveness of the violin, her husband's instrument, and that of her genius son. She quoted in her scrapbook from *The Violin, its Makers and their Imitators*: 'The singular powers centred in the violin have been beautifully expressed by Oliver Wendell Holmes, who says: - "Violins too. The sweet old Amati! the divine Stradivarius!" ' She then extends the possibilities of the violin into the human sphere with a paragraph by Maurice E Egan:

> It is a fine thing to think of a man's heart as of a good violin. It is full of rich music; its strings are drawn to their utmost tension. The master-hand touches it with his bow; it does not give forth all its rich harmonies at once. There is a prelude which suggests the wealth of noble music stored in the tense chords. Finally it comes forth in a grand increasing harmony of melodious sounds. But the strings do not loosen; they are held tight; there is no abandonment; when they relax and forget that music comes only by sacrifice, there are no more noble sounds.

In a sense of wonder, perhaps, at the phenomenon of her second son, Ann Elgar pastes a quotation from James Russell Lowell (1819-91), Longfellow's successor as professor of French and Spanish at Harvard: 'There is nothing so true, so sincere, so downright and forthright as genius. It is always truer than the man himself is, greater than he.'

Lucy tells of the appalling toll it took when the eldest boy Harry died in 1864. Ann Elgar's courage saved her husband's reason, devastated as they both were by the blow. Her response was to include in her scrapbook a 'poem on *sorrow*, lightened by sun through a minster's stained-glass window:

> And methought as I gazed, that a lesson
> From the storied pane did shine
> And patience, & hope were taught me
> By a sorrow greater than mine.'

Her faith remained indomitable, and she bade her children remember that 'God is not far off – we are *in* God His ear is close to our life, it is never taken away, even when we dream and sleep, we sigh into it.' She worshipped regularly at St.George's, Worcester, where her husband and then Elgar himself were organists. She noted in her scrapbook the death of Pope Pius IX (1846-78) and the election of Leo XIII on 9 February 1878. There follows a cutting about the appointment of Sir Lintorn Simmons as ambassador to the Holy See in October 1889. He had an audience with his Holiness the following month. The Pope's speech was then summarised: 'he expressed the great importance which he attached to the maintenance of friendly relations with the Government of England'. He spoke of Catholics' obedience to the civil law, and 'rejoiced in the liberty and peace granted to the faithful in all the vast dominions of the British Empire'. Very different was a cutting deploring the attitude of the *Daily News* towards Catholics. The paper took up 'the stupid "No Popery" argument which Mr.Gladstone was prudent enough to drop as soon as it began to burn his fingers'. They then invented the phrase 'Satanic Policy' to describe those rejoicing 'to find the religion of the majority of Irishmen ranged authoritatively on the side of order and honesty'. The *Daily News* should congratulate itself: 'To establish an intimate connection between Lord Salisbury's Government, Satan, and the Pope of Rome, is to revive, not without some hope of success, the most odious passions which have ever found their way into British politics, and which everybody who was not a fanatic believed to have been dead and buried a full generation ago.' This was the view on 1 September 1890 of *The Globe & Traveller*, describing itself as the oldest evening paper. Ann Elgar also enjoyed an advertisement for Pears soap in which it was declared 'Worthy of washing the Hands of the Pope'.

To some extent the scrapbooks chart the beginning of Elgar's musical career. His advertisement of June 1878, published without response in *The Tablet*, was pasted in by his mother: it was addressed to 'Musical Catholic Noblemen, Gentlemen, Priests, Heads of Colleges, &c., or Professors of Music' and was couched in terms of an anonymous friend's request for Elgar's advancement: 'A friend of a young man, possessed of great musical talent, is anxious to obtain partial employment for him as Organist or Teacher of Piano, Organ, or Violin, to young boys, sons of gentlemen, or as Musical Amanuensis to Composers or Professors of Music, being a quick and ready copyist.' A description of Elgar followed: 'Age 21, of quiet, studious habits, and gentlemanly bearing. Been used to good society. Would have unexceptionable references.' Locally there was increasing employment that year. There was a cutting about the Worcester Amateur Instrumental Society:

> The society was formed in 1876 for the cultivation of instrumental music by means of weekly practices under an efficient leader. After two years' successful practice it was this year resolved, in order further to encourage the study of instrumental music, to enlarge the sphere of the society by extending its benefits to those gentlemen who might not be sufficiently

advanced to join the ordinary members in their practice, and thus to afford
them the opportunity of meeting weekly for practice under a competent
leader. In furtherance of this object a separate division has been formed,
and the services of Mr.E.W.Elgar have been engaged.

Elgar's main achievement in the scrapbooks was a first London
performance of his music. *Sevillana* had already been heard in Worcester
under the Cathedral organist, William Done (1815-95), on 1 May 1884.
Eleven days later August Manns (1825-1907) conducted it at the Crystal
Palace, and Ann Elgar pasted in a ticket for the concert. She noted also a
review of the work, when Elgar conducted it with the Amateur
Instrumental Society: 'Under the careful and competent direction of Mr.
Edward Elgar the various pieces in the programme were performed with
excellent effect.' The main work was Schubert's 'Unfinished' Symphony:
'But the most enthusiastic display of the evening was called forth by a
composition from the pen of Mr. Elgar, the talented conductor of the
society, entitled "Sevillana".'
    A touching entry by Ann Elgar is a few lines of verse dated 15 July 1885
on the death of the family dog, Tip:

> What shall I write for today?
> Why do we records keep?
> When they only have to say
> Something to make us weep.
> > My faithful Tip.

Elgar was as devoted to dogs as his mother, and his reading of Walter
Scott would acquaint him with two heroic specimens, Roswal in *The
Talisman* and Bevis in *Woodstock*. By now Elgar had moved twice, to the
homes of his married sisters. First he went to Pollie Grafton (1854-1936)
at 'Loretto Villa', 35 Chestnut Walk, Worcester, remaining there from
1879 to 1883, when the Graftons left for Stoke Prior, Bromsgrove. Elgar
then transferred to the house of his eldest sister Lucy Pipe at 4 Field
Terrace, Worcester, staying till his marriage in 1889. That was where he
brought the first of his remarkable dogs.
    His name was 'Scap', short for Aesculapius, and he belonged originally
to Elgar's medical friend in Settle, Yorkshire, Dr.Charles Buck (1851-
1932). Elgar's delight in him is documented from the moment he sends
Scap a kiss in November 1883. In the summer of 1885 it was decided Scap
should come to Worcester, if Lucy and Charlie Pipe (1853-1938) would
accept him. Elgar described the progress south in a letter to Buck of 16
September: 'Scap enjoyed his journey & was very quiet the whole time. I
came "first" from Leeds & by tipping the guard was allowed to keep the

"animal" with me. He is a Christian; he had my rug spread out & lolled about, slept, pawed me all about & rode a great part of the way with his head out of the window, taking a great interest in everything.' The initial adventures continued: 'This morning I had him out at 7.30 into the river & he had his first fight with a Newfoundland brute which began it; no harm done, only I have nearly settled my black stick on the other dog, a proceeding which greatly satisfied his owner!' His exploration of the territory near Field Terrace proved satisfactory: 'The Bath Road presents a perfect paradise of new smells all of which he has duly examined and "*reported*" on. He is allowed all over the house, has his bed under the kitchen table & a private spot in my bedroom which he knows already. So much for Scap.' But there was more on 7 October: 'He has developed into a much more affectionate animal than I anticipated & loves me. When I am away he retires to my room & won't move (except for fride pork & his usual dinner) 'till I return.' Elgar had also to recount an imprudent move on the part of Ann Elgar:

> I shut him up at the shop this morning: while I went to give a lesson, he whined so his grandmother let him out, he darted down the stairs, caught his leg in *twenty concertinas* that are piled on the staircase & rolled over with all the lot into the middle of the shop! There were some ladies there & my old father enjoyed it awfully. We live in an atmosphere of "Scap", the creature's advent has curiously changed all our relationship – my father who has been a respectable citizen for 40 years is now no more than Scap's grandfather.

Symbol of a fundamental change in Elgar's life is a poem in the scrapbook by 'C.A.R.', his future wife. It is called 'Question and Answer', in which Alice Roberts pits the imaginative world of woman against the striving of man:

> What is our life? The floating of a feather
> Adown the wavy current of the breeze;
> A blossom fading in the summer weather;
> A dead leaf falling from the forest trees;
> A bubble breaking in the wind's soft kiss?
> Not this! not this!...
> And yet men tell us "we are only dreaming,"
> "Dreaming and waiting for some waking day,"
> "All we call living is but idle seeming,"
> "Imagination's work shall pass away!" –
> We meet their empty dreams with earnest strife –
> Our life *is* life!

Ann Elgar added to the scrapbook a map of the Isle of Wight, marked with crosses to show where the Elgars spent their honeymoon in 1889.

Alice Roberts came into Elgar's life in 1886 as an aspiring musician, and throughout their marriage was able to offer modest musical help, in the preparation of manuscript full scores, as an emergency pianist to help with proof-reading, or as mock-timpanist on a piece of household furniture for the same purpose. She convinced herself that it was sufficient task to nurture a genius; yet she never quite abandoned her own literary gifts. Much of her poetry from 1889 had the aim of stimulating Elgar to song, and her most ambitious achievement was the words for *From the Bavarian Highlands* (1895). In prose an essay such as *The Ideal in the Present* linked gallery visits with what Elgar was aiming at in music.

Her most sustained efforts, however, and so indicative of what she brought to the marriage, were pre-Elgar, dating from the quarter-century with her widowed mother at Hazeldine House. Two were printed, *Isabel Trevithoe* in blank verse (1878), and a two-volume novel, *Marchcroft Manor* (1882). Like Elgar himself, Alice Roberts grew up in the shadow of the Malvern Hills, and she had helped to see through the press and index a volume by the Rev.W.S.Symonds on the geology, natural history and antiquities of Wales, Devon and Cornwall. *Isabel Trevithoe* begins geologically on the Cornish coast:

> Above the sea, on hoary rocks long worn
> With wasting touch of wind and wave, high stood
> Trevithoe Court. Below, like storm-tossed flakes
> Of foam, flew restless gulls, now seeking swift
> Their lofty nests, now breasting bold the wave.
> The sea broke sullenly against a coast
> Fast bound by granite cliff, save here and there
> Where sheltered cove, with whitest sand o'erstrewn,
> E'er lulled the wrathful wave to gentler mood.

Isabel was the child of Sir Stephen Trevithoe:

> His only one, and much the father joyed
> To see her surely gain as years advanced,
> The same deep, pure delight in intercourse
> With noble mind, which, like a crystal spring,
> Had long refreshed his own aspiring soul.

After some foreign travel with her father, Isabel first met at Trevithoe Court the young man whose aspirations matched Sir Stephen's:

Lady Roberts and Alice about to visit

> There chanced to come a summer's tide had waned
> (The eighteenth summer now to Isabel),
> A stranger guest, to manhood newly grown,
> One Gilbert Ancillon. But late complete
> His college course, he left its hoary walls
> With lustre on a name illustrious.

Alice Roberts clearly has a significant future for the relationship between Gilbert and Isabel:

> Sir Stephen gladly saw his old friend's son,
> The gladlier to Trevithoe welcomed him
> As youth of promise rare; for Gilbert deep
> Had drunk the sacred stream which downward flows
> From classical fount, enriching latest days;
> Nor was each phase of modern thought forgot,
> He followed science too where'er she led,
> To fields undreamt of in the earlier days.
> Nor did the powers of mind alone point out
> The youth as one above the usual stamp.
> Inspired with ardent love for highest good,
> He grew with every year to deeper scorn
> Of all things base, to fuller sympathy
> With those oppressed by bitter want or wrong.

Gilbert's social conscience did not go down well with his own parents, who feared for the integrity of their ancient line. Among close friends he could freely discuss his passionate ideals, and now Sir Stephen proved a sympathetic listener and stimulus for visits to

> The rich-stored library, and there mused o'er
> The best-loved books; the while Sir Stephen told
> Of wise men he had known, and as they spoke
> They looked through lofty windows on the sea.

Then there was Isabel herself to sing 'lays of olden Italy' or 'newer classic strains of German song'. She might also recall a moment in Gilbert's childhood, when he had heard a girl's voice singing from an upper window in winter and now realised it was the young Isabel who had entranced him. He begged for the song again:

> Then bending o'er the notes a moment's space,
> She struck the chords, and clear and sweet rung out
> Her voice, and thus she sang her childish lay.

Alice Roberts had first written the poem at 9am on 29 December 1877, heading it 'The Snow (For a Child)'. It was revised for Isabel Trevithoe, where the third stanza now read:

> O snow, thou heal'st the smart
> Of frost's keen cruel dart;
> So soothe sad pain, O heart,
> As does the snow, the snow.

This was further changed in the author's copy with a marginal manuscript verse:

> O snow, in thy soft grave
> Sad flowers the winter brave,
> O heart, so soothe & save,
> As does the snow, the snow.

Before Elgar set the poem in 1894 as his op.26 no.1 it was again adjusted, but also doubled in length to include the melting of the snow and a desire that heart and soul might nevertheless endure in pristine purity.

At Sir Stephen's death, the entailed estate left Isabel without home or fortune. The last days at Trevithoe Court were painful, but at least in the household were two aged 'Scaps' to comfort her and reveal in the future Alice Elgar a canine affection she later suppressed:

> She knew the hour must come, and watched with pain
> The preparations slow, and watched the change
> Which crept o'er long familiar rooms and cast
> A sense of desolation all around.
> And yet the lone and changèd place seemed warm,
> And kinder far than stranger world beyond.
> Here all were griev'd with her, for e'en her dogs,
> Two favourites, which like the servitors,
> Both old and worn had grown within the house,
> Now scarce would leave her side. Uneasily
> They slunk from room to room, and with low whine
> They cast themselves down at their mistress' feet.

Initially Isabel went to live with Darcy relatives; but there the social whirl seemed pointless. She felt she must justify her existence, and went to lodge in London with an elderly widowed cousin. She had a clear conception of women's work:

Alice Roberts

> Their duties high, how they were bound to use
> Their mighty influence to clear the world
> Of wrong and endless sin, now half their fault.

Gilbert's father was aghast to hear such views, and was determined his son
should associate with her as little as possible when returned from a tour.
For Isabel herself the moment of truth came one June morning in a West
End street:

> She took her way, when, struck by piercing cry,
> She sudden turned and saw a child laid low
> By carriage passing swift. Then Isabel
> Quick sped, first gently raised, then drew the boy
> To paved way, safe from fast hurrying wheels.
> There on the dusty, trodden path she knelt
> And tender raised the half-unconscious head.

A passing workman brought water; Gilbert's father saw and walked on

> With friend as proud and lofty as himself.
> Hot flushed his brow, sore angered with the sight
> He was of Isabel, down on her knees,
> In June midday in West End street, tending
> A beggar boy. What a loss of dignity!

Gilbert found he returned to a society much changed during his three-
year absence. Particularly the women were altered:

> More free, more bold, he thought some women grown,
> No longer choice their words, refined their mien,
> And such he loathed; for lost their woman's grace,
> The crown of weaker sex, uncompensate
> By gain of manly strength; more tame were some
> But nought could stir their thought save dance or play.

He became increasingly depressed and cynical, wondering whether Isabel
too would have become equally alien to him. He happened to see her at a
reception but could observe she was different from the rest. Yet it was not
enough. The London season over, society dispersed to country retreats,
and Gilbert found himself much in the company of Lady Norah
Claireregard.

> And with dim views of marriage rising slow
> Within his brain, did Gilbert watch the girl

Now move with stately grace, now curb her steed.
And who could fail to note her wondrous eyes
Which gleamed translucently beneath her brows,
Dark as raven's wing? And Gilbert gently,
Pleased by gazing on such perfect loveliness,
Thought, could I find another bride so fair?

Out riding together, Gilbert took his chance to propose to Lady Norah in terms that were honest and practical.

Accepting his cool suit with cool regard,
"The age of love is past," she said, "a dream
Of fond romance, for our wise age unfit,"
As scornful smile passed o'er her perfect lips.

Almost at once Gilbert began to regret what he had done; but the marriage was fixed for early spring. Back in London he happened to see Isabel once more at a gallery, where both admired a picture obviously painted below Trevithoe Court. He heard of her misfortunes, about her social work, and about the injured boy she had taken to hospital. Almost in panic, as the wedding day approached, he longed to be that boy himself. Lady Norah was unaware of Gilbert's misgivings till one evening all three were invited to a friend's house. Gilbert's true feelings were then clear:

And soon was Isabel besought to sing;
She willing rose and crossed with usual grace
To where the piano stood, and heeding nought
On earth save following her footsteps sweet,
Swift followed Gilbert too, and lost in joy
He stood, as rose her voice ethereally
Above the jar of unharmonious life.

Lady Norah's image of herself had not prepared her for such a situation. She was nonplussed, yet

She silently endured, nor let a trace
Of trouble rest upon her haughty brow.

Gilbert's position was worse: he now knew his heart was not dead and that it was Isabel's; the only course was to visit her and bid farewell. She was singing again as he climbed to her lodgings. He at once requested a repeat of the song, which in 1894 became the text of another Elgar partsong, 'Fly, singing Bird'. The line 'Say I wait where anemones blow' in

the second stanza provides the code word 'anemone' which Elgar often
used when away and communicating with his wife. The following line,
'Weary, wait, till with waiting I fail' was set by Elgar in op.26 no.2 as it
appears in *Isabel Trevithoe*, though a manuscript change to the poem's
printed text produces '*Tell my love* that with waiting I fail'. Gilbert then
states his case as if it is the misfortune of a friend, but Isabel realises soon
enough he is telling his own story:

> He deeming now his heart was cold and dead,
> And caring not whate'er his fate, sought out
> A noble maid; he lightly wooed and won,
> And now the marriage day is fixed, and all
> Is ready save the laggard bridegroom cold.

He appeals to Isabel for help, and she, ever selfless, decides in her mind
that the engagement must proceed, and Lady Norah must play a different
part.

The result was a new torment to Gilbert:

> He paced
> The room with sudden fear possessed, that changed
> The Lady Norah seemed; indifferent
> No more to his own tastes. It could not be
> Her heart was warmed by love, for that the ill,
> The only ill still absent from his fate;
> For knowing neither loved they had agreed
> To wed, and thus might wander coldly on.

The following day there was a hunt at Gilbert's seat of Ancillon. It was
glorious spring weather, but Gilbert looked more gloomy than the rest:

> He moved, and ruled with ease, his fiery horse,
> While Lady Norah watched his high-born mien,
> His easy grace, with bright and love-lit eyes.
> At last to coppice near sped on the hunt,
> The chase began, and soon flew baying hounds
> And horsemen o'er the land in swift pursuit.

Gilbert drove his horse like a madman, as if completely careless of his life
and with nothing further to engage his interest:

> That day the first of all
> Rode Gilbert; now his headlong dash inspired
> The rest to ardour new, but they at last

Drew rein and sideways swerved, not daring face
A desp'rate leap o'er high and treach'rous fence.
He, roused with wild pursuit, and caring nought
For life, rode straightway at the place. His horse,
Though breathed by pace so hot, yet took the leap,
But leaped too short, and with his rider fell –
Fell, crashing down amidst the timbered fence,
In shapeless wreck. In horror paused the rest.
Eager to save they clustered round; with toil
They dragged him out from underneath his horse,
And still he breathed. Then slow they bore him home,
A senseless form, the wreck which one day's work
Had left of youth and strength.

Gilbert was now indeed the 'injured boy', and recovery was deadly slow. His parents at Ancillon Hall and Lady Norah did what they could, but he only began to rally when Isabel was at last summoned. It was clear how the future must be, and Lady Norah realised her ascendancy was over:

"Here, Gilbert Ancillon,
I now restore your troth, free, give you up.
I would not wed you now, although you prayed
Me on your knees. Unloving pact we made,
And light, but solemnly I break our bond."

Gilbert and Isabel were too much moved to have eyes for anything but each other:

So neither saw how pale
The Lady Norah's face, nor what the pain
Which quivered on her pass'nate lips, and as
Her voice she strove to steel, that none might know
The cost, it sounded harshly in their ears.

So Lady Norah left Ancillon Hall, Gilbert married Isabel, and Alice Roberts had showed the independence of spirit that would enable her in time to outface disapproval from any Ancillon Hall with its collateral aunts by marrying a man eight years her junior often to be seen serving in a music shop.

Similar ideals inform *Marchcroft Manor*, but the setting is more idyllic and social tensions largely absent. The effect of new ideas of the countryside raises local doubts, but the proper relationship between rectory and manor is satisfactorily sealed by marriage. The course of true love is interrupted only by the inept bungling of Dr.Malloney, father of the two girls who are eventually to marry the young men. He hopelessly misjudges the situation, imagines the wrong man is in love with the wrong girl, and involves the plot in impossible points of honour that take all the author's tact to submit to reason. The complications are pure comedy of errors, involving the usual heartache. They suggest a pre-echo of Bernard Shaw's 1929 speech in reply to Elgar, when describing the theatre of his early days: 'You had a heroine whose marriage was put off by improbable events, of one kind and another until it was time for the people to go home.'

The novel plunges instantly *in medias res*. Through the death of a cousin, Julian de Tressanay finds himself lord of Marchcroft Manor, as he explains to his friend Roger Osborne: 'I, who have never thought of landed property, except to expatiate on the criminality of its tenure in general, and now I, of all people, I suddenly find myself the possessor of a large domain and old baronial mansion, every stone of which could probably bear testimony to some deed of violence and oppression committed by its rapacious feudal owners.'   Alice Roberts gives an interesting description of her hero:

> Julian de Tressanay was unusually tall, his dark hair and olive complexion pointing to his foreign extraction. The expression of his face was singularly mobile, the dark eyes and rather irregular features lighting up with fire and excitement when speaking with eager gesture on subjects on which he felt strongly. He held an appointment in the Foreign Office; his duties were irksome to him, but he persevered, however, in the profession as he required some addition to his income, and furthermore, it secured to him the advantage of living in London. This was a weighty consideration, for he had thrown his whole soul into the stirring questions of the day, the improvement of the lower classes, the progress of humanity, and in London he found friends who sympathised with his aims, and scope for expounding his ideas.

The barrister Roger Osborne, on the other hand, 'scarcely reached middle height, his features were finely cut, his eyes clear and grey, his whole appearance was that of a refined gentleman whose composure it would not be easy to ruffle'. He admired Julian's convictions but could not consider them practical. Roger teased his friend but sometimes regretted the absence of enthusiasm in his own life. He was convinced he had finished with love; Julian knew he had not yet begun. The setting is mostly rural and Alice Roberts sings the praise of her land:

> English people, as a rule, are given to disparage their own country, to

explore remote and unfrequented foreign parts, scarcely knowing anything of their own country the while. Yet, dispensing with features of grandeur or sublimity, where can fairer scenes be met with than when travelling through the rich inland counties of England in the early days of August? The foliage is dark and heavy from the summer sun, but it is relieved here and there by fresh autumnal shoots; the grass fields are smooth and green after the recent mowing, while richest and most beautiful of all are the fields of golden corn and waving barley. A breath of peace and content seems to pervade the whole atmosphere; and if below the surface there are wrongs and miseries awaiting redress, yet it must be confessed that the land is fair and that one might do worse than spend one's days on the soil which is free from oppression, and which has been so long untrod by the foot of foreign invaders.

Ella Maloney, who was eventually to marry Roger, and her younger sister Olive, future bride of Julian, were both considered dreadfully spoilt by the Rector, their uncle-by-marriage. He recommended they should do some reading before receiving a visit from the intelligent young men just established at the Manor. They did nothing of the sort: 'First they went out through the low dining-room window into the garden, and as if they were not already sufficiently charming to look upon, they lingered amongst the rose trees, gathering here a bud and here a blossom, and here a spray of fragrant jessamine, which, fastened into their fresh morning dresses, rendered them both more distractingly pretty than before.'

Once Dr.Malloney's obtuseness had been overcome, and marriage pledges were fulfilled, De Tressanay and Olive made a handsome pair at the Manor:

> Julian never realized the prediction that Roger had made concerning him when he first succeeded to the Manor. He never lapsed into a common-place landowner with none but local interests. He became a distinguished politician and speaker. The old Conservative country gentlemen would shake their heads gravely and say, "A talented young man, it is a misfortune he should hold such dangerous views". Some of these grave personages, however, lived to find more than one of his audacious theories carried out and benefitting the community at large.

3 - The wizard of the north

The final verses of Tennyson's 1842 'Morte d'Arthur' include a dream:

> There came a bark that, blowing forward, bore
> King Arthur, like a modern gentleman
> Of stateliest port; and all the people cried,
> "Arthur is come again: he cannot die."

If by Elgar's day the mediaeval knight had become the Victorian gentleman, his ancestor was much in vogue at the turn of the century. Richard Hurd (1720-1808), who became bishop of Worcester in 1781, had written favourably in his *Moral and Political Dialogues* (1759) of the tilt-yard as a 'school of fortitude and honour to our generous forefathers'. He warmly praised knightly attributes of old: 'Affability, courtesy, generosity, veracity, these were the qualifications most pretended to by the men at arms, in the days of pure and uncorrupted chivalry.' The excesses of the French Revolution had shown dramatically where Enlightenment might lead. Burke (1729-97) could fulminate about the death of Marie Antoinette (1755-93) and protest that 'the age of chivalry is gone. That of sophisters, economists, and calculators, has succeeded; and the glory of England is extinguished for ever.' It was not quite so. French folly stimulated the British conservative and antiquary. George III (1760-1820) commissioned Benjamin West (1738-1820) to paint episodes from the reign of Edward III in the king's audience chamber at Windsor. Edward III became a key figure in British mediaevalism. West, an American from Pennsylvania, preserved royal favour during the war of American Independence but lost it for praise of Napoleon. His Windsor scenes include Edward's meeting the Black Prince his son (1330-76) after Crécy; the Black Prince receiving King John of France (1319-64) after the battle of Poitiers (1356); the episode with the burghers of Calais; and the foundation of the Order of the Garter (1348). Edward III was convinced that Windsor was King Arthur's birthplace, or was determined to make it so. William Beckford (1759-1844) had an Edward III gallery at Fonthill, stretching south from the great central tower. It contained seventy-two coats of arms, of the king and Garter knights, from all of whom Beckford claimed descent. On St. George's Day 1805, twenty-five new knights of the Garter were installed: 'It was his majesty's particular wish, that as many of the old customs should be kept up as possible.'

Above : Benjamin West's work for George III

Left : Dryburgh Abbey and Scott's tomb

Thus it remained at the coronation of George IV (1820-30), when there was an awed reaction from foreigners present: they were 'utterly astonished and delighted to see the revival of feudal dresses and feudal grandeur when the occasion demanded it, and that in a degree of splendour which, they averred, they had never seen paralleled in Europe'. Walter Scott was there, and he made telling use of the magnificent scene three years later in *Redgauntlet* (1824):

> At a table above the rest, and extending across the upper end of the hall, sat enthroned the youthful Sovereign himself, surrounded by the princes of the blood, and other dignitaries, and receiving the suit and homage of his subjects. Heralds and poursuivants, blazing in their fantastic yet splendid armorial habits, and pages of honour, gorgeously arrayed in the garb of other days, waiting upon the princely banqueters.

Scott describes a 'youthful Sovereign' because he transferred the scene from the coronation of George III to that of his son. Lilias Redgauntlet mentions the arrival of the king's champion, a moment when she had to play a dramatic part:

> A loud flourish of trumpets, and the voice of heralds, were mixed with the clatter of horses' hoofs, while a champion, armed at all points, like those I had read of in romances, attended by squires, pages, and the whole retinue of chivalry, pranced forward, mounted upon a barbed steed. His challenge, in defiance of all who dared impeach the title of the new sovereign, was recited aloud – once, and again.

Scott's roots in the Border lands were evocative enough. His great-grandfather of the same name was an uncompromising Jacobite known as 'Beardie', because he would not shave till the Stuarts were restored. There is a reminder of him in *Marmion* of 1808:

> The banished race of kings revered,
> And lost his land – but kept his beard.

Dryburgh Abbey, where Scott was eventually buried, was on land belonging to his grandmother. How far the family's feudal dignity extended or involved it in marauding exploits was matter perhaps less for history than Scott's imagination. Trained in the law and colleague to his attorney father for a while, both are portrayed as the Fairfords in *Redgauntlet*. Lame through a fever in boyhood, he became an expert horseman, and turned his spirited galloping on Leith Sands into the verse of Deloraine's hectic ride to Melrose in *The Lay of the Last Minstrel* (1805) and the opening of *The Lady of the Lake* (1810), where James is in single-minded chase of a stag. He and his future French wife, Charlotte, met on horseback.

A major enthusiasm at university had been German Romantic literature. He was fired by a recital in English of Bürger's *Lenore*, future inspiration for a Raff symphony (1872). With some friends he hired a tutor and attempted a *Lenore* translation of his own. He immersed himself in Schiller and Goethe, making a careful study of the latter's *Götz von Berlichingen* (1773) in praise of ancient feudalism on the Rhine. German literature became a first spur to poetry. He admired the *Reliques of Ancient English Poetry* (1765) by Bishop Thomas Percy, a source Elgar knew to the extent of wondering whether to head *The Banner of St. George* with a couple of extracts. He believed that the ballads were the product of minstrels in the employment of chieftains and lairds, and a major project of 1804 was an edition of *Sir Tristrem* of Thomas the Rhymer (fl.?1220-97). Scott was probably in error when ascribing the poem to Thomas, but he was at once plunged into the world of Arthurian romance. Of supreme importance to Scott, it seemed as if an Arthurian cycle had begun and chivalry had early flowered near his own home. He had moved from Edinburgh to the Borders with the appointment as sheriff-depute of Selkirkshire. There he had scope for local antiquarian research. From his first days as a copying clerk he had bought books, medals and memorabilia, modest foundation of the portentous collection he built up at Abbotsford.

Scott's first original work of importance was *The Lay of the Last Minstrel* :

> The last of all the Bards was he
> Who sung of Border chivalry.

Scott relishes the martial litany as he numbers the retainers of his neighbour:

> Nine-and-twenty knights of fame
> Hung their shields in Branksome hall;
> Nine-and-twenty squires of name
> Brought them their steeds to bower from stall;
> Nine-and-twenty yeomen tall
> Waited, duteous, on them all:
> They were all knights of mettle true,
> Kinsmen to the bold Buccleuch.

The notes Scott appended to his verse and novels show his magpie delight in a range of scholarship that informs all his writing. The laird of

Abbotsford was at his desk well before breakfast, adopting the Elgarian pose of country squire rather than author.

Scott's notes to *The Lay of the Last Minstrel* involve him at once in Elgarian interests. Froissart features large; there is a glimpse of Simon Magus, who should have appeared in *The Kingdom* as Peter's adversary; and Scott displays his knowledge of heraldry, a subject Elgar delighted in. Note 3 mentions the Scot's fighting method: 'Of a truth,' says Froissart, 'the Scottish cannot boast great skill with the bow, but rather bear axes, with which, in time of need, they give heavy strokes.' Froissart is cited in note 24, where Scott touches on the Moslem world he was to treat so sympathetically in *The Talisman*: 'A Saracen champion is thus described by Froissart: "Among the Sarazyns, there was a yonge knight called Agadinger Dolyferne; he was always wel mounted on a redy and a lyght horse; it seemed when the horse ranne, that he did fly in the ayre." (vol.ii, ch.71).' Note 11 mentions Simon Magus: 'The shadow of a necromancer is independent of the sun. Glycas informs us that Simon Magus caused his shadow to go before him, making people believe it was an attendant spirit.' In note 14 Scott embarks on heraldic lore: 'The arms of the Kerrs of Cessford were, *Vert* on a cheveron, betwixt three unicorns' heads, erased *argent*, three mullets sable; crest, a unicorn's head, erased *proper*. The Scotts of Buccleuch bore, *Or*, on a bend azure; a star of six points betwixt two crescents of the first.' Elgar's most elaborate excursus on heraldry was in the postscript of a letter to F.G.Edwards (1853-1909) of 19 July 1908 concerning Potters Bar, where Edwards happened to live. Having discussed exhaustively the word 'Bar', Elgar concludes with heraldry: 'P.S. Potters Bar can have no heraldic significance: ignorant novelists speak of a bar sinister, a thing which cannot exist, & the simple bar is to[o] "obvious" an[d] ordinary to be associated solely with Potter.' Elgar painted various coats of arms for the billiard room at Severn House, and he referred to the Worcester shield when writing on 18 June 1915 to Alice Stuart Wortley from the home of Hubert Leicester: 'I must use one of the Mayoral cards: you will recognise the Arms from seeing my own attempt in the Billiard room.' On 17 June 1920 Elgar wrote to Troyte Griffith about the stone for Lady Elgar's grave: 'I fear the arms must be on a lozenge; Boutell says "A Lozenge takes the place of a shield to bear the arms of Ladies, *with the sole exception of the Sovereign*". That seems conclusive. But St.John Hope in his little grammar of Eng: Heraldry says a *roundel* or *lozenge* might be used.'

In note 1 to *Marmion* Scott indicates what Malory has meant to him: 'The romance of the Morte Arthur contains a sort of abridgement of the most celebrated adventures of the Round Table; and, being written in comparatively modern language, gives the general reader an excellent idea of what romances of chivalry actually were. It has also the merit of being written in pure old English; and many of the wild adventures which it contains are told with a simplicity bordering on the sublime.' In the poem itself Scott treats of Lancelot and the consequence of his love for Guenevere:

> A sinful man, and unconfess'd,
> He took the Sangreal's holy quest,
> And, slumbering, saw the vision high
> He might not view with waking eye.

It was the rich vein of Scottish lore, however, that mainly sustained his verse and gained him a host of admirers, starting with the Prince Regent. There was a warning shot from Byron (1788-1824), though, in *English Bards and Scotch Reviewers – A Satire* as early as 1809:

> Thus lays of Minstrels – may they be the last! –
> On half-strung harps whine mournful to the blast.
> While mountain spirits prate to river sprites,
> That dames may listen to the sounds at nights;
> And goblin brats, of Gilpin Horner's brood,
> Decoy young border-nobles through the wood,
> And skip at every step, Lord knows how high,
> And frighten foolish babes, the Lord knows why;
> While high-born ladies in their magic cell,
> Forbidding knights to read who cannot spell,
> Despatch a courier to a wizard's grave,
> And fight with honest men to shield a knave.

Then in March 1812 Byron produced the first two cantos of *Childe Harold*, a compelling tale told with a wit and irony Scott had never attempted.

With characteristic generosity Scott recognised Byron's achievement at once; with characteristic resource he decided on a future as novelist, anonymous though universally suspected till 1827. Much of *Waverley* had been written in 1805; it was now resumed, only to be set aside in April 1814 when he was asked to write an article on 'Chivalry' for a supplement to the *Encyclopaedia Britannica*. Scott expressed both admiration and distaste for the institution, arguing a careful case and marshalling much evidence. Chivalry was a main factor, he felt, separating the ancient world from the modern: 'The Greeks and Romans fought for liberty or for conquest, and the knights of the middle ages for God and for their ladies.'

Scott saw clearly that chivalry was open to abuse: 'the devotion of the knights often degenerated into superstition, - their love into licentiousness, - their sprit of loyalty or freedom into tyranny and turmoil, - their generosity and gallantry into hare-brained madness and absurdity'. Scott explained how initiation in the practice of arms became more than a military matter:

> it became a religious rite, sanctified by the forms of the church which he was in future to defend. The novice had to watch his arms in a church or chapel, or at least on hallowed ground, the knight before he had received the honour of knighthood. He was made to assume a white dress, in imitation of the neophytes of the church. Fast and confession were added to vigils; the purification of the bath was imposed on the military acolyte, in imitation of the initiatory rite of Christianity.

A result was the 'infidel' was treated with the more intolerance: 'If an infidel, says a great authority, impugn the doctrines of the Christian faith before a churchman, he should reply to him by argument; but a knight should render no other reason to the infidel than six inches of his falchion thrust into his accursed bowels.' Scott outlines the role of the church in developing the idea of chivalry from enthusiasm for the crusades: 'But the Romish clergy, who have in all ages possessed the wisdom of serpents, if they have sometimes fallen short of the simplicity of doves, saw the advantage of converting this temporary zeal, which animated the warriors of their creed against the invading infidels, into a permanent union of principles, which should blend the ceremonies of religious worship with the military establishment of the ancient Goths and Germans.' Conquest of the Holy Land resulted in a 'union between temporal and spiritual Chivalry (for such was the term sometimes given to monastic establishments)'. It had called into existence the Knights of St.John of Jerusalem, the Knights Templars and the Teutonic Knights, protagonists from which feature largely in such Scott novels as *Ivanhoe* and *The Talisman.*

Scott mentions those members of the heavenly host whose tenets seemed most to accord with the spirit of chivalry: 'St.Michael, the leader of banded Seraphim, and the personal antagonist of Satan, - St.George, St.James, and St.Martin, all of whom popular faith had invested with the honours of Chivalry, were frequently selected as the appropriate champions of the militant adventurers yet on earth.' The English king warring in France at the highpoint of chivalry turned naturally to a helping hand from heaven at moments of crisis:

> Edward III, fighting valiantly in a night-skirmish before the gates of Calais, was heard to accompany each blow he struck with the invocation of his tutelar saints, Ha! Saint Edward! ha! St.George! but the Virgin Mary, to

whom their superstition ascribed the qualities of youth, beauty, and sweetness, which they prized in their terrestrial mistresses, was an especial object of the devotion of the followers of Chivalry.

Scott turns to the demands and customs of chivalry towards women: '[it exacted] a devotion to the female sex, and particularly to her whom each knight selected as the chief object of his affection, of a nature so extravagant and unbounded as to approach to a sort of idolatry.' Scott quotes Chaucer, contemporary of Edward III, typically joyous on the subject:

> To fight for a lady! Ah! Benedicite,
> It were a lusty sight for to see.

Scott notes the social mobility that might be involved: 'it was the prerogative of Chivalry to abrogate the distinction of rank, and elevate the hopes of the knight, whose sole patrimony was his arms and valour, to the high-born and princely dame, before whom he carved as a sewer.' What was the situation now, towards the end of George III's reign? It seemed to Scott as if mediaeval chivalry was no more: 'We can now only look back on it as a beautiful and fantastic piece of frostwork, which has dissolved in the beams of the sun!' Scott had no doubt, however, that its legacy lived on:

> Its effects are to be sought in the general feeling of respect to the female sex; in the rules of forbearance and decorum in society; in the duties of speaking truth and observing courtesy; and in the general conviction and assurance, that, as no man can encroach upon the property of another without accounting to the laws, so none can infringe on his personal honour, be the difference of rank what it may, without subjecting himself to personal responsibility.

Elgar's mother could have recognised the validity of such an account, and indeed for Elgar himself it was an unspoken code of conduct. The chivalrous gentleman survived the First World War with difficulty, and in such reduced numbers it might have seemed his day was done.

Waverley was completed in 1814 and the series of remarkable novels was launched. As captain of the *Jumping Jenny*, Elgar gets a splendid testimonial from Scott: 'Nanty Ewart could steer through the Pentland Firth though he were as drunk as the Baltic Ocean.' In *Redgauntlet* he is about to transport Alan Fairford in search of Darsie Latimer across the Solway Firth: 'Nanty was one of those topers, who, becoming early what *bon vivants* term flustered, remain whole nights and days at the same point of intoxication; and, in fact, as they are seldom entirely sober, can

Scott's study at Abbotsford

be as rarely seen absolutely drunk.' The *Jumping Jenny* was not made for comfort, and Nanty's concentration at the wheel did not blind him to the need of his passenger: Alan felt a movement near him, but this was just Nanty 'wrapping around him, as softly as he could, a great boat-cloak, in order to defend him from the morning air'. Alan read some Sallust on board, and Nanty showed him later he had, as well as his penchant for brandy, a 'handful of Latin, and a small pinch of Greek'. Elgar was frolicking with the Baker boys not long after correcting *Froissart* proofs in February 1901. He addressed them as 17th-century notables: 'H.H.Rupert Prince Palatine, H.G.Duke of Buckingham & the Rt.Hon. the Earl of Rochester'. To Prince Rupert he was loud in complaint: 'These from a much tried man; tried in temper, and in health, and in such wits as are left. The subscriber beseecheth your Highness to relieve him from the vexation intolerable of living in four lives at once in three separate centuries.' At the last Scott's Nanty Ewart displays all his creator's love of chivalry. When Cristal Nixon wants to implicate Nanty in his schemes to betray Redgauntlet and his fellow confederates, he flares up: 'Me help to betray poor devils, that have been so often betrayed myself! – Not if they were a hundred Popes, Devils, and Pretenders. I will back and tell them their danger.' But in a moment the altercation leads to the death of both.

Redgauntlet has much music in it, and violin music at that. The blind fiddler 'Wandering Willie' and the youthful Darsie Latimer strike up a friendship by means of their playing, and later communicate through popular tunes, fiddled or whistled, when Darsie is held by Redgauntlet against his will on the southern side of the Solway Firth. Suddenly he heard 'the unwonted sound of a violin, in the farmyard beneath my windows'. He knew at once it was Wandering Willie: 'It will not appear surprising to those who have made music their study, that, after listening to a few notes, I became at once assured that the musician was no other than the itinerant.' Darsie acknowledges the outstanding fiddler: 'the superior delicacy and force of whose execution would enable me to swear to his bow amongst a whole orchestra. I had the less reason to doubt his identity, because he played twice over the beautiful Scottish air called Wandering Willie.' Darsie thought wrily of a musical precedent: 'The history of Richard Coeur de Lion and his minstrel, Blondel, rushed, at the same time, on my mind, though I could not even then suppress a smile at the dignity of the example, when applied to a blind fiddler and myself.'

Scott's introduction to *The Talisman* (1825) shows his judicious sense of history and fine lack of prejudice: 'The period relating more immediately to the Crusades, which I at last fixed upon, was that at which the warlike character of Richard I., wild and generous, a pattern of chivalry, with all its extravagant virtues, and its no less absurd errors, was opposed to that of Saladin, in which the Christian and English monarch showed all the cruelty and violence of an Eastern Sultan; and Saladin, on the other hand, displayed the deep policy and prudence of a European sovereign.' Scott strains our credulity by introducing Saladin (1138-93) as a lone emir of the desert, and then having him enter the camp of Richard (1189-99) as a ministering physician, wielding the healing power of the 'talisman'. After the Scottish Sir Kenneth, knight of the Leopard, has encountered the whirling horsemanship of Saladin in the desert of Palestine, both warriors repose, and Scott characteristically turns his attention to the horses:

> Each was wrapt for some time in his own reflections, and took breath after an encounter which had threatened to be fatal to one or both; and their good horses seemed no less to enjoy the interval of repose. That of the Saracen, however, though he had been forced into much the more violent and extended sphere of motion, appeared to have suffered less from fatigue than the charger of the European knight. The sweat hung still clammy on the limbs of the last, when those of the noble Arab were completely dried, by the interval of tranquil exercise, all saving the foam-flakes which were still visible on his bridle and housings.

Only relaxing briefly, the combatants prepared their horses:

> The steeds, therefore, suffered themselves quietly to be taken from their food and liberty, and neighed and snuffled fondly around their masters, while they were adjusting their accoutrements for farther travel and additional toil.

Richard is sick, and Scott has him chafing at the inactivity of the army: 'does a league of monarchs, an assemblage of nobles, a convocation of all the chivalry of Europe, droop with the sickness of one man, though he chances to be King of England?' In his frustration he castigates his confederate leaders, and notably the Duke of Austria, who was later to take him captive. But already El Hakim, the Saracen skilled in medicine, purportedly sent by Saladin but in fact the man himself, is within the camp. He has demonstrated his art by tending a retainer of Sir Kenneth's. De Vaux, the king's right hand man, had reluctantly agreed that El Hakim should see Richard and equally reluctantly consented that the Scottish knight should keep his hound Roswal, a privilege usually granted only to earls: ' "Has he then a dog so handsome?" said the King.' Scott has the taciturn de Vaux lyrical in reply: ' "A most perfect creature of Heaven," said the baron, who was an enthusiast in field sports – "of the noblest Northern breed - deep in the chest, strong in the stern, black colour, and brindled on the breast and legs, not spotted with white, but just shaded into grey - strength to pull down a bull - swiftness to cote an antelope".'

Cured by the Saracen, Richard acknowledges his debt to Sir Kenneth and gives him charge over the banner of England raised on St.George's Mount. The knight of the Leopard was alone during his vigil but for Roswal. Two hours passed, but then came a playful message from Queen Berengaria (d.c.1230), feigning that Edith Plantagenet, whom he much admired, was desirous of a word with Sir Kenneth. Culpably he deserted his post, leaving Roswal to guard the standard. Teased by Berengaria's ladies, the Scot hears suddenly a savage bark and yell of agony from the Mount of St.George. Disgraced and awaiting sentence, Sir Kenneth again has recourse to El Hakim. Roswal lived and proved his sagacity by identifying his assailant as Conrade of Montferrat, seizing him by the throat and pulling him from the saddle. Philip of France (1165-1223) queries the judgment of a mere cur; Sir Walter then allows King Richard a truly Elgarian defence of Roswal:

> "recollect that the Almighty, who gave the dog to be companion of our pleasures and our toils, hath invested him with a nature noble and incapable of deceit. He forgets neither friend nor foe – remembers, and with accuracy, both benefit and injury. He hath a share of man's intelligence, but no share of man's falsehood".

Once Berengaria has confessed her guile towards Sir Kenneth and he is revealed as Prince David of Scotland, there is no impediment to his union with Edith Plantagenet.

Dogs were Scott's constant companions and he often insisted portraits of himself or the family should include them. One other novel features a canine protagonist. This was Bevis in *Woodstock* (1826), a tale of the Civil War and the year 1651, when Charles II (1660-85) was on the run after the battle of Worcester. Sir Henry Lee of Ditchley, keeper of Woodstock Park, royalist to his finger-tips, is pitted against the armed might of Oliver Cromwell (1599-1658), the one determined to safeguard Charles, the other to capture him. Scott has Sir Henry leaving church with his dog:

> wrapped in his laced cloak, and with beard and whiskers duly composed, he moved slowly through the aisles, followed by the faithful mastiff, or bloodhound, which in old times had saved his master by his fidelity, and which regularly followed him to church. Bevis, indeed, fell under the proverb which avers, "He is a good dog which goes to church"; for, bating an occasional temptation to warble along with the accord, he behaved himself as decorously as any of the congregation, and returned as much edified, perhaps, as most of them.

When Bevis apparently deserts Sir Henry to follow a stranger, the old knight recounts a story Scott remembered from Froissart. It is, Sir Henry thinks, because he has fallen on hard times since the triumph of the parliamentarians:

> "I have read, in faithful chronicles, that when Richard II and Henry of Bolingbroke were at Berkeley Castle, a dog of the same kind deserted the King, whom he had always attended upon, and attached himself to Henry, whom he then saw for the first time. Richard foretold, from the desertion of his favourite, his approaching deposition."

At once to correct Sir Henry, Bevis hinted his presence:

> There was a distant rustling among the withered leaves, a bouncing or galloping sound on the path, and the favourite dog instantly joined his master.

Charles, then twenty-two, is introduced in heavy disguise as a female fortune-teller, sufficiently conscious of her true nature to show unwelcome familiarity to Sir Henry's daughter, Alice, who responded with dignified resentment: ' "I have no reason to make my cries heard as far as Woodstock; were there occasion for my crying for help at all, it is nearer at hand".' Bevis broke through the bushes at her word and stood alert at her side. Charles establishes himself in Sir Henry's household as a royalist page, Louis Kerneguy, but this incarnation pleased Bevis no better:

> he kept up a pique against their new guest, which no advances on the part of Charles were able to soften. If the page was by chance left alone with his young mistress, Bevis chose always to be of the party; came close by Alice's chair, and growled audibly when the gallant drew near her.

Charles escapes, but Lee, his entourage, and Bevis are captured. Cromwell's first instinct is to deliver them all to the hangman. Gentler counsels prevail, and Cromwell's lieutenant explains the situation: ' "There remains only one sentenced person," said Pearson, "a noble wolf-hound, finer than any your Excellency saw in Ireland. He belongs to the old knight Sir Henry Lee. Should your Excellency not desire to keep the fine creature yourself, might I presume to beg that I might have leave?" ' Cromwell decides that Sir Henry must be reunited with Bevis, and Scott has them grow old together, dying within brief space of each other.

Mention of Froissart and reliance on him is ubiquitous in Scott. Claverhouse's speech to Morton in *Old Mortality* (1816) may therefore not be the only spur to the naming of Elgar's first concert overture.

Certainly it was a novel he knew, as he refers to it in a letter of 11 July 1916 to Alice Stuart Wortley: he had been spending his time at The Hut 'like Old Mortality renovating old inscriptions'. Scott's 'Old Mortality' was the nickname of Robert Paterson, who roamed Scotland near the end of the 18th century repairing monuments to the Cameronians. They had been strict Covenanters opposed to the policies of Charles II.

The most lovable and yet fantastic character in Sir Walter's novel is Lady Margaret Bellenden of Tillietudlem. Her moment of never to be forgotten splendour had been her entertainment of Charles himself to a breakfast. When there came the unexpected need to show hospitality to the royalist commander, Grahame of Claverhouse, the royal precedent was uppermost in Lady Margaret's mind. There were tedious vexations, as Lady Margaret made clear to her principal female attendance: ' "wherefore is the venison pasty placed on the left side of the throne, when ye may right weel remember, Mysie, that his most sacred majesty with his ain hand shifted the pasty to the same side with the flagon, and said they were too good friends to be parted?" '

Lady Margaret climbed to the battlements 'by many a winding passage and uncouth staircase'. From that vantage point a first sight of Claverhouse's approaching force would be made: 'the distant sounds of military music began to be heard from the public high-road which winded up the vale, and announced the approach of the expected body of cavalry. Their glimmering ranks were shortly afterwards seen in the distance, appearing and disappearing as the trees and windings of the road permitted them to be visible, and distinguished chiefly by the flashes of light which their arms occasionally reflected against the sun.'

And what of Claverhouse himself? Scott gives him a complex character within a frame 'in the prime of life, rather low of stature, and slightly, though elegantly, formed'. There was at once a discrepancy between his appearance and his spirit: 'The severity of his character, as well as the higher attributes of undaunted and enterprising valour which even his enemies were compelled to admit, lay concealed under an exterior which seemed adapted to the court or the saloon rather than to the field.' Such an impression was deceptive: 'But under this soft exterior was hidden a spirit unbounded in daring and aspiring, yet cautious and prudent as that of Machiavel himself.'

Henry Morton is under duress at the hands of Claverhouse, who happens to ask him, ' "Did you ever read Froissart?" ' At Morton's negative, Claverhouse continues that he has half a mind ' "to contrive you should have six months' imprisonment in order to procure you that pleasure" '. He then extols the historian's achievement:

His chapters inspire me with more enthusiasm than even poetry itself. And the noble canon, with what true chivalrous feeling he confines his beautiful expressions of sorrow to the death of the gallant and high-bred, of whom it was a pity to see the fall, such was his loyalty to his king, pure faith to his religion, hardihood towards his enemy, and fidelity to his lady-love! – Ah, bendicite! how he will mourn over the fall of such a pearl of knighthood, be it on the side he happens to favour, or on the other.

Scott's *Quentin Durward* (1823) may have come into Elgar's mind when he looked for the first time on the statue of Charles the Bold (1467-77) in the Hofkirche at Innsbruck (see p.152). A main tension in the novel is the interaction between Louis XI of France (1461-83) and Charles of Burgundy, which reaches its astonishing climax when Louis appeared on Burgundian territory at Péronne. Scott introduces Quentin in the happiest circumstances:

It was upon a delicious summer morning, before the sun had assumed its scorching power, and while the dews yet cooled and perfumed the air, that a youth, coming from the north-eastward, approached the ford of a small river, or rather a large brook, tributary to the Cher, near to the royal castle of Plessis-les-Tours.

Having a relative in Louis XI's Archers of the Royal Guard, a Scottish contingent, Durward approached the castle with the aim of joining them. There he soon found himself involved in the subtle machinations of the 'universal spider' as Louis XI was known to history. Sir Walter assesses his character with masterly precision:

Calm, crafty, and profoundly attentive to his own interests, he made every sacrifice, both of pride and passion, which could interefere with it. He was careful in disguising his real sentiments and purposes from all who approached him, and frequently used the expressions, "that the king knew not how to reign, who knew not how to dissemble; and that, for himself, if he thought his very cap knew his secrets, he would throw it into the fire".

Scott adds further characteristics:

He was by nature vindictive and cruel, even to the extent of finding pleasure in the frequent executions which he commanded.

Until 1461, when he assumed the crown, Louis had for some time taken refuge at the court of Charles's father and another Hofkirche statue, Philip the Good (1419-67) of Burgundy. For Louis as king the main concern was the increasing power of Charles the Bold. Scott describes the contrast between them: 'Charles, surnamed the Bold, or rather the Audacious, for his courage was allied to rashness and frenzy, then wore the ducal coronet of Burgundy, which he burned to convert into a royal and independent regal crown.' If Louis was crafty and cautious, Charles 'rushed on danger because he loved it, and on difficulties because he despised them'. Scott skilfully deploys their diverse characters in plots that take all the ingenuity of the young Quentin to evade on his own behalf and notably on that of the Countess Isabelle de Croye, whom he protects in all emergencies and eventually wins. Durward exhibits throughout all of chivalry's 'generosity and self-denial, of which, if the earth were prived, it would be difficult to conceive the existence of virtue among the human race'.

Elgar's letter to the *Times Literary Supplement* of 21 July 1921 deals with Scott's use of Shakespeare. There is reference to five novels but none to the many Shakespearean chapter-headings throughout the canon. Elgar cited a passage from *Waverley*:

> Yet did I mark where Cupid's shaft did light;
> It lighted not on little western flower,
> But on bold yeoman, flower of all the west,
> Hight Jonas Culbertfield, the steward's son.

The original is from Oberon in *A Midsummer Night's Dream* (Act 2, scene i):

> Yet mark'd I where the bolt of Cupid fell.
> It fell upon a little western flower;
> Before, milk-white; now purple with love's wound,
> And maidens call it, love-in-idleness.

Elgar might have recognised with happy sympathy the reading habits of Edward Waverley: 'like the epicure who only deigned to take a single morsel from the sunny side of a peach, [he] read no volume a moment after it ceased to excite his curiosity or interest'. The result was typically Elgarian:

> he had read, and stored in a memory of uncommon tenacity, much curious, though ill-arranged and miscellaneous information. In English literature he was master of Shakespeare and Milton, of our earlier dramatic authors, of many picturesque and interesting passages from our old historical chronicles, and was particularly well acquainted with Spenser, Drayton, and other poets who have exercised themselves on romantic fiction, of all themes the most fascinating to a youthful imagination, before the passions have roused themselves, and demand poetry of a more sentimental description.

With the prospect of a military future, as determined by his father, Edward Waverley broke into verse of his own:

> For ever dead to fancy's eye
> Be each gay form that glided by,
> While dreams of love and lady's charms
> Give place to honour and to arms.

Scott's invocation of Shakespeare, as quoted by Elgar, would not have escaped Waverley's notice; he need not now be too much concerned that Cecilia Stubbs would soon marry the son of his uncle's steward. Likewise he had no need to regret the abandonment of another pursuit: 'of all diversions which ingenuity ever devised for the relief of idleness, fishing is the worst qualified to amuse a man who is at once indolent and impatient'. That did not prove to be Elgar's case.

In 1745 Edward Waverley joined his regiment in Scotland. Already, as Scott relates, he had browsed freely in continental literature:

> In this respect his acquaintance with Italian opened him yet a wider range. He had perused the usual romantic poems, which, from the days of Pulci, have been a favourite exercise of the wits of Italy, and had sought gratification in the numerous collections of *novelle*, which were brought forth by the genius of that elegant though luxurious nation, in emulation of the Decameron. In classical literature, Waverley had made the usual progress, and read the usual authors; and the French had afforded him an almost exhaustless collection of memoirs, scarcely more faithful than romances, and of romances so well written as hardly to be distinguished from memoirs. The splendid pages of Froissart, with his heart-stirring and eye-dazzling descriptions of war and of tournaments, were among his chief favourites.

Elgar introduces *Ivanhoe* (1819) in his *Literary Supplement* letter under the heading of 'assimilation' of Shakespeare by Scott. He refers to a correspondent of the previous week, 'D.C.', who had linked *Ivanhoe* with *Troilus and Cressida*:

> In the last chapter of "Ivanhoe," after King Richard has proclaimed the dissolution of the Templars' Chapter of Templestowe, he rides along the front of the armed Templars challenging them to break a lance with him.
> "What, Sirs! Among so many gallant knights, will none dare splinter a spear with Richard? – Sirs of the Temple! your ladies are but sunburned if they are not worth the shiver of a broken lance!"
> This is a direct borrowing from *Troilus and Cressida*, I., iii, 280-3.

Aeneas comes to the Grecian camp to challenge a Greek warrior to meet
Hector in single combat midway between the Greek camp and the walls of
Troy.

> "If any come, Hector shall honour him;
> If none, he'll say in Troy, when he retires,
> The Grecian dames are sunburnt and not worth
> The splinter of a lance."

Elgar's familiarity with *Ivanhoe* extended also to knowledge of
Sullivan's opera (1891). He heard it on 7 March that year, and the
librettro is still at the Birthplace. Three sections were marked by Elgar.
The first was Friar Tuck's song in Act 2 scene i:

> The wind blows cold across the moor,
> With driving rain and rending tree:
> It smites the lonely hermit's door,
> But not a jot cares he;
> For close he sits within,
> And makes his merry din.

The versification was by Julian Sturgis. Scott introduces Friar Tuck in
cautious conversation with King Richard I disguised as the Black Knight:
' "Pass on, whoever thou art," was the answer given by a deep hoarse voice
from within the hut, "and disturb not the servant of God and St.Dunstan
in his evening devotions".' The hermit continues unwilling to receive a
guest: ' "You have already interrupted one *pater*, two *aves*, and a *credo*,
which I, miserable sinner that I am, should, according to my vow, have
said before moonrise".'

The other arias marked by Elgar were both sung by Brian de Bois-
Guilbert, commander of the Templars. Scott has his character outlined by
Cedric, landowner of Saxon descent little enamoured of his Norman overlords:

"Bois-Guilbert? that name has been spread wide both for good and evil.
They say he is valiant as the bravest of his order; but stained with their
usual vices, pride, arrogance, cruelty, and voluptuousness; a hard-hearted
man, who knows neither fear of earth, nor awe of heaven. So say the few
warriors who have returned from Palestine".

Voluptuous indeed, and his passion settles on Rebecca, the courageous
and beautiful Jewess, daughter to Isaac of York. Scott sets the scene:

"One thing alone can save thee, Rebecca. Submit to thy fate – embrace our
religion, and thou shalt go forth in such state, that many a Norman lady

shall yield as well in pomp as in beauty to the favourite of the best lance among the defenders of the Temple".

Rebecca's reply is to make for the parapet outside the apartment and threaten to cast herself down. The Templar is the more inflamed: ' "Rebecca! she who could prefer death to dishonour, must have a proud and a powerful soul. Mine thou must be! – Nay, start not," he added, "it must be with thine own consent".' Even now Rebecca prefers exile with her father to the Moslem lands of Granada.

Elgar's *Literary Supplement* letter next mentions Lady Penelope Penfeather, preposterous inhabitant of the valetudinary establishment based on St.Ronan's Well and its curative powers. Scott declares his aim at the outset of this contemporary novel (1823): *'celebrare domestica facta –* to give an imitation of the shifting manners of our own time'. He enlarges on the population of such spa towns:

> In such scenes, too, are frequently mingled characters, not merely ridiculous, but dangerous and hateful. The unprincipled gamester, the heartless fortune-hunter, all those who eke out their means of subsistence by pandering to the vices and follies of the rich and gay, who drive, by their various arts, foibles into crimes, and imprudence into acts of ruinous madness, are to be found where their victims naturally resort.

Lady Penelope is indeed among the most capricious and absurd of Scott's creations. Pretentious to her finger-ends, she billows with artistic and literary ambition. Her arrival at St.Ronan's Well is due to an access of wealth and brings an unquenchable desire to quote Shakespeare. Any new acquisition to the spa, in this case Francis Tyrrell, disinherited elder son of the Earl of Etherington, must endure her fixation:

> "O, confess more, sir! – Confess that to a poet a seat unoccupied – the chair of Banquo – has more charms than if it were filled even as an alderman would fill it. – What if "the Dark Ladye" should glide in and occupy it? – Would you have the courage to stand the vision, Mr.Tyrrell?"

And when Clara Mowbray enters the establishment in disarray and after the appointed time, the Shakespearean adept is at the ready:

> "Angels and ministers of grace." exclaimed Lady Penelope, with her very best tragic start – "my dearest Clara, why so late? and why thus?"

As *St.Ronan's Well* proceeds towards its sombre climax when Clara Mowbray loses her reason, it is decided there shall be a divertissement in the grounds of St.Ronan's house, part *ex tempore* and part dumb show.

The question was the subject: 'Lady Penelope declared loftily and decidedly for Shakspeare, as the author whose immortal works were fresh in every one's recollection. Shakspeare was therefore chosen, and from his works the Midsummer Night's Dream was selected.' Amid some bickering the parts were allotted: because she was taller, Miss Mowbray would be Helena, while Lady Penelope must be content with Hermia. Scott lavishes much art on Hermia's performance:

> She twisted her poor features into looks of most desperate love towards Lysander; into those of wonder and offended pride, when she turned them unto Demetrius; and finally settled them on Helena, with the happiest possible imitation of an incensed rival, who feels the impossibility of relieving her swollen heart by tears alone, and is just about to have recourse to her nails.

Elgar's mention in the July 1921 letter of Jonathan Oldbuck takes one to the centre of Scott's Shakespearian world. The eccentric character was based on George Constable, a retired lawyer and antiquary, who befriended the boy Scott when he was in Prestonpans to try bathing for the weakness of his leg. In his incomplete Memoir of his life, Scott expresses gratitude to Constable: '[he] was the first person who told me about Falstaff and Hotspur and other characters in Shakspeare. What idea I annexed to them I know not, but I must have annexed some, for I remember quite well being interested.' *Henry IV* remained Scott's favourite among the history plays, for reasons that Elgar would have echoed when at work on *Falstaff*. Oldbuck's retreat at Monkbarns in *The Antiquary* (1816) 'was surrounded by tall clipped hedges of yew and holly, some of which still exhibited the skill of the *topiarian* artist, and presented curious arm-chairs, towers, and the figures of Saint George and the dragon'. His study had the makings of a miniature Abbotsford, where he would retire 'amid a chaos of maps, engravings, scraps of parchment, bundles of papers, pieces of old armour, swords, dirks, engravings, helmets, and Highland targets'. On the walls was a 'grim old tapestry, representing the memorable story of Sir Gawaine's wedding, in which full justice was done to the ugliness of the Lothely Lady'.

When stirred to action on behalf of his young friend Lovel, 'Mr. Oldbuck equipped himself for the expedition with his thick walking-shoes and gold-headed cane, muttering the while the words of Falstaff which we have chosen for the motto of this chapter.' Here Scott's memory betrays him and he ascribes to *Henry IV* Part 2 the speech that belongs to Part 1, Act 2, scene ii: 'I am bewitched with the rogue's company. If the rascal has [have] not given me medicines to make me love him, I'll be hanged; it could not be else. I have drunk medicines.' When there is talk that Hector

M'Intyre is in the vicinity and may apply for hospitality from his uncle, Oldbuck is outraged: ' "Who?" exclaimed Monkbarns, "my nephew Hector? – the Hotspur of the North? – Why, Heaven love you, I would as soon invite a firebrand into my stackyard".' It is not just Hector, but also his dog Juno, who wreaks havoc in the household, smashing the Antiquary's vessel from a Roman tomb crucial to his theory that the legions 'had passed the defiles of these mountains'. He rounds his speech with Othello's words to Cassio:

> Hector, I love thee,
> But never more be officer of mine.

It is on *Kenilworth* (1821) that Elgar spends most time in his *Literary Supplement* letter. The novel does indeed present 'Shakespeare the man', briefly, as he waits at Greenwich for notice from Queen Elizabeth (1558-1603) on her way to the royal barge. Instead, the Earl of Leicester (c.1532-88) addresses him: 'Ha, Will Shakspeare – wild Will! – thou hast given my nephew, Philip Sidney, love-powder – he cannot sleep without thy Venus and Adonis under his pillow! We will have thee hanged for the veriest wizard in Europe. Hark thee, mad wag, I have not forgotten thy matter of the patent, and of the bears.' Sir Walter's comment is to the point: 'The *player* bowed, and the Earl nodded and passed on – so that age would have told the tale – in ours, perhaps, we might say the immortal had done homage to the mortal.' Scott has the queen and her courtiers touching on Shakespeare during their progress on the Thames; Elizabeth herself is favourable:

> And touching this Shakspeare, we think there is that in his plays that is worth twenty Bear-gardens, and that this new undertaking of his Chronicles, as he calls them, may entertain, with honest mirth mingled with useful instruction, not only our subjects, but even the generation which may succeed to us.

The novel is mainly concerned with Leicester's secret marriage to Amy Robsart, which must be kept from the queen. When the Countess hears that Elizabeth is to be received for a protracted stay at Kenilworth, Leicester's seat, she is determined to travel there and be acknowledged openly as his wife. Elgar was at least twice at Kenilworth, on two successive days during the 1912 Birmingham festival. *The Music Makers* was given its première on 1 October; the following day Elgar took Alice Stuart Wortley to Kenilworth and Stratford; the day after that Frank Schuster motored them there again. Scott had anticipated them, staying some time at the King's Arms and Castle hotel, the building of which still stands in Kenilworth High Street. With his customary passion for accuracy, Scott wished to visualise the relative positions of the great Norman keep, John of Gaunt's magnificent hall, and the new structures Robert of Leicester had himself built. The lake stretching beyond to where Henry V (1413-22) had made his 'Pleasaunce' to avoid the press of the court had recently been bridged by Leicester. In secret his unacknowledged Countess approached: 'At length the princely Castle appeared, upon improving which, and the domains around, the Earl of Leicester had, it is said, expended sixty thousand pounds sterling.' Scott lovingly describes the mighty pile:

> The outer wall of the splendid and gigantic structure enclosed seven acres, a part of which was occupied by extensive stables, and by a pleasure garden, with its trim arbours and parterres, and the rest formed the large base-court, or outer-yard of the noble Castle. The lordly structure itself, which rose near the centre of this spacious enclosure, was composed of a huge pile of magnificent castellated buildings, apparently of different ages, surrounding an inner court, and bearing in the names attached to each portion of the magnificent mass, and in the armorial bearings which were there blazoned, the emblems of mighty chiefs who had long passed away, and whose history, could Ambition have lent ear to it, might have read a lesson to the haughty favourite, who had now acquired and was augmenting the fair domain.

There Elizabeth was received with unparalleled splendour; from there the Countess departed to a hideous death. Scott draws the moral:

> We cannot but add, that of this lordly palace, where princes feasted and heroes fought, now in the bloody earnest of storm and siege, and now in the games of chivalry, where beauty dealt the prize which valour won, all is now desolate.

Kenilworth in the 17th century

4 - A history deserving great praise

The germ of Elgar's concert overture *Froissart* was a Three Choirs commission from his native city. The critic Joseph Bennett (1831-1911) was informed at once: 'I have been requested to write a short orchestral work for the Worcester Festival.' He made the point that Bennett had already reviewed a performance of his *Intermezzo moresque* at Birmingham six years previously: 'You were kind enough to notice the production of my first work at Birmingham in the 'Musical Year'; and since that time I have produced many things, some of which are published by Schott and Co.' On 12 December 1889 Bennett put a notice in the *Daily Telegraph* about the forthcoming work. On 6 April 1890 the overture was begun, and by 25 May its title was 'Froissart'. For publication Elgar turned to the main Three Choirs firm. Novello had already produced his partsong, *My Love Dwelt in a Northern Land*, and on 27 July he made contact: 'I have written for the Worcester Festival an overture for Full Orchestra & should be glad to know if I might submit the Full-score for your inspection.' Novello agreed to engrave the string parts, but printing of the wind and full score had to wait till 1901. Elgar told his mother on 8 August he 'might have been seen dancing along Oxford St: on one leg! for an hour after the interview'. He had also to tell his pregnant wife: '& "so home" as Pepys hath it. & never rested 'till my dear A. was acquent with the fax'. A few days later he informed Novello about the Keats words to be engraved on the string parts.

The words chosen by Elgar come from a Keats poem of 1816 written for his brother George as a valentine for Georgiana Augusta Wylie, his future wife. The first section, 'Hadst thou liv'd in days of old', places Georgiana in the classical world, where she might be a tenth Muse, twin to Thalia. So Keats ends the section thus:

> At least for ever, evermore,
> Will I call the Graces four.

Immediately follow the lines Elgar chose:

> Hadst thou liv'd when chivalry
> Lifted up her lance on high,
> Tell me what thou wouldst have been?

Keats by
Joseph Severn

Keats laments the 'golden cuirass' that conceals her breast, mentions her 'knightly casque' and 'alabaster steed'. He bids her unsheath the sword,

> Bane of every wicked spell;
> Silencer of dragon's yell.

Elgar backed the quotation with a drawing by Edith Lander on the title page of the MS full score of a knight and page with proudly flowing banner.

After the first performance on 10 September 1890, the *Evening Standard* considered the overture to be 'a workmanlike effort alike in thematic material, structure, and orchestration, and it deserved the warm applause it received under the composer's direction'. Joseph Bennett, a pundit 'most to be feared', concluded a well-balanced review with words of encouragement: 'Mr.Elgar has ideas and feeling as well as aspiration, and should be encouraged to persevere.' *Froissart* was launched, and the reading matter of many years had been distilled in the first of Elgar's overtly 'chivalric' works.

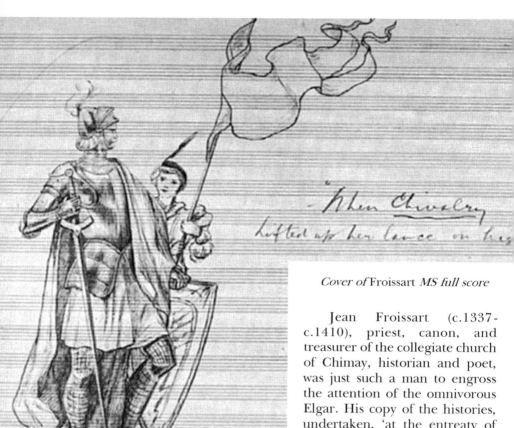

Cover of Froissart *MS full score*

Jean Froissart (c.1337-c.1410), priest, canon, and treasurer of the collegiate church of Chimay, historian and poet, was just such a man to engross the attention of the omnivorous Elgar. His copy of the histories, undertaken, 'at the entreaty of *his dear lord and master sir Robert de Namur, knight, lord of Beaufort'* remains at the Birthplace Museum. The chronicles range far and wide. He covers the period 1326-1400. His researches were not confined to France. To quote the introduction to my edition,[1] the history comprehends every considerable affair which happened in England, Scotland, and Ireland, and in Flanders. It includes also an infinite number of particulars relative to the affairs of the popes of Rome and Avignon; of Spain, Germany, Italy; sometimes even of Russia, Hungary, Turkey, Africa, and other places beyond sea; in short, of almost the whole known world.

---

[1] *Chronicles* by Sir John Froissart, translated by Thomas Johnes (London, 1939)

Froissart divides his history into four books or volumes. The first begins with the coronation of Edward III in 1327 and the accession of Philip of Valois (1328-50); it continues until 1379. Froissart then doubles back, thus giving substance to the charge of disorder in the chronicles. The reason is simple: Froissart has new information to share with the reader; so his second volume repeats in greater detail the last three years of the first and continues only to 1385, when the men of Ghent make peace with the duke of Burgundy. The third volume proceeds likewise: it retreats to 1382 and advances only to 1389 and the three-year truce between France and England. Its final set-piece is the frantic activity preparing for Isabella of Bavaria's entry into Paris. Her glorification starts the fourth volume, which ends sombrely at the dethroning and death of Richard II in 1400.

Froissart states his aim at the outset:

> That the honourable enterprises, noble adventures, and deeds of arms, performed in the wars between England and France, may be properly related, and held in perpetual remembrance – to the end that brave men taking example from them may be encouraged in their well-doing, I sit down to record a history deserving great praise.

He prays to 'the Saviour of the world' for inspiration towards 'sense and sound understanding'. Froissart was tireless in visiting the great courts of Europe. His ease of address, impartial curiosity, and the hint of immortality to his informants, ensured a steady flow of news. He heard accounts of deeds nobly done, of the counsels that went to their preparation, and biographical niceties that a man of less obvious integrity could not have elicited. Evidence from only one side was not enough; he must compare as many points of view as possible and test his findings against correspondence, statutes and treaties. Froissart expresses devotion to his task:

> And as long as through God's grace I shall live, I shall continue it, for the more I work at it, the greater pleasure I receive; like the gallant knight or squire enamoured with arms, by perseverance and attention he perfects and accomplishes himself, thus by labouring and working on this subject, I acquire greater ability and delight.

Froissart's close connection with England was through Philippa of Hainault, queen of Edward III. She did well by her adopted country, establishing Flemish weavers at Norwich, and encouraging coal-mining on Tyneside. Edward III founded Trinity College, Cambridge in 1337; Philippa's chaplain, Robert of Eglesfield, followed three years later with

Queen's College, Oxford, as tribute to her love of learning. Froissart was in her entourage 1361-64 and explains the significance of his position:

> I was secretary and amused her with handsome ditties and madrigals of love; and through affection to the service of that noble and puissant lady to whom I belonged, all the other great lords, dukes, earlys, barons, and knights of whatever nation they might be, loved me, saw me with pleasure, and were of the greatest utility to me.

Froissart was also in Scotland for six months, anticipating Walter Scott in his exploration of the Highlands. He journeyed on horseback, with his portmanteau behind, and a greyhound following.

A man of his time, and perhaps of all times, Froissart was as fascinated by the effect the Countess of Salisbury had on Edward III in his northern campaigns as he was by the virtues of Queen Philippa:

> The moment the countess heard of the king's approach, she ordered all the gates to be thrown open, and went to meet him, most richly dressed; inasmuch, that no one could look at her but with wonder, and admiration at her noble deportment, great beauty, and affability of behaviour. When she came near the king, she made her reverence to the ground, and gave him her thanks for coming to her assistance, and then conducted him into the castle, to entertain and honour him, as she was very capable of doing. Every one was delighted with her; the king could not take his eyes off her, as he thought he had never before seen so beautiful or sprightly a lady; so that a spark of fine love struck upon his heart, which lasted a long time.

The dramatic potential of this affair was not lost on the playwright who may have been the young Shakespeare.

Froissart has an ebullient description of king Edward as he crossed the Channel to engage the Spaniards and French off Sluys in June 1340:

> The king posted himself in the fore part of his own ship: he was dressed in a black velvet jacket, and wore on his head a small hat of beaver, which became him much. He was that day, as I was told by those who were present, as joyous as he ever was in his life, and ordered his minstrels to play before him a German dance which sir John Chandos had lately introduced. For his amusement, he made the same knight sing with his minstrels, which delighted him greatly.

Froissart is careful to point out that the young king remained vigilant and concerned for the fleet's aim:

From time to time he looked up to the castle on his mast, where he had placed a watch to inform him when the Spaniards were in sight. Whilst the king was thus amusing himself with his knights, who were happy in seeing him so gay, the watch, who had observed a fleet, cried out, "Ho, I spy a ship, and it appears to me to be a Spaniard".

The engagement resulted in a notable English victory, but subsequent operations on land exhausted Edward's resources and a truce in September signalled his return to England.

It has been a matter of many generations to debate whether King Arthur ever existed. Froissart has no more doubts than Edward III himself in the early 1340s, though his chronology is prudently vague:

About this time, the king of England resolved to rebuild and embellish the great castle of Windsor, which king Arthur had first founded in time past, and where he had erected and established that noble round table from whence so many gallant knights had issued forth, and displayed the valiant prowess of their deeds at arms over the world.

Froissart does not clearly distinguish between this 'round table' plan and foundation of the Order of the Garter in 1348. He knows, however, of Edward's passion for the tournament, and a notable one was held in January 1344 at the climax of his festivities to celebrate a successful campaign in Brittany the previous March. It was on the third day of jousting that the 'round table' plan was announced: it should be 'of the same manner and standing as that which Lord Arthur, formerly king of England, had relinquished, to make up a total of 300 soldiers'. There should be an annual meeting of the knights at the feast of Pentecost and a new round building was to be constructed at Windsor. The week of Pentecost had its special place in Arthurian romance, but not only there, as Uhland (1787-1862), Longfellow and Elgar knew well as context for *The Black Knight.* This ambitious scheme of Edward's was abandoned by the end of 1344, largely because he was involved in the considerable expense of the French wars.

In dealing with 1346 and the battle of Crécy, Froissart lays emphasis on an aspect of King Edward's behaviour that was later to enrage John Ruskin. The Black Prince, his son, was only two months past his sixteenth birthday, and hard pressed in the mêlée. Froissart writes as if at the king's side:

The first division, seeing the danger they were in, sent a knight in great haste to the king of England, who was posted upon an eminence, near a windmill. On the knight's arrival, he said, "Sir, the earl of Warwick, the lord Stafford, the lord Reginald Cobham, and the others who are about your son, are vigorously attacked by the French; and they entreat that you should come to their assistance with your battalion, for if their numbers should increase, they fear he will have too much to do".

The king refused to intervene, making the practical point that, should his eldest fall, he had other sons to assume his place. Froissart has him speak as a true champion of chivalry: ' "I command them to let the boy win his spurs; for I am determined, if it please God, that all the glory and honour of this day shall be given to him, and to those into whose care I have intrusted him".' Already the boyish warrior was Prince of Wales; now he was indeed to win his spurs and gain the three ostrich plumes and the motto, originally 'homout; ich dene' (courage; I serve), since sported by his successors of the principality. There was no doubting the king's pride in his son for the victory at Crécy, as reported by Froissart:

> "King Edward then came down from his post, who all that day had not put on his helmet, and, with his whole battalion, advanced to the prince of Wales, whom he embraced in his arms and kissed, and said, "Sweet son, God gave you good perseverance: you are my son, for most loyally have you acquitted yourself this day: you are worth to be a sovereign."

The king then resumed an active part in the French campaigning, laying siege to Calais in September 1346. After almost a year of siege, the Calesians were in despair and asked their governor to request a parley. The account of what followed may have come *verbatim* to Froissart from Sir Walter de Manny (d.1372), a friend and patron of his who was at Calais and later founded the Charterhouse in London. Edward was initially obdurate, demanding the unconditional surrender of Calais and vengeance on its population. Sir Walter and fellow barons pleaded otherwise, and Edward made the proposition that has so interested art and literature. Froissart alone among chroniclers gives the full story. The king yields so far as to concentrate his wrath on half a dozen of the town's most prominent inhabitants. It was Edward's intention to have them executed, but again he was thwarted: this time Sir Walter's eloquence was backed up by Queen Philippa, who had recently crossed from England. Froissart describes her intervention:

> The queen of England, who at the time was very big with child, fell on her knees, and with tears said, "Ah, gentle sir, since I have crossed the sea with great danger to see you, I have never asked you one favour: now, I most humbly ask you as a gift, for the sake of the Son of the blessed Mary, and for your love to me, that you will be merciful to these six men."

Edward was nonplussed and initially silent. Froissart then has him say: ' "Ah, lady, I wish you had been anywhere else than here: you have entreated in such a manner that I cannot refuse you; I therefore give them to you, to do as you please with them".' The queen conducted the six citizens to her apartments, and had the halters taken from their necks, after which she new clothed them, and served them with a plentiful dinner: 'she then presented them with six nobles, and had them escorted out of the camp in safety'.

Letters patent for the restructuring of the chapel at Windsor were issued on 6 August 1348; the dedication was to be to St.George and the Virgin. It was part of a revised scheme for a new order of chivalry. Froissart writes of the plan:

> He ordered it to be denominated "knights of the blue garter", and that the feast should be celebrated every year, at Windsor, upon St.George's Day. He summoned, therefore, all the earls, barons and knights of the realm, to inform them of his intentions; they heard it with great pleasure; for it appeared to them highly honourable, and capable of increasing love and friendship.

The Charterhouse, London

Of chivalric orders, only the Garter has survived. The Garter motto 'Honi soit qui mal y pense' was more concerned with Edward's claims to France than to any legendary distress over the Countess of Salisbury's stockings. The Order was founded in the afterglow of Crécy. The king was superior of the Order and St.George the main patron. The annual meeting was to involve a three-day celebration in honour of St.George, beginning on 22 April, and ending with a requiem mass for any departed brethren. The bishop of Winchester was *ex officio* prelate to the Order. Winchester also was a traditional seat of King Arthur, and by this appointment Edward III validated further the claims of Windsor. There is, moreover, at Winchester, a 'round table' associated with Arthur and his knights probably made in 1290 for the triple betrothal of Edward I's (1272-1307) children.

Edward's further operations on the continent were eclipsed by those of the Black Prince, notably at Poitiers on 19 September 1356. It was there that King John of France was taken captive, and a banquet was held in his honour. Froissart's informants furnished him with much detail:

> The prince himself served the king's table, as well as the others, with every mark of humility, and would not sit down at it, in spite of all his entreaties to do so, saying, that "he was not worthy of such an honour, nor did it appertain to him to seat himself at the table of so great a king, or of so valiant a man as he had shown himself by his actions that day".

He bade the king sup well, and that his father would fix a very reasonable ransom for him. It turned out differently. Edward and Philippa showed every consideration to the captive king, entertaining him sumptuously at the Savoy and then Windsor. But the treaty of London (1359) exacted such considerable territories from the French that it was repudiated. Edward now campaigned with the aim of a coronation at Rheims. Frustrated in this ambition, he moved towards Chartres, where Froissart reports a formidable storm: 'The hailstones were so large as to kill men and beasts, and the boldest were frightened.' The divine had intervened: 'The king turned himself towards the church of Our Lady at Chartres, and religiously vowed to the Virgin, as he has since confessed, that he would accept terms of peace.' The result on 20 October 1360 was the treaty of Calais, by which Edward gave up claims to France for Aquitaine.

Froissart devotes considerable space to the king of Cyprus. This was Peter I (1359-69), whose ambition was to launch yet another crusade, for which he canvassed European support. Froissart first introduces Peter at Avignon, papal seat from 1309: 'About Candlemas, 1362, the king of Cyprus came to Avignon: at which event the whole court was much rejoiced, and many cardinals went out to meet him, and to conduct him to the palace of pope Urban, who received him very graciously, as did the king of France, who was present.' After pleading his holy cause, Peter moved on, as reported by Froissart: 'After many days' travel in Germany, he came to a city called Prague, and found there the emperor of Germany, Charles of Bohemia, who received him magnificently.' He spent three weeks there, 'in exhorting all the Germans to assist in this holy expedition'; he then made for England, where Froissart was now resident and a witness of events at court.

Froissart is in his element:

> It would take me a day were I to attempt relating to you the grand dinners, suppers and other feasts and entertainments that were made, and the magnificent presents, gifts and jewels which were given, especially by Queen Philippa, to the accomplished king of Cyprus. In truth, he was deserving of them, because he had come a long way and at a great expense, to visit them, to exhort the king to put on the red cross, and assist in regaining countries now occupied by the enemies of God.

But Edward III played a characteristically English hand: ' "Certainly, my good cousin, I have every inclination to undertake this expedition; but I am growing too old, and shall leave it to my children".' So Peter departed. He had resources enough to take Alexandria on 10 October 1365, but the Europeans did not produce the assistance to hold it.

Froissart was greatly saddened by the death of Queen Philippa in 1369. He wrote an encomium on her life, since lost, but in the chronicles he pays her tribute enough:

> That excellent lady the queen of England (who had done so much good, and during her whole life had assisted all knights, ladies, and damsels who had applied to her, who had had such boundless charity for all mankind, and who had naturally such an affection for the Hainault nation, being the country from which she sprang,) lay at this time dangerously ill at Windsor castle, and her disorder daily increased.

She had three main requests to the king: that the agreements she had made with merchants at home or abroad should be honoured; that the legacies she had detailed for churches and servants should be paid; and that in the fulness of time Edward himself should lie beside her in Westminster Abbey. Froissart continues:

> Soon after, the good lady made the sign of the cross on her breast, and, having recommended to God the king and her youngest son, Thomas, who was present, gave up her spirit, which, I firmly believe, was caught by the holy angels and carried to the glory of Heaven; for she had never done anything, by thought or deed, that could endanger her losing it.

She died on 15 August. The Black Prince followed her on 8 June 1376, and the king just over a year later, on 21 June 1377. Edward's effigy, with evidence of the strokes that incapacitated him, remains in the Westminster Abbey Museum.

Froissart has much to say on the church schism that began with the double papal election of 1378. The Roman populace demanded of the conclave 'a Roman or at least an Italian' pope. The eventual choice was the Cardinal St.Peter. Froissart claims he was at least a hundred years old, but was carried through Rome on a white mule for so long that he survived only three days. The archbishop of Bari was next elected as Urban VI (1378-89). Froissart pinpoints the origin of the schism:

> The cardinals intended, on a proper opportunity, to make another election: for this pope, being choleric and obstinate, was neither profitable to them nor to the church; so that when he found himself invested with the powers of papacy, in consequence of which many princes of Christendom had written to him to acknowledge their obedience, he became very haughty, and desirous of retrenching the powers of the cardinals, and depriving them of several of their rights and accustomed prerogatives.

While Urban was at Tivoli, thirteen French cardinals repaired to Fondi and elected on 20 September 1378 Robert of Geneva as Clement VII (1378-94). France declared for Clement, while England supported Urban, thus further stoking the Hundred Years' War.

Urban fixed his seat at Genoa, where he sought succour from England to annoy France: there would be a general absolution for any helping to destroy the Clementists. Froissart has a nice sense of the realities:

> he should have a considerable sum of ready money, if he wished to put his plans into execution; for it was well known that the nobles of England would not, for all the absolutions in the world, undertake any expeditions, unless such were preceded by offers of money. Men at arms cannot live on pardons, nor do they pay much attention to them except at the point of death.

Nevertheless, Urban persuaded the bishop of Norwich to lead an ill-fated 'crusade' to France in 1383. Froissart burgeons into heraldry:

> the bishop of Norwich had the arms of the church borne before him, the banner of St.Peter, gules with two keys on sautoir, as being gonfalonnier of pope Urban. His pennon had his own arms, which were argent quartered with azure, with a fret or, on a field azure, and a baton gules on a field argent; and, because he was a younger brother of the Despensers, his arms were charged with a border gules.

The papal palace at Avignon

He marched against the Flemings, who were in fact supporters of Urban. His campaign reads like an anticipation of Elgar's First World War music, with capture of Dunkirk, advance to Dixmude, Poperinghe and Nieuport, culminating in the siege of Ypres. The French made sure the expedition failed. Early in 1390 Charles VI of France (1380-1422) was at Avignon and just 21, as Froissart explains: 'The king of France, the duke of Touraine and the count de Savoye, being young and giddy, neither could nor would refrain from dancing, carolling, and amusing themselves with the ladies and damsels of Avignon, though they were in the pope's palace and among the cardinals.' Urban VI had died on 18 October 1389, and there seemed a possibility to establish Clement VII in Rome. But the Roman cardinals had acted with speed by electing Boniface IX (1389-1404): 'The king of France and his lords, on hearing this, were very melancholy, and thought the schism in the church likely to continue for a long time.' It lasted, indeed, until the election of Martin V in 1417. Machinations by England and frequent threats of invasion inhibited French action in Italy and the restoration of Avignon to Roman control.

Froissart had little sympathy with the Peasant's Revolt in England (1381), and regarded it as an awful example: 'It is marvellous from what a trifle this pestilence raged in England. I will speak of all that was done, from the information I had at the time on the subject.' He considered feudal duties more demanding in England than in other countries and particulary oppressive in Kent, Essex, Sussex and Bedford. The start of disaffection was thus: 'The evil-disposed in these districts began to rise, saying, they were too heavily oppressed; that at the beginning of the world there were no slaves, and that no one ought to be treated as such, unless he has committed treason against his lord, as Lucifer had done against God.' Froissart had scant regard for a man later admired by William Morris:

> A crazy priest in the county of Kent, called John Ball, who, for his absurd preaching, had been thrice confined in the prison of the archbishop of Canterbury, was greatly influential in inflaming them with those ideas. He was accustomed, every Sunday after mass, as the people were coming out of the church, to preach to them in the market place and assemble a crowd around him; to whom he would say, - "My good friends, things cannot go on well in England, nor ever will until every thing shall be in common".

He recommended recourse to King Richard II (1377-1400), then only fourteen. Froissart only partly approves the archbishop's response: 'The archbishop of Canterbury, in being informed of this, had John Ball arrested, and imprisoned for two or three months by way of punishment; but it would have been better if he had been confined during his life, or had been put to death.' England had been ravaged by the Black Death, but it was the poll tax of 1381 that proved the last straw. On 6 June Rochester castle was seized by the insurgents, who marched on Maidstone. There Wat Tyler (d.1381) was chosen leader. Froissart maintains Tyler had fought in France, but he has no time for him: 'This Wat had been a tiler of houses, a bad man, and a great enemy of the nobility.'

Tyler and his force took Canterbury on 10 June: 'Those who had come to Canterbury entered the church of St.Thomas, and did much damage: they pillaged the apartments of the archbishop'; they also executed three citizens as traitors. The mob liberated John Ball and marched on London: 'those who had lodged at Rochester had done all they wanted, and, crossing the river, came to Dartford, but always following their plan of destroying the houses of lawyers or proctors.' It was decided the king should speak to the men about their disaffection: 'On Corpus Christi day King Richard heard mass in the tower of London, with all his lords, and afterwards entered his barge.' He proceeded along the river:

> He rowed down the Thames towards Rotherhithe, a manor belonging to the crown, where were upwards of ten thousand men, who had come from Blackheath to see the king and to speak to him: when they perceived his barge approach, they set up such shouts and cries as if all the devils in hell had been in their company.

It was impossible for Richard to land, much less to be heard. The earl of Salisbury (1328-97) made a brief speech, suggesting the mob was improperly dressed and in no state to have the king address them. Richard returned to the Tower. Froissart describes the sequel: 'When the people saw they could obtain nothing more, they were inflamed with passion, and went back to Blackheath, where the main body was, to relate the answer they had received and how the king was returned to the Tower. They all then cried out, "Let us march instantly to London".' They were able to cross London Bridge 'when crowds rushed in, and ran to those shops which seemed well stored with provision: if they sought for meat or drink, it was placed before them, and nothing refused, in hopes of appeasing them'. Froissart enlarges on their destructive zeal:

> Their leaders, John Ball, Jack Straw and Wat Tyler, then marched through London, attended by twenty thousand men, to the palace of the Savoy, which is a handsome building on the road to Westminster, situated on the banks of the Thames, belonging to the duke of Lancaster; they immediately killed the porters, pressed into the house and set it on fire. Not content with committing this outrage, they went to the house of the knights-hospitallers of Rhodes, dedicated to St.John of Mount Carmel, which they burnt, together with their hospital and church.

Finally Richard agreed to speak to the rebels at Mile End, and Froissart can but admire his courage:

> On the king's arrival, attended by the barons, he found upwards of sixty thousand men assembled from different villages and counties of England: he instantly advanced into the midst of them, saying in a pleasant manner, "My good people, I am your king and your lord: what is it you want? and what do you wish to say to me ?" Those who heard him answered, "We wish thou wouldst make us free for ever, us, our heirs and our lands, and that we should no longer be called slaves, nor held in bondage". The king replied "I grant your wish: now, therefore, return to your homes".

Wat Tyler, still obdurate, was cut down by the mayor, Sir William Walworth, and one of the king's squires, John Standwick. The royal grant of enfranchisement was revoked the following year, and the boy king's act of impetuous chivalry was set at nought.

It might initially seem remarkable that Froissart should turn his attention to the king of Armenia. This was Leo VI (1374-75) of the Lusignan family, which had ruled in Jerusalem and now held Cyprus. The Armenian kings had succeeded for a while in playing off Mongols against the Mamelukes of Egypt, but a Mongol defeat in 1303 near Damascus meant that Armenia fell gradually to the Mamelukes, until the capture of the capital Sis, and with it King Leo. He was ransomed in 1382 and removed to Paris. Froissart introduces him in 1386, when the French were planning an invasion of England: 'the number of ships, galleys, and vessels of every description, which had been collected to carry over to England the king of France and his army, were so great, that the oldest man then living had never seen nor heard of the like.' King Leo, a pensioner of Charles VI, wanted to discuss with Richard II the possibility of peace or at least a truce between France and England, threatened as he considered them by Moslem expansion.

Froissart gives him a favourable wind from Boulogne to Dover:

> The King of Armenia, on his arrival at Dover, was very well received, and conducted by some knights to the uncles of the king, who entertained him handsomely, as they knew well how to do. At a proper opportunity they asked him whither he came, and what were the reasons of his visiting England.

Leo declared his desire for peace:

> "For this war," added the king of Armenia, "is not very becoming between them: the long continuance of it has greatly emboldened and raised the pride of the Turks and Saracens. No one now makes any opposition to them; and this has been the cause why I have lost my crown and kingdom; nor have I any chance of recovering them, until a firm peace be established in Christendom. I would willingly explain this matter, which so nearly touches every true Christian, to the king of England, as I have done to the king of France".

It was clear Leo was not an emissary of Charles VI but had come on his own account; so he was despatched to London, 'where he was much stared at by the Londoners: the better sort, however, showed him every honour and respect'. He had a first audience with Richard, and was told the full council would be summoned within four days. Froissart describes the procedure:

> The king went to Westminster, where the council was assembled, and thither the king of Armenia was invited. When in the presence, the king of England was seated, according to custom, then the king of Armenia and the prelates and the lords of the council. The king of Armenia was desired to repeat what he had before told the king and a part of his council. He did so in an elegant harangue, showing how Christendom was too much weakened by the destructive wars of France and England, and that the knights and squires of the two countries thought of nothing but joining one party or other: by which the empire of Constantinople would be destroyed.

The council had agreed beforehand that the reply should be given by the archbishop of Canterbury :

"King of Armenia, it is not usual, nor has it ever been admitted, that in such weighty matters as are now in dispute between the king of England and his adversary of France, the king of England should have requests made him, with an army ready to invade his country. I will therefore declare our opinion, that you return to the French army, and prevail on them to retreat to France; and, when we shall be fully assured that every man has retired to his home, do you return hither, and we will then pay attention to any treaty you shall propose."

The king of Armenia received from Richard II the hospitality that was his due, as Froissart explains:
He dined that day with the king, who paid him every possible honour, and offered him handsome presents of gold and silver; but he refused them all, though he had need of them, and would only accept a single ring, worth one hundred francs. After the dinner, which was splendid and good, he returned to his lodgings, for he had received his answer, and on the morrow set out for Dover.

From Calais he made for Sluys and the camp of Charles VI. The French paid less attention to his efforts than the English and bade him return to Paris: 'they were resolved to sail the first fair wind for England, after the arrival of the duke of Berry and the constable. Hitherto the wind had been unfavourable: it would never have served them to land in those parts they intended to attempt, but was very fair to carry them to Scotland.' Indeed the constable of France had a rough passage from Tréguier, losing many ships, and the sailing of the expedition was postponed beyond the onset of winter, and therefore put off indefinitely. More important was the failure of the king of Armenia to be taken seriously in his bid for peace. The Hundred Years' War continued till 1453, the year Mehmet II (1451-81) took Constantinople and the great church of Hagia Sophia became a mosque.

By the time Froissart began his third volume, he was confident of immortality: 'I well know, that when the time shall come, when I shall be dead and rotten, this grand and noble history will be in much fashion, and all noble and valiant persons will take pleasure in it, and gain from it augmentation of profit.' Elgar could only concur and respond accordingly. Froissart formed the ambition to spend time at the court of Gaston III (1343-91), Count of Foix and Béarn in the extreme south-west of France. Froissart well understood the advantage of a stay there:

I well knew, that if I were so fortunate as to be admitted into his household, I could not choose a situation more proper to learn the truth of every event, as numbers of foreign knights and squires assembled there from all countries, attracted by his high birth and gentility. It fell out just as I had imagined.

The count was called 'Phoebus' because of his physical beauty. He sided with France against England and John II entrusted him with the defence of Gascony. Later he fought against the heathen in Prussia and, dying without issue, left his domains to Charles VI of France.

Froissart reached Orthez in Béarn on St.Catherine's day, 1388, after an eventful but entertaining journey, coming from Pamiers on the river Liège. It was there he met a congenial companion:

> Accidentally, a knight attached to the Count de Foix, called sir Espaign du Lyon, came thither, on his return from Avignon: he was a prudent and valiant knight, handsome in person, and about fifty years of age. I introduced myself to his company, as he had a great desire to know what was doing in France. We were six days on the road travelling to Orthez. As we journeyed, the knight, after saying his orisons, conversed the greater part of the day with me, asking for news; and when I put any questions to him, he very willingly answered them.

A main obstacle on their journey was the river Garonne, then in spate:

> On the morrow, the knight was advised to cross the Garonne (much swollen by rain), opposite the town of Cassères, in a boat; we therefore rode thither, and by our exertions the horses passed, and we ourselves afterwards with some difficulty and danger; for the boat was so small that only two horses and their men could cross at a time with those who managed the boat.

Sir Espaign was familiar with the territory they crossed and had much to tell of its history:

> As we were riding among these towns and castles, in a beautiful meadow by the side of the Garonne, the knight said, - "Sir John, I have witnessed here many excellent skirmishes and combats between the Armagnacs and Foixiens; for there was neither town nor castle that was not well garrisoned with men at arms, who engaged with and pursued each other. Do you see yonder those ruins? they are the remains of a fort which the Armagnacs raised against these two castles, and which they filled with men at arms, who did much damage to the lands of the count de Foix, on the other side

of the river; but I will tell you how they paid for it. The count de Foix one night sent his brother, sir Peter de Béarn, with two hundred lancers and four hundred peasants, laden with faggots, and as much wood as they could cut from the hedges, which they piled around the fort and set on fire, so that the fort was burnt with all in it, for none received quarter; and since that time no one has dared to rebuild it."

Their riding together, Froissart explains, always involved much talk, as they headed for the source of the Garonne along a route with handsome castles and forts. Those on the left belonged to the Count de Foix, the rest to the Count d'Armagnac:

We passed Montpesac, a fine strong castle, seated on the top of a rock, below which is the road and the town. On the outside of it, at the distance of a cross-bow, there is a pass called la Garde, with a tower between the rock and the river. Upon seeing this, I said to the knight, "Sir, this is a strong pass and a difficult country". "It is, indeed", answered the knight; "but, strong as it is, the count de Foix and his men once forced it, and advanced to Palaminich, Montesquiey, and even to Pamiers. The pass was very strong, but the English archers greatly assisted him in this conquest. Come and ride by my side, and I will tell you all about it."

The tale told, Froissart was profuse in thanks: ' "By my faith," said I to the knight, "I have heard you with pleasure".' Sir Espaign dilated on the great wealth of the Count de Foix. In his astonishment Froissart could only reply: ' "Ha, ha, holy Mary!" ' He was similarly amazed at hearing how one of the Count's knights had answered his lord's complaint on a Christmas day that the fire in the castle gallery was too small. He seized an ass laden with wood, carried it up many steps, pressed with his load through the knights and squires, and flung the ass feet upwards 'on the dogs of the hearth, to the delight of the count, and the astonishment of all, at the strength of the squire'. Froissart so relished such tales that he 'thought the road was much too short'. He explained his method of recording his experiences: 'as soon as we dismounted at our inns, I wrote all down, whether it was late or early, that posterity might have the advantage of it, for there is nothing like writing for the preservation of events.' He told Sir Espaign: ' "your history has given me much pleasure and done me service: you shall not lose a word you have said, for they shall all be chronicled".'

Froissart's reception by the Count de Foix was all he could hope for:

The knight informed him of my arrival, and I was instantly sent for; for he is a lord above all others who delights to see strangers, in order to hear news. On my entering, he received me handsomely, and retained me of his household, where I staid upwards of twelve weeks well entertained, as were my horses. Our aquaintance was strengthened by my having brought with me a book which I had made at the desire of Winceslaus of Bohemia, duke of Luxembourg and Brabant. In this book, called le méliador, are contained all the songs, ballads, roundelays and virelays which that gentle duke had composed, and of them I had made this collection. Every night after supper I read out to him parts: during which time neither he nor any one else spoke, for he was desirous I should be well heard, and took much delight in it. When any passages were not perfectly clear, he himself discussed them with me, not in his Gascon language, but in very good French.

Gaston de Foix had a high opinion of Froissart's historical endeavours: 'the history I was employed on would in time to come be more sought after than any other; "because", he added "my fair sir, more gallant deeds of arms have been performed within these last fifty years, and more wonderful things have happened, than for three hundred years before".' Froissart was therefore strengthened in his attempt, and fortified in his method:

> I will therefore illustrate, in good language, all I there learnt, to add to my materials, and to give examples to those worthies who wish to advance themselves in renown. If I have heretofore dwelt on gallant deeds, attacks and captures, of castles, towns, and forts, on hard-fought battles and skirmishes, many more will now ensue: all of which, by God's grace, I will truly narrate.

Gaston indeed deserved his 'Phoebus' sobriquet in the view of Froissart, who had ample opportunity to study his appearance and conduct within the household. He was fifty-nine at the time of Froissart's visit:

> I must say, that although I have seen very many knights, kings, princes and others, I have never seen any so handsome, either in the form of his limbs and shape, or in countenance, which was fair and ruddy, with grey and amorous eyes, that gave delight whenever he chose to express affection. He was so perfectly formed, one could not praise him too much. He loved earnestly the things he ought to love, and hated those which it was becoming him so to hate. He was a prudent knight, full of enterprise and wisdom. He had never any men of abandoned character with him, reigned prudently, and was constant in his devotions. There were regular nocturnals from the Psalter, prayers from the rituals to the Virgin, to the Holy Ghost, and from the burial service.

Froissart testifies to the Count's generosity:

> He had every day distributed as alms, at his gate, five florins in small coin,
> to all comers. He was liberal and courteous in his gifts; and well knew how
> to take when it was proper, and to give back where he had confidence. He
> mightily loved dogs above all other animals; and during the summer and
> winter amused himself much with hunting. He never liked any foolish
> works nor ridiculous extravagancies; and would know every month the
> amount of his expenditure.

Froissart explains that the Count had coffers in his apartment, from
which to give money to the knights, squires or gentlemen who might visit.
None went empty away. He was easy of access, ready for discourse, but
laconic in his advice and answers.

Supper was daily a festive occasion, beginning late and following an
established ritual:

> When he quitted his chamber at midnight for supper, twelve servants bore
> each a lighted torch before him, which were placed near his table and gave
> a brilliant light to the apartment. The hall was full of knights and squires;
> and there were plenty of tables laid out for any person who chose to sup.
> No one spoke to him at his table, unless he first began a conversation. He
> commonly ate heartily of poultry, but only the wings and thighs.

Froissart gives evidence for Gaston's delight in music: 'He had great
pleasure in hearing minstrels, as he himself was a proficient in the science,
and made his secretaries sing songs, ballads and roundelays.' Froissart
noted the splendour of the chapel music: 'I there heard organs play as
melodiously as I have ever heard in any place.' He noted his impartiality,
too, towards pope and antipope: 'On Christmas day were seated at his
table four bishops of his own country, two Clementists and two Urbanists.'
But what most delighted Froissart was the constant press of paragons of
chivalry:

> There were knights and squires to be seen in every chamber, hall and
> court, going backwards and forwards, and conversing on arms and amours.
> Every thing honourable was there to be found. All intelligence from distant
> countries was there to be learnt; for the gallantry of the count had brought
> visitors from all parts of the world. It was there I was informed of the
> greater part of those events which had happened in Spain, Portugal,
> Arragon, Navarre, England, Scotland, and on the borders of Languedoc;
> for I saw, during my residence, knights and squires arrive from every
> nation.

The port of Genoa

It is with some glee that Froissart launches an expedition in 1390 to the north coast of Africa: 'I have delayed for a long time speaking of a grand and noble enterprise that was undertaken by some knights of France, England and other countries, against the kingdom of Barbary.' Froissart vouches for the entertainment value of his tale: 'such events as I have to relate are greatly amusing.' The expedition was instigated by the Genoese, as he explains: 'The cause of their forming this armament was, that the Africans had attacked the country of Genoa, plundering the islands belonging to them.' The Genoese were well received in France, where many knights foresaw an accession of honour and considered praiseworthy any attempt to extend the Christian faith. Froissart claims that the expedition was to be essentially aristocratic: 'the Genoese were extremely bound not to suffer any servants to embark, but solely such as were gentlemen, and men who could be depended upon.'

Froissart takes delight in the appearance of the flotilla:

It was a beautiful sight to view this fleet, with the emblazoned banners of the different lords glittering in the sun and fluttering in the wind; and to hear the minstrels and other musicians sounding their pipes, clarion and trumpets, whose sounds were re-echoed back by the sea. When all were embarked, they cast anchor, and remained that night at the mouth of the harbour.

After passing Elba, they were driven by a violent storm into the Gulf of Lions and regrouped on Sardinia:

> When all was ready, and the men at arms had re-embarked on board their galleys, the admiral gave orders for the trumpet to sound, and the fleet to get under weigh. The sea was now calm, and the weather fine: it was a pleasure to see the rowers force their vessels through the smooth surface, which seemed to delight in bearing these Christians to the shores of the infidels.

The careful historian confesses an alibi: 'As I, John Froissart, ths author of these chronicles, was never in Africa, I sought all the information I could from those knights and squires who had been on this expedition, and made several journeys to Calais to learn the truth of all that passed.' He describes the instant reaction of the North Africans:

> On their first noticing the fleet, they sounded, according to custom, a number of bells on the towers, to alarm and inform the country that an enemy was on the coast. There were encamped near the town a large body of barbarians and infidels, whom the kings of Tunis and Bugia had sent thither to defend the coast.

The approach to the harbour produced an unexpected sight: 'the town seemed to be hung with cloths or tapestry, somewhat similar in appearance to coverlids of beds.' When dampened, these fabrics proved an effective defence against arrows and stones.

The Christian forces disembarked, and the central position was reserved for the commander:

> The duke of Bourbon, as commander in chief, was lodged in the centre of the army, with all honour, and powerfully guarded. The device on his banner, powdered over with flowers-de-luce, was a figure of the Virgin Mary in white, seated in the centre, and an escutcheon of Bourbon at her feet.

There wese regular skirmishes during the nine weeks of the siege, but the Saracens wanted to discover why they were being attacked. The Christians replied as follows: 'in consequence of their ancestors having crucified and put to death the son of God, called JESUS CHRIST, a true prophet, without any cause or just reason, they were come to retaliate on them for this infamous and unjust judgment.' The Moslems laughed at the answer, and said it was the Jews, not they. But there were moments when the

supernatural seemed to be on the side of the Christians. Froissart was told
that after a let-up in the skirmishing, the Moslems planned a major attack,
which was mysteriously checked:

> As the Saracens approached, they saw before them a company of ladies
> dressed in white: one of them, their leader, was incomparably more
> beautiful than the rest, and bore in front a white flag, having a vermilion
> cross in the centre. The Saracens ware so greatly terrified at this vision that
> they lost all their strength.

The August heat, effects of wine and onslaught of flies laid the
Christians low with fever. It seemed that a Saracen proposal for a combat
between ten from each side might end the siege and the expedition. The
Moslems boasted their religion: 'They maintain that their faith is more
perfect than yours; for it has continued since the beginning of the world,
when it was written down; and that your faith has been introduced by a
mortal, whom the Jews hung and crucified.' Pontius Pilate was not present
to ask, 'What is truth?'; but Lord de Coucy had a nice perception what was
chivalry: 'How do we know if their opponents are gentlemen? They may,
if they choose, bring to the combat ten varlets, or knaves, and, if they are
defeated, what is the gain?' In the event no Moslem took up the challange.
An unsuccessful attack on the town and French suspicion that the Genoese
were in league with the Saracens sapped any remaining enthusiasm for the
expedition, and North Africa was left to Islam. Perhaps the campaign had
not been as greatly amusing to either side as Froissart had foretold. Yet
warfare retained its glamour, the more so when false faiths were involved.
Nor is it at all surprising that Elgar could conjur from Froissart's pages a
concert overture of equivalent ardour and élan.

5 - Go forth to meet the shadowy future

The Longfellow *Hyperion* admired by Ann Elgar was a major influence on Elgar's early life. He sent a copy to Helen Weaver (1860-1927) after his Leipzig visit in January 1883, as reported by her friend Edith Groveham: 'I remember how much he loved Longfellow's prose - & we did not even know Longfellow wrote prose, he sent Helen the book containing *Hyperion* - & being all about the Heidelberg student life we loved it.' *Hyperion* treats of many places besides Heidelberg, and the Elgars' first continental trip together in 1892 involved a number of them. Elgar could deposit with Novello most of *The Black Knight*, a setting of a poem in *Hyperion*, before they joined Minnie Baker, sister of WMB (1858-1935), at Margate. They left for Dover and Cologne on 25 July.

At graduation in 1825, Longfellow was offered the newly founded professorship in modern languages at Bowdoin University, Maine, provided he undertook some European travel. This took him for protracted stays in France, Spain, Italy and Germany; in England he passed briefly through London, Oxford and Stratford before embarking for New York in Liverpool. For the moment he had wandered enough, as he wrote on the return journey in August 1829: 'Travelling has its joys for him whose heart can whirl away in the sweep of life and the eddies of the world, like a bubble catching a thousand different hues from the sun; but happier is he whose heart rides quietly at anchor in the peaceful haven of home.' In September 1831 Longfellow married Mary Storer Potter, whose death four years later was to prove the starting point for *Hyperion*.

Europe beckoned again in April 1835, as Longfellow had been appointed to the Smith professorship at Harvard. This time England came first. There was dinner with John Gibson Lockhart (1794-1854) and his wife Sophia, daughter of Sir Walter Scott, an early hero of Longfellow's. He had also an introduction from Ralph Waldo Emerson (1803-82) to Thomas Carlyle, a meeting described by Mary Longfellow: 'Mr Carlyle, of Craigenputtoch, was soon after announced, and passed a half-hour with us much to our delight. He has very unpolished manners and a broad Scottish accent, but such fine language and beautiful thoughts that it is truly delightful to listen to him.' At the time Carlyle was writing his *History of the French Revolution* (1837), and Mrs.Carlyle told how John Stuart Mill (1806-73) was responsible for the accidental burning of much of the MS. Longfellow and Carlyle shared a love of German literature. Longfellow had read some *Wilhelm Meister*, which Carlyle had

Carlyle by Millais

translated, and Mrs.Carlyle told them her husband placed Goethe second only to Jesus Christ. One night Longfellow read further in Carlyle: 'It is nearly two o'clock in the morning, and I have just finished The Life of Schiller; a truly noble delineation of the life, character and writings of that great and good man. I shall lie down to sleep with my soul quickened and my good resolutions and aspirations strengthened.'

The London month was followed by embarkation to Hamburg in the hands of a Scottish captain: 'a rough old fellow, with a carrotty wig, and a face like a rotten apple'. They moved on to Copenhagen and Stockholm; and in the Cathedral of Uppsala Longfellow saw an ancient wooden image of the god Thor. A rough passage brought them to Amsterdam, where their child was born prematurely and did not live. Mary was well enough for a move to Rotterdam; but she did not rally, as Longfellow told his father on 28 November 1835: 'I am much grieved to say that Mary is not so well to-day. She is very feeble, and the physician tells me that her situation is dangerous.' She died the following day.

Her death marks the beginning of *Hyperion* and its epigraph from *Wilhelm Meister*:

> Who ne'er his bread in sorrow ate,
> Who ne'er the mournful midnight hours
> Weeping upon his bed has sate,
> He knows you not, ye Heavenly Powers.

In Greek mythology Hyperion was a Titan and father of Helios the sun. Longfellow explained the choice of title to George Greene (1811-83) in a letter of 23 July 1839: '*Hyperion* is the name of the book, not of the hero. It merely indicates that here is the life of one who in his feelings and purposes is a "son of Heaven and Earth", and who though obscured by clouds yet "moves on high".' Paul Flemming, the hero of *Hyperion*, was exactly in Longfellow's position: 'The friend of his youth was dead. The bough had broken "under the burden of the unripe fruit". And when, after a season, he looked up again from the blindness of his sorrow, all things seemed unreal.' Longfellow's brother Samuel[1] (1819-92) brings him to the Rhine: 'At Dusseldorf, stopping for half an hour, he strayed into a Roman Catholic church; and the solemn stillness at the elevation of the Host, the kneeling crowd, and the soft, subduing hymn, chanted to the music of the organ, soothed and cheered him.'

The Elgars reached the Rhine at Cologne on 25 July 1892, the end of the day they left England. Next morning they were up early. Despite 'E.

[1] Longfellow, Samuel: *Life of Henry Wadsworth Longfellow with Extracts from His Journals and Correspondence* (London, 1886)

dreaful headache' they went into the Cathedral. Longfellow and Flemming could have seen only the uncompleted building that nevertheless inspired Schumann to the fourth movement of the 'Rhenish' Symphony. Thomas Hood (1799-1845) called it 'a broken promise to God', and Wordsworth invoked the aid of heaven:

> O for the help of Angels to complete
> This Temple - Angels governed by a plan
> Thus far pursued (how gloriously!) by Man.

The poem was written in 1820, and 60 years later national honour gloriously concluded the plan, as the Elgars could appreciate before leaving for Bonn.

Longfellow also moved on to Bonn, where he visited the Cathedral and called on August Wilhelm Schlegel (1767-1845), translator of Shakespeare; 'a man bowed under some three-score years, with an intellectual and pleasant countenance and courteous manners'. In the afternoon Longfellow continued by carriage to Rolandseck. Paul Flemming 'was now pursuing his way along the Rhine to the South of Germany. He had journeyed the same way before, in brighter days and a brighter season of the year, in the May of life and in the month of May. He knew the beauteous river all by heart, every rock and ruin, every echo, every legend.'

In Bonn the Elgars 'drove to Beethoven's house'. Perhaps they remembered that even as a statue Beethoven (1770-1827) had displayed characteristic indifference to royalty in his stance. Queen Victoria was a guest of honour at the unveiling in 1845 and noted in her diary: 'Unfortunately, when the statue was uncovered, it turned its back.' There the Elgars took to the river on a 'Dampfschiff', and had a 'lovely day up the Rhine', though 'boat rather crowded' and they 'heard much about the Hudson'. They passed the great mountain range described in *Hyperion*: 'Beyond, rose the summits of the Siebengebirg. Solemn and dark, like a monk, stood the Drachenfels, in his hood of mist and rearward extended the curtain of mountains, back to the Wolkenburg, - the Castle of the Clouds.' At the foot of the Drachenfels, legend has it, Siegfried received the sword Nothung and slew the dragon. The Elgars could not fail to note the island of Nonnenwerth and may have known that Liszt (1811-86) and the Countess d'Agoult (1805-76) spent summers there, whence Marie wrote to Sainte-Beuve (1804-69) in Paris: 'Every day I see from my window ten or twelve ships passing up and down the river. Their smoke fades away in the branches of the larches and poplars. None of them stops! Nonnenwerth and its island recluses have no business with the rest of humanity!'

Hyperion expresses Longfellow's admiration for the great river: 'O, the pride of the German heart in this noble river! And right it is; for, of all the rivers of this beautiful earth, there is none so beautiful as this.' For Longfellow and the Elgars, the immediate goal was Coblenz. Longfellow reached it 'in the afternoon in time to cross the river and stand upon the esplanade of Ehrenbreitstein in the gathering twilight'. This, the greatest castle on the Rhine, was considered invincible until the French starved it out in 1799. It gave its name to Kenelm Digby's *Broad Stone of Honour or the True Sense and Practice of Chivalry*. It was a happy accident that Turner (1775-1851), when painting castles of the Rhine, mistranslated this name as the 'Bright' Stone of Honour. The result in his many versions of the rock and castle is the subtlest play of light. The confluence of the two rivers, the Rhine and the Mosel, which gave its name to Coblenz, had been known as the Deutsches Eck since the time of the Teutonic Knights' presence in 1216; but not until 1892 was it deified by the monstrous equestrian statue of the German emperor Wilhelm I (1861-88).

Meanwhile the Elgars steamed on past what Longfellow describes as 'ancient castles, grim and hoar, that had taken root as it were on the cliffs'. It was also the territory of Byron's Childe Harold, largely responsible for making Walter Scott a novelist, who now viewed strongholds mostly ruined by French armies, whether of Louis XIV (1643-1715), the Revolution, or Napoleon (1799-1815):

> There Harold gazes on a work divine,
> A blending of all beauties; stream and dells,
> Fruit, foliage, crag, wood, cornfield, mountain, vine,
> And chiefless castles breathing stern farewells
> From grey but leafy walls, where Ruin greenly dwells.
> And there they stand, as stands a lofty mind,
> Worn, but unstooping to the baser crowd,
> All tenantless, save to the crannying wind,
> Or holding dark communion with the crowd.
> There was a day when they were young and proud;
> Banners on high, and battles pass'd below;
> But they who fought are in a bloody shroud,
> And those which waved are shredless dust ere now,
> And the bleak battlements shall bear no future blow.

Stolzenfels was the first castle to pass. In *Hyperion*, Paul Flemming stops there:

> Because, right above him on the high cliff, the glorious ruin of Stolzenfels is looking at him with its hollow eyes, and beckoning to him with its gigantic finger, as if to say, - "Come up hither, and I will tell thee an old tale".

The first words of the ancient castle were those Ann Elgar had quoted in her scrapbook, beginning, 'Beware of dreams!' The cavernous voice of the ruin continued:

> "In ancient times, there dwelt within these halls a follower of Jesus of Jerusalem, - an Archbishop in the Church of Christ. He gave himself up to dreams; to the illusions of fancy; to the vast desires of the human soul. He sought after the impossible. He sought after the Elixir of Life."

This was Archbishop Werner of Trier (1388-1418), who busied himself in the castle with alchemical experiments. The Elgars saw something very different. The mediaeval remains had been incorporated by Karl Friedrich Schinkel (1781-1841) into a castle that would have delighted Sir Walter Scott with its turrets and crenellations. This is where Queen Victoria lodged after the Beethoven celebrations.

The Elgars left their Rhine steamer at Mainz. It was 9.30 pm on 26 July 1892, at the end of a long day. They had only the following morning to see anything of the city and 'firebranded round Mainz'. One hopes that they, Longfellow and Flemming, saw the fine equestrian statue of St. Martin soaring above the roofline of the Cathedral, had time for a quick glance at the Baroque statue of St.Boniface in the market-place, and lingered rather longer by his monument inside the Cathedral. Born Wynfrith (c.672-754) of a good family near Exeter, he was consecrated bishop in 722 and assumed the name Boniface as apostle of Germany. It was Boniface who gave Mainz the primacy among the prince archbishops heading those responsible for the election of the German king and Holy Roman Emperor. The Elgars were in the museum and could not have missed the massive sandstone slab with sculptures of the electors and their king. Longfellow had been delighted with the tomb of Frauenlob, the Minnesinger (c.1260-1318): 'Below it is a bas-relief, representing the poet's funeral. He is carried to his grave by ladies, and thereby won the name of Frauenlob.' If the Elgars missed him, they could have paid him vicarious respect while listening to *Die Meistersinger* (1868) in Bayreuth on 31 July or when seeing the house of Hans Sachs (1494-1576) in Nuremberg two days later. Mastersingers claimed Frauenlob as a seminal influence and wrote new words to his tunes.

On that 2 August, Longfellow had been in Elgar's mind. He wrote to his Grafton nephews and nieces at Stoke Prior, outlining some of the astonishments to be found in 'Bayern'. He went on to mention the most prominent feature of Nuremberg:

> There is a very old Castle in this town & your mother will show you a poem
> by Longfellow about the town which is one of the oldest in this country: &

at the old castle there is a tower where they keep all the old instruments of torture, but we did not care to see them. Then in all these towns there are every now & then fountains in the middle of the streets where the poor people fetch water from & most of them are very handsome &, here specially, they are splendid looking things & works of art.

Longfellow had indeed been in the city during his first German stay and published the 'Nuremberg' poem in his *Belfry of Bruges* volume (1845). It reads like a versification of Alice Elgar's diary:

In the valley of the Pegnitz, where across broad meadow-lands
Rise the blue Franconian mountains, Nuremberg, the ancient, stands.
Quaint old town of toil and traffic, quaint old town of art and song,
Memories haunt thy pointed gables,
                like the rooks that round them throng:
Memories of the Middle Ages, when the emperors, rough and bold,
Had their dwelling in thy castle, time-defying, centuries old;
            ***
On the square the oriel window, where in old heroic days
Sat the poet Melchior singing Kaiser Maximilian's praise.
Everywhere I see around me rise the wondrous world of Art:
Fountains wrought with richest sculpture standing in the common mart;
And above cathedral doorways saints and bishops carved in stone,
By a former age commissioned as apostles to our own.
            ***
Not thy Councils, not thy Kaisers, win for thee the world's regard;
But thy painter, Albrecht Dürer, and Hans Sachs thy cobbler-bard.

With less than a week to go before their return to England, the Elgars reached Heidelberg on 11 August 1892. Longfellow had written glowingly to his father about the place on 24 January 1836: 'Fortunately, Heidelberg is a very beautiful place. The town stands between steep and high mountains on the Neckar, just where the valley, before so narrow that you can almost throw a stone across, spreads out trumpet-mouthed into the broad plain of the Rhine.' He is much struck by the castle: 'Overlooking the town stand the ruins of a magnificent old castle, - the finest I have seen in Europe, excepting the Alhambra.' Longfellow has Paul Flemming spend a last evening before the tower of Elizabeth, British princess and 'winter queen' of Bohemia (1596-1662):

At intervals, the wind of the summer night passed through the ruined castle and the trees, and they sent forth a sound as if Nature were sighing in her dreams; and for a moment, overhead, the broad leaves gently clashed together, like brazen cymbals, with a tinkling sound; and then all was still, save the sweet, passionate song of nightingales, that nowhere sing more sweetly than in the gardens of Heidelberg Castle.

With various excursions to neighbouring regions, the Heidelberg section of *Hyperion* takes a third of the book. A Harvard professor, and resident in a German university town, Longfellow now made use in the 'romance' of lectures he gave on the 'Lives of Literary Men'. Samuel Longfellow gives the details:

> Considerable portions of these lectures were afterwards woven into Hyperion, and may be read there. Among them were the chapters on Jean Paul, on the Lives of Scholars, and on Literary Fame, in the first Book; the sketch of an artist's life in Rome and the pictures of the Middle Ages, which in the third Book are feigned to be read from Mary Ashburton's sketch-book; and the chapter on Hoffmann and his writings in Book fourth.

The day after arriving in Heidelberg, Elgar wrote to his mother: 'I must send a line from <u>here</u> about which we have read & thought so much. I have marked with a cross our hotel which is <u>above</u> the Castle: it is exquisitely lovely here & we are just going exploring.' Actual mention of *Hyperion* was in connection with 'the beer scandal'. Paul Flemming and his friend the Baron happened one evening to pass a student tavern, where they were invited in by Von Kleist, who was 'universally acknowledged, among his young acquaintance, as a "devilish handsome fellow"; notwithstanding a tremendous scar on his cheek, and a cream-coloured moustache, as soft as the silk of Indian corn'. They first saw an initiation of young Nasty-Foxes, 'looking wild, and green, and foolish'. They were 'obliged to pass under a pair of naked swords, held crosswise by two Old-Ones, who, with pieces of burnt cork, made an enormous pair of moustaches on the rosy cheeks of each'. They then watched Branders, those who had been a term at the university, traversing a table on chairs with lighted paper in their hair. A pale quiet-looking student, who was trying to make his poodle sit upright at his side with a pipe in its mouth, was insulted by a student already far gone. A challenge was at once issued, and each had to drain three brimming tankards of beer. The challenger was victorious, as the other collapsed in the midst of the third glass. It was then that Von Kleist made his dramatic entry:

> At this moment a majestic figure came stalking down the table, ghost-like, through the dim, smoky atmosphere. His coat was off, his neck bare, his hair wild, his eyes wide open, and looking straight before him, as if he saw some beckoning hand in the air, that others could not see. His left hand

was upon his hip, and in his right hand he held a drawn sword extended, and pointing downward. Regardless of every one, erect, and with a martial stride, he marched directly along the centre of the table, crushing glasses and overthrowing bottles at every step.

One student dashed a full glass of beer into his face, and chaos ensued. Von Kleist left the tavern with six duels to fight. The Elgars left Heidelberg for High Mass in Cologne Cathedral and their return to England.

Hyperion was also a useful depository for translations of German poems that Longfellow made for his Harvard classes, sometimes improvised and sometimes more carefully worked. They are dotted around throughout the book, but the greatest concentration occurs on the afternoon of a rainy day in the hotel at Interlaken in the third Book. Paul Flemming is with Mary Ashburton, the thinly disguised Frances Appleton (d.1861), who was to be Longfellow's second wife. Flemming happens to pick up a volume of poetry lying on the table, and the author is Ludwig Uhland (1787-1862): ' "I have opened at random upon the ballad of the Black Knight. Do you repeat the German after me and I will translate".' He begins by reading the first line to Miss Ashburton, but she refuses to have anything to do with such sounds: ' "Well, then, listen. I will improvise a translation for your own particular benefit".' And so he does, producing the ten stanzas exactly as set by Elgar in a work he was now to complete and which would be as significant for his choral future as *Froissart* had been for his orchestral. The future might well be shadowy to a man of Elgar's temperament, but he was now well equipped to meet it.

Mary Ashburton considered the *Black Knight* 'rather too grim and ghostly for this dull afternoon'. Flemming then gives a sample passage from a Harvard lecture: ' "It begins joyously enough with the feast of Pentecost, and the crimson banners at the old castle. Then the contrast is well managed. The knight in black mail, and the waving in of the mighty shadow in the dance, and the dropping of the faded flowers, are all strikingly presented to the imagination".' He ends with a sentence that Elgar, in unprofessorial mood, might have echoed: ' "However, it tells its own story, and needs no explanation".'

In June 1836 Longfellow left Heidelberg with an ultimate goal of Italy. His brother Samuel explains that at Innsbruck he had to change his mind:

At the police station they refused for some reason to *viser* his passport for Italy. In vain he remonstrated; they would only sign it for Switzerland, and to Switzerland he must go. So, after looking at the fine bronze statues that guard the tomb of Maximilian in the Kapuciner Church, and sketching an outline of that of Alfred, he set out in the afternoon by post for Bregenz, along the banks of the Inn.

" 'Twas Pentecost, the Feast of
    Gladness,
When woods and fields put off all
    sadness.
Thus began the king, and spake:
  ' So from the halls
    Of ancient Hofburg's walls
A luxuriant spring shall break.'

" Drums and trumpets echo loudly,
Wave the crimson banners proudly.
From balcony the king looked on;
  In the play of spears,
    Fell all the cavaliers
Before the monarch's stalwart son.

The Black Knight *by Birket Foster*

Among the statues guarding the tomb of the Emperor Maximilian I is no
'Alfred'. There are many Albrechts, but it is more likely that Longfellow
was struck by the apparently anomalous presence of King Arthur, just as
Elgar was when he first visited the church in August 1894.

Hyperion has Paul Flemming reach Innsbruck by a thoroughly
dramatic route, scaling mountain heights and crossing awesome chasms
on the way. From the Furca pass he could see the Jungfrau:

> His soul within him was wild with a fierce and painful delight. The
> mountain air excited him; the mountain solitudes enticed, yet maddened
> him. Every peak, every sharp, jagged iceberg, seemed to pierce him. The
> silence was awful and sublime. It was like that in the soul of a dying man,
> when he hears no more the sounds of earth.

Despite a hint of the *Gerontius* poem to come, the scene is of course
Wagnerian, as he was to embody it in the last two acts of *Die Walküre*
(1870). Flemming continues his awed progress:

> A sudden turn in the road brings you in sight of a lofty bridge, stepping
> from cliff to cliff in a single stride. A mighty cataract howls beneath it, like
> an evil spirit, and fills the air with mist; and the mountain wind claps its
> hand and shrieks through the narrow pass. Ha! Ha! This is the Devil's
> Bridge. It leads the traveller across the fearful chasm, and through a
> mountain gallery into the broad green, silent meadow of Andermath.

There were even more spectacular wonders ahead:

> Ere long he reached the magnificent glacier of the Rhone; a frozen
> cataract, more than two thousand feet in height, and many miles broad at
> its base. It fills the whole valley between two mountains, running back to
> their summits. At the base it is arched, like a dome; and above, jagged and
> rough, and resembles a mass of gigantic crystals, of a pale emerald tint,
> mingled with white. A snowy crust covers its surface; but at every rent and
> crevice the pale green ice shines clear in the sun. Its shape is that of a
> glove, lying with the palm downwards, and the fingers crooked and close
> together. It is a gauntlet of ice, which, centuries ago, Winter, the king of
> the mountains, threw down in defiance to the Sun; and year by year the
> Sun strives to lift it from the ground on the point of his glittering spear.

Paul Flemming misjudged any affection Mary Ashburton might feel for
him. Longfellow had summoned a parallel from 14th-century chivalry to
express his delight in her: 'Old Froissart tells us, in his Chronicles, that,
when King Edward beheld the Countess of Salisbury at her castle-gate, he
thought he had never seen before so noble nor so fair a lady.' Gently

rejected, Flemming was a second time emotionally stricken within the year. Now bound for Innsbruck, he was in the company of an English friend, who tried to comfort him by quoting 'Sir John Suckling's Song' from Act 4 of his play *Aglaura* (1638) :

> Why so wan and pale, fond lover ?
> Pr 'ythee why so pale ?
> Will, if looking well can't move her,
> Looking ill prevail ?
> Pr'ythee why so pale ?

The last line of the third stanza is sound sense: 'The devil take her!' Elgar set the poem as a partsong for a Worcester concert in March 1881. The work is since lost, but a sketch at Elgar's Birthplace shows he set the more correct version, 'Why so pale and wan?' It must be a moot point whether he took the poem from *Hyperion*. Flemming and his companion persevered through a wild night, and the disappointed lover had bouts of restless sleep:

> He slept again at intervals; and at length, though long after midnight, reached Innsbruck through sleeping and waking; his mind filled with dim recollections of the unspeakably dismal night-journey; - the climbing of hills, and plunging into dark ravines: the momentary rattling of the wheels over paved streets of towns, and the succeeding hollow rolling and tramping on the wet earth; the roar of waters, leaping through deep chasms by the roadside; and the wind through the mountain-passes, sounding loud and long, like the inextinguishable laughter of the gods.

They did not linger in Innsbruck:

> They did not fail, however, to visit the tomb of Maximilian in the Franciscan Church of the Holy Cross, and gaze with some admiration upon the twenty-eight gigantic bronze statues of Godfrey of Bouillon, and King Arthur, and Ernest the Iron-man, and Frederick of the empty pockets; kings and heroes, and others, which stand leaning on their swords between the columns of the church, as if guarding the tomb of the dead.

Longfellow remembered them years later, when writing a poem to commemorate his friend Bayard Taylor (1825-78) :

> As the statues in the gloom
> Watch o'er Maximilian's tomb.

Flemming and the Englishman were now ready for Salzburg:

Maximilian kneels on his cenotaph

After gazing awhile at these motionless sentinels, they went forth, and strolled through the public gardens, with the jagged mountains right over their heads, and all around the tall, melancholy pines, like Tyrolese peasants, with shaggy hair; and at their feet the mad torrents of the Inn, sweeping with turbid waves through the midst of the town. In the afternoon, they drove on towards Salzburg, through the magnificent mountain passes of Waidering and Unken.

By the time Paul Flemming reached Salzburg he was in a raging fever, and he remained dangerously ill for a week. He had nightmare visions and hallucinations:

He was lying with his hands crossed upon his breast, and his eyes looking up at the white curtains overhead. He thought them the white marble canopy of a tomb, and himself the marble statue lying beneath.

It was morning and the Cathedral clock opposite his hotel struck ten :

When the clock ceased striking, the eight-and-twenty gigantic bronze statues from the Church of the Holy Rood in Innsbruck stalked into the chamber, and arranged themselves along the walls, which spread into dimly-lighted aisles and arches.

It was no wonder Longfellow had Flemming haunted by the Maximilian statues. They had a profound effect on the Elgars too, judging from their repeated visits to the church.

In 1894 the Elgars were in Bavaria from 2 August till 18 September. They spent only the first night in Munich, but there was obviously purposeful walking ahead, as the next day Alice Elgar slightly overdid her umlauts when noting that they bought 'a Rücksack & E.'s booful mantel'. It was then Garmisch and the Bethells' establishment where the Fittons from Malvern, including the future 'Ysobel' of the 'Enigma' Variations, joined them on 9 August. Further evidence of adventure came on 5 August: 'A's boots' first appearance at Garmisch', and on 13 August they 'Bought another Rücksack'.

The Elgars were now ready for departure to Innsbruck, their most southerly point, and Elgar himself began a supplementary account of the journey. They started from Garmisch on Tuesday, 14 August: 'Doubtful looking morning but fine all day tho' cloudy.' Wild deer came close to them on the way, as they walked to Mittenwald, town of violin makers. They saw the statue to Mathias Klotz (1653-1743), founder of the violin school, by the church, but had 'fruitless endeavours to find some one to repair A's umbrella'. The next day it was the feast of the Assumption, and they went to the church with its 'fine ceiling' for 'Blessing of flowers -

bunches carried by children'. There were 'Statues with real hair' and the
Mittenwald church band was the 'best we have heard so far'. They moved
on to the sight of 'lonely curious shaped peaks' now that they had crossed
the frontier into Austria. They had the surprise of a '**Snake in road**' but
lunched pleasantly at Seefeld: '(Sardines butter hot potatoes   sehr gut)'.
Benediction was just beginning at the church, so they 'walked across the
pastures to a curious roman-looking chapel. Christ over altar with <u>real</u>
hair'. In the afternoon they had 'Hot milk at 4.15 at a little Gast Haus just
before Zirl   fine view of Inn Thal & vast snowy mountains in distance afar
beyond Innsbrück.' That was the Elgars' first hint of the terrain crossed
by Paul Flemming and first evidence that Elgar had caught the umlaut
disease. From Zirl they took the train to Innsbruck, where they stayed for
three nights at the Hotel d'Europe.

That same evening they 'Walked to Fransiskan Kirche   saw monument
to <u>King Arthur</u>'. Elgar's account of 16 August has much about his interest
in Maximilian: 'walked in old town & again to Church to see monument
Silberne Kapelle &c&c.' The Silver Chapel was the burial place of
Maximilian's great-grandson, Frederick II, Archduke of the Tirol (1564-
95) - it was he who made a magnificent museum of the Unterschloss at
Schloss Ambras, where the Elgars went in the afternoon. There he had
taken in 1570 the busts of Roman emperors Maximilian had originally
planned for his tomb. On return to Innsbruck, Elgar 'Saw Church again &
monument'. On 17 August, their last full day in Innsbruck, it was 'again to
Max. Monument'. In the afternoon, Elgar was alone. He saw 'much new
snow on mountains   E wildly rushing after engines   Lovely effects of sun
setting - lights on snow & distant peaks'. They left Innsbruck the following
morning and were back in Garmisch on the evening of 19 August. Elgar
summed up: 'A very lovely & ever to be remembered little excursion.'

What was it that so fascinated the Elgars with Maximilian and his tomb,
so that they returned repeatedly to the church not only in 1894, but in
subsequent years? For the funeral monument the Elgars visited so often
Maximilian planned the most lavish expenditure. To watch over him in
death there were to be forty more than lifesize statues of heroes, his family
and collaterals; 100 smaller statues of saints connected with the Habsburg
family; and thirty-four busts of Roman emperors to emphasise the
continuity of the imperial idea. All were to be cast in bronze, a formidable
task in the case of the largest statues. Where were the craftsmen to attempt
the work? And where, indeed, was the building to house this array, all to
be concentrated on the great central cenotaph on which the figure of the
emperor kneels? In the end only twenty-eight of the standing figures were
produced, and Maximilian was sufficiently sensitive to local problems to
entrust the King Arthur and Theodoric (c.454-526) to the workshop of
Peter Vischer (1460-1529) in Nuremberg. The saints were reduced to

twenty-three and the Roman emperors to twenty-one, though still including the disreputable Caligula (37-41), Nero (54-68) and Domitian (81-96). The Hofkirche or Court Church was specially built to receive the statues by the Emperor Ferdinand I (1556-64), grandson of Maximilian, and the monument was ready for display in 1563.

Maximilian I, crucial figure in the Habsburg empire, was crowned king of the Romans in 1507. The Venetians refused him permission to cross their territory, and he had to be content to declare himself Roman Emperor Elect the following February, with the tacit approval of Pope Julius II (1503-13). Dynastic marriages achieved the vast territories inherited by his grandson Charles V (1519-58) and almost at once divided by him. Maximilian's less public diplomacy involved support for Perkin Warbeck (c.1474-99) as Richard, duke of York. Warbeck was given a place of honour at the funeral of Maximilian's father, Frederick III (1452-93) and was recognised as Richard IV of England. In return Warbeck made Maximilian his heir, so that he should succeed to the Yorkist heritage. It was small wonder that Henry VII (1485-1509) was suspicious: 'the cautious Tudor distrusted the flighty Habsburg'. A bad storm in the English Channel, however, allowed Henry some redress.

Queen Isabella of Spain had died in 1504, and her daughter Juana was now married to Philip the Fair (1504-6), son of Maximilian, both of them to become supporting statues in the Hofkirche. They sailed for Spain on 10 January 1506, but appalling weather drove them to Melcombe Regis (now Weymouth) in Dorset. They were conducted to Windsor with due ceremony and received by Henry. There was an exchange of chivalric courtesies. Philip became a Knight of the Garter, and Prince Henry of Wales a Knight of the Golden Fleece. The opportunity was taken to draw up a treaty advantageous to the Tudor king, but there were signs and portents that boded ill for the Habsburg. The vane of St.Paul's Cathedral, a brazen eagle and therefore also Habsburg symbol, had fallen during the storm and smashed the sign of a nearby inn, an eagle. This was considered an evil omen for Philip the Fair, who died later that year. The inordinate grief of his widow deranged her mind, and history knows her as Juana the Mad.

Maximilian was fascinated with mediaeval glitter and later times regarded him as a last example of knighthood. In the *Broad Stone of Honour*, Kenelm Digby devotes space to Maximilian. The 'Orlandus' book tells of his prowess in arms:

> In 1495, when the Emperor Maximilian held his first diet at Worms, there rode into the city a French knight, named Claude de la Barre, of formidable aspect, who was thought to have been sent by his king. Scarcely had he found a place in the inn, when he hung out his shield under the window, and sent a herald about to challenge all German knights to come and joust with him.

No German knight would attempt the contest, until the 'stout Caesar Maximilian' had his shield hung near that of the French knight. The encounter was appointed for nine days later :

> Both appeared in full armour, neither spoke a word to the other. Fear and uncertainty marked the countenance of every spectator, as the trumpets sounded for the third time, when the lances were couched, and the shock took place. Then the combatants threw away their spears, and assailed each other with shining swords. The Frenchman aimed a stout thrust at the emperor, but his armour turning the edge, he had soon the advantage, and laid on so thick, that after a desperate struggle, he obliged his adversary to yield himself prisoner.

For the last twenty years of his life Maximilian was much concerned with artistic matters. Lacking the resources to plan great building works, he wondered about an equestrian monument for himself in Augsburg, a memorial in the imperial Cathedral of Speyer and above all an unparalleled funerary display. He planned three biographies in terms of Arthurian romance. In *Weisskunig*, Maximilian as chivalrous hero is in a world where 'Knights calling themselves the King of Troy and the King of Europe perform deeds of great courage, while observing rituals known to them and their audiences from the literature they cherish'. Such were the romances concerning Tristan and Parsifal. Kenelm Digby quotes in his 'Godefridus' book: 'In the White King it is said, that young Maximilian had a great inclination to examine into the origin and antiquity of noble families, and for this purpose learned men were appointed, who should do nothing else but search through convents and libraries, in order to discover facts relating to heroic houses.' Digby has more to say in the 'Orlandus' book:

> In the Weiss Kunig, it is related how the young Maximilian learned to shoot with the cross-bow and the English bow, to hunt with falcons, and to pursue mountain game, to chase stags, with goats, chamois, wild boars, marmots, and hares. There is an engraving representing savage rocks and precipices; the young prince having crossed a torrent and shot a chamois, while two attendants are left on the other side in astonishment at his boldness. Near Innsbruck, I have seen the cleft in the side of the rock, nearly perpendicular, on which he is said to have stood, unable to get forwards or backwards, so that he was obliged to descend by the aid of a rope, which was let down to him from above.

Then there is *Theuerdank*, an account in verse of Maximilian's journey to Mary of Burgundy (1457-82) in August 1477 for the purpose of marriage. *Freydal*, also in verse, is entirely concerned with games of combat and masquerades; but its 265 woodcuts are based on actual episodes from Maximilian's life.

Unable to construct a triumphal arch to celebrate his reign (the Innsbruck arch was erected only in 1765, to commemorate the wedding of the future Leopold II (1790-92)), Maximilian turned to the woodcut to provide not only the great arch his purse would not otherwise allow but also the triumphal procession to pass beneath it. The procession has 137 woodcuts, mainly by Hans Burgkmair (1473-1531) and leads off with 'a naked man riding on a griffin', who blows 'a strange twisted horn'. Apart from fifers, drummers and trumpeters, there are five main musical 'cars' in the Triumph. The lutes and viols are led by Artus, on a car drawn by two elks, whose banner proclaims his skill:

> Now lutes and viols harmonize
> In elegant and courtly wise;
> Thus bade by his Imperial might
> Have I produced this fair delight,
> Blending these tuneful instruments
> As well befits such great events.

Master Paul Hofhaimer (1459-1537) is on a car with regal and positive drawn by a camel. His banner reads:

> Regal and positive I play with ease.
> The organ, too, with many keys
> I make resound with artful voices
> So that each listener rejoices -
> All with a master's understanding,
> Our noble Emperor thus commanding.

The choral car is drawn by two wisents (European bison) in charge of George Slatkonia, bishop of Vienna (1456-1522):

> With voices high and low conjoint,
> With harmony and counterpoint,
> By all the laws of music moved,
> My choir I constantly improved.
> But not alone through my intent -
> Give thanks to royal encouragement!

If Elgar was curious enough to investigate Maximilian's musical establishment, he would have found there also such names as Henricus Isaac (c.1456-1517) and Ludwig Senfl (c.1486-1543); and he might have remembered that part of the procession appeared in his mother's scrapbook.

Maximilian, Mary of Burgundy (left), Maria Bianca Sforza (right)
and Philip the Fair on the Triumphal Arch

On the Triumphal Arch the central portal depicts Maximilian's family tree. There are twenty-four historical panels featuring the main military and political events of the emperor's career. Eleven panels are more occupied with private matters, such as Maximilian's skill in languages, his interest in jousting and heraldry, and his part in the discovery of Christ's robe at Trier. At the bottom of the arch are three coats-of-arms at the right: they belong to Johannes Stabius, who devised the literary plan of the arch; Jörg Kolderer, who prepared the preliminary sketches; and Albrecht Dürer (1471-1528), personally responsible for some of the woodcuts. Maximilian declared his aim:

> Whoever prepares no memorial for himself during his lifetime has none after his death and is forgotten along with the sound of the bells that toll his passing. Thus the money that I spend for the perpetuation of my memory is not lost; in fact, in such a matter to be sparing of money is to suppress my future memory.

The Innsbruck Hofkirche has ensured Maximilian's memory cannot be suppressed. Elgar was surprised to find King Arthur among Maximilian's guardian statues; but the emperor based much of his life and its ideals on Arthur and the Round Table. In the Triumphal Procession Arthur also appears, next to Odobert of Provence; but Maximilian's historians seem to have lost their nerve when it came to the family tree on the Triumphal Arch; there Arthur does not appear. Elgar would have noticed at once the hopeful anachronism in the quartering of Arthur's shield, where already the English lion and French fleur-de-lys appear; and Alice Elgar might have remarked the striking resemblance between Maximilian's Arthur and her own 'EDU'.

To take the most notable statues in chronological order, one of the most magnificent is that of Theodoric, perhaps based on a sketch by Dürer. Edward Gibbon (1737-94) paid him apt tribute: 'Italy revived and flourished under the government of a Gothic king, who might have deserved a statue among the best and bravest of the ancient Romans.' He was later identified with Dietrich von Bern, who finally vanquishes Gunther and Hagen in the *Nibelungenlied* (c.1200). Chlodwig or Clovis (c.466-511) has a surcoat richly decorated with fleurs-de-lys. From the centre of a chain round his neck hangs a crucifix, symbolic of his conversion to Christianity in 496 or 506 after a victory over the Alemanni. Gregory of Tours (c.540-94) is less than generous towards him: 'he killed many other kings and several of his close kinsmen, fearful lest they should supplant him or diminish his authority'. Godfrey of Bouillon (c.1060-1100), last of the Nine Worthies, and Kenelm Digby's 'Godefridus', was cast in the workshop of Stephan Godl, whom Maximilian had brought from Nuremberg in 1508, and whose official task was the 100

Habsburg saints. Godfrey wears a cap surrounded with a crown of thorns and armour covered with crosses to signify his rule of Jerusalem as advocate of the Holy Sepulchre at the end of the First Crusade. Sir Walter Scott describes him in *Count Robert of Paris*. The Emperor Alexius (1081-1118) asks: ' "Whom have we next? Godfrey Duke of Bouillon - leading, I see, a most formidable band from the banks of a huge river called the Rhine. What is this person's character?" ' Nicephorus answers him: ' "this Godfrey is one of the wisest, noblest, and bravest of the leaders who have thus strangely put themselves in motion; and among a list of independent princes, as many in number as those who assembled for the siege of Troy, and followed, most of them, by subjects ten times more numerous, this Godfrey may be regarded as the Agamemnon".'

Maximilian's first marriage brought him close connection with the House of Burgundy and its eventual rule. The statue of Philip the Good (1396-1467) was also cast in Godl's workshop (1520-21). Stern featured, he wears a broad-brimmed hat with drapery extending round the neck. There is chain mail beneath his surcoat, which is richly ornamented with fabulous animals and fleurs-de-lys; he has also a short cape with fleurs-de-lys, rampant lions and bends. His long sword has panels of a man on horseback, a fabulous creature, and a woman with billowing robes. In 1429 he asked to postpone election to the Order of the Garter; his Order of the Golden Fleece was founded in January 1430 when he married Isabel of Portugal. Its patrons were Jason as pagan hero and Gideon from the Bible. The fall of Constantinople in 1453 made Philip and his nobility think of a crusade. Their naval ships made an appearance in the eastern Mediterranean and the Black Sea. The Golden Fleece itself turned thoughts towards the east. Philip's statue displays the Order. The Burgundian court was then at its most brilliant. Rogier van der Weyden (c.1399-1464) painted portraits of Philip and his son Charles and Jan van Eyck (c.1395-1441) joined the ducal chamber. Musically there were such luminaries in the household as Binchois (c.1400-60), Du Fay (1397-1474), and the English Robert Morton, who may be identical with the bishop of Worcester who died in 1497.

The statue of Charles the Bold was also cast in the Godl workshop. The likeness is from a painting, now apparently lost, but still available in 1534; shorn of his beard, however, Charles lacks some boldness. In his struggle with Louis XI, with whom he had been partly brought up, he secured the alliance of Edward IV of England, and married his sister, Margaret of York, as his third wife in 1468. Like Maximilian I, his future son-in-law, he was a belated representative of chivalry, with a wide knowledge and culture. He supported the production of elaborate and magnificent manuscripts, and is said to have written songs and a motet, perhaps under the guidance of Du Fay. Charles's statue has flared hat surrounded by a twisted band. He is in full armour, with coat of mail beneath the outer pleating of many sections held together with studs. He has grieves, gauntlets, and armed shoulder-pads. He wears the Order of the Golden Fleece suspended from an elaborate chain. Scott describes him in *Quentin Durward* as he goes forth to the celebrated meeting with Louis XI at Péronne:

> Dressed in his ducal mantle, and attended by his great officers, and principal knights and nobles, he went in gallant cavalcade to meet Louis XI. His retinue absolutely blazed with gold and silver; for the wealth of the Court of England being exhausted by the wars of York and Lancaster, and the expenditure of France limited by the economy of the Sovereign, that of Burgundy was for the time the most magnificent in Europe.

Mary of Burgundy, daughter of Charles the Bold, was Maximilian's first wife and mother of Philip the Fair. The casting of her statue was begun in 1513, and there was an often-copied portrait, since lost, to work from. She wears a headdress tapering to a conical point, a typical Burgundian dress with squarecut neck and elaborate patterning, and a necklace of intricate detail; her rounded shoe has a very high instep. In her left hand she holds a partly open missal, but she was as devoted to hunting as Maximilian himself. He took as second wife in 1495, largely for political reasons, Bianca Maria Sforza (1472-1511), niece of Ludovico il Moro (1494-99), patron of Leonardo da Vinci (1452-1519) and of Josquin des Prez (c.1450-1519). The casting of her statue in 1525 was ordered by Ferdinand I. The elaborate crown is surmounted with stylised crosses, and her long hair is caught up in an ornamental wimple. The long dress of many folds is supported by elegant shoulder straps, and the embroidered sleeves are puffed at the shoulders.

Maximilian's father, the Emperor Frederick III, had to wait till 1524 for the casting of his statue. The features are those of an old man, careworn, with sunken cheeks and down-turned mouth; his hooked nose is similar to that of Maximilian. He wears a crown with cross on top, has a richly ornamented sceptre in his left hand and a short sword in his right, while an orb rests on a cushion by his foot. He was the last of the Holy Roman Emperors to be crowned in Rome (March 1452). He was driven from Vienna in 1490 by Matthias Corvinus (1458-90) and handed over the government to Maximilian, retiring to Linz for the study of botany, astronomy and alchemy.

Philip the Fair, son of Maximilian, had his statue cast in 1516, ten years after his sudden death, though the sketch for the finished work was made in Philip's lifetime. Through his mother, he was heir to the Burgundian empire; through his marriage to Juana of Spain in 1496 he became king of Castile. His is the fine portrait of a young contemporary. He wears fluted armour and a pleated gown, and has on his head the

Mary of Burgundy

crown of Castile adorned with pomegranates. His marriage and those of his father are among the carved marble scenes that surround the central mausoleum. If most of the scenes are concerned with military exploits and diplomatic coups, the four guardian figures of the ensemble, seated at the four corners, just below the level of Maximilian himself, have been chosen to represent the essential virtues of the emperor's reign. They are Fortitude, Justice, Prudence, and Temperance.

In the course of their repeated visits to the monument, the Elgars must have become familiar with all twenty-eight of the statues in a detail beyond anything set out here. Perhaps King Arthur, dignified and commanding, may have remained their favourite. Paul Flemming, mindful of his sickbed experience in Salzburg, may have wished to forget them all. Longfellow himself, whose favourite opera was *Don Giovanni,* may idly have wondered which statue should come to dinner. But the emperor has ordained their permanent stability.

Maximilian had access to the gold mines of Hungary, and the copper of Styria and Bohemia; but his finances were such that he was nicknamed 'Max ohne Geld'. Kenelm Digby takes up the matter in his 'Orlandus' section:

"I am not the king of gold," said the Emperor Maximilian to his father, "but of men." The epithet of "Maximilian the moneyless" might indeed have indicated a culpable neglect of economy, which was dangerous in a sovereign; for though it is but little to learn that it was used as a reproach by the vulgar class of mankind, we are obliged to respect the judgment of the impartial historian.

The bells have ceased tolling for Maximilian and the Habsburgs, but the money he spent on his monument was not lost.

Samuel Longfellow explains that it was on a far more modest memorial, at St.Gilgen, his brother found the epigraph for his 'romance':

And it was in this church-yard that he read, on the wall of its little chapel, the inscription which he afterward made the motto of Hyperion, and which has been the watch-word of life to so many who read it in those pages. It is a little mortuary chapel, holding a few rude wooden seats, and having an extraordinary frieze of human skulls arranged just under its ceiling. There are several funeral tablets affixed to the walls, and on one of these - a tablet of metal, not marble, is the inscription :

* * *

Look not mournfully into the Past, It comes not back again.
Wisely improve the Present. It is thine.
Go forth to meet the shadowy future, without fear, and with a manly heart.

6 - The war and waste of clashing creeds

A.J.Jaeger (1860-1909), the 'Nimrod' of the 'Enigma' Variations, reported to Parry that Elgar had no great opinion of *The Light of Life* (1896) but it was very different with *Scenes from the Saga of King Olaf* (also 1896), which he was still looking back on with pleasure as late as December 1922, in a letter to Ivor Atkins: 'it seems strange that the strong (it is *that*) characteristic stuff shd. have been conceived & written (by a poor wretch teaching all day) with a splitting headache after dinner & at odd, sustained moments - but the spirit and will was there.' Rosa Burley (1866-1951), the Malvern headmistress who was part of the teaching round, did not approve of Longfellow as choice for yet another Elgar work after *The Spanish Serenade*, *The Black Knight*, and the Froissart *Rondel*. Longfellow died in March 1882, and two years later a memorial bust of him, despite displeasure from Cardinal Newman, was placed in Westminster Abbey next to Chaucer, an apt position in view of the *Tales of a Wayside Inn*, from which the 'Olaf' scene was taken. Longfellow's *Tales* were directly inspired by Chaucer's 'Canterbury' set. Rosa Burley had vehemently joined the critical reaction against Longfellow. Elgar had not; nor had his collaborator on *King Olaf*, H.A.Acworth (1848-1943), whose life's work in India gave him topics in common with Alice Elgar, as did his translations from the Indian.

Hyperion had revealed Longfellow's delight in the Middle Ages, as when he transfers some of his thoughts to Mary Ashburton in chapter 5 of Book III:

> It is only when I stand amid ruined castles, that look at me so mournfully, and behold the heavy armour of old knights, hanging upon the wainscot of Gothic chambers; or when I walk amid the aisles of some dusky minster, whose walls are narrative of hoar antiquity, and whose very bells have been baptized, and see the carved oaken stalls in the choir, where so many generations of monks have sat and sung, and the tombs, where now they sleep in silence, to awake no more to their midnight psalms; - it is only at such times that the history of the Middle Ages is a reality to me, and not a passage in romance.

Longfellow and Elgar shared many literary interests. On his first French visit the poet is in quest of Quentin Durward, writing to his brother Stephen from Paris on 19 November 1826:

Longfellow statue at Cambridge, Massachusetts

So down I went in spite of mud and mire, in search of these wonderful caverns, and also of Plessis-les-Tours, which lies somewhere on the same route. I persuaded myself, when I came to the ford of the river, that it was the same at which Quentin Durward crossed. But Plessis-les-Tours I could not find; nobody knew anything about it.

Dickens (1812-70) may not have rated highly with Alice Elgar, but Longfellow writes joyously to his father on 30 January 1842 about his first American visit :

> You see by the papers that Dickens has arrived. He is a glorious fellow; and the greatest possible enthusiasm arises among all classes. He has not a moment's rest, - calls innumerable, invitations innumerable. - and is engaged three deep for the remainder of the stay, in the way of dinners and parties. He is a gay, free-and-easy character; with a fine bright face, blue eyes, and long dark hair.

That October Longfellow stayed with him in London; from there he wrote to Charles Sumner (1811-74), lifelong friend and fearless anti-slavery campaigner:

> I write this from Dickens's study, the focus from which so many luminous things have radiated. The raven croaks from the garden, and the ceaseless roar of London fills my ears.

He goes on to say he has read Dickens's *American Notes* (1842):

> It is jovial and good-natured, and at times very severe. You will read it with delight and, for the most part, approbation. He has a grand chapter on Slavery. *Spitting* and *politics at Washington* are the other topics of censure. Both you and I would censure them with equal severity, to say the least. He gives due laud to the New-York oysters.

There was much enjoyment of Ruskin. The Mary Ashburton of *Hyperion* had now become Longfellow's second wife Frances, and on 19 November 1849 she read to him: 'In the evening, to the sound of wind and rain upon the casement, F. read to me Ruskin's Seven Lamps of Architecture, one of the most remarkable books of the time. What a magnificent breadth and sweep of style in the elevated passages!' Ruskin had admiration in return, as noted by Samuel Longfellow: '"Longfellow, in his Golden Legend, has entered more closely into the temper of the monk, for good and for evil, than ever yet theological writer or historian, though they may have given their life's labor to the analysis."'

The Longfellows tried *Sartor Resartus*, to be quoted by Elgar in his

Birmingham lecture; the poet commented: 'What a figure Carlyle will make in the history of this age!' In November 1858 Longfellow recorded: 'Got Carlyle's History of Frederick, and begin reading. Graphic introductory chapters; then a dull morass of *Kurfürsten* and the like, with great shadows stalking through the mist. Finally, half through the first volume, the history begins and is very interesting.'

Arthur Clough (1819-61) came to dinner in February 1853, and brought Matthew Arnold's latest volume of poems, including both 'Tristram and Iseult' and 'Empedocles on Etna'. Longfellow found them 'Very clever; with a little of the Tennysonian leaven in them'. In July 1859 Longfellow was engrossed in 'Tennyson's new poem, Four Idyls of the King. Eagerly devour the first of them, which is charming - reminding one of Chaucer's "Griselda".' The titles were 'Enid', 'Vivien', 'Elaine' and 'Guinevere'. He liked the first and third best. In the final sequence of 1891, known to Elgar, they became 'The Marriage of Geraint', 'Geraint and Enid', 'Merlin and Vivien', 'Lancelot and Elaine', and 'Guinevere'. In August 1859 a Longfellow friend, James Fields, was on the Isle of Wight and gave 'the spirited outline sketch of the Idyllic Poet serenely ploughing the windy acres'. Frances also received Jessamine from Tennyson's garden.

Longfellow was very musical, often at the opera and in the concert hall. He was familiar with such singers as Giuditta Grisi (1805-40), Jenny Lind (1820-87) and Adelina Patti (1843-1919). *Don Giovanni* (1787) remained the greatest of all operas, as is clear from the diary of 17 April 1850: 'Ah what a delicious opera! what a trio; what arias; what accompaniments! San Quirico, as Leporello, played capitally; he is a real *buffo*, and seems to have just stepped down from a stage in the streets of Naples. Beneventano is too stout for the Don, and too vulgar, - a bandit in brown boots.' The following September he was at a concert that impressed him: 'At Jenny Lind's first concert. Rain, pitiless rain. A crowd. She is very feminine and lovely. Her power is in her presence, which is magnetic, and takes her audience captive before she opens her lips. She sings like the morning star; clear, liquid, heavenly sounds.' On 3 December 1853 there was some Wagner: 'With Mrs.Howe at the Germania Concert. It was mostly Wagner's music, - beginning with the celebrated overture to Tannhäuser. Strange, original, and somewhat barbaric.' In January 1855 they heard *I Puritani* (1835) with Giuditta Grisi and Giovanni Mario (1810-83). 'Grisi is grand, with her superb style and tragic bursts of passion. A splendid woman. Her voice has lost some of its power and freshness; but still she sings right royally.'

In January 1856 there was *Norma* (1831). 'After dinner went to the opera and heard 'Norma', whose beautiful music I like; but the opera itself - its Druids and Romans and sheeted chorus and prima donnas, looking as if they had just jumped out of bed - has grown very tedious to me. I was in an ab-Normal condition.' On 16 February there was considerable contrast: 'At the opera, "The Prophet" by Meyerbeer, - founded on the history of John of Leyden and the Anabaptists. It is a grand opera, with startling, splendid passages, and an air of power all through it.' At the beginning of March it was the turn of Beethoven, who in fact topped Longfellow's list of composers: 'The Beethoven Festival, and Inauguration of Crawford's bronze statue of the great musician, in the Boston Music Hall. A beautiful spectacle, with a introductory poem by W.W.Story, very good and very well delivered.' On 1 April Beethoven evoked some Latin verbs: 'After dinner, went to hear Beethoven's "Fidelio". Singers and orchestra weak; the music simple and beautiful, and old-fashioned. But Beethoven's music, like the Latin verbs *odi* and *memini*, though past in form has always a present signification.'

Part of the 'Saga of King Olaf' was written as early as 1849, when Longfellow seems to have conceived it as opening to what is now 'The Golden Legend'. A diary note of 10 December clarifies his intentions: 'A bleak and dismal day. Wrote in the morning "The Challenge of Thor," as "Prologue" or "*Introitus*" to the second part of Christus.' Longfellow's final 'prologue' solution was to have Lucifer and the powers of the air attempt to tear down the cross from the spire of the same Strasbourg Cathedral where Sir Walter Scott located in *Anne of Geierstein* (1829) a momentous meeting between Margaret of Anjou (1430-82) and the Earl of Oxford (? 1408-1462). In April 1850 Longfellow, poet but also Harvard professor, made the sort of *cri de coeur* Elgar was to make as professor:

> The seventy lectures to which I am doomed next year hang over me like a dark curtain. Seventy lectures! who will have the patience to hear them? If my eyes were sound and strong I should delight in it. But it will eat up a whole year, and I was just beginning so cheerily on my poem, and looking forward to pleasant work on it next year!

This was to be 'The Golden Legend' (1851). In October, at the age of 43, he was yet more weighed down by the university: 'I seriously think of resigning my professorship'; and he goes on: 'Few men have written good poetry after fifty.'

A diary entry of 20 January 1852 gives an appropriately icy mention of the saga world:

> Very cold; chilling body and soul. I sat by the fire wondering how the old Icelandic scalds could sing at all. No wonder that their stricken faculties uttered themselves in such broken accents, such glacial metres, such abrupt and jagged songs!

Ole Bull

He investigated also the Finnish *Kalevala*, which gave him the rhythm for Hiawatha (1855). In December 1855 Ole Bull (1810-80), future 'musician' in the *Tales of a Wayside Inn*, came twice to dinner. On the first occasion he was a fellow-guest with Thackeray (1811-63) and James Fields, when he 'played and chanted old Norse melodies, which were very striking'. Next time the cast was the same, and there was 'music on the Cremona'. He was a prodigious violinist, effective rival to Paganini (1782-1840) as composer and player. In January 1841 Clara Schumann had been critical of him as a man: '*Ole Bull* entertained during the meal, but he talks too much about *nothing* (though not without imagination and vitality). He doesn't let anyone get a word in edgewise, and bores people.' As a player he seemed worse, when he performed the 'Kreutzer' sonata with Mendelssohn and showed himself 'a thoroughly bad musician who knows *Beethoven* only by name but will never understand him'. Thackeray was more merciful: 'there was a mad-cap fiddler, Ole Bull, who played most wonderfully'; he was also intriguing as a man 'and charmed me still more by his oddities and character. Quite a figure for a book'.

In January 1859, Longfellow saw possibilities in the King Olaf story and clarified his mind about 'The Challenge of Thor', written almost ten years back: 'The thought struck me this morning, that a very good poem might be written on the Saga of King Olaf, who converted the North to Christianity. Read the old Saga in the Heimskringla, Laing's translation. It is very curious. 'The Challenge of Thor' will serve as a prelude.' The *Heimskringla*, brief sagas about the kings of Norway by Snorri Sturluson (1178-1241), became Longfellow's essential source for 'Olaf'; 'The Challenge', however, was his own invention.

Longfellow was back with the sagas in February 1860: 'Gave part of the morning to the *Heimskringla*.' The following month he was planning a poetic treatment of the saga: 'Arrange the several cantos of "King Olaf"'; and at the beginning of November he was busy with more research: 'Go down to the college library to look up some Icelandic sagas.' The Laing translation used by Longfellow gives a graphic account of Snorri's life. He was both poet and lawyer. He first went from Iceland to Norway and the court of King Haakon in 1218. He settled differences between merchants of the two countries and brought Iceland peaceably under the control of Norway. His dealings were less than scrupulous and led to a breakdown in relations with the king, who had him murdered in Iceland by his son-in-law. Snorri was author also of the prose *Edda*, used by Wagner in forging the *Ring*. Samuel Laing (1780-1868) came from Orkney and served with Sir John Moore (1761-1809) in the Spanish expedition. Unlike Moore, he survived, and his *Heimskringla* came out in 1844. Carlyle acknowledged his debt to Laing in his *Early Kings of Norway* (1875), declaring that the version deserved 'to be reckoned among the great history books of the world'. With 'The Challenge of Thor' Longfellow presented at once the clash of faiths.

Snorri delves further, giving an account of Olaf's birth in 968. On the death of his father King Trygve, his pregnant mother fled to a small island in a lake, where Olaf was born and named after his grandfather. Astrid wished to take her child to her brother at the court of Yaroslav the Wise in Novgorod (1015-54), but he was captured by Estonian Vikings. Eventually recognised, he was taken to Novgorod, where he stayed nine years. Snorri extols him: 'Olaf was the handsomest of men, very stout and strong, and in all bodily exercises he excelled every Northman that ever was heard of.' Not unnaturally jealousy arose at Yaroslav's court, where also the sons of Edmund Ironside (1016) had found refuge from Canute (1017-35). Olaf took to the seas and plunder.

He married in Vendland, but after his wife's death, did his worst against Friesland, Saxland and Flanders. Snorri then sends him to England: 'He sailed all the way north to Northumberland, where he plundered; and thence to Scotland, where he marauded far and wide. Then he went to the Hebrides, where he fought some battles; and then southward: to Man, where he also fought.' There is relief when Olaf reaches the Scilly Isles, where he heard of a seer who could foretell the future. This hermit proved a turning-point in Olaf's career: ' "Thou wilt become a renowned king and do celebrated deeds. Many men wilt thou bring to faith and baptism, and both to thy own and others' good".' The hermit ascribed his powers to the God of the Christians, and all were baptised. Longfellow, Acworth and Elgar are almost at the ready, but the dog Vige must first be aquired.

Olaf's second marriage was to Gyda, daughter of the King of Ireland. Snorri has Olaf taking to the sea again:

> As they required to make a foray for provisions on the coast, some of his men landed, and drove down a large herd of cattle to the strand. Now a peasant came up, and entreated Olaf to give him back the cows that belonged to him. Olaf told him to take his cows, if he could distinguish them: "but don't delay our march."

Now it was Vige's chance to show his skill:

> The peasant had with him a large house-dog, which he put in among the herd of cattle, in which many hundred head of beasts were driven together. The dog ran into the herd, and drove out exactly the number which the peasant had said he wanted; and all were marked with the same mark, which showed that the dog knew the right beasts and was very sagacious.

Vige looks forward certainly to Sir Walter's Roswal and Bevis, and maybe even to Elgar's Aesculapius, to say nothing of the bulldog Dan who features in 'GRS' of the 'Enigma' Variations and his post-war dogs. Snorri tells the inevitable sequel: 'Olaf then asked the peasant if he would sell him the dog. "I would rather give him to you," said the peasant. Olaf immediately presented him with a gold ring in return, and promised him his friendship in future. This dog was called Vige, and was the very best of dogs, and Olaf owned him long afterwards.'

Longfellow's visit to the college library on 2 November 1860 finally clarified his mind, and most of the Olaf Saga was shaped by the end of the month. It was also a significant month politically, as stated in the diary entry of 7 November: 'Lincoln is elected. Overwhelming majorities in New York and Pennsylvania. This is a great victory; one can hardly overrate its importance. It is the redemption of the country. Freedom is triumphant.' On the last day of the month Longfellow could report significant progress on the Saga: 'With all kinds of interruptions, I have contrived this month to write nearly the whole of a poem, "The Saga of King Olaf," in a series of lyrics'. Samuel Longfellow adds a note that fifteen sections were written that month. On 9 December Longfellow was back with his Saga: 'In the evening finished "Iron Beard," which ends the "Saga." Another stone rolled over the hill.'

The year 1861 produced tragedy public and private for Longfellow. On 30 January he records the steady approach of civil war: 'Slowly the events of Secession unroll.' Halfway through February he wrote that 'The dissolution of the Union goes slowly on. Behind it all I hear the low murmur of the slaves, like the chorus in a Greek tragedy, prophesying Woe, woe!' The crisis occurred on 12 April: 'News comes that Fort Sumter is attacked. And so the war begins!' In July of the same year Frances Longfellow died. Samuel Longfellow tells what happened:

> On the ninth of July 1861, his wife was sitting in the library with her two little girls, engaged in sealing up some small packages of their curls which she had just cut off. From a match fallen upon the floor, her light summer dress caught fire. The shock was too great, and she died the next morning.

After Longfellow's own death an unpublished poem was discovered, dated to the 18th anniversary of the day she died. Among his works it appears as *The Cross of Snow*:

> In the long, sleepless watches of the night,
>   A gentle face - the face of one long dead -
>   Looks at me from the wall, where round its head
>   The night-lamp casts a halo of pale light.
> Here in this room she died; and soul more white
>   Never through martyrdom of fire was led
>   To its repose; nor can in books be read
>   The legend of a life more benedight.
> There is a mountain in the distant West.
>   That, sun-defying, in its deep ravines
>   Displays a cross of snow upon its side.
> Such is the cross I wear upon my breast
>   These eighteen years, through all the changing scenes
>   And seasons, changeless since the day she died.

Perhaps echoes of the *Tannhäuser* overture entered Longfellow's home in November 1861, when Charles Sumner brought Michael Bakunin (1814-76) to dinner. Maybe they knew, or maybe they didn't, that March 1861 was the month Wagner had suffered his *Tannhäuser* fiasco in Paris, and that with much of *The Ring* and *Tristan* complete, he was now embarked on plans for *Die Meistersinger*. Longfellow, like Wagner, was fascinated by Bakunin:

> Mr.B. is a Russian gentleman of education and ability. - a giant of a man, with a most ardent, seething temperament. He was in the Revolution of Forty-eight; has seen the inside of prisons, - Olmutz, even, where he had Lafayette's room. Was afterwards four years in Siberia; whence he escaped in June last, down the Amoor, and then in an American vessel by way of Japan to California.

While work on the *Wayside Inn* continued, the civil war remained a haunting presence. At the beginning of September 1862 Longfellow wrote:

> Yesterday we had report of a great battle at Manassas, ending in defeat of the Rebels. The moon set red and lowering; and I thought in the night of the pale, upturned faces of young men on the battle-field, and the agonies of the wounded; and my wretchedness was very great. Every shell from the cannon's mouth bursts not only on the battle-field, but in far-away homes, North or South, carrying dismay and death.

But on 23 September Longfellow's hopes in President Lincoln were justified: 'Good news this morning. Emancipation of the slaves! On and after January 1, 1863, "all persons held as slaves within any State, or designated part of a State, the people thereof shall then be in rebellion against the United States, shall be then and thenceforward and forever free."' As Bakunin might have remarked, Alexander II (1855- 81) had freed the serfs in February 1861. At the end of March 1863 Charles Longfellow, the eldest son, 'received a commission as second lieutenant of cavalry'. Two months later Longfellow reported an extraordinary event: 'In town saw the first regiment of blacks march through Beacon Street. An imposing sight, with something wild and strange about it, like a dream.'

Finally fifteen thousand copies of the *Tales of a Wayside Inn* were published on 25 November 1863, first of three series, but less than a week before Longfellow received a telegram that his son was severely wounded. On 28 December he wrote to an English friend about it: 'In the last battle on the Rapidan he was shot through both shoulders with a rifle-ball, and had a very narrow escape of it. He is now at home, and doing very well.' Longfellow goes on to write about the *Tales*, that the Red Horse Tavern at Sudbury not far from Boston, in origin an old colonial house, does indeed exist; and all the characters, except the landlord, were based on people he knew. The 'musician' is Ole Bull, whose violin is commandeered for many an interlude. Clara Schumann would not have been surprised that his story in Part 1, 'The Saga of King Olaf', is easily the longest of the seven tales. Longfellow introduces him at once:

> Before the blazing fire of wood
> Erect the wrapt musician stood;
> And ever and anon he bent
> His head upon his instrument,
> And seemed to listen, till he caught
> Confessions of its secret thought, -
> The joy, the triumph, the lament,
> The exultation and the pain;
> Then, by the magic of his art,
> He soothed the throbbings of its heart,
> And lulled it into peace again.

Longfellow's student was a man after the young Elgar's heart:

> He loved the twilight that surrounds
> The border-land of old romance,
> Where glitter a hauberk, helm and lance,
> And banner waves, and trumpet sounds,
> And ladies ride with hawk on wrist,
> And mighty warriors sweep along,
> Magnified by the purple mist,
> The dusk of centuries and of song.
> The chronicles of Charlemagne,
> Of Merlin and the Mort d'Arthure,
> Mingled together in his brain
> With tales of Flores and Blanchefleur,
> Sir Ferumbras, Sir Eglamour,
> Sir Launcelot, Sir Mogadour,
> Sir Guy, Sir Bevis, Sir Gawain.

Ole Bull himself could not have asked for a more glowing tribute than the one Longfellow gives him:

> Last the Musician, as he stood
> Illumined by that fire of wood;
> Fair-haired, blue-eyed, his aspect blithe,
> His figure tall and straight and lithe,

And every feature of his face
Revealing his Norwegian race;
A radiance, streaming from within,
Around his eyes and forehead beamed,
The Angel with the violin,
Painted by Raphael, he seemed.
He lived in that ideal world
Whose language is not speech, but song;
Around him evermore the throng
Of elves and sprites their dances whirled;
The Strömkarl sang, the cataract hurled
Its headlong waters from the height;
And mingled in the wild delight
The scream of sea-birds in their flight,
The rumour of the forest trees,
The plunge of the implacable seas,
The tumult of the wind at night,
Voices of eld, like trumpets blowing,
Old ballads, and wild melodies
Through mist and darkness pouring forth,
Like Elivagar's river flowing
Out of the glaciers of the North.

In 1862 Longfellow had visited the publisher James Fields: 'He gives me a picture of Stradivarius in his workshop among his violins. I feel as if I should like to make musical instruments and could do it, if my head were not full of other things, - as Don Quixote thought he could have made good toothpicks and bird-cages, if his head had not been full of adventures.' Elgar's violin by Nicola Gagliano (fl.c.1740-80) was a product of Naples; Ole Bull's instrument came from the most famous of all violin towns:

The instrument on which he played
Was in Cremona's workshops made,
By a great master of the past.
Ere yet was lost the art divine;
Fashioned of maple and of pine,
That in Tyrolean forests vast
Had rocked and wrestled with the blast:
Exquisite was it in design,
Perfect in each minutest part,
A marvel of the lutist's art;
And in its hollow chamber, thus,

> The maker from whose hands it came
> Had written his unrivalled name, -
> "Antonius Stradivarius."

Elgar is ready to take up the musician soon after he begins an 'Interlude':

> And then the blue-eyed Norseman told
> A Saga of the days of old.
> "There is," said he, "a wondrous book,"

at which point Elgar launches his music. Longfellow almost demands a musical setting:

> And in each pause the story made
> Upon his violin he played,
> As an appropriate interlude,
> Fragments of old Norwegian tunes
> That bound in one the separate runes,
> And held the mind in perfect mood,
> Entwining and encircling all
> The strange and antiquated rhymes
> With melodies of olden times.

Elgar's 'Challenge of Thor' sets Longfellow *verbatim* and complete. For 'King Olaf's Return' Longfellow's fourteen stanzas, gathered from far and wide in Snorri, have been reduced to eight in Elgar's setting. Estonia and Novgorod are omitted, as are stanzas dealing with Olaf's astonishing prowess. The sheer bravado of a couple is worth quoting:

> When at sea, with all his rowers,
> He along the bending oars
>   Outside of his ship could run.
> He the Smalsor Horn ascended,
> And his shining shield suspended
>   On its summit, like a sun.

> On the ship-rails he could stand,
> Wield his sword with either hand,
>   And at once two javelins throw;
> At all feats where ale was strongest
> Sat the merry monarch longest,
>   First to come and last to go.

Elgar and Acworth now play fast and loose with Longfellow's order and indeed that of Snorri's *Heimskringla*. Longfellow has Iron-Beard in section VII, where he is a likeable old brute:

> He was the churliest of the churls;
> Little he cared for kings or earls;
> Bitter as home-brewed ale were his foaming passions.

Physically he was formidable:

> Huge and cumbersome was his frame;
> His beard from which he took his name,
> Frosty and fierce, like that of Hymer the giant.

To Olaf he was defiant and peremptory:

> "Such sacrifices shalt thou bring,
> To Odin and to Thor, O King,
> As other kings have done in their devotion!"

Elgar and Longfellow smash the pagan gods and lay Ironbeard low; then Olaf gives the Longfellow Drontheimers the inevitable choice:

> King Olaf from the doorway spoke:
> "Choose ye between two things, my folk,
> To be baptized or given up to slaughter!"

Their decision was eminently sensible:

> And seeing their leader stark and dead,
> The people with a murmur said,
> "O King, baptize us with thy holy water!"

It was Acworth's task to knock Longfellow's blunt stanzas into a 'Conversion' scene that should give adequate scope for a tenor Olaf, bass Ironbeard, and a well-behaved chorus. This he did with notable success. Longfellow's 'Gudrun' scene can be split happily enough (if that's the word) between murderous soprano, chorus and tenor. Its ten stanzas need no adjustment, and its conclusion has the off hand manner of genuine saga-ing:

> And forever sundered ride
> Bridegroom and bride!

Longfellow is also in sole charge, with no help from Acworth, of 'The Wraith of Odin'. Snorri, however, made the apparition's identity clear from the outset; Wagner was to call him Wotan or Wanderer: 'It is related that once on a time King Olaf was at a feast at this Augvaldsness, and one

Gudrun's bridal night

eventide there came to him an old man very gifted in words, and with a broad-brimmed hat upon his head. He was one-eyed, and had something to tell of every land.' Snorri has the bishop urging bedtime on Olaf: 'Now, when the king had sat late into the night, the bishop reminded him it was time to go to bed, and the king did so. But after the king was undressed, and had laid himself in bed, the guest sat upon the footstool before the bed, and still spoke long with the king; for after one tale was ended, he still wanted a new one. Then the bishop observed to the king it was time to go to sleep, and the king did so.' Elgar deprives us only of Longfellow's bishop:

> And ever, when the tale was o'er,
> The King demanded yet one more;
> Till Sigurd the Bishop smiling said,
> " 'Tis late, O King, and time for bed."
> Dead rides Sir Morten of Fogelsang.

Elgar toyed with the idea of setting Longfellow's 'Thora of Rimol' scene, which concerns the flight and death of Earl Hakon after Olaf's return to Norway. Snorri has Thora 'a woman of great influence, and one of the earl's best beloved'. She devises a hiding-place for Hakon: 'There is but one place about the house where they could never expect to find such a man as you, and that is the swine-stye.' Perhaps so, but it was there 'his base thrall Karker' murdered him.

The next woman Elgar tackled instead was 'Queen Sigrid the Haughty'. Snorri and Longfellow give two reasons for the collapse of the marriage plans: the ring Olaf sent proved not to be gold so 'she ordered the ring to be broken in pieces, and it was found to be copper inside'; then there was the question of faith, with Sigrid obstinate for her ancestral gods. Snorri describes the sequel: 'Then King Olaf was enraged, and answered in a passion, "Why should I care to have thee, an old faded woman, and a heathen jade?" and therewith struck her in the face with his glove.' Longfellow and Snorri agree sometimes word for word; Acworth and Elgar, in recasting the scene for soprano, tenor and chorus of maidens, cannot bear Olaf to cheat over the ring, and soften the most offensive of his insults.

Longfellow's 'The Skerry of Shrieks', a bloodcurdling scene rejected by Acworth and Elgar, described the end of Ehvind Kallda, 'a sorcerer', according to Snorri, 'and particularly knowing in witchcraft'. Snorri continues: 'Eyvind went from his ship to the land with his followers, and there they played many of their pranks of witchcraft. Eyvind clothed them with caps of darkness, and so thick a mist that the king and his men could see nothing of them.' Each had his 'Tarnhelm', but Olaf devised a watery end for them: 'Then the king ordered them all to be taken out to a skerry which was under water in flood tide, and there to be left bound. Eyvind and all with him left their lives on this rock, and the skerry is still called the Skerry of Warlocks.'

'Thangbrand the Priest' proved too much for Acworth and Elgar in the end, to say nothing of their potential audience, though there had been an idea of setting him for bass solo after 'The Wraith of Odin'. Snorri sketches his personality: 'When King Olaf Trygvesson had been two years king of Norway, there was a Saxon priest in his house who was called Thangbrand, a passionate, ungovernable man, and a great man-slayer; but he was a good scholar and a clever man. The king would not have him in his house upon account of his misdeeds; but gave him the errand to go to Iceland, and bring that land to the Christian faith.' Longfellow takes over:

> He was quarrelsome and loud,
>   And impatient of control,
> Boisterous in the market crowd,
>   Boisterous at the wassail-bowl,
>   Everywhere
>   Would drink and swear,
> Swaggering Thangbrand, Olaf's Priest.

His conversion efforts were not a success. Snorri sums up: 'Thangbrand was two years in Iceland, and was the death of three men before he left it.'

Longfellow's next two sections, based closely on Snorri, were too strong meat for any possible Elgar listener. 'Raud the Strong', according to Snorri, 'was a great idolater, and very skilful in witchcraft'. In his search for Raud, Olaf sailed north from Drontheim and encountered foul weather. Longfellow continues the tale in 'Bishop Sigurd at Salten Fiord':

> And the sea through all its tide-ways
> Swept the reeling vessels sideways,
> As the leaves are swept through sluices,
>   When the flood-gates open wide.
>
> " 'Tis the warlock! 'tis the demon
> Raud!" cried Sigurd to the seamen;
> "But the Lord is not affrighted
>   By the witchcraft of his foes."

Far from it. When the bishop had taken all the proper religious precautions, the ships entered the fjord, 'and the sea was curled about their keel track like as in a calm'. Longfellow follows Snorri to the last detail of Raud's hideous end:

> Then between his jaws distended,
> When his frantic struggles ended,
> Through King Olaf's horn an adder,
>   Touched by fire, they forced to glide.
>
> Sharp his tooth was as an arrow,
> As he gnawed through bone and marrow;
> But without a groan or shudder,
>   Raud the Strong blaspheming died.

'King Olaf's Christmas' in Longfellow's sequence, queried by Elgar for possible setting, tells how Halfred the Iceland scald was given by Olaf a sword without a scabbard, then told to sing a song with 'sword' in every line:

> Then the Scald took his harp and sang,
> And loud through the music rang
>   The sound of that shining word;
> And the harp-strings a clangour made,
> As if they were struck with the blade
>   Of a sword.

Laing, in his version of Snorri, gives the actual words Halfred made up:

> This sword of swords is my reward.
> For him who knows to wield a sword,
> And with his sword to serve his lord,
> Yet wants a sword, his lot is hard.
> I would I had my good lord's leave
> For this good sword a sheath to choose:
> I'm worth three swords where men swords use,
> But for the sword-sheath now I grieve.

Olaf complained that 'sword' did not appear in one of the lines; Halfred replied: ' "But there are three swords at least in two other lines" '; and the scald got his scabbard.

In Longfellow's scheme, 'The Building of the Long Serpent', a scene Elgar wondered whether to include after the Olaf-Thyri duet, is closely modelled on Snorri except for the builder's name, Thorberg Skafhogg in the saga, Thorberg Skafting in the poem. The dimension of seventy-four ells is identical in both. The climactic moment, when deep scoring appears mysteriously on one side of the finished ship, is dealt with thus by Longfellow:

> Straight the master-builder, smiling,
> > Answered thus the angry King:
> "Cease blaspheming and reviling,
> Olaf, it was Thorberg Skafting
> > Who has done this thing!"
>
> Then he chipped and smoothed the planking,
> > Till the King, delighted, swore,
> With much lauding and much thanking,
> "Handsomer is now my Dragon
> > Than she was before!"

Longfellow now makes his only departure from Snorri's sequence, and deals immediately with 'The Crew of the Long Serpent', which in the saga comes after Olaf's decision to recover Thyri's lands. Snorri cites more than forty names and hints at many more. Longfellow confines himself to six but implies a large complement:

> In the fore-hold Biorn and Bork
> Watched the sailors at their work:
> > Heavens! how they swore!
> Thirty men they each commanded,
> Iron-sinewed, horny-handed,
> Shoulders broad, and chests expanded,
> > Tugging at the oar.

'A Little Bird in the Air', set *in toto* by Elgar, was created by Longfellow from scraps and hints in Snorri. The next section, 'Queen Thyri and the Angelica Stalks', has Longfellow matching Snorri: 'It is related that the king one day early in spring was walking in the street, and met a man in the market with many and, for that early season, remarkably large angelica roots.' Thyri will have none of them, and Longfellow makes her as impossible as most of the other women in his Saga:

> But she cast them from her,
> Haughty and indignant,
> On the floor she threw them
> > With a look of scorn.

Acworth and Elgar had already endured the baleful Gudrun and Sigrid, so Thyri should be more tractable. Acworth has her almost pleased with the angelica:

> Sweet are thy words, but O! meseems,
> A sweeter gift would be,
> The boon that haunts Queen Thyri's dreams,
> Her dowry over sea.

Olaf is so relieved to find a Norsewoman who does not wish to do him in that he is ready to indulge in a love duet.

'King Svend of the Forkèd Beard' in Longfellow follows Snorri's essential point: 'Sigrid was King Olaf Trygvesson's greatest enemy; the cause of which, as before said, was that King Olaf had broken off with her, and had struck her in the face.' By concentrating on three of Longfellow's nine stanzas, with some cutting and rejigging, Acworth and Elgar produced the Choral Recitative beginning:

> After Queen Gunhild's death,
> So the old Saga saith,
> Plighted King Svend his faith,
> To Sigrid the Haughty.

Longfellow's stanzas end with the sailing of the three Norse kings against Olaf and hints of treachery to come. The scheming of Sigvald, whereby Olaf is lured to the island where the kings have their ships assembled, does not concern Elgar and his librettist. Longfellow's 'King Olaf and Earl Sigvald' is based closely on Snorri. The sea-battle begins with Longfellow's 'King Olaf's War-Horns', using much Snorri *verbatim*: 'The king replied, high on the quarterdeck where he stood, "Strike the sails; never shall men of mine think of flight. I never fled from battle. Let God dispose of my life, but flight I shall never take".' Longfellow describes Olaf on board:

> King Olaf stood on the quarter-deck,
> With bow of ash and arrows of oak,
> His gilded shield was without a fleck,
> His helmet inlaid with gold,
>   And in many a fold
> Hung his crimson cloak.

Olaf despises the 'soft Danes and Swedes', but respects the courage of Eric the Norseman, son of Earl Hakon, who had died in Thora's pigsty. With his 'Einar Tamberskelver' section, Longfellow elaborates considerably on Snorri, sending Einar for the moment triumphant to board the main enemy ship. Snorri makes no mention of Michael the Archangel:

> Then, with a smile of joy defiant
> On his beardless lip,

> Scales he, light and self-reliant,
>   Eric's dragon-ship.
> Loose his golden locks were flowing,
>   Bright his armour gleamed;
> Like Saint Michael overthrowing
>   Lucifer he seemed.

The final scene of the battle in Longfellow is 'King Olaf's Death-Drink'. Snorri gives a graphic description of the last moments: 'Kolbiorn the marshal, who had on clothes and arms like the king's, and was a remarkably stout and handsome man, went up to the king on the quarter-deck. The battle was still going on fiercely even in the fore-hold.' Earl Eric's men had boarded the *Long Serpent*, and the end came: 'King Olaf and Kolbiorn the marshal both sprang overboard, each on his own side of the ship.' Longfellow concentrates on Olaf's mysterious fate:

> While far on the opposite side
> Floats another shield on the tide,
> Like a jewel set in the wide
>   Sea-current's eddying ring.

> There is told a wonderful tale,
> How the King stripped off his mail,
> Like leaves of the brown sea-kale,
>   As he swam beneath the main;

> But the young grew old and gray,
> And never, by night or by day,
> In his kingdom of Norroway
>   Was King Olaf seen again!

In 'The Death of Olaf' Acworth and Elgar made a long choral movement from bits and pieces of Longfellow. Snorri's rich gallery of characters in the battle featured also in Longfellow, but now they are abandoned, with much barbaric splendour. Yet the generalised verse has excitement enough, even if at the end the doubts and possibilities of Snorri and Longfellow are ruled out:

> Above him rolls the sullen surge,
>   That stormy heart has rest.

Longfellow's coda, 'The Nun of Nidaros', is his own invention, owing nothing to Snorri except the name of Astrid. Acworth and Elgar cut lines here and stanzas there. Longfellow sets the scene in more detail:

In the convent of Drontheim,
Alone in her chamber
Knelt Astrid the Abbess,
At midnight, adoring,
Beseeching, entreating
The Virgin and Mother.

Astrid is of course the mother of the dead Olaf, a fact that can easily be forgotten by the end of Elgar's *Scenes*. It was also decided by librettist and composer that the message of the 'Epilogue' should come anonymously rather than from St.John the Divine:

She heard in the silence
The voice of one speaking,
Without in the darkness,
In gusts of the night-wind
Now louder, now clearer,
Now lost in the distance.

The voice of a stranger
It seemed as she listened,
Of some one who answered,
Beseeching, imploring,
A cry from afar off
She could not distinguish.

The voice of Saint John,
The beloved disciple,
Who wandered and waited
The Master's appearance,
Alone in the darkness,
Unsheltered and friendless.

St.John at Trondheim Cathedral

The last four lines set by Elgar are put in the past by Longfellow and mark the start of another 'Interlude' in his *Tales of a Wayside Inn*:

A strain of music closed the tale,
A low, monotonous, funeral wail,
That with its cadence, wild and sweet,
Made the long Saga more complete.

Ole Bull as the 'musician' had rounded off his scald's narration, and now came the 'theologian's' turn:

> 'Thank God,' the Theologian said,
> 'The reign of violence is dead,
> Or dying surely from the world;
> While Love triumphant reigns instead,
> And in a brighter sky o'erhead
> His blessed banners are unfurled.
>
> And most of all thank God for this:
> The war and waste of clashing creeds
> Now end in words, and not in deeds,
> And no one suffers loss, or bleeds,
> For thoughts that men call heresies.

He proceeds to tell a tale about Torquemada, the Grand Inquisitor.

7 - The banner of Britain's might!

Elgar wrote to Novello on 13 December 1896 about some points in Shapcott Wensley's text for *The Banner of St.George*. He was unhappy, for instance, at the first words of the royal victim, Princess Sabra: 'If it may be suggested I should much like some other phrase to be substituted for the opening of the Princess' speech - "*Dear Friends*" - which remind one somewhat of 'Chadband'.' This was the unctuous reverend humbug of Dickens's *Bleak House*, described by his creator as 'a large yellow man, with a fat smile, and a general appearance of having a good deal of train oil in his system'. For a celebration of Queen Victoria's Diamond Jubilee in 1897 the associations were wrong, and the words were changed, so that Sabra should acquire the requisite imperial dignity:

> 'Fear not,' she cries, 'the darkest hour of night
> Is oft the harbinger of silver dawn'.

Elgar's St.George is 'skilled in Dragon Management and Virgin Reclamation' to quote a poem of U.A.Fanthorpe. But George's dragon is a late arrival, a 12th-century addition to the legend, to make of him a knight of Christian chivalry, ready sometimes to bargain for the conversion of a place before agreeing to rescue a princess. In the Greek church he tramples the dragon of the Apocalypse; but it is St.George as martyr who is important to the earlier mediaeval tradition. Indeed for Elgar's hero there is no princely banquet or royal alliance. He is off at once:

> 'For I must bear the cross in other lands,
> And strive and suffer, till the morn shall dawn,
> That brings for me the martyr's fadeless crown!'

Various traditions have it that he was crushed by a millstone, had his flesh raked, was attacked with a burning torch or dragged by a horse. Eusebius of Caesarea (265-340) may be the first to mention St.George when he speaks in Book VIII (v.l) of 'a certain person by no means obscure' who tore up in Nicomedia a decree against the churches: this when two emperors were in the city. He suffered accordingly. The apocryphal *Acts of St.George* have him a tribune in the Roman army, beheaded under Diocletian (284-305) for refusing to sacrifice. A Coptic text from Qasr Ibrim in Nubia names his parents as Polychronia and Gerontius. He has associations with Joppa and Lydda, but in Chapter xxiii of the *Decline and Fall* Gibbon takes advantage of the almost total lack of information about his life to affirm that 'the infamous George of Cappadocia has been transformed into the renowned St.George of England, the patron of arms, of chivalry, and of the garter'. Gibbon has him profiteering from the sale of bacon to the army and becoming the Arian archbishop of Alexandria. The mob murdered him, and Julian the Apostate was after his library.

Martyrs do not usually rescue princesses and, like the dragon, she comes late to the tale. Many churches were dedicated to him and his fame had spread from the Middle East to Europe before his princess appears. Constantine (306-37) is said to have built a basilica over his supposed tomb at Lydda. Accounts of his deeds, martyrdoms and miracles proliferated in many languages. Gregory of Tours testified to the existence of his relics in France, and Clovis, future sentry for Maximilian I at Innsbruck, dedicated a monastery near Cambrai in his name. Pope Boniface IV (608-15) converted the Pantheon at Rome into a church (610), setting up altars and installing reliquaries, including one for St.George. Zacharias (741-52), the last Greek pope, discovered (751) St.George's head in Rome. At least five heads were known in the Middle Ages, including one 'with an helmet of gold' given by Edward IV to the chapel at Windsor Castle.

Tradition brings the cult of St.George to Britain in the 6th century. The agent was Antonius, a mythical count of Britain, who made him patron of heavy cavalry, and thus an inspiration for the Round Table knights. He was said to have come as tribune of Beirut on Diocletian's orders, when he became friends with the empress, Queen Helen. She was easily identified with Helena (c.250-c.335), mother of Constantine and discoverer of the True Cross. So he could become friendly with Constantine while both were serving in York. Together they could visit the tomb of Joseph of Arimathea at Glastonbury, a supposed kinsman of George. Richard Johnson, author of *The Most Famous History of the Seven Champions of Christendome* (c.1597), locates George's birthplace in Coventry. Having rescued the daughter of an Egyptian sultan, he brings her to England, and their son is Guy of Warwick. Some romances have Guy delivering Winchester from Olaf Trygvesson in 993.

St.George was well established in England by the time of the Conquest. Aelfric the Grammarian (c.955-c.1010) includes him among his *Lives of the Saints*, alliterative sermons in the metres of old English poetry. The tympanum of the south doorway at St.George's, Fordington, was carved about the time of the Conquest. Pevsner's *Dorset* describes it as dedicated to St.George. He is shown centrally on horseback, thrusting his spear into the mouth of an enemy, while another lies prostrate and a third appears truncated with arms raised. Behind the warrior saint are two soldiers kneeling at prayer, with shields and weapons propped against a wall. The *Gesta Regum Anglorum* by William of Malmesbury (c.1095-1143), the most important historian in England after Bede (673-735), connects the saint with Robert II of Normandy (c.1054-1134), eldest son of William the Conqueror (1066-87) who never gained the English throne. Robert Curthose stirred himself from a mainly indolent life to join the First Crusade (1096-9). St.George was said to have appeared before the battle of Antioch (1098), wearing white armour with a red cross, and led the troops to victory. He was manifest again during the siege of Jerusalem in July 1099. Such wonders attained swift currency in western Europe and Britain and were celebrated by troubadours. Coeur-de-Lion in Palestine (1191-2) was well aware of St.George's evocative power, having put the army under his protection as the result of a dream, it was said. In *The Talisman*, Walter Scott makes the saint central to the crusaders' camp, when he positions the ensign of England:

> It was displayed upon an artificial mound, nearly in the midst of the camp, which perhaps of old some Hebrew chief or champion had chosen as a memorial of his place of rest. If so, the name was now forgotten, and the

St.George at Fordington Church

Crusaders had christened it Saint George's Mount, because from that commanding height the banner of England was supereminently displayed, as if an emblem of sovereignty over the many distinguished, noble, and even royal ensigns, which floated in lower situations.

Richard showed his devotion to the saint by repairing his church at Lydda.

It was during the reign of Edward I that England prospered as a military nation and the martial St.George became the country's patron. He was the first monarch to display the saint's red cross on royal banners (along with the arms of St.Edmund the Martyr (939-46) and St.Edward the Confessor (1042-66)), and to emblazon the surcoats of his soldiers likewise. His grandson Edward III consolidated St.George's position. The chapel in Windsor Castle, previously dedicated to the Confessor, was from August 1348 to be under the auspices of the Virgin Mary and St.George. Edward's abortive Round Table scheme seems not to have involved St. George, but he was central to the Order of the Garter and its ceremonies.

Edward early followed his grandfather's example in cultivation of the saint, and the Milemete treatise (1326-7), now at Christ Church, Oxford, shows St.George arming the young man. Both have elongated bodies, with faces almost obscured by the bulk of their helmets. Edward already holds the spear given him by the saint and is about to receive the shield decorated with lions passant. Edward possessed a relic of the saint's blood and appeared with him in a painting (c.1355-63) in St.Stephen's chapel, Westminster, being led by St.George towards the altar.

In St.George's, Windsor, there were many reminders of the saint. Originally there was a statue of him with the dragon, a painting of him with Edward the Confessor on the rood screen, and a reliquary with three of his bones. The panels of an alabaster reredos, brought from Nottingham in ten carts drawn by eighty horses, may well have contained St.George scenes. But the most impressive testimony comes from the wooden desk-ends on the south side of the choir, probably designed by a Flemish sculptor (1477-84). Ten carvings concern the saint, princess and dragon, with a final four detailing the martyrdom. The first shows St.George in full armour making obeisance to the Virgin and Christ child. The next four subjects are incorporated more or less effectively in the Shapcott Wensley libretto. A dumpy princess is shown taking leave of her dumpy parents; the bearded king wears a gigantic crown, while the queen mops her eye and the princess has a delightful lamb on a lead, since in former days the dragon was content with sheep till supplies ran down. The mounted St.George dominates the next scene, while the princess regards him appealingly and the lamb, perhaps sensing the situation is saved, munches away beneath the horse. Maximum drama ensues when St.George drives his spear into the dragon's neck, with the princess

St.George, Princess and lamb triumphant

grateful in the background, parents and inhabitants observing with astonishment. The dragon is now a crumpled heap beneath the triumphant St.George, but the princess goads it sufficiently to lead it towards the city. Only the shoes of St.George have survived on the next panel; perhaps he demands from the king the town's conversion or is offered the princess in marriage. The tortures were unsuitable for the Diamond Jubilee but had their place in mediaeval legend. St.George is first shown about to be stripped of his garments. He then lies on a board to be dismembered, while a wretched little creature ladles his parts into a cauldron, and the emperor Dacian (Persian in some traditions) is among the eager spectators. The saint is on a latticed sledge being dragged through the city by two horses, from one of which the rider has just tumbled. In the final scene Dacian attempts poison; there is a prostrate victim beneath the upright George, while a demon grins from Dacian's crown.

By the time of Poitiers, St.George is an ubiquitous aid to the English. Froissart has the Black Prince address his small band of followers thus:

> If, through good fortune, the day shall be ours, we will gain the greatest honour and glory in this world: if the contrary should happen, and we be slain, I have a father and beloved brethren alive, and you all have some relations, or good friends, who will be sure to revenge our deaths. I therefore entreat of you to exert yourselves, and combat manfully; for, if it please God and St.George, you shall see me this day act like a true knight.

He bade his banner advance 'in the name of God and St.George'. Deity and English saint were attentive to such pleas so that King John of France became a prisoner and went to Windsor in his turn.

It was Henry V who followed most closely the chivalric example of Edward III and was even more successful in his French campaigns. The beginning of Shakespeare's Act 3 has him urging on his men by the scaling ladders of Harfleur:

> 'I see you stand like greyhounds in the slips,
> Straining upon the start. The game's afoot:
> Follow your spirit; and upon this charge,
> Cry, God for Harry, England, and Saint George.'

The England that was now 'Guarded with grandsires, babies, and old women' was bade pray to St.George for the king's safety. There was a tradition that St.George had appeared to the English over the field of Agincourt in 1415, as previously to the Crusaders. A carol of the mid-15th century records the event:

Enfors we us with all our might
To love Seint George, our Lady knight

Worship of virtu is the mede,
And seweth him ay of right:
To worship George then have we hede,
Which is our soverein Lady's knight.

He keped the mad from dragon's dred,
And fraid all France and put to flight.
At Agincourt - the crownecle ye red -
The French him se formest in fight.

In his vertu he wol us lede
Agaiuis the Fend, the ful wight,
And with his banner us oversprede,
If we love him with all our might.

In Act 2 scene v of *Henry V,* bluff Hal is wooing the French princess:

'If ever thou beest mine, Kate, as I have a saving faith within me tells me thou
shalt, I get thee with scambling, and thou must therefore needs prove a good
soldier-breeder: shall not thou and I, between Saint Denis and Saint George,
compound a boy, half French half English, that shall go to Constantinople,
and take the Turk by the beard? Shall we not? what say'st thou, my fair
flower - de - luce?'

Henry V promoted the cult of St.George in many ways. At the
beginning of his reign, on 26 June 1413, Archbishop Chichele elevated
St.George's day to a 'greater double feast'. In May 1416 there came to
Windsor for the Garter ceremony the future Holy Roman Emperor
Sigismund, king of Hungary from 1387, king of Bohemia from 1419, and
eventually to receive the imperial crown at Rome in 1433, four years
before his death. He brought with him to England the heart of St.George,
and a golden image of the saint. The Garter knights greatly valued
possession of the heart, which was carried in their annual processions.
Celebrations in honour of Sigismund involved a series of 'sotylties' or
'soteltes'. It seems these were large cakes or pies featuring episodes in the
career of St.George, such as his arming by an angel, the fight with the
dragon and the princess's leading the defeated dragon back to the city.
The Bedford *Book of Hours* in the British Library shows the duke
kneeling before the saint. In this case St.George wears the monarch's
Garter robes and may have the features of the recently dead Henry V. No
sovereign has achieved closer identification.

When crowned in 1429 at the age of eight, Henry VI (1422-71) had another sotyltie that foretold his father's speech to Kate in the Shakespeare play. On either side of the Virgin Mary were St.Denis and St. George. The following year the boy went for coronation as king of France, and a poem of well-wishing for the journey includes a St.George stanza:

> Seynt george, oure ladyes knight
> On whom alle englond hath byleve,
> Shew us thy helpe to god almyght,
> And kepe oure kyng from alle myscheve.
> Thou art our patronesse knyght y-preve
> To defend wyth fyght oure ladyes fe,
> Seynt george, by oure helpe yn all oure greve,
> Salvum fac regem domine.

Later in his reign (1440) Henry founded Eton College, where St.George still slays the dragon on a buttress of the antechapel.

One of Scott's most dramatic scenes in *Anne of Geierstein* concerns the exiled widow of Henry VI, Queen Margaret of Anjou . She appears a tall form outside the Cathedral of Strasbourg. The Earl of Oxford and his son Arthur are travelling under the assumed name of Philipson on a mission to Charles the Bold of Burgundy, watchful statue in the Hofkirche at Innsbruck. The Philipsons and Queen Margaret repair for Mass,

> as it was performed by a priest at the altar of a chapel, divided from the main body of the splendid edifice, and dedicated, as it appeared from the image over the altar, to Saint George; that military Saint, whose real history is so obscure, though his popular legend rendered him an object of peculiar veneration during the feudal ages.

A short while after the service, a bell summoned a congregation to High Mass in the main body of the Cathedral: 'its sound withdrew from the sequestered chapel of St.George the few who had remained at the shrine of the military saint, excepting the father and son, and the female penitent who kneeled opposite to them.' At length she approached them and spoke in a slow solemn voice: '"Do you here worship," she said, "the St.George of Burgundy, or the St.George of merry England, the flower of chivalry?"' Philipson answered that his service was to '"the saint to whom this chapel is dedicated, and the Deity with whom I hope for his holy intercession, whether here or in my native country".' The Queen chides him for praying in disguise at a foreign shrine, forgetting his origin and former greatness: '"that you have worshipped in the royal fane of Windsor - that you have there bent a *gartered* knee, where kings and princes kneeled around you".' It hardly matters that there is no St.George's chapel

Charles the Bold in the Innsbruck Hofkirche

in Strasbourg Cathedral or was ever an altar dedicated to him inside the building: there was, however, a shrine to him in the cloister.[1]

When eventually the Philipsons reach the camp of Charles the Bold, he greets them with his favourite oath: ' "You merchants, by St.George, are a wily generation".' Oxford, as he now appears to Charles, argues that the Duke can hardly trust his new ally, the Yorkist Edward IV. Charles is brisk in his doubts: ' "By St.George, I will not dissemble with you! It is in that very point that my doubts trouble me. Edward is indeed my brother-in-law, but I am a man little inclined to put my head under my wife's girdle".' His scheme was to pit Edward against the hated Louis XI: ' "With spring I take the field with an army superior to both, and then, St.George for Burgundy!" ' Oxford urges him to take up the cause of Margaret of Anjou and fight Louis on her behalf: ' "Do I live to hear the noble Duke of Burgundy, the mirror of European chivalry, say, that no reason has been shown to him for an adventure where a helpless queen is to be redressed - a royal house raised from the dust?" ' The Duke shrewdly distinguishes between the play of tournaments and deadly warfare:

'I tell thee, John of Oxford, when thou and I wore maiden armour, such words as fame, honour, *los*, knightly glory, lady's love, and so forth, were good mottos for our snow-white shields, and a fair enough argument for splintering lances - Ay, and in tilt-yard, though somewhat old for these fierce follies, I would jeopard my person in such a quarrel yet, as becomes a knight of the order. But when we come to paying down of crowns, and embarking of large squadrons, we must have to propose to our subjects some substantial excuse for plunging them in war.'

Reference is to the Order of the Garter, with which he was invested while Edward IV was on the run in Holland towards the end of 1470. William Caxton (c.1422-91) was one of those present and reported the oration of John Russell in his *Prologues and Epilogues* (lxxx).

Charles's association with St.George and the Duke's many oaths are commemorated in a golden reliquary (c.1457-71) at Liège Cathedral containing a finger of St.Lambert, ill-starred bishop of an ill-starred Maastricht, martyred missionary to Brabant. Saint and Duke appear in the innocence of youth. George is in the act of either assuming or removing his helmet, while the kneeling Charles in front of him looks with mingled awe and astonishment at the tubular container of the relic that he holds in both hands. Scott has Charles the Bold vehement when the Earl of Oxford hopes his daughter ' "Will one day wed some powerful prince, who may be the stay of your Highness's house".' There was a blunt reply: ' "Never! by

[1] Information courteously supplied by the archivist of Strasbourg Cathedral

Saint George, never!" answered the Duke sharply and shortly. "I will have
no son-in-law, who may make the daughter's bed a stepping-stone to
reach the father's crown".' In a sense it was so: Charles the Bold was killed
in battle on 5 January 1477; and his daughter Mary married the Habsburg
Maximilian I the following August and provided a veritable 'stepping-
stone' to the Burgundian lands. All three have their ghostly presence in
the Hofkirche at Innsbruck. In an engraving of 1508, Hans Burgkmair
represented Maximilian himself as St.George. He is shown on horseback,
and with him are the dead dragon and rescued princess; only the arms
betray Maximilian's identity.

The European fame of St.George had a firm literary foundation in the
Legenda Aurea of Jacobus de Voragine (1230-98), a Dominican friar who
became bishop of Genoa. It contains much ecclesiastical lore, homilies for
saints' days, and lives of the saints among whom is St.George. An early
English translation was made in about 1438, but this was supplanted by
Caxton's some fifty years later, which was sumptuously published by
William Morris's Kelmscott Press in 1892. It is now that the dragon
becomes an essential part of the legend. The town of Silene (spelt Sylene
on the Salisbury Breviary of 1424-5, f.448, in the Bibliothèque Nationale,
Paris, and refined to Sylenë by Shapcott Wensley for Elgar), somewhere in
Libya, is beset by a dragon living in the marshes nearby. Its pestilential
breath is a constant nuisance, and the townsfolk hope to pacify it with the
daily offering of sheep. When the flocks are seriously depleted, the
citizens make the sacrifice that of a sheep and a child drawn by lots. When
the king's only daughter is chosen, the royal household begs to be
excused. The Sileniens are adamant, threatening to fire the king and his
palace. The princess is decked for the ordeal as a bride for marriage.
Then comes St.George. The princess is initially reluctant that anyone
should risk his life against the monster, but St.George insists and wounds
it. The princess is urged to lead the dragon towards the city with her
girdle. There the saint will despatch the monster if all become Christian.
St.George himself performs the multiple baptism and instructs the
building of a church. If offered a reward of coin, land or the princess's
hand, he generally refuses.

Crusaders brought back stuffed crocodiles from the East, which may
account for the location of Silene and the dragon. The slaying of a dragon
is the crowning achievement of many heroes, as in the case of Siegfried at
the Drachenfels or of Arthur himself. Pre-conquest England used the
dragon as an ensign of war. Uther Pendragon, for instance, future father
of Arthur, had a vision of a flaming dragon in the sky, which the seers
interpreted as a sign of his future rule: 'he ordered two dragons to be
fashioned, like to those he had seen in the circle of the star, one of which
he dedicated in the cathedral of Winchester, the other he kept by him to

be carried into battle.' So it was that the King Arthur in Innsbruck has dragons featured on his armour.

St.George's victory over the dragon may be interpreted as the conquest of pagan cults by the Roman church, or its suppression of heresies. Sigismund of Hungary, Garter knight from 1416, instituted the Order of the Vanquished Dragon two years later to signal his victory over the Hussites. On the other hand, Elizabeth I takes on a George-like role as a doughty champion freeing her people from the errors of Rome and the coils of the Pope. The Pope, indeed, is sometimes roughly treated in dragon iconography, appearing as a shapeless monster with triple tiara pinned to the ground by a Protestant St.George against a backdrop of Protestant churches. In such a scene the rescued princess is the true, reformed church. Many a dragon has the curled and twisted tail of a serpent, suggestive of evil as old as Eden. The more baneful the traditions a dragon might suggest, the more valiant was the saint and satisfactory his victory.

It must be assumed that Elgar's St.George, clattering in for the Diamond Jubilee was Protestant. A mighty combatant for Catholic chivalry and a Catholic St.George was Kenelm Digby, older contemporary at Trinity, Cambridge, of Tennyson, Thackeray and Edward FitzGerald, who knew him by sight: 'A grand swarthy fellow, who might have stepped out of the canvas of some knightly portrait in his Father's house - perhaps the living image of one sleeping under some cross-legg'd effigies in the church.' The subtitle of *The Broad Stone of Honour* is 'The True Sense and Practice of Chivalry'. It is divided into four books, 'Godefridus', 'Tancredus', 'Morus', and 'Orlandus'. The first two are named after crusading heroes, Godfrey of Bouillon, watcher at the Maximilian tomb, and Tancred, Godfrey's lieutenant in the capture of Jerusalem who achieved also an operatic life under such as Campra (1660-1744) and Rossini (1792-1868). Sir Thomas More (? 1477-1535) presides over book three as advocate against those rejecting Christian chivalry, while book four invokes Ariosto (1474-1535) to give 'a more detailed view of the virtues of the chivalrous character, when it was submitted to the genuine and all-powerful influence of the Catholic faith; and Orlando may be symbolical of this more generous chivalry'.

In 'Tancredus' Digby writes of St.George and the Garter:

> Knights of the Garter, the decoration of which illustrious order still remains, were admonished at their installation to wear the symbols of their order, that 'by the imitation of the blessed martyr and soldier of Christ, Saint George, they may be able to overpass both adverse and prosperous adventures; and that, having stoutly vanquished their enemies, both of body and soul, they may not only receive the praise of this transitory combat, but be crowned with the palm of eternal victory'.

Godfrey of Bouillon in the Innsbruck Hofkirche

Digby's pages glow with Arthurian tales and countless excerpts from Froissart. He ends the first part of 'Orlandus' with a quotation from Caxton as *laudator temporis acti*:

> The exercises of chivalry are not used and honoured as they were in ancient time, when the noble acts of the knights of England that used chivalry were renowned through the universal world. O, ye knights of England, where is the custom and usage of noble chivalry? What do ye now but go to the bains and play at dice? Alas! what do ye but sleep and take ease, and are all disordered from chivalry? Leave this, leave it, and read the noble volumes of St.Graal, of Launcelot, of Tristrem, of Galaod, of Perceval, of Perceforest, of Gawayn, and many more; there shall ye see manhood, courtesy, and gentilness (*Of the Order of Chyvalry and Knyghthood*).

Yet all was not lost in Caxton's day, still less in Kenelm Digby's. He has to admit that the amusements of chivalry had been made more than ever alive 'in the pages of Ste.Palaye, Büsching, La Colombière and Scott'. The Tournament of Eglinton was only a few years in the future, inspired by such as Digby. He writes of Homeric games, of a boys' tournament at Rome, said to have been invented by Ascanius, son of Aeneas (see Virgil's *Aeneid*, Book V, 545) and suggests that the French were the first to establish regular tournaments. He claims it was in the reign of Henry the Fowler (919-36), the king of Wagner's *Lohengrin*, that tournaments began in Germany. The English took them up under Stephen (1135-54), the Italians adopted them, and the crusaders spread them to Constantinople. The clergy, however, looked at them askance. The author of St.Bernard's life (1090-1153) has no time for them: 'A large company of noble warriors came to Clairvaux when the time of Lent was near beginning; they were almost all youths devoted to secular warfare, seeking those execrable vanities, which are commonly called tournaments.'

Clairvaux was the last place to be sympathetic. Was not this the same Bernard whom a legend not of today claims that he strode into Speyer Cathedral on the Rhine and greeted an image of the Virgin with the words 'O clemens, o pia, o dulcis Virgo Maria'; when the Virgin replied 'Salve, Bernarde', the saint declared roundly it was unfitting for a woman to speak in church, and the statue has said nothing since. Moreover, Saint Bernard was zealous for the Second Crusade, and Digby makes another point about church hostility; St.George might have fewer numbers to support:

> The number of deaths at tournaments was very great. At Cologne, on one occasion, the lists resembled a field of battle; moreover, it was said that

they prevented the nobles from assisting Europe against the Turks in the East. On these accounts the church prohibited them, and at length ecclesiastical burial was refused to all who fell in tournaments. The hatred of the clergy against them may be instanced in the monk of St.Denis who, describing the hanging of a certain proud knight, says that the executioner cried, 'Laissez aller'; the expression of the heralds, to signify the commencement of these games.

A bishop of Worcester was among those who added his prohibition, a fact Elgar may not have reckoned with when orchestrating the *Severn Suite* and its 'Tournament'.

Saint Bernard's disapproval was remarkably ineffective, as Digby relates: 'At tournaments in Edward III's time, women sometimes appeared on horseback armed with daggers and in armour. Ramon Muntaner describes a Spanish woman, in the reign of Peter of Aragon, who put on armour, and took a French knight prisoner, having killed his horse ('Orlandus' II).' Digby calls Edward III the 'most chivalrous king that ever reigned in England'; and Chaucer was his poet, creator of a knight who had wandered far:

> A knight ther was, and that a worthy man,
> That fro the time that he firste began
> To riden out, he loved chevalrie,
> Trouthe and honour, fredom and curtesie.
> Ful worthy was he in his lordes werre,
> And thereto had he ridden, no man ferre,
> As wel in Christendom as in Heathenesse,
> And ever honoured for his worthinesse.
>
> At Alisandre he was whan it was wonne.
> Ful often time he hadde the bord begonne
> Aboven alle nations in Pruce.
> In Lettowe hadde he reysed and in Ruce,
> No cristen man so ofte of his degre.

By the time of Queen Victoria's Diamond Jubilee mediaeval knights and their tournaments had been transformed by imperial experience. There was almost constant warfare, small-scale mostly, but a Crimean War or Indian Mutiny might flare up. St.George retained his armour as England's patron, but mediaeval equipment was mainly for the dead. Queen Victoria had always enjoyed portraits of Prince Albert in armour, and he is represented thus in his Memorial Chapel at Windsor, built originally by Henry III (1216-72) but eventually a shrine to the Prince Consort and Victoria's grandson, the Duke of Clarence (1864-92). The white effigy of Prince Albert has a short mail shirt beneath elaborate armour; round his neck is the Order of the Garter. Two angels kneel by his head, and a long sword supported by both hands reaches almost to the recumbent figure of his dog Eos curled round his feet. The cenotaph inscription sums up the Prince's life: 'I have fought the good fight. I have finished my course.' Virtues and angels surround the base of the monument. But it is Alfred Gilbert's (1854-1934) tribute to the young Duke of Clarence which dominates the chapel. Alice Elgar noted his death in her diary on 14 January 1892, when Elgar was prostrate with 'flu. The funeral was on 20 January when Elgar was still unwell. Minnie Baker sent a volume of Lear Nonsense to cheer him, and sale of the Hazeldine furniture began. Gilbert is best remembered for his statue of Eros at Piccadilly Circus in memory of the Earl of Shaftesbury. Gilbert was delighted with the commission, and wrote to his mother about it:

> But I'll do it yet, and you shall go with me to St.George's Chapel to see my work and my children after us. This is the surrounding for an Artist after all. He must be moved, his imagination must be appealed to. He must be moved, attend, even tho' it be called worldly. It is the most worldly things which awaken the deepest suggestions. Think of the beautiful Princess, who one would imagine God himself would not dare to afflict, bowed down like the humblest peasant with the grief for her first born.

The Duke is in military uniform, of Victoria's day not Edward III's, but a helmeted and very youthful St.George with his left arm round a highly decorative crucifix preserves the mediaeval associations. The slender stem of the cross reaches the ground between the fantastic footwear of the saint. An angel poises a crown above the Duke's head, as he was next in line to the throne as eldest son of the future Edward VII.

At the beginning of her reign, Victoria was sceptical about such schemes as the Eglinton Tournament. It made an instant appeal to the potential knights, as noted by Grantley Berkeley (1800-81) in *My Life and Recollections* (1865):

> I know of nothing that ever seized on the minds of the young men of fashion with such force as it did, or held out apparently so many romantic attractions. I can safely say that, as far as I was concerned, I was seized with an extraordinary desire to be one of those who would enter the lists, without at first considering the consequences . . . All that I thought of for the moment was a Queen of Beauty; brave deeds, splendid arms, and magnificent horses.

St.George by Alfred Gilbert

The Queen was not altogether displeased when the British climate made a fiasco of the event, writing in her diary of 2 September 1839 of a conversation with Lord Melbourne (1779-1848):

> Talked of the horrid weather; of its having poured so at the Tournament, the Queen of Beauty having been obliged to go in a *close carriage*, and that the whole thing had turned out to be the greatest absurdity. Lord M. said he heard from Lord Compton, that is *he* had not seen Lord Compton, but 'a *lady* told me,' (I guess who this *mysterious* lady is from whom he hears so much) that there never was anything like it; the Tent had not been waterproof; all the rain came in, and they were drenched, and Lord Eglinton had to send home the various people who he could not lodge, to their various Inns, etc. etc. I said it served them all right for their folly in having *such* a thing &c.

Then the young Queen herself, after marriage to the Prince Albert who had been educated at Bonn on the castled Rhine and was steeped in the legends of his land, danced an anachronistic quadrille in a court of mediaeval chivalry. The occasion was a costume ball given at Buckingham Palace on 11 May 1842. After some hesitation, she and the prince had decided to attend as Froissart's patroness Queen Philippa and Edward III. They were determined to get the costumes right, and there are sketches by Victoria of what they were to wear. She was delighted with the result: 'Nothing could have gone better than the whole did, & it was a truly splendid spectacle.' The royal household represented the court of Edward III, with two equerries in armour. There were also characters from the Waverley novels, including Sir Kenneth of Scotland from *The Talisman*, though presumably without Roswal, and Merry Muscovites. Chaucer was represented, Bulwer-Lytton (1803-73) went as an Elizabethan ancestor, while Robert Peel (1788-1850) reincarnated a Van Dyck portrait. *The Times* of 14 May was lyrical:

> Her Majesty's fancy dress ball on Thursday night was a scene of such brilliance and magnificence, that since the days of Charles II, with the solitary exception of one fête given in the reign of George IV, there has been nothing at all comparable to it in all the entertainments given at the British Court.

The Queen was so delighted with the ball's success that she commissioned Edwin Landseer (1802-73) to paint herself and Albert in their Plantagenet costumes. Landseer gave the faces of monarch and consort a moonlike vacancy, reserving human interest for the two small pages crouched to the left of the picture.

The royal interest in chivalry, divided this time between King Arthur and Edward III, is evident in the decorative scheme for the new Houses of Parliament. Prince Albert was chairman of the Royal Commission on the Fine Arts that was to advise on the way ahead. He took his duties seriously enough to commission experimental frescoes by such artists as William Dyce, Daniel Maclise (1806-70) and Landseer for a summer house at Buckingham Palace, since destroyed. Subjects were taken mainly from Scott and Shakespeare. Prince Albert also brought over for consultation Peter Cornelius (1783-1867), who had painted frescoes for Leo von Klenze's (1784-1864) Glyptothek and Alte Pinakothek in Munich, buildings well known to the Elgars on their Bavarian visits. William Dyce painted in 1847 the fresco at Osborne House on the Isle of Wight showing Neptune resigning the empire of the sea to Britannia. If Neptune has since reclaimed it, this does not detract from the flair of Dyce's fresco or from the significance of a conversation he had with Prince Albert about Arthurian romances as the English equivalent of the *Nibelungenlied*. The Parliament project was put out to competition, and among the winners were Charles Cope (1811- 90), Dyce and Maclise.

For the House of Lords Cope painted Edward III conferring the Order of the Garter on the Black Prince. He had the precedent of Benjamin West's achievement in the King's Audience Chamber at Windsor (1787-9), a series of seven 'Edward III' paintings commissioned by George III, for which a picture of St.George and the dragon provides an overall context. In the Lords there are two frescoes by Maclise, the *Spirit of Chivalry* and the *Spirit of Justice*. 'Chivalry' is an idealised figure of Victoria herself holding a laurel wreath in her left hand. On one side of her are three helmeted and crowned knights; on the other a bishop with crook and mitre, and civil dignitaries. In the foreground are an elderly harpist and young lutenist, while a youthful knight, with hands on sword and scabbard, gazes ardently at 'Chivalry'. The central figure of 'Justice' holds a pair of scales in her right hand. Supporting her is the Archangel Michael with drawn sword. Foreground victims appealing for their rights include a manacled black slave and chubby little boy who seems thoroughly at ease with the world.

Dyce's contribution is in the Queen's Robing Room, and his themes are Arthurian. 'Courtesy' shows 'Sir Tristram harping to La Beale Isoud' and is set in Ireland before the plot becomes too tangled. Tristram plays his harp, while Isoud looks bashfully at hers. 'Mercy' has an imperious Guenevere as central figure, while in front of her a kneeling 'Sir Gawain swears to be merciful and "never to be against ladies".' Gawain's oath is needed, since he had just cut off a lady's head by mistake. In 'Religion', Sir Galahad, Sir Perceval and his sister, and Sir Bors see a vision of Christ and the four evangelists amid swirling clouds. 'Generosity' illustrates the moment before the castle of Joyous Gard in which Malory depicted 'King Arthur unhorsed by Sir Bors and spared by Sir Launcelot'. Sir Bors would kill the king, but Launcelot stays him: 'I will never see that most noble king that made me knight neither slain nor shamed.' In 'Hospitality' (by Dyce but completed by Cope) Arthur with sword aloft stands on a dais and welcomes Tristram as he enters the crowded Gothic court on horseback. An aged harpist and couple of singing boys make music for the occasion.

After the Prince Consort's death in 1861 it seemed to the British as if they had no queen. E.F.Benson puts it succinctly in *As we were* (1930):

> For many years she retired into a complete seclusion, and made no public appearance of any sort. Though for a time she would not even see her ministers, her devotion to her duty reasserted itself and she worked as hard as ever, but her labours were as secret and invisible as those of the queen-bee in the central darkness of the hive.

By the time of the Golden Jubilee she was again a public figure and a *Te Deum* by Prince Albert had been sung in Westminster Abbey. At evening the boys of Eton College had organised a torchlight procession to Windsor Castle. Augustus Hare described their arrival: 'Most unspeakably weird, picturesque, inspiring, beautiful, and glorious was the sight, when, with a burst of drums and trumpets, the wonderful procession emerged under the old gate of Edward III.' Hare felt it a scene to transport the mind: 'I am sure that the beloved figure in the white cap seated in the wide-open central window felt it so, and was most deeply moved by the sight and sound of so much loyal and youthful chivalry.' Gratifying if unusual news from India may also have come to the Queen's ears, when Lord Dufferin the viceroy wrote to Sir Henry Ponsonby, her private secretary: 'inform Her Majesty that all the ladies of Calcutta are buying Jubilee bustles'.

At the time Elgar was celebrating the Diamond Jubilee, the situation seemed yet more splendid. The empire comprised almost a quarter of the globe and its inhabitants. The century was nearing its end as a British century. Gladstone felt this was the moment for the Queen to abdicate; most of the British did not. London had become the heart of the world as a string of villages. *Le Figaro* felt that the British empire had now surpassed the Roman, an idea Elgar was to express in the following year's *Caractacus*, dedicated to the Queen. The *New York Times* seemed about to rejoin the motherland, in the way Shaw was to envisage in the *Apple Cart* of 1929: 'We are a part, and a great part, of the Greater Britain which seems so plainly destined to dominate this planet.' The women's association of Brooklyn clinched the matter by singing 'God save the Queen' at a jubilee meeting. The Austrian emperor Franz Josef (1848-1916) called at the British Embassy in Vienna wearing the Order of the

Thomas Holloway advertises the Jubilee

Garter and the uniform of the British regiment to which he belonged.

Jubilee Day was 22 June, a week after Elgar completed his *Te Deum and Benedictus* for Hereford. The previous evening the Queen held a banquet at Buckingham Palace, and for the first time since her widowhood did not wear black. The procession to St.Paul's was an astonishing affair and graphically described in the diary of Lady Monkswell:

> First came the Naval Brigade with guns, and the ten or twelve colonial premiers and their wives in carriages, each followed by the mounted troops of their colony, such strange, fine looking horsemen. The excellent premiers and their wives who in their continent are quite small people, had never had such a good day in their lives, and were chiefly grinning from ear to ear with joy and pride. They were very well cheered. Secondly came Captain Ames, the tallest man in the British Army, six feet eight inches, and his four troopers, seven or eight batteries of Horse Artillery, divided by what seemed to my aching sight endless squadrons of Dragoon Guards, Hussars, the Scots Greys, and the 17th Lancers. Thirdly the splendid troops of native Indian Cavalry, the Indian princes in their magnificent native costumes and riding the most splendid horses. The last, riding alone, was Sir Pertab Singh, ADC to the Prince of Wales, and the great polo player. He looked one mass of gold.

It is worth pausing a moment over Sir Pertab (or Pratap, 1845-1922), as Alice Elgar may have done when reading about the procession and remembering that Sir Pratap's Jodhpur was only some 200 miles from the Kota, where her father had distinguished himself in the Mutiny, 40 years before. There was a special cheer for Sir Pratap, rightly so. He had been fearless in his young days, wrestling with wild boars. At the Golden Jubilee he had felt the Queen would prefer him to stay at Buckingham Palace rather than Claridge's or the Savoy. His chivalry and courtesy were legendary, as when he had been willing to take the fourth corner of an Englishman's coffin, to the horror of local brahmins. At the age of 70 he was with his troops in Palestine when they took Haifa; at moments of crisis he told his men they had the choice of death by the enemy or execution by him.

Lady Monkswell's account reaches its climax with the approach of Victoria herself:

> the sixteen carriages ending with the cream-coloured ponies, and the Queen. She was sitting quite upright and brisk in the carriage, not looking flushed or overcome, but smiling and bowing. She was dressed in grey and black, and held in her hand the very long-handled black lace parasol lined with white, given her by Mr.Charles Villiers, the oldest M.P. She held it high up so that we could see her face.

She had sent a jubilee message by telegraph around the world: 'Thank my beloved people. May God bless them.' *The Times* summed up the occasion: 'History may be searched, and searched in vain, to discover so wonderful an exhibition of allegiance and brotherhood amongst so many myriads of men.' The Queen spoke afterwards to the Bishop of Winchester: ' "From what point did you see the procession" then recollecting, she said, "Oh! you were on the steps of St.Paul's. I" she added, "was unfortunate - I had a very bad place and saw nothing"'

Poets responded variously. Housman (1859-1936) had marked the earlier jubilee with sombre irony:

> It dawns in Asia, tombstones show
>   And Shropshire names are read;
> And the Nile spills his overflow
>   Beside the Severn's dead.
>
> We pledge in peace by farm and town
>   The Queen they served in war,
> And fire the beacons up and down
>   The land they perished for.
>
> 'God save the Queen' we living sing,
>   From height to height 'tis heard;
> And with the rest your voices ring,
>   Lads of the Fifty-third.
>
> Oh, God will save her, fear you not:
>   Be you the men you've been,
> Get you the sons your fathers got,
>   And God will save the Queen.

Celebrating the Diamond Jubilee, Francis Thompson (1859-1907) imagines first the vigil of the previous night, peopled by poets lately dead, Tennyson to lead and Coventry Patmore last, all of them with Elgarian associations:

>   I saw
> In the cloud-sullied moon a pale array,
> A lengthened apparition, slowly draw;
> And as it came,
> Brake all the street in phantom flame
> Of flag and flower and hanging, shadowy show
> Of the tomorrow's glories, as might suit
> A pageant of the dead.

Thompson draws them on with music:

> First went the holy poets, two on two,
> And music, sown along the hardened ground,
> Budded like frequence of glad daisies, where
> Those sacred feet did fare;
> Arcadian pipe, and psaltery, around,
> And stringèd viol, sound
> To make for them melodious due.
> In the first twain of those great ranks of death
> Went One, the impress recent on his hair
> Where it was dinted by the Laureate wreath:
> Who sang those goddesses with splendours bare
> On Ida hill, before the Trojan boy;
> And many a lovely lay,
> Where Beauty did her beauties unarray
> In conscious song.

***

> A Strength beside this Beauty, Browning went,
> With shrewd looks and intent,
> And meditating still some gnarlèd theme.
> Then came, somewhat apart,
> In a fastidious dream,
> Arnold, with a half-discontented calm,
> Binding up wounds, but pouring in no balm.
> The fervid breathing of Elizabeth
> Broke on Christina's gentle-taken breath.
> Rossetti, whose heart stirred within his breast
> Like lightning in a cloud, a Spirit without rest,
> Came on disranked; Song's hand was in his hair,
> Lest Art should have withdrawn him from the band,
> Save for her strong command;
> And in his eyes high Sadness made its lair.
> Last came a Shadow tall, with drooping lid,
> Which yet not hid
> The steel-like flashing of his armèd glance;
> Alone he did advance,
> And all the throngs gave room
> For one that looked with such a captain's mien.

The most surprising and far-sighted tribute came from Rudyard Kipling :

> Far-called, our navies melt away;
>   On dune and headland sinks the fire:
> Lo, all our pomp of yesterday
>   Is one with Nineveh and Tyre!
> Judge of the Nations, spare us yet,
>   Lest we forget - lest we forget!

Kipling foresaw trouble ahead, as he wrote to J.W.Mackail: 'The big smash is coming one of these days, sure enough, but I think we shall pull through not without credit. It will be the common people - the third-class carriages - that'll save us.' His only son John was born in the August of Jubilee year. Victoria foresaw not so much a 'big smash' as a constant struggle to preserve the *status quo*. She sometimes wondered 'why nobody was to have any-thing anywhere but ourselves': meanwhile she could enjoy the fact that any geographical feature in the world might be named after her; could study Hindustani with her Munshi and try out a word or two on her Indian troops; could define the empire in her own down-to-earth way as an instrument 'to protect the poor natives and advance civilisation'; rejoice in the fact that she had more Moslem subjects than the Sultan of Turkey; nor be too much concerned that, while on one side of her in the procession rode the Prince of Wales, on the other rode that sometimes tiresome Kaiser Wilhelm II.

8 - So much I know, not knowing how I know

The career of Charles George Gordon was as remarkable as his character. After spectacular military success, he was known to an admiring public as 'Chinese Gordon'. Promoted colonel and made CB at home, given highest honours by the Chinese, Gordon wanted no limelight and became commander of the Royal Engineers at Gravesend, spending time and resources on relieving the poor and seeing to the education of local boys. The young Herbert Kitchener, commissioned just before his 21st birthday, dined regularly in his Brompton mess near Chatham, adorned with portrait of Gordon as a Chinese mandarin. Twenty-five years later his own portrait was beside it.

Gordon's working connection with Egypt began in 1874. He had a good relationship with the Khedive Ismail (1863-95), both concerned to restrict the slave trade on the Upper Nile, the one with a determination based on high moral concern, the other in a more desultory fashion through a network of corrupt officials. Egypt had only shadowy control over equatorial provinces nominally in her sphere. By diplomatic finesse, strength of character, and unwavering integrity Gordon established an ascendency almost single-handed, since most of his assistants succumbed to the climate.

The Khedive now made Gordon governor-general of the Sudan. Because of the ravage of diseases, he determined to go to Khartoum alone 'with an infinite and Almighty God to direct and guide me'. His personal magnetism again achieved success, and an Anti-Slavery Convention between the British and Egyptian governments was signed in August 1877. Egyptian finances, however, were in chaos. Educated in Paris, the Khedive had observed the realisation of Haussmann's (1809-91) plans; the result was much effective layout and rebuilding in Cairo. The Suez Canal was opened in November 1869 and the opulence of the entertainments for the astonishing concourse of celebrities was crippling, even if *Aida* came two years late.

The Khedive's eventual reaction was to set up a commission of enquiry into Egyptian finances with Gordon as president. Gordon agreed on condition that none of the European debt commissioners served. This was unacceptable, and the result was deposition and exile (June 1879) for the Khedive. After further frustrating experiences in the Sudan and South Africa, where Gordon saw much of Cecil Rhodes (1853-1902), he spent most of 1883 in Palestine. There he formed daring theories about the

General Gordon

Tomb of Christ, having already convinced himself that the Garden of
Eden was in the Seychelles. He was in communication with the Palestine
Exploration Fund, among whose sponsors was George Grove (1820-1900),
and for whom Kitchener later undertook an important mapping task. An
article by Gordon was published after his death in the *Palestine
Exploration Fund Quarterly Statement* (April 1885). Entitled 'Eden and
Golgotha', the article plunges in: 'I have formed a theory with respect to

the position of Eden.' The theory involved many gnomic utterances: 'Seychelles is granitic, all other islands are volcanic'; 'Aden, query Eden'; 'Mussulman tradition places Eden at Ceylon'; 'I do not go into the question whether or not the Tree of Knowledge is not the *Lodoicea seychellarium* and the Tree of Life the *Artocarpus incisa*, though for myself I do not doubt it.' Both trees were on the luxurious island of Praslin, the one known popularly as 'Coco de mer', the other the 'Breadfruit'. Eve's teeth would have had a hard time with the fruit of the former. In Jerusalem conviction came soon: 'The morning after my arrival at Jerusalem I went to the Skull Hill, and felt convinced that it must be north of the Altar. Leviticus i, 11, says that the victims are to be slain on the side of the Altar northwards.' He continues: 'The Latin Holy Sepulchre is west of the altar, and therefore, unless the types are wrong, it should never have been taken as the site.' Gordon preferred a place outside walled Jerusalem, and those incredulous of 'Gordon's Tomb' were succeeded by Anglicans grateful for this quiet 'Garden Tomb'. Many Protestants are convinced by Gordon's arguments that this is the Tomb of Christ.

In the Sudan Mohamed Ahmed (1843-85), a boatbuilder from Sennar, had proclaimed himself the Mahdi in August 1881. It was a view of Mecca that the Mahdi, foretold by the prophet Mohamed, would coincide with Antichrist, and that Christ would descend to join forces with him. The orthodox declared Mohamed Ahmed an imposter, but his movement, aiming at a march on Egypt, overthrow of the heretical Turks, and conversion of the world, achieved formidable strength. A British army was annihilated on 5 November 1883. Sir Evelyn Baring (1841-1917) was now British agent and consul general in Egypt. He urged evacuation of the Sudan, with safe abandonment of their various outposts by the Egyptian garrisons. There was strong journalistic pressure in Britain, notably from the *Pall Mall Gazette*, that the man for the job was Gordon. Baring, who was dubious about Gordon, made a valid point in his *Modern Egypt*, written in 1908 after he became Earl of Cromer (vol.I, p.435): 'The arguments in favour of newspaper influence are too commonplace to require mention. But newspaper government has certain disadvantages.' Baring was in constant correspondence with Lord Granville (1815-91), the foreign secretary. In December 1884 he wrote: 'The Egyptian Government are very much averse to employing General Gordon, mainly on the ground that, the movement in the Soudan being religious, the appointment of a Christian in high command would probably alienate the tribes who remain faithful.' Looking back on the events that were to unfold in the Sudan, Baring regretted much, but could not fault the public admiration for Gordon (I, 430):

The public enthusiasm which General Gordon's name evoked led to some disastrous consequences, yet I cannot bring myself to condemn it. It was, in fact, eminently creditable to the British public. There was nothing mean or self-seeking about it. It was a genuine and generous tribute to moral worth, and it showed that, even in this material age, moral worth has a hold on the public opinion of at least one great civilised country.

Gordon's brief was to evacuate the Sudan, an aim with which he concurred; but Baring was in touch with Granville on 21 January 1884, while Gordon was on his way to Egypt: 'It is as well that Gordon should be under my orders, but a man who habitually consults the Prophet Isaiah when he is in a difficulty is not apt to obey the orders of any one.' Gordon reached Cairo on 24 January and left for the Sudan two days later. Baring wrote to Granville on 28 January: 'It is impossible not to be charmed by the simplicity and honesty of Gordon's character. My only fear is that he is terribly flighty and changes his opinions very rapidly.' This was confirmed by the series of contradictory telegrams with which Baring was bombarded from Khartoum, and from a letter Gordon wrote to his sister: 'No man in the world is more changeable than I am.'

By now Gordon had in his possession a small edition of *The Dream of Gerontius*. The precise chronology is not easy to unravel. Four years later E.A.Maund wrote to Gordon's sister on 30 January 1888:

> It may interest you to know how it was that General Gordon had this little Roman Catholic poem with him in Khartoum.
>
> The day he left, your brother related to me how his spiritual life was changed by what he experienced at his father's deathbed, as, gazing on his lifeless form, he thought: "Is this what we all come to?"; this led to a long discussion of death, when I remarked that some of his ideas reminded me of Dr.Newman's little Book, *The Dream of Gerontius*. Whereupon he said he should like to read it; and I promised to send it after him to Egypt. Your brother in a postcard, dated from Khartoum, 7-3-84, acknowledging the book says:
>
>> "My Dear Mr.Maund, - Your letter of 25 January arrived today . . . , Thanks for the little book."

Gordon may have received *The Dream of Gerontius* in Cairo, but had time to acknowledge it only two weeks after reaching Khartoum on 18 February. Clearly he had read it with care by then, the day he handed it on to Frank Power, the *Times* correspondent, with a dedication on the fly leaf: 'Frank Power, with kindest regards of CG Gordon 18-2-84'. Below the dedication Power added a note for his sister Mary:

Dearest M

     I send you this little book which General Gordon has given me. The pencil marking thro' the book is his

     Frank Power   Khartoum

     Lord Wolseley (1833-1913), adjutant general of the British army, with wide experience of Egypt, was of the opinion that, even before Gordon reached Khartoum, he would probably need rescuing. He had first met Gordon in the Crimea and greatly admired him: 'absolutely ignored self in all he did, and only took in hand what he conceived to be God's work'. On 4 April Gordon wrote in his journal: 'No human power can deliver us now, we are surrounded.' Four days later Wolseley made the essential point: 'Time is the most important element in this question.' On 13 April the prime minister, W.E.Gladstone, wrote to the Marquess of Hartington (1833-1908), secretary of state for war: 'I have never heard mention in Cabinet or otherwise of sending English troops to Khartoum, unless in the last and sad necessity of its being the only means of rescuing him.' In May there was a mass protest meeting in Hyde Park urging support for Gordon, then a public subscription towards an expeditionary force. The majority of the cabinet voted on 25 July for a relief expedition. Gladstone hesitated till the end of the month. Then parliament voted the necessary funds and Wolseley was in Cairo on 9 September. The following day Frank Power left Khartoum in a steamer to try and speed the expeditionary force, if it existed; but the ship struck a rock and he was murdered on 18 September.

     The last page of Gordon's diary is dated 14 December: 'Now MARK THIS, if the Expeditionary Force, and I ask for no more than two hundred men, does not come in ten days, the town may fall; and I have done my best for the honour of my country. Good-bye.' Lord Charles Beresford, who had commanded the royal yacht *Osborne* and was to be a notable Elgarian friend, was now in charge of the naval brigade. He only just avoided death through a ferocious Dervish assault at the wells of Abu Klea on 17 January 1885. His memoirs give a graphic account: 'they came down upon us with a roar like the roar of the sea, an immense surging wave of white-sashed black forms brandishing bright spears and long flashing swords and the terrible rain of bullets poured into them by the Mounted Infantry and the guards stayed them not.' Beresford writes of the Gardner machine gun which jammed after firing seventy rounds. All those handling the gun were killed except Beresford. He was flattened beneath the Dervish charge, lay stunned under a pile of bodies, and then scrambled to safety. Beresford was too ill to accompany the steamers heading to Khartoum; it was they who heard on the afternoon of 27 January that Gordon had been killed the previous day.

     Queen Victoria was appalled and took dramatic action: 'telegraphed *en clair* to Mr.Gladstone, Lord Granville, and Lord Hartington, expressing how dreadfully shocked I was at the news, all the more so when one felt it might have been prevented.' Gladstone, the 'Grand Old Man' now became 'M.O.G.' in the public mind, 'Murderer of Gordon'. Wolseley, who gave up smoking for ever in grief at his failure to rescue Gordon, never forgave Gladstone, writing in his journal of 4 February 1885: 'it was owing to his influence, active measures for the relief of Gordon were not undertaken in time.' His comment on Gladstone's retirement in 1896 was scornful: 'The arch traitor Mr.Gladstone has reached the end of his ignoble career; an "extinct volcano" that can no longer vomit forth destruction to his country.'

In Egypt Sir Evelyn Baring admitted Gordon had died magnificently (II, 10): 'History has recorded few incidents more calculated to strike the imagination than that presented by this brave man, who, strong in the faith which sustained him, stood undismayed amidst dangers which might well have appalled the stoutest heart.' He echoed the view of his Queen and British opinion when he continued: 'But no soldier about to lead a forlorn hope, no Christian martyr tied to the stake or thrown to the wild beasts of ancient Rome, ever faced death with more unconcern than General Gordon.' It was to be ten years before reconquest of the Sudan became a matter for informed political discussion.

Meanwhile John Henry Newman, created cardinal in 1879, was in considerable distress at the Birmingham Oratory. Ignorant of the fact that Gordon died that day, he wrote on 26 January 1885 to Lord Blachford (1811-89), an Oxford friend and contributor to the Tractarian movement, who as Frederic Rogers had been under-secretary of state for the colonies from 1860 to 1871, when he became a peer: 'As to the expedition, has not Gladstone made imprudent promises, which it will be frightful to keep?' He spoke of his personal concerns: 'I suppose everyone is as anxious as I am about the Nile expedition - those who have relations on it far more so.' Two of the old boys from the Oratory school were serving under Beresford. Rudolph de Lisle was killed at Abu Klea and Francis Pollen was down with fever. Newman explained the details: 'Poor young de Lisle, a clever fellow'; moreover he was 'the third of a large family 3 of whom have died in the course of the year, and a comrade and great friend of one of the young Pollens, who, having to tow a boat up the rapids swimming, is invalided with fever. Other of our boys are there too.'

Then, in early April 1885, Newman received from Dublin a completely unexpected letter:

> Seeing that you are a large subscriber to the 'Memorial Fund' for General
> Gordon, it strikes me, that you would be pleased to see the enclosed little
> book. It was given to my brother the late Mr.Frank Power by General

John Henry Newman by George Richmond

Herbert Kitchener as Sirdar by von Herkomer

Gordon soon after his arrival in Khartoum. As you will see by the front page the pencil marking through the book is done by General Gordon himself I need not say how highly I prize it, for many reasons so I will feel obliged if you will return it to me at your earliest convenience.

It was the *Dream of Gerontius* copy Gordon had given Power the previous year. Newman replied at once, on 7 April:

Your letter and its contents took away my breath. I was deeply moved to find that a book of mine had been in General Gordon's hands, and that, the description of a soul preparing for death.

I send it back to you, with my heartfelt thanks, by this post in a registered cover. It is additionally precious, as having Mr.Power's writing in it.

Father William Neville, to be Newman's executor, and with whom Elgar had to negotiate when proposing abbreviations to *The Dream of Gerontius* and also when Worcester Cathedral sought to Anglicise the text, was set to transcribing Gordon's markings into several copies of the poem. The first was sent to the Anglican Richard Church, dean of St.Paul's in London, long a close friend of Newman's. The dean expressed his gratitude on 10 April: 'All our party are alive to the interest of the book - one result was that they all went to get copies of the small edition.' Elgar, and then Alice Roberts, also possessed the poem with its Gordon markings.

In Egypt Baring noted that since 1895 avenging Gordon was a matter of keen debate. He ascribed this to an access of imperialist sentiment in Britain. When the decision was taken in 1896, Kitchener was to command. He had met Gordon twice and been in Egypt at the time of his death. He had expressed concern for Gordon in a letter to his father as early as March 1884: 'I do not think England will stand Gordon being deserted. It is the most disgraceful thing I ever knew, had they taken anyone's advice that knew anything about the country Gordon would be safe now.' Since 1892 Kitchener had been Sirdar, commander-in-chief, of the Egyptian army. He had campaigned in the north of the Sudan and lunched with the Queen at Windsor on his return. Various trophies had been sent to her without his seeing them; when he viewed them on display, he had to improvise descriptions for her. A so-called 'Crusader sword' was found to have an English inscription on it. But Victoria enjoyed the occasion and noted in her diary for 18 November 1896: 'a striking, energetic-looking man, with rather a firm expression, but very pleasing to talk to'. He lunched with her again three days later, when about to depart for Egypt and the Sudan.

Sir Evelyn Baring was not sure he liked Kitchener; but he admired him: 'Young, energetic, ardently and exclusively devoted to his profession, and, as the honourable scars on his face testified, experienced in Soudanese warfare, Sir Herbert Kitchener possessed all the qualities necessary to bring the campaign to a successful issue.' Wolseley, having to operate at speed, had used the river and risked the cataracts. Kitchener planned a broad gauge railway for supplies, borrowing locomotives from Cecil Rhodes and hoping eventually to realise the dream of a Cape to Cairo train service. Baring confessed that the 'general plan of campaign arranged in Cairo was executed to the letter'. There had been appalling setbacks: 'Storms of unprecedented violence occurred, with the result that large stretches of the railway embankment were washed away and had to be reconstructed.' On 1 January 1898 Kitchener sent Baring 'an historic telegram, which virtually sealed the fate of the Soudan'. He forecast an important battle and requested reinforcements. When it came to the battle of the Atbara, he had only two words for the troops: 'Remember Gordon'. There was terrible slaughter at the battle of Omdurman on 2 September 1898, when 10,883 dervishes were killed. It is hardly reassuring that almost twice that number of British troops died on the first day at the Somme, 1 July 1916, less than a month after Kitchener had been drowned in the black waters off Orkney.

Kitchener planned a memorial service for Gordon on Sunday, 4 September 1898, in front of the ruined palace where he died and where the British and Egyptian flags flew again. The 'Dead March' from *Saul* and *Scipio* march were played; 'Abide with me' was sung, apparently Gordon's favourite hymn. Father Brindle gave a special benediction, mentioning Gordon and the Sudan: 'Give back to it days of peace - send it rulers animated by his spirit of justice and righteousness - strengthen them in the might of Thy power that they may labour in making perfect the work to which he devoted, and for which he gave, his life.' Kitchener was too moved to dismiss the parade, and another had to do it.

Queen Victoria received a telegram the next day: 'a most touching account, and most dramatic, of his entry into Khartoum and of a memorial service held to the memory of poor Gordon on the spot where he was killed! Surely he is avenged!' She created him Lord Kitchener of Khartoum, but her vigilance and instinct did not fail her when she felt Kitchener guilty of an error of judgment. The Mahdi had died only some five months after Gordon. Kitchener feared his tomb might be a nationalist rallying point, so he destroyed it and cast the Mahdi's body into the Nile. The Queen was displeased:

> it savours in the Queen's opinion too much of the Middle Ages not to allow
> his remains to be buried in private in some spot where it would not be

considered as of any importance politically or an object of superstition. The graves of our people have been respected and those of our foes should, in her opinion, also be.

Nevertheless she signed a cheque for £40,000 on behalf of a grateful nation towards the £100,000 Kitchener needed for the foundation and endowment of Gordon College in Khartoum: 'to give them the intellectual force to act as governors of their own destinies'. The Mahdi's tomb has since been rebuilt.

Alice Elgar's diary makes no mention of the Kitchener expedition, mainly because there was hectic activity over Elgar's completion of *Caractacus* and its first performance on 5 October 1898. Elgar, however, clearly realised the significance of Kitchener's entry into Khartoum, so that General Gordon was much in his thoughts. The result was a letter to Jaeger of 20 October, just one day before he may have had the initial idea for the 'Enigma' Variations:

> Gordon Sym.
>
>   I like this idee but my dear man *why* should I try ?? I can't see - I have to earn money somehow & its *no good* trying this sort of thing even for a 'living wage' & your firm wouldn't give 5£ for it - I tell you I am sick of it all: why can't I be encouraged to do decent stuff & not hounded into triviality.

Yet the Gordon idea remained a matter for discussion over the next seven months. F.G.Edwards (1853-1909) wondered if he might insert a paragraph about the symphony in *The Musical Times*. On the 'Enigma' day itself he replied discouragingly:

> No: please not: it would be nearer the mark to say that 'E.E. having achieved the summit (or somewhat) of his amb[itio]n retires into private life & bids adieu (or a diable) to a munificent public'
>
>   Anyhow 'Gordon' simmereth mighty pleasantly in my (brain) pan & will no doubt boil over one day

Jaeger next heard in a letter of 24 October that Elgar had 'sketched a set of Variations (orkestry) on an original theme'; but 'Gordon' returned on 11 November when he said that '*un*officially, poor old Worcester wants a Symphony!' He made the usual complaint, 'none of this will pay me a cent!' but continued:

> Now as to Gordon: the thing possesses me, but I can't write it down yet: I *may* make it the Worcester work, if that engagement holds   so don't, please, pass on the idea to anybody else just yet. I would really like Edwards

180 *Elgar and Chivalry*

to announce it but I must first get to know if the Dean & Chapter would object to the subject in an English Cathedral!

The 1899 Worcester festival was the first at which Ivor Atkins (1869-1953) would be the principal conductor and he naturally wanted a major Elgar showpiece. Elgar gave a firm enough undertaking about 'Gordon' for Atkins to include it in a draft programme of 29 December 1898. Elgar also acquiesced on 16 February 1899 in Edwards's idea for a *Musical Times* paragraph. After mentioning the Variations, he continued: 'Other compositions are nebulous at present. The Symphony for Worcester *is* to be entitled 'Gordon' - appealing to the feelings &c.&c.' Ten days later Elgar was equally positive to Jaeger:

> Sorry! I thought you understood about Gordon - I imagined I told you that I had annexed the idea - I only wanted to see my way to ease and affluence to write it - that has not arrived but anyhow I'm making a shot at it. you won't be afraid of gongs - I'm not the man to make a noise (??).

Elgar was referring to *Caractacus* Scene II, where the druid maidens have the assistance of a small gong discreetly played, but where the 'Invocation' to Taranis has a large gong crashed *fff* at the words,

> Thrice the sacrificial knife
> Reddens with a victim's life.

The *Musical Times* paragraph was published on 1 March 1899:

> Mr.Edward Elgar has several interesting compositions 'on the stocks.' Chief among them is the new symphony for the Worcester Festival, which is to bear the title 'Gordon'. As in the case of Beethoven's No.3, Mr.Elgar has selected a great hero for his theme, though one of a very different type from that of the 'Eroica.' The extraordinary career of General Gordon - his military achievements, his unbounded energy, his self-sacrifice, his resolution, his deep religious fervour - offers to a composer of Mr.Elgar's temperament a magnificent subject, and affords full scope for the exercise of his genius; moreover, it is a subject that appeals to the sympathies of all true-hearted Englishmen.

But it was not to be: Worcester had to be content with the Variations plus extended finale and a slightly revised *Light of Life*. Elgar informed Atkins of his decision on 9 May, again pleading the financial case. Atkins wondered if it might be possible to raise a subsidy towards publication, but Elgar would have none of it. A last plea from Jaeger was answered by Elgar on 5 November 1899 with a new excuse:

It's no good trying any patriotic caper on in England: we applaud the 'sentiment' in other nations but repress it sternly in ourselves: - anything like 'show' is repugnant to the *real* English - whom you don't know or understand yet nor ever will -

There followed an apology for talking rot, as Alice Elgar had said his remark was 'rude & untrue'.

With 'Gordon' abandoned, and an important Birmingham commission for 1900 to be fulfilled, it was decision time for the next major work. Should it be the biblical 'Apostles' scheme, or a setting of *The Dream of Gerontius?* A crisis of confidence was resolved on 1 January 1900, when G.H.Johnstone from Birmingham agreed with Elgar for *Gerontius* (1900). Newman had written the poem in 1865 and dedicated it to the memory of Father John Joseph Gordon (1811-53). The copy General Gordon gave to Frank Power has the words 'Joanni Joseph' separated by a pencil mark from the name 'Gordon', as if the general wished in some way to associate himself not only with the content of the poem but also its dedication. John Joseph had been a cadet in the Indian army and was stationed in Calcutta. After discussions with Archdeacon Corrie, he decided on holy orders. He went to Trinity, Cambridge in 1833, just after Tennyson, Thackeray and FitzGerald. In May 1841 he attended services in St.Mary's, Oxford: 'Newman both read and preached wonderfully, my heart was swelling the whole time.' After three Anglican curacies he was received into the Roman church on 24 February 1847. Newman himself takes up the story in 1856, three years after Father Gordon had died at the age of 41 (Newman writes in the third person):

> The Father is accustomed to say that there is nothing which has touched him more, or has remained more deeply engraven on his mind, than the generous confidence with which Father Gordon committed himself to him, without as yet having any personal knowledge of him. At the time that Father Gordon was received, our Father was in Rome, whither he had gone to present himself before the Pope [Pius IX], and to ask leave of His Holiness to set up the Congregation of St.Philip in England.

Newman had many of the attractive qualities of Philip Neri (1515-95), who had gathered round him a group of young men to meet in the attics of his church, which they called the 'Oratory'. Devoted to music, he was ultimately responsible for the word 'oratorio'. In 1575 Gregory XIII (1572-85) granted him the church of S.Maria Vallicella, which was eventually rebuilt to become the Chiesa Nuova, where was established 'a Congregation of secular priests and clerics known as the Oratory'. While the Elgars were in Rome, Carice reported an excursion on 16 March 1908:

'we all three went to the Palazzo Massimo to see the Chapel where S.Philip Neri performed a miracle, open only today. We passed through the courtyards, so gloomy, & through many of the rooms, in one of which were *lovely* painted leather (Spanish) wall papers. XVIth century furniture. Very nice chapel, mass going on & sweet music. Went on to Chiesa Nuova, but had no time to see it properly.' The miracle was the raising to life of Paolo dei Massimi.

Father Gordon's work was much admired by Newman:

> In some departments of missionary and Oratorian work, he stood by himself with an excellence of his own. We all recollect what animation he imparted to any undertaking which he began; how interesting was his conversation; how impressive were his instructions; how his remarks struck home; how very mild, how courteous was his manner (what the world calls gentlemanlike), tempering the impetuosity of his reasoning by the meekness and gentleness of his bearing; and then, besides, how he could bring people together, mark out their work for them, and keep them to it; how skilfully and efficiently he managed the schools; what vigour he imparted to the singing of the Oratory Hymns, the first collection of which in a printed form is due to his zeal.

Newman describes how Gordon had taken a leading part in choosing the Edgbaston site, where the building of the Birmingham Oratory began in December 1850, but was soon stricken with illness. He was sent twice to Sussex but showed little improvement. Newman continues:

> In the Autumn, when the Father had need of friends in Italy, in order to collect evidence for the serious trial in which he was engaged, Father Gordon was one of the two Fathers deputed by the Congregation for that purpose. He was selected, among other reasons, because of his state of health, which it was hoped a southern climate would benefit.

The trial was the action for libel brought against Newman by D.Giacinto Achilli because of a passage in his *Lectures on the Present Position of Catholics in England* (1850). The lectures contain also enough to account for Elgar's sense of alienation as a Catholic. Rumour had it that an underground store-room at the Oratory was a dungeon, an idea with which Newman plays only half in fun:

> and fifty years hence, if some sudden frenzy of the hour roused the anti-Catholic jealousy still lingering in the town, a mob might have swarmed about our innocent dwelling, to rescue certain legs of mutton and pats of butter from imprisonment, and to hold an inquest over a dozen packing-cases, some old hampers, a knife-board, and a range of empty blacking bottles.

An altogether grimmer humour informs another extract: 'We are regarded as something unclean, which a man would not touch, if he could help it: and our advances are met as would be those of some hideous baboon, or sloth, or rattlesnake, or toad, which strove to make itself agreeable.'

Father Gordon returned in February 1852. The trial took place in June and Newman was called for judgment on St.Cecilia's day, 22 November: 'It was too much for Fr.Gordon: faithful to his own loyal heart; on that day he was seized with a pleurisy, and when the Father returned from London on the morrow with his process still delayed, he found him in bed. It was the beginning of the end.' The strain of the legal proceedings had taken its toll on Newman too. He was ordered to rest and was invited by James Hope (1812-73), married to Sir Walter Scott's granddaughter, to visit Abbotsford for Christmas and the New Year. Jealous for his religious detachment in the midst of social duties, Newman initially declined on 29 October:

> Your offer is a most tempting one, but it is impossible. It would be so great a pleasure to spend some time with you - and then I have ever had the extremest sympathy for Walter Scott that it would delight me to see his place. When he was dying I was saying prayers (whatever they were worth) for him continually, thinking of Keble's words, 'Think of the minstrels as ye kneel'.

In the end, with a retrial impending in the Achilli affair and all its attendant worry, Newman accepted.

Newman had hardly reached Abbotsford on 17 December, a house now converted to Roman Catholicism, when he wrote Father Gordon an enchanting account of his journey north, as eventful as any similar railway trip of the 21st century: 'the train was half an hour late; and by the time I got to Derby that half hour had become an hour. Accordingly I gave up all hope of the Express; but there it was at the Derby station Waiting for me'. At Newcastle there were desperate measures:

> I flung myself on the mercy of a Samaritan of a policeman, who literally ran with me to the ticket office, and then to the refreshment-room, where, with great fear lest it would get into my head (which it didn't) I swallowed down a glass of sherry, and carried off to the carriage some sandwiches.

He ended with religious matters: 'The Blessed Sacrament, I am glad to say, is in the house.'

Rest for Newman involved no break in correspondence. He was constantly in touch with the Oratory, as in a letter to Austin Mills on

Christmas Eve: 'the Post goes hence irregularly, by love, not by obedience, by accident not be law.' Now that he was chaplain to Abbotsford, he had specific religious questions about the number of drops of water in the chalice for Mass, whether 'the Great Host of Mass' might be broken up, and whether incense was at all used for the 'Missa Cantata'. He supposed this last depended on local custom, 'and what the local custom is at Abbotsford, Sir W.Scott alone can tell'. When he mislaid his glasses, Hope gave him 'a pair of Sir W.S.'s tortoise shell - so you must not be frightened'. Hope threw in a *Midsummer Night's Dream* quote (Act 5 scene i), that Newman would now have 'a poet's eye in a fine frenzy rolling'.

It was not only the health of Father Gordon that concerned Newman; Abbotsford itself was under imminent threat of losing its heir, Walter Scott Lockhart (1826-53), who had joined the army at 20 and was now a sick man at Versailles. He died on 10 January, and Newman was much moved that he should be in Sir Walter's home when his direct male line came to an end. Newman wrote a detailed account of Abbotsford to Father Gordon on 7 January:

> The House itself is dark and the rooms low. The first floor passage is not so broad (not above half) as the 'Newman Alley' leading to my room from our corridor. Very dark withal, and winding. I could shake hands with the nursery maids in the rooms opposite me, without leaving my own room - and sometimes of a morning or evening in going down stairs, seeing nothing, I hear a step approaching, and am obliged to stand still where I am, for fear of consequences, and then a little light figure shoots past me on the right or left, she having better eyes than I. Once there was an awful moral stoppage, neither daring to move.

He reverted to the weather, which was all that could be expected of the borderland in winter, having found use for a discarded Catholic weekly:

> Every other day is stormy, and I have found the Tablet of great use in acting as a blower to my grate - where a portion of it has remained steadily for hours till it was fairly crumbled into tinder. The rooms are small; I am surprised there is not more draught than there is; but as for light, it was not much after ½ past 3 one day that I left off attempting to employ the sun's light. The House is lighted with gas, even in the bedroom it is very good gas.

Indeed the gas installation was one of Abbotsford's features to which Sir Walter had given much care and of which he was most proud.

Newman's diary takes him south on 25 January: 'left Abbotsford for Birmingham   F Joseph sitting up - I came unexpected - I was quite shocked at the change'. Indeed his condition was now hopeless, and his mother insisted he return to Bath, where Newman was able to see him once more: 'his life hangs on a spider's web'. Before his death he said to his brother Robert, an Anglican clergyman: 'I do not say that I do not fear to die; for death must always be a fearful thing. God's justice is very terrible, but then in the crucifixion, God's mercy appears so very great, so awful that it supports us under the awfulness of His Justice.' He died on 13 February 1853, and five days later Newman wrote to the Oratory priest now installed at Abbotsford: 'He is an inexpressible loss to us - to me a special loss; never could anyone be more loyal to me personally than he has been from first to last. I shall say Mass to him every week for a long time to come.' Newman then quotes from the same Book VI of the *Aeneid* as Elgar was to make use of at the head of his *Dream of Gerontius* full score: 'His saltem accumulem donis, not inanibus'. In Virgil Anchises mourns the unfulfilled promise of Marcellus, nephew of Augustus, who was to die young. Dryden translates:

> This gift which parents to their children owe,
> This unavailing gift, at least, I may bestow.

'Unavailing' was certainly *not* the word for Newman's Masses.

Progress on the Edgbaston Oratory was now a major concern. Newman sang his first Mass there and moved in three days after Father Joseph's death. On 4 March 1853 he reported to Cardinal Wiseman (1802-65) at Westminster: 'As we creep in head foremost, I have gone up first, these three weeks, and am battling with the workmen, who, like aboriginal inhabitants, do not brook being dispossessed.' Dedication of the church took place on St.Cecilia's day. In this first Oratory church at Edgbaston there was a 'Bona mors' chapel at the end of a passage leading from the south transept. There Newman could meditate on the dead and rehearse phrases that were to play an integral part in his *Dream of Gerontius* poem.

Newman wrote the poem in an extraordinary burst of inspiration. Two manuscripts survive. The first is on 52 scraps of paper with many erasures and corrections. The fair copy, also with emendations, has the dates 17 January and 7 February 1865 at the beginning and end. It is interesting that the most significant changes came towards the conclusion of the poem. Elgar and Jaeger could not possibly know that Newman too had made major revisions after the Soul's 'I go before my judge'. Newman's additional lines, written out after the end of the poem, would have been splendid ammunition for Jaeger in his conviction that Elgar must also produce a fitting sequel to that momentous sentence. Newman also revised his version of the psalm sung by the Souls in Purgatory, and originally appended to it a seven-verse hymn of 1857 for a choir of angelicals, beginning:

> Help, Lord, the souls which Thou hast made,
> The souls to Thee most dear,
> In prison for the debt unpaid
> Of sins committed here.
>
> Those holy souls, they suffer on,
> Resigned in heart and will,
> Until Thy high behest is done,
> And justice has its fill.

The poem aroused considerable interest and involved Newman in correspondence playful and serious. On 16 June 1865 he wrote to John Telford, the minister at Ryde, who felt there should have been more on the Virgin: 'I have set down the dream as it came before the sleeper. It is not my fault, if the sleeper did not dream more. Perhaps something woke him. Dreams are generally fragmentary. I have nothing more to tell.' Newman's letter neatly disposes of much speculation about what in *Gerontius* is meant to be 'dream' and what reality. Later, on 11 October, he wrote to an Oxford friend and constant correspondent, Thomas Allies:

> I assure you I have nothing more to produce of Gerontius. On the 17th of January last it came into my head to write it. I really cannot tell how, and I wrote on till it was finished, on small bits of paper. And I could no more write anything else by willing it, than I could fly. I am greatly honoured by the good Nuns of Notre Dame in Liverpool having got their children to act it.

That was one of the less expected tributes to the poem. The *Dream* and its dedication gave special pleasure to Father Joseph's mother and his brother William, also a Catholic priest. Newman wrote briefly to him on 23 January 1866: 'I am glad to have done a thing pleasing to you and to your Mother - I was promoted to it by that never-sleeping remembrance which I have of your dear Brother.'

Doctrinally Rome tended to have a certain wariness about Newman, and in 1867 he deputed Ambrose St.John, Catholic grandson of a former dean of Worcester, to put his case to the Prefect of Propaganda. When Newman wrote to St.John on 19 April (Good Friday), he made some telling points; it seemed Rome was more concerned with the question of disobedience than any detail of faith: 'It is not advisable you should get into any dispute about faith - and you might refer to my *works*. By the bye, I doubt whether it will be prudent to show to any one my Gerontius, as prosaic minds may find heresy in my poetry.' He goes on to make what seems an anachronistic remark: 'Every man has his price. Ignatius declares that a Cardinal or Monsignor's price is English snuff.'

Newman published his *Verses on Various Occasions* in 1868, with *The*

Dream of Gerontius as major poem. Among the first to acknowledge his copy was Matthew Arnold, who wrote from the Athenaeum on 20 January 1868:

I value the gift more than I can well say. I think almost all the more important of the Poems I was already acquainted with, but I am glad of any opportunity which makes me read them again. In addition to their other merits, I find their simple clear diction come very refreshingly after the somewhat sophisticated and artificial poetic diction which Mr.Tennyson's popularity has made prevalent.

He then alludes to their deeper qualities:

But the more inward qualities and excellencies of the Poems remind me how much I, like so many others, owe to your influence and writings; the impression of which is so profound, and so mixed up with all that is most essential in what I do and say, that I can never cease to be conscious of it and to have, an inexpressible sense of gratitude and attachment to the Author.

Gladstone added his view on 24 January:

I have been greatly delighted with the volume. That which I may call its chief ornament, I mean the Dream of Gerontius, it is not new to me. I have read it several times, and more than once read aloud to friends. Opinions will form themselves independent of competence, and I own that to me it seems the most remarkable production in its very high walk since the unapproachable Paradiso of Dante, and his less but not very much less wonderful Purgatorio. I am truly glad that now going forth with your name it will attract the attention it deserves.

Newman was again at Abbotsford in July 1872, for a fortnight. This time Hope-Scott was unwell. He had assumed the Scott name in 1853 after the death of Walter Scott Lockhart. Since then Hope-Scott's first wife Charlotte had died (1858), as also had his second (1870), Lady Victoria Fitzalan Howard, eldest daughter of the 14th Duke of Norfolk (1815-60). On his first visit, when writing to Father Joseph, Newman had described the Hopes and Arundels as 'quite Saints'. He did not know 'which of them is in the Chapel most', and concluded: 'Indeed it is impossible to be in a more simply religious house, which was not a convent.' The cast had now changed, but much was the same, as he wrote on 11 July to Ambrose St.John: 'The Blessed Sacrament is reserved in the Chapel, as when I was here before, and brings before me vividly Lord Arundel praying before it. A blessing must come on all of his.' In another letter he noted that 'This Presbyterian region has now several lights set upon high candlesticks.'

Cardinal Newman by Millais

It was the 15th Earl of Norfolk (1847-1917), acquainted with the Elgars from October 1902 and largely responsible for the two coronation arrangements Elgar was involved in, who approached Newman with a scheme that was also to have Elgarian associations. He wrote on 6 April 1881: 'A great wish has been long felt by many of your friends to obtain a good picture of you that we could present to some public gallery in London.' He continued: 'Some of us have now made an arrangement in virtue of which Millais has agreed to paint your portrait if you will consent to sit for him. I may say that Protestants as well as Catholics have been interesting themselves in this matter.' Newman felt he must accept at once, sensitive to the compliment but not relishing the time he would need to be in London. On 1 June he wrote to Millais, agreeing that the first sitting should be on Monday, 27 June, but hoping he would not be needed beyond the Saturday: 'I am of a great age now, and am obliged to take it into account.' He was indeed over 80. Millais was quite informal with the Cardinal. He indicated the sitter's chair on a dais, and instructed: 'Oh, your eminence, on that eminence if you please.' To which he added, 'Come, jump up, you dear old boy!' Newman obeyed, and felt Millais had been 'very merciful in the length of time he exacted of me'. Millais was pleased with the result, rightly considering it one of his finest portraits. In the *Athenaeum* of 29 April 1882, F.G.Stephens (1828-1907) judged it 'a masterpiece to be reckoned with the greatest works that the Italians produced when portrait painting occupied the best hours of Titian, Tintoret, Sebastiano, and Bronzino'. Or was it not more like Velazquez, 'this splendid study of deep rose red and carnation tints'? In November Newman reported that Millais had been exhibiting the picture in Bond Street, 'but now it is with the engraver'. Thus Alice Stuart Wortley was able to give Elgar a print of it in 1904.

At the end of the *Dream of Gerontius* full score Elgar added the Ruskin quotation that has since proved so apt. The paths of Newman and Ruskin hardly crossed. There is no mention of the latter in Newman's mature correspondence, and at Oxford, where they certainly coincided, their only contact seems to have been meetings concerning Gothic architecture. Ruskin's mother was resident in Oxford while her son was at Christ Church from January 1837. Indeed she had rooms opposite St.Mary's when the Tractarian movement was at its height. Temperamentally Calvinist, she had been sufficiently disturbed when Ruskin had fallen in love at 16 with Adèle-Clotilde Domecq, Catholic daughter of her husband's colleague in the sherry trade. But Ruskin showed no interest in the sermons and readings by Newman that so captivated much of intellectual Oxford.

By a strange irony it was Millais who was to link through his art the Ruskin married to Effie and the aged Cardinal. During the fateful summer of 1853 he began the painting of Ruskin at a Glenfinlas waterfall. Ruskin wrote to his father about it on 6 July: 'I think you will be proud of the picture - and we shall have the two most wonderful torrents in the world, Turner's St.Gothard and Millais' Glenfinlas.' Ruskin regarded Millais as a potential successor to Turner (1775-1851), subject to his own guidance; but he was pleased with the finished portrait, as he wrote to Millais on 11 December 1854, five months after his marriage to Effie had been annulled: 'I am far more delighted with it now than I was when I saw it in your rooms. As for the wonderment of the painting there can of course be no question.' Millais also painted Effie at a different Glenfinlas waterfall, sketching her at other places. He explained to Holman Hunt on 17 July 1853: 'The dreariness of mountainous country in wet weather is beyond everything. I have employed myself painting little studies of Mrs.Ruskin.' Millais and Effie were married on 3 July 1855, and the future Alice Stuart Wortley was their third daughter (1862-1936). Millais wanted nothing more to do with Ruskin, who continued to write judiciously and generously about Millais's art. Elgar met the Stuart Wortleys in Sheffield at the beginning of October 1902. More and more she became an Elgarian Egeria, and it may have been a natural chivalry towards her that withheld Ruskin from Elgar's literary references, most notably in his Birmingham lectures as professor of music.

The Ruskin Elgar quoted at the end of *Gerontius* had died on 20 January 1900, almost at its beginning. In 1860 Ruskin had produced the last of his *Modern Painters* volumes; thenceforward he became social rather than art critic, and 'Of King's Treasuries' was an 1864 lecture given in Manchester and published as part of *Sesame and Lilies*. In 1871 Ruskin began the reissue of many works, and was glad this volume should be the first. In the new preface he emphasised the need for books, and books of good quality: 'For we none of us need many books, and those which we need ought to be clearly printed, on the best paper, and strongly bound.' In a young man's library every volume should have

> its assigned place, like a little statue in its niche, and one of the earliest and strictest lessons to the children of the house being how to turn the pages of their own literary possessions lightly and deliberately, with no chance of tearing or dogs' ears.

Ruskin deplores the neglect of fine books, a royal treasury indeed:

> kings and statesmen lingering patiently, not to grant audience but to gain it! - in those plainly furnished and narrow ante-rooms, our bookcase shelves, - we make no account of that company, - perhaps never listen to a word they would say, all day long!

Ruskin makes his distinction: 'for all books are divisible into two classes, the books of the hour, and the books of all time'. It is then that Ruskin defines the good book of all time:

> The author has something to say which he perceives to be true and useful, or helpfully beautiful. So far as he knows, no one has yet said it; so far as he knows, no one else can say it. He is bound to say it, clearly and melodiously if he may; clearly, at all events. In the sum of his life he finds

Ruskin by Millais

this to be the thing, or group of things, manifest to him; - this, the piece of true knowledge, or sight, which his share of sunshine and earth has permitted him to seize. He would fain set it down for ever; engrave it on rock, if he could; saying, "This is the best of me; for the rest, I ate, and drank, and slept, loved, and hated, like another; my life was as the vapour and is not; but this I saw and knew: this, if anything of mine, is worth your memory." That is his "writing;" it is, in his small human way, and with whatever degree of true inspiration is in him, his inscription, or scripture. That is a "Book."

Appointed the first Slade professor of art at Oxford in 1869, Ruskin gave his inaugural lecture on 8 February of the following year. Crowds were such that the lecture had to be transferred from the University Museum to the Sheldonian Theatre. In June 1903 Selwyn Image (1849-1930) remembered the performance:

> This slight, almost insignificant man towered over his audience. He had the fire and force of a prophet. His eyes flashed upon you. Always beginning in a low voice, slowly and quietly, he grew more and more full of sparkle and vigour as he proceeded. But he never lost command of himself, or became the plaything of his eloquence. Towards the end of his lecture he generally grew more quiet. Those perorations, those incomparable perorations, were delivered very gravely, with the most exquisite sense of cadence, of rhythmic modulation.

It was clear from Ruskin's text that art was not to be the exclusive subject of his professorship: 'There is a destiny now possible to us - the highest ever set before a nation to be accepted or refused. We are still undegenerate in race; a race mingled of the best northern blood. We are not yet dissolute in temper, but still have the firmness to govern and the grace to obey.' He then addressed the young men in his audience: 'Will you, youths of England, make your country again a royal throne of kings; a sceptred isle?' He urged an expansionist future on England: 'she must found colonies as fast and as far as she is able, formed of her most energetic and worthiest men; - seizing every piece of fruitful waste ground she can set her foot on.' Small wonder that Cecil Rhodes was impressed and inspired.

Perhaps the aged seer at Brantwood, not quite clear in his mind, rowing with his delicate fingers the *Jumping Jenny* on Coniston Water, now himself a Lakeland Nanty Ewart, reading *Old Mortality* or *Redgauntlet* to his household by candlelight, is a more attractive figure. His chivalrous captains of industry, owing much to Carlyle, the idealism of his St.George's Guild, the various Ruskin communities in America, had been part of a noble dream that would fade before the most materialistic century the world had yet seen, and the most bloodthirsty. At his death G.F.Watts sent a laurel-wreath cut from his own tree; he had done this previously only for Tennyson, Leighton (1830-96) and Burne-Jones. On the 1907 monument to Queen Victoria at Lancaster, Ruskin is carved to stand between Turner and Millais, which is essentially where, when all is forgiven, he properly belongs. That Sullivan (1842-1900) is the only musician represented, means that the great Queen and her magnificent entourage were prepared to be amused.

Meanwhile Elgar knew, now that Novello had printed the *Gerontius*

Ruskin in the Jumping Jenny

full score for the May 1902 performance in Düsseldorf where Richard Strauss (1864-1949) made his speech of commendation, that the MS must rest at the Oratory. Novello queried: 'in an old damp, mouldy Church?' Elgar was not to be deflected. He dated the gift 'Sept.17: 1902', the month his mother had died, adding a few words: 'I offer this M.S. to the Library of the Oratory, with the deepest reverence to the memory of Cardinal Newman whose poem I have had the honour to attempt to set to music.'

9 - Pride, pomp and circumstance of glorious war!

Queen Victoria urged her statesmen to constant vigilance: 'If we are to *maintain* our position as a *first-rate* Power, we must, with our Indian Empire and large Colonies, be *Prepared* for *attacks* and *wars, somewhere* or *other,* CONTINUALLY.' Harry Acworth, librettist of *Caractacus,* would have cordially agreed. He had served in India, and the Elgars at Forli were surrounded with Indian trophies. It was Jaeger at Berners Street, the Novello headquarters, who raised objection to some lines in the final chorus of *Caractacus*:

> Britons, alert! and fear not,
> Though round your path of Pow'r,
> The menial cohorts gather,
> And jealous tyrants low'r.

In his response of 21 June 1898 Elgar relented a little but was ready for a duel: 'by all means will I ask Acworth to eliminate the "truculent" note in the lines: any nation but ours is allowed to war whoop as much as they like but I feel we are too strong to need it.' Acworth, he was sure, did not indicate Jaeger's Germany by 'menial', but 'more probably hill tribes & such like - jealous evidently refers to anybody you like. Now - "pluck ye by the ear" if you feel aggrieved I will bring my sword up & give you as pretty a fight as you can wish - in Berners st - but I warn you I am probably a better swordsman than you'. Moreover he now had at his disposal the swords of Sir Henry Gee Roberts, recently burnished; to reinforce the point, Elgar's letter of three days later has a clash of swords between two combatants, drawn by Elgar to represent a Jaeger with hair flying into the air, and a grimly hatted composer with beaked nose and weapon liberally tipped with 'Gore'.

The 'Opposing cohorts' (Acworth's revision) of October 1899 would not have regarded themselves as 'menial'. Arthur Conan Doyle (1859-1930), with most of the Sherlock Holmes stories behind him, was based at a field hospital in Bloemfontein for much of the South African War (1899-1902). In *The Great Boer War* (1901) he has given a striking description of the Afrikaner character:

> Take a community of Dutchmen of the type of those who defended
> themselves for fifty years against all the power of Spain at a time when

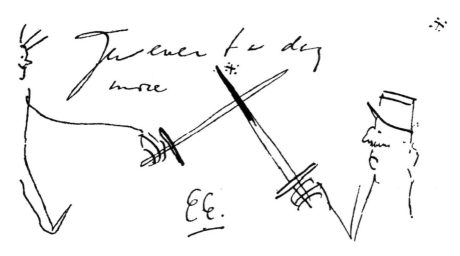

Elgar's threatened duel

Spain was the greatest power in the world. Intermix with them a strain of those inflexible French Huguenots who gave up home and fortune and left their country for ever at the time of the revocation of the Edict of Nantes. The product must obviously be one of the most rugged, virile, unconquerable races ever seen upon earth. Take this formidable people and train them for seven generations in constant warfare against savage men and ferocious beasts, in circumstances under which no weakling could survive, place them so that they acquire exceptional skill with weapons and in horsemanship, give them a country which is eminently suited to the tactics of the huntsman, the marksman, and the rider. Then, finally, put a finer temper upon their military qualities by a dour fatalistic Old Testament religion and an ardent and consuming patriotism. Combine all these qualities and all these impulses in one individual, and you have the modern Boer - the most formidable antagonist who ever crossed the path of Imperial Britain.

Many in England failed to realise the scale of the struggle ahead, Elgar probably among them. He wrote to Jaeger on 24 November 1899: 'I say, they asked me to suggest something for a patriotic-T.Atkins-fund-Boer-war-fund-Concert - I said perhaps the *Flying Dutchman*! wd. do. jape.' Conan Doyle makes other shrewd points about the background to the war and its nature: 'At the same time they mark the beginning of a new military era, for they drove home the fact - only too badly learned by us - that it is the rifle and not the drill which makes the soldier.' He adds more on the terrain and its inhabitants: 'A handful of people by the right of conquest take possession of an enormous country over which they are dotted at such intervals that it is their boast that one farmhouse cannot see the smoke of another.' President Kruger (1825-1904) was now serving his fourth term as ruler of the Transvaal. *The Times* spoke of 'an islet of blind, uncompromising conservatism of the mediaeval type' and characterised Paul Kruger's position within it: 'The autocrat of this islet is PRESIDENT KRUGER, who is, doubtless, a very worthy man according to his lights, but who was unfortunately born at least a hundred years too late.' With a dry and precise humour Kruger began a speech to the inhabitants of the Transvaal in strict order of precedence: 'Burghers, friends, thieves, murderers, newcomers, and others'. It was the plight of the newcomers that eventually caused the war.

Shiploads of troops left for South Africa on the outbreak of hostilities. As correspondent to the *Morning Post*, Winston Churchill (1874-1965) was among the first. His despatches appeared also as books in May and October 1900: 'all Southampton was cheering wildly along a mile of pier and promontory when at 6 p.m. on October 14, the Royal Mail steamer Dunottar Castle left her moorings and sailed with Sir Redvers Buller for the Cape.' Conan Doyle lists some of the commanders: 'never in picturesque days of old did a more knightly company ride in the forefront of England's battle.' Queen Victoria had wished Kitchener to be in command from the outset; again she was probably right, though she wrote to him that South Africa would be a very different matter from the Sudan. Buller (1839-1908) arrived in Cape Town at the end of October, and already the situation was serious: Kimberley, Mafeking and Ladysmith were three small towns the Boers were determined to secure. Buller's instructions in London were to take Bloemfontein and then strike at Pretoria. He now felt he must divide his forces and make for the beleaguered towns. Cecil Rhodes was at Kimberley and Baden-Powell (1857-1941) at Mafeking, to name those most vividly remembered for good or ill. Conan Doyle has reservations about Rhodes, magnificently commemorated with a copy of the dynamic 'Physical Energy' statue by Watts (the original is in Kensington Gardens): 'That great man has done good service to the Queen both before and since, but it must be a prejudiced admirer who will not acknowledge that our position in Africa would in some respects have been stronger had he never devoted his energy to Imperial Politics.'

With characteristic impatience Churchill was at the front in no time, combatant and correspondent in one. On 14 November he joined an expedition on one of the threatened railways: 'An armoured train! The very name sounds strange; a locomotive designed as a knight-errant; the agent of civilisation in the habiliments of chivalry. Mr.Morley attired as Sir Lancelot would seem scarcely more incongruous.' Ambush awaited them:

Paul Kruger in
Vanity Fair

The long brown rattling serpent with the rifles bristling from its spotted sides crawled closer to the rocky hillock on which the scattered black figures of the enemy showed clearly. Suddenly three wheeled things appeared on the crest, and within a second a bright flash of light - like a heliograph, but much yellower - opened and shut ten or twelve times.

After valiant attempts to continue the journey, Churchill was a prisoner: 'And then, above the rain storm that beat loudly on the corrugated iron, I heard the sound of a chaunt. The Boers were singing their evening psalm, and the menacing notes - more full of indignant war than love and mercy - struck a chill into my heart.'

Churchill was chaffed by his captors: ' "Oh no, old chappie, you can never beat us. Look at Mafeking. We have taken Mafeking. You will find Baden Powell waiting for you at Pretoria. Kimberley, too, will fall this week. Rhodes is trying to escape in a balloon, disguised as a woman - a fine woman." Great merriment at this. "What about Ladysmith?" "Ten days. Ten days more and then we shall have some whisky".' This was far from the truth, but the English newspapers were guilty of making siege epics from the stories of the three towns, which were suffering more from boredom than excitement, more from discomfort than from imminent danger. Churchill in captivity enlarges on one of the reasons the war perhaps had to be fought: ' "Educate a Kaffir! Ah, that's you English all over. No, no, old chappie. We educate 'em with a stick. Treat 'em with humanity and consideration - I like that. They were put here by the God Almighty to work for us. We'll keep them in their proper places".'

Churchill came to an important decision within a month, writing a note of farewell on 10 December to the Secretary of War, South African Republic: 'Sir, - I have the honour to inform you that as I do not consider that your Government have any right to detain me as a military prisoner, I have decided to escape from your custody.' This he did, adroitly and successfully. He had one consolation: 'no one in the world knew where he was'; nor did he know himself. His sole companion 'was a gigantic vulture, who manifested an extravagant interest in his condition and made hideous and ominous gurglings from time to time'. After he had reached safety, a telegram came from London dated 30 December 1899: 'Best friends here hope you won't go making further ass of yourself.'

On 4 January 1900 Elgar wrote to Jaeger about arrival of the printed score of the 'Enigma' Variations: 'I rcd. *the* score all safely & some odd parts for all of which thanks: how lovely the score looks, I am so delighted with it & only wish it were a harbinger of peace & good will - but -'. The Variations were the first major Elgar work to appear in full score from Novello. Meanwhile the situation in South Africa was not encouraging. While Churchill was on the run, the Boers had been notably successful, as

Churchill escaping by Joseph Nash jnr.

Conan Doyle makes clear: 'The week which extended from December 10th to December 17th, 1899, was the blackest one known during our generation, and the most disastrous for British arms during this century. We had in the short space of seven days lost, beyond all extenuation or excuse, three separate actions.'

Conan Doyle was scathing about the methods of the British commanders: they seemed more suitable for 'hill tribes & such like': 'Our own loose formations, our adherence to volley firing, and in this instance the use of our artillery all seem to be legacies of our savage wars.' He broadened his criticisms:

> There may be a science of war in the lecture room at Camberley, but very little of it found its way to the veldt. The slogging valour of the private, the careless dash of the regimental officer - these were our military assets - but seldom the care and foresight of our commanders. It is a thankless task to make such comments, but the one great lesson of the war has been that the army is too vital a thing to fall into the hands of a caste.

But Conan Doyle's most deadly scorn was reserved for the European powers that rejoiced in every British setback: 'It is singular to glance at the extracts from the European press at that time and to observe the delight and foolish exultation with which our reverses were received.' He could partly excuse the French, the Russians, and the Vatican:

> That this should occur in the French journals is not unnatural, since our history has been largely a contest with that Power, and we can regard with complacency an enmity which is the tribute to our success. Russia, too, as the least progressive of European States, has a natural antagonism of thought, if not of interests, to the Power which stands most prominently for individual freedom and liberal institutions. The same poor excuse may be made for the organs of the Vatican.

Germany's hostility seemed to Doyle incomprehensible: 'But what are we to say of the insensate railing of Germany, a country whose ally we have been for centuries? In the days of Marlborough, in the darkest hours of Frederick the Great, in the great world struggle of Napoleon, we have been the brothers-in-arms of these people.' More recent history might have offered an explanation and warned Doyle that German unification, whether under Otto Bismarck or indeed Helmut Kohl, would fundamentally affect affairs in Europe.

At the beginning of the new century chivalry still flourished, and Conan Doyle was quick to recognise it in a Boer commander, Piet Joubert (1834-1900): 'He came from that French Huguenot blood which has strengthened and refined every race which it has touched, and from it he derived a chivalry and generosity which made him respected and liked even by his opponents.' At home, too, there was heart-warming assurance:

> But if there were any who doubted that this ancient nation still glowed with the spirit of its youth his fears must soon have passed away. For this far-distant war, a war of the unseen foe and of the murderous ambuscade, there were so many volunteers that the authorities were embarrassed by their numbers and their pertinacity. It was a stimulating sight to see those long queues of top-hatted frock-coated young men who waited their turn for the orderly room with as much desperate anxiety as if hard fare, a veldt bed, and Boer bullets were all that life had that was worth the holding. Especially the Imperial Yeomanry, a corps of riders and shots, appealed to the sporting instincts of our race.

It was the three small towns under siege that dominated interest at home. Churchill described Ladysmith as 'a twenty-acre patch of tin houses and blue gum trees, but famous to the uttermost ends of the earth'. He recounts an attempt to raise the spirits of the besieged town:

> That night we tried to congratulate or encourage Ladysmith, and the searchlight perseveringly flashed the Morse code on the clouds. But before it had been working half an hour the Boer searchlight saw it and hurried to interfere, flickering, blinking, and crossing to try to confuse the dots and dashes, and appeared to us who watched this curious aerial battle - Briton and Boer fighting each other in the sky with vibrations of ether - to confuse them effectually.

The main threat to the garrison was the Boer artillery, but it was capriciously used. There might be a bombardment of ferocious accuracy followed by days of comparative idleness: on Christmas Day the Boers fired Christmas puddings at the town. Buller failed repeatedly to relieve the town, but Churchill overheard two artillerymen: 'Said one: "We ought to have the Queen up here, in her little donkey carriage." "Ah, we'd do it all right then," replied his comrade.'

There were four possible courses for the Boers. They might bombard Ladysmith into submission, which they failed to do for lack of concentrated effort; they could take it by storm, a form of fighting to which they were least suited; they might so invest the place that famine must ensue; they could wait for disease to do their work. In the end Buller broke through on 28 February 1900, and the following day Alice Elgar noted: 'E. to Links. Ladysmith relieved.' On 2 March she could add: 'Sent Ist part of "Dream of Gerontius" to Novello. Town decorated.'

Winston Churchill gives a superb account of his approach to Ladysmith:

Never shall I forget that ride. The evening was deliciously cool. My horse was strong and fresh, for I had changed him at midday. The ground was rough with many stones, but we cared little for that. Beyond the next ridge, or the rise beyond that, or around the corner of the hill, was Ladysmith - the goal of all our hopes and ambitions during weeks of almost ceaseless fighting.

Steadily he rode on, 'wildly, recklessly, up and down hill, over the boulders, through the scrub'. At last it was Ladysmith: 'We turned the shoulder of a hill, and there before us lay the tin houses and dark trees we had come so far to see and save.'

The relieving army entered Ladysmith on 3 March at 11 a.m., with Sir Redvers Buller at the head. But it was not quite the force the defenders expected to see, as Churchill explains:

All through the morning and on into the afternoon the long stream of men and guns flowed through the streets of Ladysmith, and all marvelled to see what manner of men these were - dirty, war-worn, travel-stained, tanned, their uniforms in tatters, their boots falling to pieces, their helmets dinted and broken, but nevertheless magnificent soldiers, striding along, deep-chested and broad-shouldered, with the light of triumph in their eyes and the blood of fighting ancestors in their veins. It was a procession of lions.

Kimberley had less strategic value than Ladysmith, but the De Beers diamond mines were there, and so was Cecil Rhodes, who arrived on 13 October 1899, two days before the siege began. Conan Doyle contrasts scrub and diamonds: 'There might almost seem to be some subtle connection between the barrenness and worthlessness of a surface and the value of the minerals which lie beneath it.' He elaborates the point later: 'Kimberley was unique, the centre of the richest tract of ground for its size in the whole world. Its loss would have been a heavy blow to the British cause, and an enormous encouragement to the Boers.' He proceeds to enlarge on his view of Cecil Rhodes, whose capture would also have been a glittering prize:

This remarkable man who stands for the future of South Africa as clearly as the Dopper Boer stands for its past, has, both in features and in character, some traits which may, without extravagance, be called Napoleonic. The restless energy, the fertility of resource, the attention to detail, the power of terse comment - all these recall the great emperor. So does the simplicity of private life in the midst of excessive wealth. And so finally does a want of scruple where an ambition is to be furthered.

For the assistance of Colonel Robert Kekewich, in charge of the Kimberley garrison, De Beers had raised an irregular force of 3000, the largest contingent among the defenders. Rhodes felt this gave him a proportionate authority in the town. Conflict between Rhodes and Kekewich was inevitable. The *Times* exacerbated the situation by its use of the siege diary written by the Hon.Mrs.Rochfort Maguire, a close friend of Rhodes. She extolled the 'wonderful fruit gardens and long vine-covered walks' created by Rhodes. Otherwise Kimberley was dreary: 'The town itself is exceedingly unattractive, dry and dusty, no fine buildings, and the houses mostly miserable tin shanties.' Mrs.Maguire notes the food situation: 'Horseflesh was first served out on January 8, and from that date on it became almost the staple food of the white and coloured population. Towards the end we had a few mules and donkeys thrown in, which were pronounced a great treat; but we never had recourse to dogs or cats.' When supplies became shorter still, Rhodes started a soup kitchen.

Conan Doyle remained guarded in his view of Rhodes, differing from Mrs.Maguire and therefore from the British press: 'it is a fact that the town would have been more united, and therefore stronger, without his presence. Colonel Kekewich and his chief staff officer, Major O'Meara, were as much plagued by intrigue within as by the Boers without.' Indeed there came a moment when Lord Roberts (1832-1914), who had arrived in Cape Town on 10 January 1900 in overall command with Lord Kitchener as his number two, authorised Kekewich to arrest Rhodes should he continue to prove impossible. As at Ladysmith, there was indiscriminate bombardment of Kimberley: 'The shells, following the evil precedent of the Germans in 1870, were fired not at the forts, but into the thickly populated city.' Relief came on 15 February, with mounted New Zealanders prominent among the advanced guard. Conan Doyle thought that was extraordinary enough: 'Macaulay in his wildest dream of the future of the much-quoted New-Zealander never pictured him as heading a rescue force for the relief of a British town in the heart of Africa.'

It was the siege of Mafeking that most fully caught the public imagination in England, partly because it lasted longest, a total of 217 days. Colonel Robert Baden-Powell was in charge almost by mistake. He should have been raising regiments in Bechuanaland and Rhodesia: instead he was at Mafeking, sitting tight. Conan Doyle had keen admiration for him:

> In the Matabele campaign he had out-scouted the savage scouts and found his pleasure in tracking them among their native mountains, often alone and at night, trusting in his skill in springing from rock to rock in his rubber-soled shoes to save him from their pursuit. There was a brain quality in his bravery which is rare among our officers. Full of veldt craft and resource, it was as difficult to outwit as it was to outfight him.

His resource seamed limitless:

> From drawing caricatures with both hands simultaneously, or skirt
> dancing, to leading a forlorn hope, nothing came amiss to him; and he had
> that magnetic quality by which the leader imparts some of his virtues to his
> men. Such was the man who held Mafeking for the Queen.

Nor was Victoria unappreciative: 'I continue watching with confidence and
admiration the patient and resolute defence which is so gallantly
maintained under your ever resourceful command.'

Yet was there also a hint of the Malvern composer, strangely military
in appearance but sensitive to his finger ends, and now occupied with the
mysterious truths of his masterpiece? As English readers could know from
the *Times*, Colonel Baden-Powell also needed communion with the
natural world around him:

> In the noisy day he yearns for the noiseless night, in which he can slip into
> the vistas of the veldt, an unobtrusive spectator of the mystic communion
> of tree with tree, of twilight with darkness, of land with water, of early morn
> with fading night, with the music of the journeying winds to speak to him
> and to lull his thoughts. As he makes his way across our lines the watchful
> sentry strains his eyes a little more to keep the figure of the colonel before
> him, until the undulations of the veldt conceal his progress. He goes in the
> privacy of the night, when it is no longer a season of moonlight, when,
> although the stars are full, the night is dim.

Messages of relief to come arrived from General Roberts and, as Conan
Doyle commented: 'if trouble may be allayed by sympathy, then theirs
should have lain lightly. The attention of the whole empire had centred
upon them, and even the advance of Roberts's army became secondary to
the fate of this gallant struggling handful of men who had upheld the flag
so long.' The *Times* correspondent wondered how much longer the siege
would last: 'We have not yet equalled the siege of Azoth, which Herodotus
tells us lasted for 29 years, nor come within appreciable measure of the
siege of Troy.'

Roberts and Kitchener now put into operation the plan originally
conceived for Sir Redvers Buller. They would take Bloemfontein,
Johannesburg and Pretoria as well as relieving the last of the three towns.
Mafeking's turn came on 17 May 1900.

Conan Doyle describes the overwhelming joy that seized the English-
speaking world :

> Many who had looked at their maps and saw this spot isolated in the very
> heart of Africa had despaired of ever reaching their heroic fellow-

The Queen and Munshi hear dispatches

countrymen, and now one universal outbreak of joy-bells and bonfires from Toronto to Melbourne proclaimed that there is no spot so inaccessible that the long arm of the empire cannot reach it when her children are in peril.

So it was in 1900, and Alice Elgar responded accordingly on 19 May: 'Heard of relief of Mafeking. Joy - Flags.' Elgar himself was in Hereford and wrote more guardedly to Jaeger the next day: 'I'm glad you're enjoying the hawful spirits of us - I was in Hereford yesterday and the folks were really mad I think.' But Mafeking caused an upsurge of interest in *The Banner of St.George*, with some outlandish publicity material. Elgar added a postscript to a letter of 1 June to Jaeger about it: 'I can't help (it'll only cost the firm 1d. stamp to return the packet) sending you the enclosed whole *bag of tricks re* St.George - it has amused us vastly. also the flag-tickets, bills & general mild excitement.'

It now seemed as if the war was entering its final stages. Conan Doyle could not forgive Paul Kruger:

> It is heart-sickening to think of the butchery, the misery, the irreparable losses, the blood of men, and the bitter tears of women, all of which might have been spared had one obstinate and ignorant man been persuaded to allow the State which he ruled to conform to the customs of every other civilised State upon the earth.

Lord Roberts had entered Bloemfontein on 13 March 1900 and remained there six weeks. The pressing need was to re-establish railway communication with the Cape. But Conan Doyle mentions another reason why the army remained static until 1 May: 'This long delay was absolutely necessary in order to supply the place of the ten thousand horses and mules which are said to have been used up in the severe work of the preceding month.' Much occupied with his medical work at Bloemfontein, Conan Doyle had nevertheless only admiration for the behaviour and restraint of the troops: 'The most stringent orders were issued against looting or personal violence, but nothing could exceed the gentleness and good humour of the troops. Indeed there seemed more need for an order which should protect them against the extortion of their conquered enemies.'

Churchill describes the extraordinary mix of men now gathered in Bloemfontein:

> It is five o'clock in the afternoon. The Market-square is crowded with officers and soldiers listening to the band of the Buffs. Every regiment in the service, every Colony in the Empire is represented; all clad in uniform khaki, but distinguished by extraordinary variety of badges.

Churchill considered each conversing group a sample of imperial federation: 'The City Volunteer talks to a Queensland Mounted Infantryman, who hands his matchbox to a private of the line. A Bushman from New Zealand, a Cambridge undergraduate, and a tea-planter from Ceylon stroll up and make the conversation general.' While talk turned to the likely duration of the war, Lord Roberts appeared:

> The conversation stops abruptly. Everyone looks round. Strolling across the middle of the square, quite alone, was a very small grey-haired gentleman, with extremely broad shoulders and a most unbending back. He wore a staff cap with a broad red band and a heavy gold-laced peak, brown riding boots, a tightly-fastened belt, and no medals, orders, or insignia of any kind. But no one doubted his identity for an instant, and I knew that I was looking at the Queen's greatest subject.

It seemed to Conan Doyle that April in Bloemfontein that 'the real glories of the British race lie in the future, not in the past. The Empire walks, and may still walk, with an uncertain step, but with every year its tread will be firmer, for its weakness is that of waxing youth and not of waning age.' Elgar would have concurred, at any rate for a few years yet. But Conan Doyle the doctor was now at full stretch:

> All through the campaign, while the machinery for curing disease was excellent, that for preventing it was elementary or absent. If bad water can cost us more than all the bullets of the enemy, then surely it is worth our while to make the drinking of unboiled water a stringent military offence, and to attach to every company and squadron the most rapid and efficient means for boiling it - for filtering alone is useless. An incessant trouble it would be, but it would have saved a division of the army.

Churchill noted 'a handsome building surrounded in the classic style by tall white pillars, and, surmounted by a lofty dome'. It looked like 'a Parliament House, but for the Red Cross flag which flies from the summit and proclaims that, whatever may have been its former purposes, the spacious hall within is at last devoted to the benefit of humankind'.

On the way to Johannesburg the troops passed the area of greatest wealth to South Africa, as noted by Conan Doyle:

> This long distant hill was the famous Rand, and under its faded grasses lay such riches as Solomon never took from Ophir. It was the prize of victory; and yet the prize is not to the victor, for the dust-grimed officers and men looked with little personal interest at this treasure-house of the world. Not one penny the richer would they be for the fact that their blood and their energy had brought justice and freedom to the gold fields.

The astonishing wealth of the area was surrendered without a battle by the Boers, and on the last day of May the British army entered Johannesburg. Doyle was both exultant and cautionary:

> Upon May 31st, without violence to life or destruction to property, that great town which British hands have done so much to build found itself at last under the British flag. May it wave there so long as it covers just laws, honest officials, and clean-handed administrators - so long and no longer!

There was no lingering at Johannesburg: the ultimate prize was to be the capture of Pretoria, made indeed with little extra effort on 5 June. Churchill describes the scene:

> At two o'clock Lord Roberts, the staff, and the foreign attachés entered the town and proceeded to the central square, wherein the Town Hall, the Parliament House, and other public buildings are situated. The British flag was hoisted over the Parliament House amid some cheers. The victorious army then began to parade past it.

Churchill half expected to find President Kruger 'seated on his stoep reading his Bible and smoking a sullen pipe'; but it was quite otherwise. Conan Doyle sums up:

> And now what had come of it all? A handful of faithful attendants, and a fugitive old man, clutching in his flight at his papers and his moneybags. The last of the old-world Puritans, he departed poring over his well-thumbed Bible, and proclaiming that the troubles of his country arose, not from his own narrow and corrupt administration, but from some departure on the part of his fellow burghers from the strict tenets of the dopper sect. So Paul Kruger passed out from the active history of the world.

The hope now was that the Boers would sue for peace and the war would be over within the year. It was not to be, and the Boers now instituted a long-drawn-out guerilla warfare that maintained hostilities into the next reign and over two more years. How significant was it that Elgar finished composition of *The Dream of Gerontius* on 6 June? At the time it would have been difficult to say. On 3 August 1900, the day Elgar completed the orchestration, Alice Elgar wrote to Mrs.Kilburn: 'It seems to me that E. has given a real message of consolation to the world.' So it has proved.

Churchill, before leaving South Africa, summed up the first stage of the war:

By the unbroken success of his strategy Lord Roberts had laid the Boer Republic low. We had taken possession of the Rand, the bowels whence the hostile Government drew nourishment in gold and munitions of war. He had seized the heart at Bloemfontein, the brain at Pretoria. The greater part of the railways, the veins and nerves, that is to say, was in our hands. Yet, though mortally injured, the trunk still quivered.

Conan Doyle pays his tribute to the state of the troops:

> Lean and hard, inured to warfare, and far from every temptation of wine or women, the British troops at this stage of the campaign were in such training, and marched so splendidly, that the infantry was often little slower than the cavalry.

But an entirely new situation was developing, and the view of Jan Smuts (1870-1950) was prevailing among the apparently defeated: 'that guerilla war was better suited to the genius of the Boer people than regular field operations'. The Boers found the leaders they needed, Christian De Wet (1854-1922) and Johan De La Rey (1847-1914).

The new conditions were quickly demonstrated, as reported in the *Times* at the beginning of July: 'And so it was that, after General Baden-Powell with his column had marched on towards Pretoria, we, a mere post, holding the important town of Rustenburg on the line of communications, suddenly found ourselves threatened by armed Boers, who, like Roderick Dhu's warriors, seemed to spring from the rocks.' Walter Scott's *Lady of the Lake* had provided accurate parallel (Canto Fifth. The Combat. IX):

> Instant, through copse and heath, arose
> Bonnets and spears and bended bows;
> On right, on left, above, below,
> Sprung up at once the lurking foe.

De Wet's aim was to disrupt British communications, and his capture became increasingly important. It seemed in mid-August as if this would be a certainty at Oliphant's Nek; but the *Times* takes up the dismal story:

> It seemed now as if nothing could save the Boer convoy, English generals being on all sides, and the only road of escape being held by General Baden-Powell. At 2.30 came the awful news. De Wet had found Oliphant's Nek open and was now marching out. No one can describe the feelings of both officers and men. Here we had been enduring forced marches, heavy days of fighting, privations of all sorts, including want of food and blankets, but of these we had thought nothing when we believed that at last we had our man. And then to find that the bird had flown!

Plans for the 1900 Hereford festival had been laid before it was realised how long the war would drag on. Hubert Parry had been commissioned to write a 'Thanksgiving Te Deum'; this was 'to commemorate the noble achievements of the British Forces in South Africa'. For the *Musical Times* of 1 September 1900 Jaeger described it as 'hewn in granite, noble structures erected in the architectural style of Bach, a wealth of new thought expressed in the beautiful classical language bequeathed to us by the immortal Leipzig cantor'. He was less complimentary when writing to Elgar about it on 12 July: 'Parry! oh. Parry!! very much Parry!!! Toujours Parry!!!! Fiddles sawing all the time!!!!! DEAR old Parry!!!!!! Now if you could compose & Skoughre like that!!' Stanford also produced an appropriate work for Hereford. This was a setting of *The Last Post*, a poem by W.E.Henley (1849-1903). Elgar was represented by his *Te Deum and Benedictus* of three years previously and by the wonderfully unwarlike Scene 3 of *Caractacus*.

For the Birmingham festival at which *The Dream of Gerontius* was first performed on 5 October, Parry had written *The Soldier's Tent*, a scena for baritone and orchestra, to be sung by Plunket Greene (1865-1936), also participating in the Elgar. The words were from *The Bard of Dombovitza*, translated by Alma Strettell and Carmen Sylva. At Birmingham it went reasonably well and was also an acknowledgment of British warfare far away. But with his *De Profundis* he suffered almost as much as Elgar. Parry's diary of 29 September expresses his irritation: 'To rehearsal in afternoon. Elgar's Dream of Gerontius gave a vast amount of trouble and kept chorus and orchestra at work till past 5.30. No use trying to get anything out of "De Profundis" with them all tired out.' The result was a 'Terrible performance of "De Profundis". Ist sopranos came in a bar too soon in the opening passage and ruined it. And it all went as flabbily as possible. Nothing to be got out of the chorus by any means.' So Elgar was not the only victim. Deep depression followed the *Gerontius* débâcle, but Elgar was reluctantly returning to form by 26 October, when he wrote to Jaeger: 'Seriously, my dear friend, look at the position: e.g. - I'm asked to write something for the Phil: - well I've practically got a Concert overture ready: the P. wont pay anything.' He then went into the finances, postulating a net loss: 'Now what's the good of it?   Nobody else will perform the thing - if I take it to your firm they might print the strings but the result wd. be the same.' By 4 November he was more cheerful: 'Don't say anything about the prospective overture yet - I call it "Cockayne" & it's cheerful and Londony - "stout and steaky".'

Among those who suffered from enteric fever and eventually died at Pretoria in October 1900 was Prince Christian Victor of Schleswig-Holstein, whose mother was Princess Helena, third daughter of Queen Victoria. The prince was a professional soldier in the 60th Rifles, who at 31 had been on

Kitchener's staff during the lead-up to Omdurman and Khartoum in 1898. His death was noted by the Queen in her journal of 1 November 1900, when she was still at Balmoral. She went to a memorial service at Crathie church in the same year as she had mourned her second son, Alfred:

> This morning the beloved boy was to be laid to rest, with the soldiers he loved so well, and there were to be services at St.George's Chapel and at the Chapel Royal. We went at twelve to the church here, where there was a simple touching service, much the same as we had for dear Affie at Osborne. I was much moved. A great number of people were present, all the neighbours, and my own people, who show the greatest feeling. The sun was shining brightly, which was very pleasant, and made it less gloomy, but my tears flowed again and again.

It was also an occasion for Victoria to write to Lord Kitchener on 16 November 1900: 'The Queen knows how fond Lord Kitchener was of our darling Christian Victor, who was much attached to Lord Kitchener.' She continued in sorrow: 'The Queen feels much upset and shaken by this event and the loss of her grandson who was very useful to her, and at whose birth she was present. The war drags on, which is very trying.'

At the end of that November Lord Roberts left for England and Kitchener was in command. There was much to do in reorganising his forces, a task that took two months. But such was the optimism in Pretoria that the *Times* correspondent could write on 21 January 1901:

> The war drama itself was over, but there remained the epilogue. This epilogue - very different as it was from the play proper - required that the stage should be reset and the properties rearranged. This task demanded both time and hard work. So the curtain was rung down, and the audience - that is, the public - had to wait while Stage Manager Lord Kitchener and his staff of generals and brigadiers prepared the stage for the last great scene of all. And now everything is ready.

Kitchener's scheme for bringing the guerilla war to an end was then explained:

> For the purposes of the new plan of campaign the whole area affected by guerilla warfare has been treated as a military chess board, and the squares will be covered by groups of brigades, to every unit of which a clearly defined area of operation has been allotted. Each brigade has its own ground to cover and will move in an arranged direction, clearing the ground as it goes.

On 23 November 1900 Alice Elgar reported that her husband had equipped himself with a 'Trombone study'. In the postscript to a Jaeger letter of 7 December Elgar declared, 'I'm learning the Trombone'; and for good value he drew a massively concentrated self-portrait and a note emerging from the instrument *fffz* and *diminuendo*. References to the instrument multiply in correspondence and diary. On Christmas Eve Elgar wrote to Martina Hyde, and added near the end of a mainly business letter: 'I am learning the trombone.' On 8 February Mrs.Elgar reported to Jaeger news of a remarkable musical occasion: Der Tondichter & I have just been playing 'Nimrod' as a duet for *Trombone* & piano!' At the end of the letter she appended an excuse for her 'most curious & unliterary English The trombone must have scattered my Senses somewhat.' When Elgar wrote to Joseph Bennett in anticipation of *Cockaigne*'s first performance, he was now the avowed trombonist:

> The work is in regular form somewhat extended: in the 'working-out part' sundry contrapuntal japes occur, and certainly a military band passes, but there's nothing to give the astucious mystagogue (that's you as analyst!) much trouble in describing. As I play the trombone myself the parts for this family are rather more dressed than usual, I think, so if you would be well advised you might hear it, by telephone, at 109, Finchley-road.

Queen Victoria died on 22 January 1901, and Elgar ended his letter to Jaeger of the same day, 'God save the King!' Almost her last thoughts had been for South Africa: ' "What news is there from Lord Kitchener ? What has been happening in S.Africa?" ' Kitchener was much exercised by the size of the country, which seemed to swallow up all his troops. On 23 February the *Times* gave a vivid account of the problem:

> As a matter of fact, none of the guerillas still carrying on the struggle south of the Vaal show any inclination to fight. They are just like quicksilver. They gather, and as soon as an armed body comes into contact with them they disperse to the four winds, to gather again at some distant centre. This is the whole secret of the prolonged hostilities. There is no enemy with sufficient cohesion or confidence to risk an engagement, and the whole of the Imperial resources are frittered away in the pursuit of phantom commandos ever dissolving like the mirage of the South African veldt. These commandos will gather to overwhelm a small detached post or to capture a train. Then, having divided the spoil, they turn their prisoners adrift and scatter, to concentrate 50 miles away from the scene of their success.

It seemed on 28 February as if there might be a chance to end the war. Mrs. Louis Botha, wife of the Transvaal commandant-general had come to Pretoria some days before with a proposal that Botha (1862-1919) and Kitchener should meet. Kitchener leapt at the opportunity and proposed generous peace terms, having to yield only on his wish to secure the vote for the indigenous black population. His aim was to secure a stable South Africa, with Boer and Briton in equilibrium. Joseph Chamberlain (1836-1914) as colonial secretary rejected the terms, and the war continued. Kitchener expressed his frustration to St.John Brodrick (1856-1942) at the Foreign Office: 'We are now carrying the war on to put 2-300 Dutchmen in prison at the end of it. It seems to me absurd and wrong, and I wonder the Chancellor of the Exchequer did not have a fit.' In England Lloyd George (1863-1945) pointed a nice distinction between Chamberlain and Kitchener: 'There was a soldier who knew what war meant; he strove to make peace. There was another man, who strolled among his orchids 6,000 miles from the deadly bark of the Mauser rifle. He stopped Kitchener's peace!'

At the beginning of 1901 Elgar was revising *Froissart* for publication of the full score, and wrote to Jaeger about it on 12 January: 'I am sending you all the Froissart I have - what jolly *healthy* stuff it is - quite shameless in its rude young health! deary me! was I ever like that?' About the Keats epigraph he wrote: 'Put the Motter where you darn please - I wanted it everywhere.' The same letter makes clear that chivalry would be lifting up her lance again in more of Elgar's 1901 music: 'In haste & joyful (Gosh! man I've got a tune in my head).' Which was probably the first hint of the trio tune in *Pomp and Circumstance* March no.1. 'Dorabella' of the 'Enigma' Variations heard it on 10 May, as she reported in *Memories of a Variation*: ' "Child, come up here. I've got a tune that will knock 'em - knock 'em flat", and he played the Military March No.1 in D. I *was* thrilled; the whole thing carried one along so splendidly.' Elgar indicated the off-key start on E flat; and then ' "Talk of jokes - what about the trombones here" - pointing to a passage - "they'll have some fun!" ' And Dorabella ended her diary for the day: 'Nice evening. Heard Cockaigne and the Quick Marches. Oh! my goodness - for a Military Band!!' It gave Jaeger much pleasure that the first German performance of the 'Enigma' Variations should be in his native Düsseldorf, on 7 February 1901. He wrote about it four days later, mentioning the German attitude to the Boer conflict: 'I hope & believe that this will be the beginning of the Variations' tour through Germany. I was so glad to see or hear that the D'dorf audience did not let its *political* bias darken its judgement of an English work of art.' Elgar responded the next day: 'I'm really glad they did not hiss Buths.' Far from it.

From May 1901 Kitchener was Acting High Commissioner in South Africa, in command of politics and the war. It was during this stage of his duties that Kitchener had to face press and public disquiet over the 'concentration camps', to which Boer women and children were sent as result of a scorched-earth policy to bring the Boers to their knees. Conditions were unhygienic and there were many unnecessary deaths, but agitation in England was aiding the Boer cause. The *Times* sprang to Kitchener's defence: 'It is the right of British subjects to be tried by their peers, and it is not fair that people who have never seen a tent except with strawberries and cream inside should judge Boer refugee camps by an English drawing-room standard.' By now Kitchener was weary of the war; as he wrote to Lord Roberts in October 1901: 'I think I hate the country, the people, the whole thing, more every day.' But in the midst of his frustration he devised policies that brought the war to an end within six months. He had blockhouses built to divide the veldt into paddocks and connected them with barbed wire and telegraph; he formed two regiments from surrendered Boers: he no longer brought civilians into 'concentration' camps; he armed 16,000 Africans. After tortuous negotiations skilfully masterminded by Kitchener, peace came eventually on 31 May 1902.

The première of the *Pomp and Circumstance* Marches was given in Liverpool under Alfred Rodewald (1861-1903) on 19 October 1901. Three days later Henry Wood (1869-1944) gave them in London, and the effect was electric. Arnold Bax (1883-1953) described it as

> the night that Queen's Hall was invaded by one of London's most stupendous fogs. Sir Henry's back and the faces of the orchestral players were as figments in the baseless fabric of a dream. At the end of *Land of Hope and Glory* there arose such a heartening din as could never before have startled Queen's Hall. The very fog was disturbed into dense and delirious whorls and eddies. It seemed to me that the excitement would never abate.

Henry Wood on the rostrum was of the same impression and had to take a measure he was never to repeat, as he recounted in *My Life of Music* :

> I shall never forget the scene at the close of the first of them - the one in D major. The people simply rose and yelled. I had to play it again - with the same result; in fact, they refused to let me go on with the programme. After considerable delay, while the audience roared its applause, I went off and fetched Harry Dearth who was to sing *Hiawatha's Vision* (Coleridge-Taylor); but they would not listen. Merely to restore order, I played the march a third time. And that, I may say, was the one and only time in the history of the Promenade concerts that an orchestral item was accorded a double encore. Little did I think then that the lovely, broad melody of the

trio would one day develop into our second national anthem - *Land of Hope and Glory*.

With characteristic showmanship and good sense, Wood had reversed the order of the two marches, so that Stanford referred to them accordingly when writing to Elgar on 22 November, a month later:

> I was up aloft in the Gallery. I found myself in a minority in liking No 1 better than No 2 - for which you may curse me or not as you like. Anyhow the public like the other best: it is their affair, & you have translated Master Rudyard Kipling into Music in No 2 certainly, & said 'blooming beggar' in quite his style. (He always reads (but does not print) those two words in a less polite fashion!) Anyhow they both came off like blazes, & are uncommon fine stuff.

Novello was concerned and Jaeger was vexed that the marches were to be published by Boosey. He urged on 26 October that the rest of the series should come to Novello; meanwhile nos.1 and 2 besieged him:

> The beastly things are worrying me into an illness. The Tunes, damn them, Keep buzzing in my empty head, & the orchestral effects, harmonies & all your Monkey tricks dance about & within me.

Edward VII lost no time in stamping an architectural presence on the start of his reign. He instigated in 1901 the Queen Victoria Memorial Scheme, for which Aston Webb (1849-1930) won the competition. The Mall was much altered. Laid out originally by Charles II (1660-85) as an avenue with four rows of trees, it was greatly widened by Webb. Gradually his plan took shape, involving the Admiralty Arch to the east, the statue group in memory of Queen Victoria by Thomas Brock (1847-1922) as focus of the Parisian *rond-point* in front of Buckingham Palace, which also acquired a new façade. The splendour and opulence of the scheme was a fitting introduction to the reign; Elgar was equally to exert himself in the *Coronation Ode*, planned to celebrate the crowning of the king in June 1902 as fitting climax to the festivities marking the end of the Boer War. Elgar had been introduced to his librettist, A.C.Benson (1862-1925), Eton schoolmaster and son of the former Archbishop of Canterbury, by Sir Walter Parratt (1841-1924), organist of St.George's, Windsor, and Master of the King's Music. Benson and Elgar were working on the plan at the end of 1901. Benson wrote a detailed letter on 3 December, outlining the numbers he would write. Words for the bass solo were already done and clearly based on reports of fighting in the Boer War:

> See that thy squadrons haste, when loosed are the hounds of hell: -
> Then shall the eye flash fire, and the valorous heart grow light,
> Under the drifting smoke, and the scream of the flying shell,
> When the hillside hisses with death, - and never a foe in sight.

Then there was the question of the finale. Elgar wanted to introduce the trio tune of *Pomp and Circumstance* no.1. Jaeger feared any words would 'sound downright vulgar' but Elgar was not deflected and Benson was willing to try: 'A finale on the lines you indicate - though the metre is a hard one - if you could string together a few nonsense words, just to show me how you would wish them to run, I would construct it, following the air closely.' So was 'Land of Hope and Glory' born. Organ and military band were to be added to the *Ode*'s large symphonic orchestra. Elgar described the bass solo as 'frankly military, or rather naval & military & means "fight".' At the text's 'Strong to arise and go, if ever the war-trump peal' Elgar made a marginal note: 'Trumpets, Cornets Trombones &c. (as much brass at this pitch as possible)'. Not for nothing was he son-in-law to Sir Henry Gee Roberts; not for nothing had he learnt the trombone; not for nothing was he to see himself as a troubadour 'turned on to step in front of an army and inspire the people with a song'. As motto for the *Pomp and Circumstance* Marches he took fiery words by Lord de Tabley (1835-95) :

> Like a proud music that draws men to die
> Madly upon the spears in martial ecstasy,
> A measure that sets heaven in all their veins
> And iron in their hands.
> I hear the Nation march
> Beneath her ensign as an eagle's wing;
> O'er shield and sheeted targe
> The banners of my faith most gaily swing,
> Moving to victory with solemn noise,
> With worship and with conquest, and the voice of myriads.

10 - For Christian service and true chivalry

One of the more remarkable facts about Elgar's 'Apostles' project is that he seems to have had only the vaguest idea of the task's magnitude. He had the superb achievement of *Gerontius* behind him, knew how much of Newman's poem he had needed to cut, had the experience of countless festival oratorios for ready recall, and yet he could not envisage how many words, let alone notes, his initial plan might involve. He was to begin with Christ in the synagogue at Nazareth and end at Antioch, where the disciples were first called Christians. Initially this vast scheme was to be encompassed in a single work. The relentless approach of the 1903 Birmingham festival caused exhaustion and worry as Elgar realised his outline plan could not possibly be realised. Since there was no alternative, Birmingham accommodated the various foreshortenings he suggested. The *Apostles* would now end with the Ascension, any thought of continuing with the church in Jerusalem, let alone the message to the Gentiles, having been abandoned. The scheme was now expanded to three oratorios, of which the second, eventually called *The Kingdom*, was to extend the church to Elgar's goal of Antioch, and a *Last Judgement*, perhaps based mainly on the *Apocalypse* of St.John and *The City of God* by St.Augustine (354-430), would complete the trilogy. Similar crises dogged *The Kingdom* of 1906, so that it ended at the point where Part 1 of the original 'Apostles' should have reached. It was no wonder Elgar could see no further ahead. His Catholic faith was wavering, he was now firmly established as a metropolitan rather than provincial composer, and he owed the world a symphony. Musical bits and pieces for *The Last Judgement* lingered in sketch form as hint that he might some day undertake the work; ultimately it seemed they would have a symphonic destiny of their own, in the no.3 commissioned in 1932 by the BBC.

At what point Elgar decided on William Morris's words from *The Earthly Paradise* as a suitable text to round off his *Apostles* we cannot guess; nor at what stage in his literary explorations he came to know that lengthy and uneven poem. The fact that *The Apostles* ended as it did gave splendid significance to the Elgars' visiting at the conclusion of the 1903 festival the Birmingham church of St.Philip (now the Anglican Cathedral), where they saw not only the glorious *Ascension* of Burne-Jones but the *Last Judgement* at the west end. It was appropriate that the church authorities had turned to Burne-Jones, since he was a Birmingham man. His parents had been married in St.Philip's, and he was christened there.

He and Morris, who was from a more affluent Essex background, met at
Exeter College, Oxford. Admiration for Newman reinforced an intention
to enter the Church; but via Ruskin they came to the Pre-Raphaelites,
eventually seeing *The Return of the Dove to the Ark* (1851) by Millais,
which was on show in Oxford, and Holman Hunt's *The Light of the World*
(1851-3) at the Royal Academy.

Plans to enter the Church were transformed into a scheme for an
Arthurian Brotherhood, based on Malory's *Morte d'Arthur* and Kenelm
Digby's *The Broad Stone of Honour.* Their first important joint project

Mary Magdalene at Simon's door by Rossetti;
Elgar, The Apostles, *'In Caesaria Philippi'*

was under the auspices of Dante Gabriel Rossetti, who described Burne-Jones as 'one of the nicest fellows in Dreamland'. The task was to decorate the debating chamber in the new Oxford Union, now the library. It was the summer of 1857, the year of Elgar's birth, and of General Roberts's involvement in the Indian Mutiny. The subject William Morris chose was 'How Sir Palomydes loved La Belle Iseult with exceeding great love out of measure, and how she loved not him again but rather Sir Tristram.' Burne-Jones treated Merlin and Nimuë, a subject that retained its hold on him at least as late as *The Beguiling of Merlin* (1873-4), now in the Lady Lever Art Gallery, Port Sunlight. Burne-Jones gives a splendid account of the torture Morris might submit to in the service of art:

> For the purposes of our drawing we needed armour, and of a date and design so remote that no examples existed for our use. Therefore Morris, whose knowledge of these things seemed to have been born in him, and who never at any time needed books of reference for anything, set to work to make designs for an ancient kind of helmet called a basinet, and for a great surcoat of ringed mail with a hood of mail and the skirt coming below the knees. They were made for him by a stout little smith who had a forge near the Castle.

Burne-Jones describes the sequel in the debating chamber:

> One afternoon when I was working high up at my picture, I heard a strange bellowing in the building, and turning round to find the cause, saw an unwonted sight. The basinet was being tried on, but the visor, for some reason, would not lift, and I saw Morris embedded in iron, dancing with rage and roaring inside. The mail coat came in due time, and was so satisfactory to its designer that the first day it came he chose to dine in it.

It was almost a Pre-Raphaelite habit to marry *de haut en bas*, certainly so in the case of Holman Hunt, Rossetti, and also Morris; Elgar took the opposite path. Morris's first independent home, the 'Red House' designed by Philip Webb (1831-1915) in Kent, was mediaeval in spirit and near the pilgrims' route to Canterbury. Rossetti thought it 'more a poem than a house', and Burne-Jones was much involved in its decoration. The drawing-room walls were decorated with scenes from the romance of Sir Degrevaunt; a cupboard in the hall had Nibelung episodes; and in the lower passage were comical birds and shrubs. Morris himself experimented with stained glass, prophetic of his initial successes with the firm he set up in 1862, with Burne-Jones a main designer. Major commissions came from George Frederick Bodley (1827-1907), first pupil of the Gilbert Scott, who in two years' time was to take over the

'restoration' of Worcester Cathedral. The activities of the firm involved
tapestry, embroidery, metalwork, woodwork, and whatever might escape
from the brutalising cycles of the commercial world as defined by Ruskin
in *Unto this Last* (1860). Morris admitted his debt: 'It was through him
that I learned to give form to my discontent, which I must say was not by
any means vague.'

   At Oxford Morris developed a facility in writing verse that guaranteed
quantity if not always quality. Bernard Shaw was to describe this: 'He could
sling rhymes together without having to think about them, and used to

Oxford Union murals and Morris ceiling

look at me with incredulous disgust when I told him that when I wanted a rhyme I had to try down the alphabet.' *The Defence of Guenevere* (1858) presented the queen as stricken but proud, indeed unrepentant in its final lines:

> Her cheek grew crimson, as the headlong speed
> Of the roan charger drew all men to see
> The knight who came was Launcelot at good need.

His next major poem was *The Life and Death of Jason* in 1867. Thus he had worked a mediaeval vein and a classical. This was to be the basis of his main poetical production, *The Earthly Paradise*. The Chaucerian sequence of stories followed only five years after Longfellow's *Tales of a Wayside Inn*. There are twelve classical myths, one for each month, told by the elders of 'a nameless city in a distant sea'. These include 'The Story of Cupid and Psyche', inspiration for a series of Burne-Jones paintings; the love of Alcestis, which was quoted by Elgar; and 'Pygmalion and the Image', a lead again followed up by Burne-Jones. The tales of the wanderers, those who had vainly sought 'The Earthly Paradise' across the ocean and, after many bizarre adventures, decided to call it a day, were from various sources. Among them were 'The Lovers of Gudrun' from Norse tradition, with more on Longfellow's and Elgar's King Olaf; 'The Fostering of Aslaug', which concerns the child of Siegfried and Brünnhilde; and 'The Hill of Venus', basis for the opening of Wagner's *Tannhäuser*, particularly as sensualised for the disastrous Paris performances of 1861.

Morris disarms us with a six-verse 'Apology', claiming to be everything he most certainly was not. Did the opening hint at Newman's *Dream of Gerontius*, published three years before? It would be pleasant to think so, in view of Morris's early admiration for Newman:

> Of Heaven or Hell I have no power to sing,
> I cannot ease the burden of your fears,
> Or make quick-coming death a little thing,
> Or bring again the pleasure of past years,
> Nor for my words shall ye forget your tears,
> Or hope again for aught that I can say,
> The idle singer of an empty day.

The fourth verse is perhaps more Elgarian in some of his moods, again with a reference to the end of Virgil *Aeneid* Book VI, where Anchises tells how false dreams ascend through the ivory gate:

Morris by Watts

Dreamer of dreams, born out of my due time,
Why should I strive to set the crooked straight?
Let it suffice me that my murmuring rhyme
Beats with light wing against the ivory gate,
Telling a tale not too importunate
To those who in the sleepy region stay,
Lulled by the singer of an empty day.

Morris's prologue deals with the wanderers, and explains them in the following argument:

> Certain gentlemen and mariners of Norway, having considered all that they had heard of the Earthly Paradise, set sail to find it, and after many troubles and the lapse of many years came old men to some Western land, of which they had never before heard: there they died, when they had dwelt there certain years, much honoured by the strange people.

Morris begins in pre-industrial Ruskinian vein:

> Forget six counties overhung with smoke,
> Forget the snorting steam and piston stroke,
> Forget the spreading of the hideous town:
> Think rather of the pack-horse on the down,
> And dream of London, small, and white, and clean,
> The clear Thames bordered by its gardens green.

From Norway, to escape plague, they made for Bremen and west through the Channel, where they encountered the navy of Edward III, full sail for France, with the Black Prince on board. Morris has transported us to the domain of Froissart and the year 1346. The narrator among the wanderers tells how they were bidden to come aboard and face the king; he urges them to join the expedition and win glory on the fields of France. The wanderers affirm their only loyalty is to the quest, and the king desists:

> Broad-browed he was, hook-nosed, with wide grey eyes
> No longer eager for the coming prize.

Edward, claiming to be 'of Odin's blood', gave them a horn and ring, a safe pass, and the blessing of a warrior no longer certain about the value of military success.

Morris's calendar of the year's months charts also increasing despair over his marriage. November was the month for 'The Lovers of Gudrun' and a month of pain for Morris:

> Yea, I have looked, and seen November there:
> The changeless seal of change it seemed to be,
> Fair death of things that, living once, were fair:
> Bright sign of loneliness too great for me,
> Strange image of the dread eternity,
> In whose void patience how can these have part,
> These outstretched feverish hands, this restless heart?

Gudrun, wooed by those she despised and deprived of the man she loved best, takes Morris into the world of sagas he was to make more and more his own and was twice to involve a visit to Iceland. It is from there, in the wanderer's tale, that Kiartan Olafsson, inspired by hearsay of King Olaf's prowess and strange faith, decides on a personal encounter in Norway. Snorri Sturluson has him 'considered to be the most agreeable and hopeful man of any born in Iceland', and the wanderer describes the circumstances of the expedition's arrival:

> Now tells the tale that safe to Drontheim came
> Kiartan with all his fold, and the great fame
> Of Olaf Tryggvison then first they knew,
> When thereof spake the townsmen to the crew:
> But therewithal yet other news they heard,
> Which seemed to one and all a heavy word:
> How that the king, from the old customs turned,
> Now with such zeal toward his new faith burned,
> That thereby nothing else to him was good
> But that all folk should bow before the Rood.

Elgar and Longfellow knew all about that, to say nothing of an Ironbeard now at ease, perhaps, among the Valkyries of Valhalla. Snorri arranges a submarine meeting for Kiartan and the king:

> It happened one fine day that many set out to swim for amusement, and among them was a man who distinguished himself above the others in all bodily exercises.

None would take up the challenge of swimming against this man.

Morris reading to 'Ned' by Burne-Jones

'Then I will make a trial', said Kiartan, casting off his clothes, and springing into the water. Then he set after the man, seizes hold of his foot, and
dives with him under water. They come to the surface, and without
speaking a word dive again, and are much longer under water than the
first time. They come up again, and without saying a word dive a third
time, until Kiartan thought it was time to come up; this, however, he could
in no way accomplish, which showed sufficiently the difference in their
strength. They were under water so long that Kiartan almost drowned.

Soon enough he realised his adversary had been King Olaf. So rude a
baptism was followed by observation of a high Mass at Michaelmas. It
seemed at Yule an armed clash might occur, but the king's arguments,
more accommodating than in Longfellow, eventually prevail:

> Great love there grew 'twixt Kiartan and the king
> From that time forth, and many a noble thing
> Was planned betwixt them; and ere Yule was o'er
> White raiment in the Minster, Kiartan bore,
> And he and his were hallowed at the font.

It was June when an elder told the story of 'The Love of Alcestis'.
Morris sets the scene with care:

> Now in the early June they deemed it good
> That they should go unto a house that stood
> On their chief river, so upon a day
> With favouring wind and tide they took their way
> Up the fair stream; most lovely was the time
> Even amidst the days of that fair clime,
> And still the wanderers thought about their lives,
> And that desire that rippling water gives
> To youthful hearts to wander anywhere.

The god Apollo approaches the seat of Admetus in his royal house of
Pherae, travel-stained and desirous of employment:

> A staff he bore, but nowise was he bent
> With scrip or wallet; so withal he went
> Straight to the King's high seat, and standing near,
> Seemed a stout youth and noble, free from fear
> But peaceful and unarmed; and though ill clad,
> And though the dust of that hot land he had
> Upon his limbs and face, as fair was he
> As any king's son you might lightly see,

> Grey-eyed and crisp-haired, beautiful of limb,
> And no ill eye the women cast on him.

Request was made for keep and work. Apollo emphasises to Admetus his care of flocks, echoing the sense of an epithet he bore, 'Lykeios', the wolf-god, and so averter of wolves; and his power as musician, player of the lyre and inspiration of the Muses. Admetus loved him, yet was in awe whenever he met him apparently distracted and staring towards the east, where his own horses were harnessed to draw the chariot of the sun. There were occasions, too, when the effect of the music in the palace seemed overwhelming:

> Within the King's hall, would he seem to wake
> As from a dream, and his stringed tortoise take
> And strike the cords unbidden, till the hall
> Filled with the glorious sound from wall to wall,
> Trembled and seemed as it would melt away,
> And sunken down the faces weeping lay
> That erewhile laughed the loudest; only he
> Stood upright, looking forward steadily
> With sparkling eyes as one that cannot weep,
> Until the storm of music sank to sleep.

When spring came round, Admetus was absent six days for the wooing of Alcestis; but her father set such outlandish conditions he did not see how he could prevail and win the bride. Disconsolate, he wandered to the shore and came in sight of his herdsman, singing free from care:

> The while the heifers' bells about him rang
> And mingled with the sweet soft-throated birds
> And bright fresh ripple: listen, then these words
> Will tell the tale of his felicity,
> Halting and void of music though they be.

The song that follows, from which Elgar detached the last three lines as final comment on the full score of *The Apostles*, can hardly be said to express Apollo's happiness, if a god can experience such. The world indeed was a lovely place, but man would delve and woman spin to scant avail despite the deafness of the gods to their pleas and the hollowness of much achievement. Zeus, secure on high, had little care for what had been so lovingly created but was now badly tended by mortals who lived so short a time.

SONG

O dwellers on the lovely earth,
Why will ye break your rest and mirth
To weary us with fruitless prayer;
Why will ye toil and take such care
For children's children yet unborn,
And garner store of strife and scorn
To gain a scarce remembered name,
Cumbered with lies and soiled with shame?
And if the gods care not for you,
What is this folly ye must do
To win some mortal's feeble heart?
O fools! when each man plays his part,
And heeds his fellow little more
Than these blue waves that kiss the shore
Take heed of how the daisies grow,
O fools! and if ye could but know
How fair a world to you is given.

O brooder on the hills of heaven,
When for my sin thou drav'st me forth,
Hadst thou forgot what this was worth,
Thine own hand had made? The tears of men,
The death of threescore years and ten,
The trembling of the tim'rous race -
Had these things so bedimmed the place
Thine own hand made, thou couldst not know
To what a heaven the earth might grow
If fear beneath the earth were laid,
If hope failed not, nor love decayed.

He stopped, for he beheld his wandering lord,
Who, drawing near, heard little of his word,
And noted less: for in that haggard mood
Nought could he do but o'er his sorrows brood.

Of course Elgar was aware of Apollo's song *in toto*, and knew well the import of the two stanzas, with their implied rebuke to man and the chief of Classical gods. Did Elgar mean the three lines to stand in isolation, or would he also have others understand that he too had often upbraided his fellow men and inveighed against God, a notable example being the letter to Jaeger of 9 October 1900, six days after the woeful *Gerontius* première:

I always said God was against art & I still believe it. anything obscene or
trivial is blessed in this world & has a reward - I ask for no reward - only to
live & to hear my work. I still hear it in my heart & in my head so I must
be content. Still it is curious to be treated by the old-fashioned people as a
criminal because my thoughts & ways are beyond them.

Perhaps he bore in mind also the so sad fate of Admetus and Alcestis.

Apollo's year of service to Admetus ran its course, and he told the king
he must now depart. He bade him join him the following morning for a
final word that the king must hear in solitude at the summit of a nearby
hill. There they climbed in silence and Apollo revealed something of his
divine nature. The name and presence of Apollo was a matter of dread
even to the gods of Olympus, but he instructed Admetus to have no fear
and consider him a friend, should ever fortune cease to smile. Morris
describes his final moments with Admetus:

Alcestis and Love *by Burne-Jones*

He ceased, but ere the golden tongue was still
An odorous mist had stolen up the hill,
And to Admetus first the god grew dim,
And then was but a lovely voice to him,
And then at last the sun had sunk to rest,
And a fresh wind blew lightly from the west
Over the hill-top, and no soul was there;
But the sad dying autumn field-flowers fair,
Rustled dry leaves about the windy place,
Where even now had been the godlike face,
And in their midst the brass-bound quiver lay.

Married to Alcestis, Admetus lived a happy life till mortal sickness
came upon him. Summoned to his aid, Apollo came:

Whether it were but parcel of their dream,
Or that they woke to it as some might deem,
I know not, but the door was opened wide,
And the King's name a voice long silent cried,
And Phoebus on the very threshold trod.

His message was a hard one but with a ray of hope: Admetus might live if
any could be found ready to die in his stead. Only Alcestis was willing to
surrender her life for his, though not without a struggle and much agony
of mind:

But now Alcestis rose, and by the bed
She stood, with wild thoughts passing through her head.
Dried were her tears, her troubled heart and sore
Throbbed with the anguish of her love no more.

Her journey was to be a lonely one through the land of shades, for now
was the decision taken and she must die. Admetus, on the other hand,
could live:

He has awakened: but not thin and wan
His face was now, as of a dying man,
But fresh and ruddy; and his eyes shone clear,
As of a man who much of life may bear.
And at the first, but joy and great surprise
Shone out from those awakened, new-healed eyes;
But as for something more at last he yearned,
Unto his love with troubled brow he turned,
For still she seemed to sleep: alas, alas!
Her lonely shadow even now did pass

> Along the changeless fields, oft looking back,
> As though it yet had thought of some great lack.

Morris and the elder of the city set in a distant sea close the poem still with an air of mystery:

> And for Admetus, he, too, went his way,
> Though if he died at all I cannot tell,
> But either on the earth he ceased to dwell,
> Or else, oft born again, had many a name.
> But through all lands of Greece Alcestis' fame
> Grew greater, and about her husband's twined,
> Lived, in the hearts of far-off men enshrined.

Alice Elgar might well have been pensive over the story of Alcestis; but in October 1903, with the Classical and Norse worlds subsumed in the splendour of the *Apostles* first performance, the Elgars took their final Birmingham impression from the church of St.Philip, built by the same Thomas Archer (?1668-1743) who went on to design St.John, Smith Square, now London's most 'musical' church. The stained glass is of superb quality, the grandest achievement of Burne-Jones and the William Morris firm. The two men had been in France during the summer of 1855 and had visited Chartres. A result was a fine tale Morris wrote while still at Oxford, *The Story of the Unknown Church*. The trees are not the pines of Spetchley or *The Dream of Gerontius*, but Elgar would have responded to the description of the abbey's surroundings:

> The Abbey where we built the Church was not girt by stone walls but by a circle of poplar trees, and whenever a wind passed over them, were it ever so little a breath, it set them all a-ripple; and when the wind was high, they bowed and swayed very low, and the wind, as it lifted the leaves, and showed their silvery white sides, or again in the lulls of it, it let them drop, kept on changing the trees from green to white, and white to green; moreover, through the boughs and trunks of the poplars, we caught glimpses of the great golden corn sea, waving, waving, waving for leagues and leagues; and among the corn grew burning scarlet poppies, and blue corn-flowers; and the corn-flowers were so blue that they gleamed, and seemed to burn with a steady light, as they grew beside the poppies among the gold of the wheat.

It is as if Morris is describing also the glass of Chartres Cathedral. His characterisation of mediaeval glass seems to link both Chartres and Birmingham: 'The windows of that date that are left us are very deep and rich in colour, red and blue being the prevailing tints.' Elgar described

The Last
Judgement
*by Burne-
Jones*

their visit to St.Philip's at the end of the Birmingham festival on 17 October 1903, how they 'walked up it to see the stained glass & on turning round were struck by Burne-Jones' Ascension (It is mine - or mine is it . . the sun shining thro' it Very impressive ending to our glorious week'. They were making for the 3.20 train, and the afternoon sun would have been behind the west window, where is in fact *The Last Judgement* (1897), completed after Morris's death. If Elgar mistook this vast design, with white-robed Christ and gently trumpeting angel, for the *Ascension*, the fault is maybe more that of Burne-Jones than his. The deep blues and reds of the *Ascension* at the east end are perhaps more suggestive of some episode in Christ's ministry. If there was confusion, it hardly matters; Burne-Jones had made his effect.

Inspired by visits to the Glaspalast exhibitions in Munich (1893 and 1894), by shows at the New Gallery in London, visits to the studio of G.F.Watts, by some rather uninteresting books, and by the music Elgar was composing around her, Alice Elgar wrote an essay in the mid-1890s entitled 'The Ideal in the Present'. At the outset she put her question: 'How will the latter half of the 19th Century be characterised by the historian of the future?' She contrasted the major discoveries of yesteryear and now:

> Formerly great discoveries and inventions lay more in vast regions beyond our sphere. Copernicus, Galileo, Newton pointed to new paths of thought, but they led through realms of far and abstract knowledge; they did not give us, as have modern discoverers, means of traversing empires in rapid bodily presence or in transmitted thought; they did not light our hours of actual palpable darkness or convey our every thought and wish to far distant destinations.

She points out the astonishing increase in material prosperity, but now 'a new shadow appears - Demos, - claiming his share'. Yet despite late Victorian problems and restless ambitions, there was matter for rejoicing: 'Yet in the midst of our hurried life and massive incomprehension of lofty art, we must remember with joy and astonishment that there is an ideal side even to this age, weary, worn out and sordid as it seems in many respects.' There was little comfort to be found at the Academy or indeed most English exhibitions:

> At a far higher level was the choice of Subjects in the last two Exhibitions at Munich; the peculiarly trying and trite events so dear to the English public were entirely absent, and the eye could wander over the walls without fear of meeting the wearisome Changes rung on babies and their antics and similar pictures which sadden the heart in galleries at home. Notwith-

standing the general elevation of taste abroad, the proud thought that our very highest painters need fear no rivalry, proved a soothing reflexion.

She then plays her trump cards on behalf of English art:

Think that this age has seen the birth of two painters of the absolutely ideal: Burne-Jones and Watts - the name of Rossetti rises to one's lips in conjunction with theirs but though the subjects he chose were highly poetical and artistic and sometimes religious, they did not represent so entirely an imaginative side of life and thought as many of the works of his two great contemporaries.

Alice Elgar treats first of Burne-Jones: 'Step for a moment aside out of the roar and hurry of London Streets full of the excitement and anxiety of life; - enter a quiet gallery. A magic presence seems to banish the noise and rush of town from the mind and excitement and anxiety fade as a refreshing touch seems to reach the jaded spirit.' She writes about four Burne-Jones pictures: *The Golden Stair, The Days of Creation, Le Chant d'Amour* and *Love among the Ruins*. In 1870 he had resigned from the Old Water-Colour Society and hardly exhibited for the next seven years. He re-appeared in 1877 with eight paintings at the Grosvenor Gallery in New Bond Street, founded that year by Sir Coutts Lindsay (1824-1913). For W.S.Gilbert (1836-1911) it was the 'Greenery-Yallery Grosvenor Gallery'. Among the Burne-Jones works was a *St.George* of a rather rueful countenance. He is in full armour, and on his silver shield is depicted the naked princess, in considerable distress because the dragon is coiled round her legs and its head is making for her breasts. To reassure us that all is well, a heap of slain dragon is piled behind the saint's legs. A striking work in the same exhibition was *The Beguiling of Merlin*, an Arthurian subject treated by Tennyson as 'Vivien' in 1859 and then in 1871 renamed 'Merlin and Vivien'. The figure of Nimuë was modelled on Maria Zambaco, a striking Greek beauty with whom Burne-Jones had a tempestuous affair at the beginning of the 1870s. Nimuë has snakes in her hair, and F.G.Stephens considered 'Nimuë's face in its snaky intensity of malice is marvellous, not so the weak and womanish visage of Merlin'. As astute a critic as Sidney Colvin, Slade professor at Cambridge, director of the Fitzwilliam Museum and future Elgarian, was enchanted by Burne-Jones's offering: 'We have among us a genius, a poet in design and colour, whose like has never been seen before.' Ruskin, Slade professor at Oxford, was equally impressed. The Grosvenor Gallery closed in 1890, but already Lindsay's assistants, Joseph Comyns Carr (1849-1916) and Charles Hallé (1846-1914), son of the Hallé orchestra's founder, had departed to create the New Gallery in 1888, taking Burne-Jones with them.

So it was at the New Gallery that Burne-Jones had a notable retrospective in the winter of 1892-3, an exhibition the Elgars saw on 1 May 1893, a fortnight after the première of *The Black Knight* on 18 April. The first painting to attract the attention of Alice Elgar was *The Golden Stair*, originally shown at the Grosvenor Gallery in 1880:

> The picture represents no love story, no legend of any age, you are lifted into a world of pure imagination. The maidens are rapt and content in their own existence, fulfilling some law absolutely unknown to us - we know not whence they come or whither they go. We ask what their life, their thoughts, but wait in vain for a reply.

F.G.Stephens had watched the work take shape in Burne-Jones's studio and saw in it the influence of Piero della Francesca (1416-92), whom Burne-Jones had much admired in a recent visit to Arezzo. Burne-Jones was not sure what the picture meant: 'he wanted everyone to see in it what they could for themselves. He was often amused by the anxiety people had to be told what they ought to think about his pictures as well as by their determination to find a deep meaning in every line he drew.' Alice Elgar wrote an extended poem about the picture:

As down an amber staircase slow
They came and spoke in whispers low.
Still hovered o'er each face the fire
Which lofty praise and high desire
Awake in spirits pure. Their hymn
Was scarcely hushed; afar and dim
Soft echoed yet the sound of bell,
Of viol, lyre attunèd well.
'Oh ye with clear eyes bright,
Oh ye with grey robes light,
Whence come ye maidens fair
Adown the Golden Stair?'
Then slowly smiling answered they
In words which seemed a low sweet lay,
'In other world than thine we dwell
And morn and eve our praises swell
As climbing slow the amber stair
We reach a pure, serener air.
But not for thee to know our life
Where sheltered well from heat and strife
We pass adown the Golden Stair
Nor time nor age can touch us there'.

The Golden Stair
by Burne-Jones

* * *

For nothing earthly do they care,
But ever dreaming onward fare,
With pensive distant air
Adown the Golden Stair.

Alice Elgar next writes about *The Days of Creation*, which was in the opening Grosvenor Gallery show. Henry James felt that Burne-Jones was now 'quite at the head of the English painters of our day, and very high among the painters of this degenerate time'. He continued:

> In the palace of art there are many chambers, and that of which Mr.Burne-Jones holds the key is a wondrous museum. His imagination, his fertility of invention, his exquisiteness of work, his remarkable gifts as a colourist, cruelly discredited as they are by the savage red walls at the Grosvenor - all these things constitute a brilliant distinction.

The Days of Creation is one of Burne-Jones's series paintings, with the six days each in its separate frame with two-line Latin inscription above from *Daniel* 2, part of verses 20-22, 'Blessed be the name of God for ever and ever: for wisdom and might are his: And he changeth the times and the seasons: he knoweth what is in the darkness, and the light dwelleth with him.' The acts of creation are represented each in an orb held by an angel: light; the firmament; earth, sea, plants and trees; sun, moon and stars; birds, animals and creatures of the sea; man and woman. The angelic presence increases from one to six as the days are numbered, retaining throughout a characteristic Burne-Jonesian detachment. Alice Elgar admires the matter and the manner:

> Take again 'The Days of Creation'. The sublime subject, beyond the reach of human thought or imagining, is treated in the most lofty and ideal sense. No attempt is made to render any image of the Creator in human form, the only form possible for us to imagine, but we see merely a picture of His works held up in a mirror as it were to reflect in triumphant repose the 'works that He has done.' It is held up to our eyes by the great Angels, 'those Ministers of His who do His bidding.'

Alice Roberts may have seen *Le Chant d'Amour* at the Grosvenor Gallery in 1878. Henry James certainly did and was again perceptive, noting first the sort of criticisms that would be made: 'It will be a matter of course to say that the subjects are unreal, the type of figure monotonous and unpleasant, the treatment artificial, the intention obscure'; but he admired 'the beautiful, rapt dejection of the mysterious young warrior' and wondered 'where to look for a more delicate rendering of a lovesick swain'. The 'Chartres colours abound in a scene where Love the blind organ-blower seems to have interrupted his task. All three characters appear to be in suspended animation.' F.G.Stephens thought the background had come straight from *The City of Dreadful Night,* a poem Elgar may already have known when he saw the painting in 1893. Alice Elgar continues her essay:

> Leaving the lofty heights of primaeval Creation and turning to scenes of the latterday Earth, the same touch raises and idealizes all. Look at the 'Chant d'Amour.' Does it not seem as if Love were a solemn devotion and worship, a dedication of the most passionate thoughts and feelings to something higher than the trifling fancy of the moment, to something higher than coarse and animal affections. See the pure faces of the Earnest lovers celebrating their joy in one another's presence, not in artificial and glaring surroundings, heated ball rooms or crowded salons, but out in God's own universe amidst the flowers He has sown, their happiness attuned the while to lofty strains of harmony.

Le Chant d'Amour *by Burne-Jones*

Love Among the Ruins was shown at the New Gallery the following season, and the Elgars saw it with 'BGN' of the 'Enigma' Variations on 29 March 1895. Burne-Jones took the title and general idea from a poem of Browning's; there the city is so ruinous that it has become mainly pasture for sheep. Burne-Jones goes no farther than briars, column-drums, an interruption to the music-making, and a look of foreboding on the part of the girl. Alice Elgar comments thus:

> We may call to mind another instance 'Love among the Ruins.' From one corner of the picture a young man and a young girl witness the deserted and wrecked remains of a city. No thought of triumph comes to them, rich as they are in their youth, their love, and their beautiful young life. On the contrary an overwhelming dread and pain are depicted on the girl's face as she clings to her companion who, with manly tenderness endeavours to shield her from the anguish of the scene before her eyes. In this place of utter desolation they seem like ideal beings possessing joy and good gifts but rapt in regret for the sorrowful sight before them.

Alice Elgar's last Burne-Jones choice was *Vesper, or The Evening Star,* sometimes known as *Hesperus.* A first attempt at the idea was shown at the Old Water-Colour Society in 1870; the definitive version would have been seen by the Elgars at the New Gallery in 1893. F.G.Stephens in the

Love among the Ruins *by Burne-Jones*

Athenaeum of 1870 (p.586) first described the picture as 'grand poetry expressed in bad grammar'. The Elgarian view was more generous :

> Could there be a painting of more exquisite refinement and beauty than
> 'The Evening Star'? pictured as a fair maiden floating at Eventide over a
> city set in a perfect scene of land and sea. Peace and harmony emanate
> from the clear evening light and grace flows from every fold of her raiment
> as it flutters in the wind. She moves along, a fair emblem of coming rest,
> in the exquisite purity of an ideal vision.

Ruskin could not understand why Burne-Jones took such delight and trouble with the draperies of his figures: 'Why should the tuckings in and out of muslin be eternally interesting?'

Alice Elgar's essay prepares to consider another artist: 'Let us pass on now to the work of Watts.' Both Elgars had visited the Watts studio in Melbury Road, Kensington on 11 April 1891. When financial problems at *Holland House* necessitated selling part of the estate, *Little Holland House*, where Watts had been living, was to be demolished. On Tennyson's suggestion, he commissioned a house on the Isle of Wight from Philip Webb, architect of Morris's *Red House*. He also had a house built in the new Melbury Road, Kensington, by Frederick Pepys Cockerell (1833-78). Sidney Colvin was an early visitor, after Watts had resumed his portrait of Gladstone. He described him as a 'fine genius' and went on to say that he 'was of course quite unchanged: his beautiful simplicity of character did but increase with age, his high ambitions both in decorative painting and monumental sculpture continued with increase rather than abatement.' Initially Watts called his new home 'Little Holland House' in memory of the demolished building. Julia Margaret Cameron (1815-79) saw that the original loss contained new hope:

> Not so, the seed hath struck deep root, and see
> Four Studios rising where one used to be
> Attracted hither by the master mind
> That ever sought through art to elevate mankind.
> Still doth the master here pursue this aim
> Beneath a roof identical in name
> With the demolished home we so deplore
> Spreading its fame yet wider than before.

From 1880 Watts invited the public to visit his studio free every Sunday afternoon, though it was on a Saturday that the Elgars went. What exactly they saw on that occasion it is impossible to say. Alice had probably seen some Watts at the Grosvenor Gallery. *Love and Death* was his main exhibit at the opening in 1877, and with it a portrait of Burne-Jones. Oscar Wilde

Love and
Death
by Watts

was much impressed by the former as one of Watts's 'poems painted on canvas'. He continued: 'There are perhaps few paintings to compare with this in intensity of strength and in marvel of conception.' Henry James was equally favourable: ' "Love and Death" is an allegory, an uncomfortable thing in painting, but Mr.Watts's allegory is eminently pictorial.' He warned further: 'The picture has a certain graceful impressiveness, and the painter has rendered with peculiar success the air of majestic fatality in the pale image which shows no features.' Over the next ten years Watts exhibited nearly sixty paintings at the Grosvenor. The Watts retrospective of 1881-2 was the first devoted to a living British artist.

Alice Elgar selected three paintings for comment: 'Think of the Enigma "The Embodied Striving of the mind of Man to pierce the Unseen, the Unknowable" - of "Hope" in aerial raiment of soft translucent tints resting on the mysterious globe of Earth, listening for a word with which to make glad the heart of that Earth - look at "Love and Life", the ideal of Love in its best and highest influence, saving, leading and raising its fellow soul through the difficulties and over the stony and steep paths of the world. Scarcely a picture of his which does not elevate our thoughts and point to some great lesson, some teaching clothed in the most exquisite of forms and colour, lessons which we should do well to take seriously to heart.' The first version of *Hope* was shown at the Grosvenor Gallery in 1884. Watts gave examples of *Love and Life* to both the United States and France. *The Ideal in the Present* next considers a special aspect of Watts's work:

> To Watts also, belongs the rare glory that in the representation of the nude female figure, he clothes it with such a noble ideality that far from its having a debasing influence, or appealing to any lower side of human nature, it stands vested with a sacred purity, an emblem as it were, of what should be encompassed with reverence.

On this occasion she may have been thinking of the *Psyche* shown at the Grosvenor in 1880, a figure of wondrous tenderness, and in an attitude of repose suggesting neither anticipation nor loss, or *The Three Goddesses* (Aphrodite, Hera and Pallas) exhibited the following year. When the Elgars visited the Munich Glaspalast in 1893, there were twenty-four paintings by Watts and a sculpture. Among the paintings was *Love and Death*. There was also *The Dweller in the Innermost* which Watts described in a letter to Walter Crane (1845-1915) as

> a stuttering that I should never have expected even you to follow or make any sense of. I myself can hardly give a mental form to the confused ideas which it endeavours in some slight way to focus, vague murmurings rather than fancies which constantly beat me and rather prevent any kind of work than aid.

Above all there was *The Happy Warrior*, seen at the Grosvenor Gallery in 1884, and now making such an impression in Munich that it was purchased by the Bavarian state. Watts regretted the waning of chivalry (1879): 'Had it been encouraged to penetrate all ranks in the army of life, many of our greatest difficulties might never have arisen.' Mary Seton Tytler, later Watts's second wife (his first short-lived marriage was to Ellen

The Three Goddesses *by Watts*

Terry (1847-1928), the actress and high-spirited correspondent of Bernard Shaw), recorded her impressions when she visited his studio in 1870: '[he] so distinctly suggested to me the days of chivalry that I believe I should not have been surprised if, on another visit, I had found him all clad in shining armour.' Watts worked a number of chivalric subjects. They started with *Aspirations*, which shows a young man ready for fight; *The Red Cross Knight* has a warrior shielding a woman; *Sir Galahad*, which was worked up again at the request of a master for the chapel at Eton, portrays the Arthurian knight resting from fight; and *The Happy Warrior*, with his helmet cast back, has died fighting and is rewarded with a vision of his Ideal. The title for this painting comes from Wordsworth's poem *Character of the Happy Warrior*, which begins:

> Who is the happy Warrior ? Who is he
> That every man in arms should wish to be?
> - It is the generous Spirit, who, when brought
> Among the tasks of real life, hath wrought
> Upon the plan that pleased his boyish thought:
> Whose high endeavours are an inward light
> That makes the path before him always bright.

And Wordsworth ends:

> Who, whether praise of him must walk the earth
> For ever, and to noble deeds give birth,
> Or he must fall, to sleep without his fame,
> And leave a dead unprofitable name -
> Finds comfort in himself and in his cause;
> And, while the mortal mist is gathering, draws
> His breath in confidence of Heaven's applause:
> This is the happy Warrior; this is He
> That every man in arms should wish to be.

The painting that inspired Elgar most directly in connection with *The Apostles* was by the Russian Kramskoi. Elgar saw in it 'my ideal picture of the Lonely Christ as I have *tried* (and tried hard) to realise . . . the Character'. He had come across a photograph of it at the home of Canon Gorton (1854-1912), his host at the Morecambe Competitive Festival in 1903, when *The Banner of St.George* was to be performed by the massed choirs. Ivan Nikolaevich Kramskoi (1837-87) was leader of the Thirteen Contestants who had revolted in 1863 against the St.Petersburg Academy demand that competition for the annual gold medal could be only on a stipulated subject, in this case 'The Banquet of the Gods in Valhalla'. They

The Happy Warrior *by Watts*

resigned from the Academy and formed a successful co-operative group, which led in 1870 to the 'Society for Travelling Art Exhibitions'. Pavel Tretyakov (1832-98), patron and collector, gave encouragement and assistance. There were two main results: the paintings by the 'Wanderers' found place in provincial collections; and Tretyakov himself purchased some of the best works for his own collection, which was eventually given to the city of Moscow in 1892.

Before entering the Academy, Kramskoi had worked in photographers' studios; his fine series of portraits are remarkable likenesses but have also a psychological insight that makes them hauntingly memorable. Fellow artists are wonderfully captured, but he is often at his most telling when portraying the lined faces of peasants, and especially the old. Tolstoy appears in the fulness of his power, while the poet Nekrasov is a valetudinarian in white gown on a white sofa. Most famous and enigmatic of his portraits is *The Unknown Woman* of 1883, shown a little arrogant in her barouche against a lightly touched and wintry St.Petersburg sky. Early in his career, Kramskoi had sketched a *Moses striking Water from the Rock*. In 1872-4 he produced *The Temptation of Christ* which so fascinated Elgar. It was an attempt to embody the toilsome human search for moral truth. Kramskoi's Christ is an isolated and concentrated figure shown against the hard and pitiless rocks of the Palestinian desert. This is far from any Pre-Raphaelite Christ, far indeed from the Christ figures in the Burne-Jones stained glass in St.Philip's. As so often in Kramskoi, the colours of this dawn scene give no enrichment, still less distraction from the huddled figure. It is almost a Gethsemane, but without the garden. Kramskoi himself said: 'This is no Christ, it is an image of the sorrows of humanity which are known to all of us.' Gorton was able to secure Elgar a copy of the picture, which is now at the Birthplace. Dostoievsky sat for Kramskoi, and both are buried in the same Alexander Nevsky cemetery, searching interpreters of their age.

11 - By Cam and Tiber

A.C.Benson, formerly an Eton master, but now a fellow of Magdalene College, Cambridge, wrote in 1905 a biography of Edward FitzGerald, author of *Euphranor*, the book that prevented Elgar from catching any fish on 25 August 1907. It was a book such as to intrigue an Elgar already possessed of the great tune that was to be the protagonist in Symphony no.1; at the same time it was a surprising book to come from so desultory an author. Benson sums up his life at the outset: 'It was the career of a lonely, secluded, fastidious, and affectionate man; it was a life not rich in results, not fruitful in example. It is the history of a few great friendships, much quiet benevolence, tender loyalty, wistful enjoyment.' He was at school in Bury St.Edmunds and had the chance to wander among the sad fragments of the great abbey. He went on to Trinity College, Cambridge, where Thackeray was a main friend, and the Tennysons (Frederick, 1807-98; Alfred, 1809-92) were contemporaries. An early poem, *The Meadows in Spring*, says much:

> And there I sit
> Reading old things,
> Of knights and lorn damsels
> While the wind sings -
> Oh, drearily Sings! . . .
> But close at the hearth,
> Like a cricket, sit I,
> Reading of summer
> And chivalry -
> Gallant chivalry!

FitzGerald lived most of his life in Suffolk, disliking the railways that threatened to bring metropolitan civilisation with them. He describes a typical morning:

> Here is a glorious sunshiny day: all the morning I read about Nero in Tacitus lying at full length on a bench in the garden: a nightingale singing, and some red anemones eyeing the sun manfully not far off. A funny mixture all this: Nero, and the delicacy of Spring: all very human, however.

Benson mentions his friendships: 'he goes out a drive with Dickens, Thackeray, and Tennyson, a precious carriage-full. Dickens he finds 'unaffected and hospitable, but sees nothing in his face which would indicate genius, except "a certain acute cut of the upper eyelid".' FitzGerald's friendship with Carlyle dates from 1842: in letters he often referred to him as 'Gurlyle', Thackeray's name for him. Carlyle had engaged Dr.Arnold (1795-1842) of Rugby to visit the field of Naseby with him to get accurate matter for his *Cromwell* (1845). Most of the battlefield belonged to FitzGerald's father, who had erected an obelisk to mark the highest point. The researchers took this as the scene of the hottest engagement, so that their topography went much awry. FitzGerald called on Carlyle to put him right and then did some excavations at Naseby. He found fragments of skeletons close packed. Carlyle was awestruck: 'there are the very jaw-bones that were clenched together in deadly rage, on this very ground one hundred and ninety-seven years ago!'

FitzGerald called *Euphranor* (1851) 'a pretty specimen of a chiselled cherry-stone'; but his genius as a prose writer, like Elgar's, went into his letters. *Euphranor* remains his one attempt (apart from the Bernard Barton biography of 1849) at an original prose work. It is in the manner of a Platonic dialogue, owing also much to Lucian (c.125-c.200) and Peacock (1785-1866). It is set in Cambridge, and at the beginning Euphranor is rejoicing in the splendour of a May day and rouses the doctor narrator for a trip on the river. Gathering up Lexilogus, the bookworm, they crossed Trinity Great Court and made for the Cam. They

Trinity Great Court, Cambridge by Ackermann

take a boat and discuss Kenelm Digby and *The Broad Stone of Honour.*
The doctor preferred the earlier 'Protestant' edition, but Euphranor, with
leanings towards Newman and the Oxford movement, spoke up for
Digby's larger Catholic version. They walk across the fields to Chesterton,
where Lexilogus visits an elderly relative and the rest go to the Three
Tuns Inn. There they meet Lycion, the man of fashion, smoking a cigar.
He takes up the Digby theme and speaks about the absurdity of the
Eglinton Tournament, supposing that Digby 'would take us back to the
days of King Arthur'. He imagined that Don Quixote had settled all that.

The doctor broadens the discussion to ask whether Carlyle has not
spoken of a 'Chivalry of Labour'? Henceforward not '*Arms* and the Man'
but '*Tools* and the Man' are to be subject of the world's epic. Euphranor
has little time for Carlyle: 'As Tennyson says, King Arthur, who was carried
away wounded to the island valley of Avilion, returns to us in the shape of
a "modern gentleman".' Aristotle is invoked by the doctor on behalf of the
young: 'they live by Hope, for Hope is of the future, but Memory of the
past, and to Youth the Future is everything, the Past but little.'

When writing to Walford Davies about Symphony no.1, Elgar allied
himself with the young, expressing 'a *massive* hope in the future'.
Euphranor points the moral, explaining 'how Lamb's friend, looking
upon the Eton boys in their Cricket-field, sighed "to think of so many fine
Lads so soon turning into frivolous Members of Parliament!" ' The
argument follows another Elgarian line when turning to the virtues of
dogs and horses. The doctor enlarges on this: 'The Horse, you know, has
given his very name to Chivalry, because of his association in the Heroic
Enterprises of Men.' Moreover, he used to be buried with our ancestors.
And the Muse 'sings of those who believe their faithful Dog will
accompany them to the World of Spirits'.

In education the doctor pleads for the traditional establishments of
England, citing the Eton of Henry VI 'under the walls of his Royal Castle,
all reflected in the water of old Father Thames, as he glides down the
valley; and Winchester with her William of Wykeham entomb'd in the
Cathedral he built beside his School'. The doctor is wary of sacrificing 'the
Living Man to the Dead Languages' or of dissipating the young 'among
the Fine Arts, Music, Poetry, Painting, and the like'. He would 'make
Gymnastic a necessary part of their education'. Euphranor is incredulous:
'But you would not have Eton Boys compelled to climb and tumble like
monkeys?' The doctor is rather for military exercises 'which no less a Man
- although a Poet - than John Milton, enjoin'd as the proper preparation
for War, and, *I* say, carrying along with them a sense of Order, Self-
restraint, and Mutual Dependence, no less necessary in all the relations of
Peace'. Hamlet had foregone his '*Custom of Exercises*' while studying at
Wittenberg, presumably including the cricket that would have bowled his

uncle out at once.

The case of Hamlet leads them on to discuss presence of mind, of which the doctor gives a graphic example:

> As when the Hunter's horse falling with him in full cry, he braces himself, between saddle and ground, to pitch clear of his horse - as Fielding tells us that brave old Parson Adams did, when probably thinking less of his horse than of those Sermons he carried in his saddle-bags.

Euphranor thought Parson Adams lucky to have a horse at all and imagined the hunter would go the way of the gladiator and boxer: 'perhaps the very Horse he rides gradually to be put away by Steam into some Museum among the extinct Species that Man has no longer room or business for'.

The discussion continues on how the young may shape up to face the dangers that still threaten. Euphranor has recourse to the *Clouds* of Aristophanes and a passage between Right Logic and Wrong: 'It is, you see, Old Athens pleading against Young.' The latter is castigated for relinquishing the discipline and exercises that reared the men of Marathon for 'the Warm Bath, the Dance, and the Law Court' and is addressed in a speech that Euphranor had translated:

> O listen to me, and so shall you be stout-hearted and fresh as a Daisy:
> Not ready to chatter on every matter, nor bent over books till you're hazy:
> No splitter of straws, no dab at the Laws, making black seem white so cunning:
> But scamp'ring down out o' the town, and over the green Meadow running.

Euphranor admitted that the decline in the youth of Athens, satirised by Aristophanes, continued till the citizens could contribute little but declamation and despatches when Rome came to assist against Philip of Macedon.

The day was advancing, and they realised they could not be in College for 3.30 dinner; so the doctor offered dinner at the inn. They tried to persuade Lycion to join a walk, but he preferred billiards. Lexilogus returned from visiting his aunt and heard that Digby and his books had been their essential subject. They left the road to walk in the fields, and Euphranor quoted some Chaucer:

> Embrouded was he as it were a Mede,
> Alle ful of Fresshe floures, white and rede,

adding, 'What a picture was that, by the way, of a young Knight!' Lexilogus did not know his Chaucer, so Euphranor obliged from memory with the description of the 'yonge Squier'. Discussion followed on his qualities, Euphranor teasingly praising his artistic gifts, while the doctor insisted on his strength, horsemanship and raids on the Continent. There was more on Chaucer and his pilgrims from the doctor, while Euphranor mentioned that John Lydgate (?1370-1449), the monk-poet of Bury St.Edmunds abbey, had spoken of Chaucer and his encouragement of fellow-poets. The doctor characterised him also as a man of affairs: 'employ'd by Princes at home and abroad. And ready to fight as to write'. A man after the doctor's heart, thought Euphranor.

Shakespeare was of similar calibre, added the doctor, who strongly believed in the poaching story of the dramatist's youth. His London career as player, playwright and manager was sketched by the doctor, who concluded:

> to Stratford he finally retired, where he built a house, and planted Mulberries, and kept company with John-a-Combe, and the neighbouring Knights and Squires - except perhaps the Lucys - as merrily as with the Wits of London; all the while supplying his own little 'Globe' - and, from it, 'the Great globe itself,' with certain manuscripts, in which (say his Fellow-players and first Editors) Head and hand went so easily together as scarce to leave a blot on the pages they travell'd over.

Was that not also the way of Sir Walter Scott? commented Euphranor, 'in that love for Country home, and Country neighbour - aye, and somewhat also in that easy intercourse between Head and hand in composition which those who knew them tell of.' The doctor expressed his own enthusiasm: ' "Magician of the North" they call'd him in my own boyish days; and such he is to me now; though maybe not an Archi-magus like him of Stratford.' Euphranor attributed to Carlyle the view 'that Sir Walter's Characters are in general fashioned from without to within - the reverse of Shakespeare's way - and Nature's'. The doctor sprang at once to Scott's defence, naming Carlyle 'old Sartor' after his *Sartor Resartus*:

> if the Sartor's charge hold good, it must lie against the Heroes and Heroines of the later, half-historical, Romances; in which, nevertheless, are scenes where our Elizabeth, and James, and Lewis of France figure, that seem to me as good in Character and Circumstance as any in that Henry the Eighth, which has always till quite lately been accepted for Shakespeare's.

But as for the Scottish novels, in which 'Highlander, Lowlander, Royalist, Roundhead, Churchman or Covenanter' were so depicted that the tales had taken on the validity of household history, the doctor found himself in a quandary: 'I declare that I scarce know whether Macbeth's blasted heath would move me more than did the first sight of the Lammermoor Hills when I rounded the Scottish coast on first going to Edinburgh; or of that ancient "Heart of Mid-Lothian when I got there".'

The doctor now takes on the part of FitzGerald himself as longstanding friend of Tennyson, and recalls a touching moment during the poet's visit to Scotland:

> he found himself beside that 'bonnie Doon' and - whether it were from recollection of poor Burns, or of 'the days that are no more' which haunt us all, I know not - I think he did not know - but, he somehow 'broke' as he told me, 'broke into a passion of tears'.

The doctor had known Tennyson break down only once before, when they had been reading about the destruction of Troy in Book II of the *Aeneid*. The doctor calls Chaucer and Wordsworth to witness:

> As all who knew him know - a Man at all points, Euphranor - like your Digby, of grand proportion and feature, significant of that inward Chivalry, becoming his ancient and honourable race; when himself a 'Yonge Squire,' like him in Chaucer 'of grete strength,' that could hurl the crow-bar further than any of the neighbouring clowns, whose humours, as well as of their betters, - Knight, Squire, Landlord and Land-tenant, - he took quiet note of, like Chaucer himself. Like your Wordsworth on the Mountain, he too, when a Lad, abroad on the Wold; sometimes of a night with the Shepherd; watching not only the Flock on the greensward, but also
>
> > The fleecy Star that bears
> > Andromeda far off Atlantic seas
>
> along with those other Zodiacal constellations which Aries, I think, leads over the field of Heaven.

It was now afternoon, and they turned back towards the inn. Lexilogus had not spoken much, and the doctor asked him about Herodotus (c.480-c.425) and Strabo (b.c.63 BC), whose books he had noticed on his table. He learnt something 'about the courses of the Nile and the Danube, and the Geography of the Old World: till, all of a sudden, our conversation skipt from Olympus, I think, to the hills of Yorkshire - our own old hills - and the old friends and neighbours who dwelt among them.' Then up rode Phidippus, another Yorkshireman, in real life FitzGerald's much admired friend, William Kenworthy-Browne, a man 'quick to love and quick to fight - full of confidence, generosity and the glorious spirit of Youth'. His character was opposite to that of the sedentary FitzGerald; that was the attraction. Kenworthy-Browne's copy of *Euphranor* had the following dedication: 'This little book would never have been written, had I not known my dear friend William Browne, who, unconsciously, supplied the moral.' The doctor suggested Phidippus should join them for dinner at Chesterton, 'where his Mare might have her Dinner too - all of us Yorkshiremen except Lycion'. There was to be a boat-race later, which Phidippus must watch. He was not taking part himself: 'he must yet see his own Trinity keep the head of the River.'

At the inn Euphranor and Lycion played billiards a while, 'Lycion very lazily, like a man who had already too much of it, but yet nothing better to do'. When the meal was announced, there was 'that slight hesitation as to precedence which Englishmen rarely forget on the least ceremonious occasions, - Lexilogus, in particular, pausing timidly at the door, and Euphranor pushing him gently forward'. Lycion talked of a ball he had attended recently, and mentioned three beautiful young ladies from a neighbouring county who had proved excellent at the waltz. The doctor remarked that dancing was out for him unless he could find a 'concave partner'; but he made suggestions for a couple of the young men: Euphranor must 'advertise for a "Strong-minded" Female, able to read Plato with him, and Wordsworth, and Digby, and become a Mother of Heroes'. As to Phidippus there seemed to be no need of a suggestion after all, as he had chosen his 'Diana'.

They all made for the Cam, and the scene was familiar enough: 'Townsmen and Gownsmen, with the tassell'd Fellow-commoner sprinkled here and there - Reading men and Sporting men - Fellows, and even Masters of Colleges, not indifferent to the prowess of their respective Crews.' At last conversation was stilled:

> suddenly the head of the first boat turn'd the corner; and then another close upon it; and then a third; the crews pulling with all their might compacted into perfect rhythm; and the crowd on shore turning round to follow along with them, waving hats and caps, and cheering, 'Bravo, St.John's!' 'Go it, Trinity!' - the high crest and blowing forelock of Phidippus's mare, and he himself shouting encouragement to his crew, conspicuous over all - until the boats reaching us, we also were caught up in the returning tide of spectators, and hurried back toward the goal.

The head of the river was now St.John's. Phidippus 'remained engaged in eager conversation with his defeated brethren', while Lycion 'got into better company elsewhere'. It was left for the doctor to walk with Euphranor and Lexilogus 'across the meadow leading to the town, whither the dusky troops of Gownsmen with all their confused voices seem'd as it were evaporating in the twilight, while a Nightingale began to be heard among the flowering Chestnuts of Jesus'. And so Elgar closed the book, shouldered his rod, packed his bags for the day and returned fishless to Plas Gwyn.

In point of fact a return visit to Cambridge after his student days had

Jesus College, Cambridge by Ackermann

not struck FitzGerald at all favourably, as he wrote to W.F.Pollock (1815-88) on 14 August 1839: 'Cambridge looked very ghastly, and the hard-reading, pale, dwindled students walking along the Observatory road looked as if they were only fit to have their necks wrung.' FitzGerald gave Edward Cowell (1826-1903) his opinion of *Euphranor*: 'Not but I think the Truth is told: only, a Truth every one knows! And told in a shape of Dialogue really something Platonic: but I doubt rather affectedly too.' Benson, long the Eton schoolmaster, and aware that FitzGerald's advocacy of the *corpus sanum* had been all too readily heeded, concentrates on other aspects of *Euphranor*: 'Yet the little book remains, penetrated with the delicate fragrance of a poetical spirit, with the strong sense of beauty, and with the pathos of the brevity of happiness, which was the dominant strain in FitzGerald's mind.'

It is almost as if Benson is writing about FitzGerald's masterpiece. He started studying Persian in 1853, encouraged by his friend Cowell, later professor of Sanskrit at Cambridge. On 27 December he wrote to Frederick Tennyson about it: 'I also amuse myself with poking out some Persian which E.Cowell would inaugurate me with.' Omar Khayyám was born at Nishapur and died in 1123. He seems to have been a tent-maker, perhaps following his father's trade. He was both mathematician and astronomer. His skill in algebra induced the Sultan Malik-Shah (1072-92) to summon him in 1074 for the purpose of furthering his astronomical studies and reforming the calendar. His 500 four-line epigrams were a sideline and gathered together under the title 'ruba'is'. Some are mystic, others pantheistic and also agnostic. They were separate entities, not grouped according to any pattern.

FitzGerald writes to Cowell on 5 June 1857, when staying with Phidippus, about his pleasure in Omar:

> When in Bedfordshire I put away almost all Books except Omar Khayyám!, which I could not help looking over in a Paddock covered with Buttercups and brushed by a delicious Breeze, while a dainty racing Filly of W.Browne's came startling up to wonder and snuff about me.

He then turned some Omar into 'Monkish Latin, like "Dies Irae" &c.' That deserved an apology to Cowell:

> You will think me a perfectly Aristophanic Old Man when I tell you how much of Omar I could not help running into such bad Latin. I should not confide such follies but to you who won't think them so, and who will be pleased at least with my still harping on our old Studies.

He wrote again to Cowell on 1 July: 'June over! A thing I think of with Omar-like sorrow. And the Roses here are blowing - and going - as abundantly as even in Persia. I am still at Geldestone, and still looking at Omar by an open window which gives over a Greener Landscape than yours.' It was also the time of the Indian Mutiny, and on 3 October 1857 FitzGerald was anxious for Cowell, based in Calcutta: 'I hope things will not be so black with you and us by the time this Letter reaches you!' He goes on to mention the main Indian concern of the moment: 'Only all are trembling for Lucknow crowded with Helplessness and Innocence! I am ashamed to think how little I understand of all these things: but have wiser men, and men in Place, understood much more? or, understanding, have they *done* what they should?'

Work continued on the *Rubáiyát*, and on 3 September 1858 FitzGerald could report to Cowell its conclusion:

> My Translation will interest you from its *Form*, and also in many respects in its *Detail*: very unliteral as it is. Many Quatrains are mashed together: and something lost, I doubt, of Omar's Simplicity, which is so much a Virtue in him. But there it is, such as it is.

A couple of months later he told Cowell it was 'most ingeniously tesselated into a sort of Epicurean Eclogue in a Persian Garden'. The *Rubáiyát* made little impression initially, but had remarkable success when taken up by

Rossetti and Swinburne. A letter of appreciation from Ruskin did not arrive until 1873, ten years after Burne-Jones had received it for forwarding. Benson has much of interest on similarities between Omar and FitzGerald:

> Omar was a sentimentalist, and a lover of beauty, both human and natural; so was FitzGerald. Omar tended to linger over golden memories of the past, and was acutely alive to the pathos of sweet things that have an ending; and such was FitzGerald. Omar was penetrated with a certain dark philosophy, the philosophy of the human spirit at bay, when all refuge has failed; and this was the case with FitzGerald.

Benson turns to music in describing FitzGerald's method with the Persian original: 'It was as though FitzGerald had found some strict and solemn melody of a bygone age, and enriched it with new and honeyed harmonies, added melancholy cadences and sweet interludes of sorrow.' Alfred Tennyson paid delightful tribute to FitzGerald's memory and the *Rubáiyát* in the 1885 dedication to *Tiresias*. For ten weeks Tennyson had stayed at the home of FitzGerald, by then a convinced vegetarian:

> but none can say
> That Lenten fare makes Lenten thought,
> Who reads your golden Eastern lay,
> Than which I know no version done
> In English more divinely well;
> A planet equal to the sun
> Which cast it, that large infidel
> Your Omar; and your Omar drew
> Full-handed plaudits from our best.

Like Elgar, FitzGerald retained his admiration for Scott throughout his life. In his preface to *Polonius* (1852), a collection of aphorisms, some original, others culled from his wide reading and including thoughts of Bacon (1561-1626), Carlyle and J.H.Newman, he refers to his beloved Scott:

> When Sir Walter Scott lay dying, he called for his son-in-law, and while the Tweed murmured through the woods, and a September sun lit up the towers, whose growth he had watched so eagerly, said to him, 'Be a good man; only that can comfort you when you come to lie here!' '*Be a good man!*' To that threadbare Truism shrunk all that gorgeous tapestry of written and real Romance!

He wrote to W.F.Pollock about one of the novels he had been reading lately:

The Pirate is, I know, not one of Scott's best: the Women, Minna, Brenda, Norna, are poor theatrical figures. But Magnus and Jack Bunce and Claud Halcro (though the latter rather wearisome) are substantial enough: how wholesomely they swear! and no one ever thinks of blaming Scott for it. There is a passage where the Company at Burgh Westra are summoned by Magnus to go down to the Shore to see the boats go off to the Deep Sea fishing, and 'they followed his stately step to the Shore as the Herd of Deer follows the leading Stag, with all manner of respectful Observance.' This, coming in at the close of the preceding unaffected Narrative, is to me like Homer, whom Scott really resembles in the simplicity and ease of his Story.

At the end: 'I finished the Book with Sadness; thinking I might never read it again.'

Like Newman, he describes a visit to Scott's home:

But I did get to Abbotsford, and was rejoiced to find it was not at all Cockney, not a Castle, but only in the half-castellated style of heaps of other houses in Scotland; the Grounds simply and broadly laid out before the windows, down to a field, down to the Tweed, with the woods, which he left so little, now well aloft and flourishing, and I was glad.

FitzGerald then mentions the grave of Scott's dog:

I could not find my way to Maida's Grave in the Garden, with its false quantity,
                    Ad januam Domini, etc.,
which the Whigs and Critics taunted Scott with, and Lockhart had done it.

The trouble was the first syllable of 'januam', which should be short to take its proper place in a dactyl; unfortunately it is long. John Gibson Lockhart, Scott's son-in-law and a Balliol man, should have known this, though he understood well enough that a faithful Roman dog would have had his post at the 'janua' or house-door of his master. FitzGerald goes on to quote Scott: ' "You know I don't care a curse about what I write": nor about what was imputed to him, in spite of Gurlyle, who sent me an ugly Autotype of Knox whom I was to worship instead.' FitzGerald wanted to visit Scott's own grave, but in his emotion confused Dryburgh with Jedburgh:

Then I went to see Jedburgh Abbey, in a half-ruined corner of which he lies entombed - Lockhart beside him - a beautiful place, with his own Tweed still running close by, and his Eildon Hills looking on. the man who drove me about showed me a hill which Sir Walter was very fond of visiting, from which he could see over the border, etc. This hill is between Abbotsford and Jedburgh: and when his Coach horses, who drew his Hearse, got there, to that hill, they could scarce be got on.

FitzGerald also writes to Carlyle about the Abbotsford pilgrimage, but refuses to concur with his judgment of Scott: 'Oh, I know you think Scott a brave, honest, good-natured man, and a good Storyteller, only not a Hero at all. And I can't help knowing and loving him as such.'

FitzGerald was bothered with his eyes as early as 1869, and organised neighbour boys for reading sessions. He explained to Fanny Kemble (1809-93) that one evening 'the boy was so disturbed by a mouse that he had to be dismissed.' He wrote to her again on 25 April 1879:

> I - We - have finished all Sir Walter Scott's Scotch Novels; and I thought I would try an English one; Kenilworth - a wonderful Drama, which Theatre, Opera and Ballet (as I once saw it represented) may well reproduce. The Scene at Greenwich, where Elizabeth 'interviews' Sussex and Leicester, seemed to me as fine as what is called (I am told, wrongly) Shakespeare's Henry VIII. Of course, plenty of melodrama in most other parts: - but the Plot wonderful.

By the winter of 1881 he has to rely entirely on his boys:

> I can read but little, and count of my Boy's coming at Night, to read Sir Walter Scott, or some Travel or Biography, that amuses him as well as me. We are now beginning the *Fortunes of Nigel,* which I had not expected to care for, and shall possibly weary of before it ends; but the outset is nothing less than *delightful* to me.

Benson writes of FitzGerald's essential achievement: 'To enrich the world with one imperishable poem, to make music of some of the saddest and darkest doubts that haunt the mind of man - that is what many far busier and more concentrated lives fail to do.' Elgar would readily have concurred in the year of the 'great beautiful tune' and the months in Rome that turned the 'lovely river piece' and embryo string quartet towards Symphony no.1.

When the Elgars departed from Capri on 12 February 1907, Canon and Mrs.Gorton, their hosts, 'watched till steamer started. Very touching & we had a bad choke at leaving him.' The following day they were in Rome and welcomed by the Bethells. They made almost at once for St.Peter's: 'E. most impressed with vastness.' They had only ten days in Rome on this occasion, but were indefatigable sightseers. They were at the Capitol and visited the museums, though Elgar did not much care for the equestrian statue of Marcus Aurelius (161-80). They were in the Vatican: 'saw the sculpture gallery & the Stanze - Sculpture wonderful. E.

delighted. Again to S.Peter's.' It was already clear they must come back to Rome. On the Sunday they went to Mass in one of the Piazza del Popolo churches and walked on the Pincian Hill in sunny weather. The next day they were at the Baths of Diocletian , and saw the great display of Roman antiquities in the National Museum. Elgar was 'quite overcome by the great bust of Juno' found on the Palatine and perhaps the portrait of an empress in guise of the goddess. This was to be a focal point for Elgar during the following winter. Filling in her diary later, Lady Elgar was uncertain whether 19 February was the day they visited St.John Lateran, second of the main Roman basilicas. The following day Elgar had an appointment with Lorenzo Perosi, music director of the Sistine Chapel since 1898. Elgar's first mention of him was in a letter of 16 February to F.G.Edwards: 'The way the journalists have evolved a Perosi boom is remarkable - & we haven't hear a note yet.'

Robert Newman's London Musical Festival of May 1899 at Queen's Hall, during which the 'Meditation' from *The Light of Life* was heard, included also three Perosi oratorios, all written in 1898. Henry Wood did not conduct them but was unimpressed, as he states in *My Life of Music* (p.126):

> Perosi's oratorios bored me; some of our early Victorian Mus.Docs. had
> produced more vital and interesting works. We had a second and a third
> dose of these compositions at the eighth and ninth concerts in the shape
> of the Resurrection of Lazarus and the Resurrection of Christ. I hardly
> know which I disliked the more.

The first had been the *Transfiguration of Christ*; but Elgar was emphatic to Edwards: there would be no Perosi at Worcester. In February 1907, however, with eleven oratorios to his name, the thirty-four-year old Perosi could not have been more accommodating. Elgar spent a delightful morning with him at the Vatican, 'E. returned *enchanted* with Borgia rooms & Pinturicchio &c. & Perosi's rooms.' The day before they left Rome, Perosi repeated the invitation to include Lady Elgar: 'saw the Borgia rooms & then the Gardens, & the Librarian took us into the Library All wonderful & beautiful.' On 23 February they left Rome, and the last diary reference concerns the third basilican church: 'View of S.Paolo from train.'

It would be interesting to know when Elgar first became fascinated with Piranesi. Was he, for instance, a subject touched on by E.W.Whinfield, an early Elgarian mentor in artistic matters? Did he see prints in London long before he owned any in 1915 and 1919? He could hardly fail to see them in Rome even during this first ten days. Piranesi (1720-78) created the Romantic vision of Roman antiquity and of the city itself. He first came there in 1740 with the Venetian ambassador to the new Pope, Benedict

XIV (1740-58). He was already trained as architect, stage designer and etcher. The ruins of Rome offered startling inspiration to the young man. Before leaving three years later he completed the twelve plates of a work he called on the title page, 'Part 1 of Architecture and Perspectives'. It was a glorious mixture of jumbled ruins, with people clambering among gigantic structures and some scattered skulls, and idealised buildings for some future day based on the utmost magnificence of ancient Rome. There was a 'large sculpture gallery', a 'dark prison', 'magnificent bridge', 'hall in the manner of the ancient Romans', receding stairways linking superb columned halls, a 'royal courtyard' and so on.

Already Piranesi was travelling the path that would direct the rest of his life. This first publication was an attempt to show how the Eternal City might again equal its own past. He also left with Roman booksellers a series of commercial prints illustrating famous buildings of the city, ancient and modern. These were sold to travellers and used in guidebooks. The excavations at Herculaneum attracted him to Naples, and back in Venice he profited from the recent etched work of Tiepolo (1696-1770) and Canaletto (1697-1768).

He returned to Rome in 1747, establishing himself on the Via del Corso, opposite the French Academy. He was already producing the large format landscapes that were to be the mainstay of his reputation. In 1748 he published an edition of his own. This was the *Roman Antiquities from the Period of the Republic and the First Emperors drawn and etched by the Venetian Architect Giambattista Piranesi, and dedicated by him to the Most Illustrious and Most Reverend Monsignor Giovanni Bottari, Private Chaplain of Pope Benedict XIV, one of the Keepers of the Vatican Library, and Canon of S.Maria in Trastavere.* Battari was a considerable scholar, had written on Classical and Christian Rome, and was associated with important Roman libraries.

The Elgars returned to Rome on 7 November 1907. Elgar was not taken with the apartment at first, but the following day he was beginning to like it. It could hardly have been more central. Carice was with her parents and, after Elgar had done some work on the quartet, she went with him 'on the Pincian Hill, down through the Piazza del Popolo' on the same 9 November that he also wrote to Alfred Littleton (1845-1914): 'We are here all safely & find our flat very simple but comfortable & a glorious view: it is really one of the best situations in Rome & the walks on The Pincian are at our door almost which is most convenient for Alice.' Wherever they went, Piranesi had been before. He began his *Views of Rome drawn and etched by Giambattista Piranesi, Venetian Architect,* in the late 1740s; the series continued until his death. The prints might be sold individually or gathered into collections the more numerous as the years went by. After two introductory plates and the title page comes a

'Fantasy of ruins with a statue of Minerva' as frontispiece. Then immediately one is taken to St.Peter's, with a view of the piazza and its central obelisk once set up in Alexandria by Virgil's poet friend and governor of Egypt, Cornelius Gallus (c.70-26 BC). Next one enters the great basilica and moves on to the interior of S.Paolo fuori le Mura. The other two basilicas, St.John Lateran and S.Maria Maggiore are viewed from outside. The four churches are magnificently displayed, all placed diagonally on the print, as was Piranesi's habit, except the St.Peter's piazza. Cloud effects add to the atmosphere of terribilità Piranesi can so readily conjure.

Elgar's niece, May Grafton, was also of the party, and on 14 November Carice reports that the three of them went an expedition that took them past the Fontana Trevi as far as the Colosseum:

> saw the fountain, with the horses by Pheidias & Praxiteles, & by some side-streets to the Capitol; we saw the eagles & the evil wolves, ja! & the two basalt lions at the foot of the steps. We went up the steps & just looked round, but did not go into the galleries, but went down the Via Campidoglio on the left & began gradually to see the whole Forum. We went into this, & walked about for a little, the sun was behind us & we had all the light on the Forum itself. We saw the arches of Severus, Titus & Constantine, & the latter's great Basilica. Then we went on into the Colosseum & spent a few minutes there . . . The extraordinary size is overpowering.

St.Peter's by Piranesi

The next day Carice, and her father were in the Sistine chapel '& studied the ceiling & the *Last Judgment*, and the Frescoes'; they returned via the Piazza Navona, the Pantheon, and the Piazza Colonna, with its pillar commemorating the conquests of Marcus Aurelius. Piranesi has superb views of the Pantheon in his publication of 1762 dedicated to Robert Adam (1728-92). The last shows the magnificent building intact and imagined in the splendour of its original setting. The title of the volume indicates that Piranesi's fame had travelled far: *The Campus Martius of Ancient Rome, the Work of G.B.Piranesi, Fellow of the Royal Society of Antiquaries, London*. It is not to Piranesi's discredit that the Society was no more 'royal' in 1762 than it is now. Elgar had come to an important decision by 3 December 1907, as he explained to Alfred Littleton, chairman of Novello: 'I promised Beale I would let him know as to an oratorio - the final one of the series - for the next Birmingham festival. I have to-day written definitely & finally to give up the idea.' He complained of noise from neighbouring pianos and doubted he would compose anything while in Rome: 'In any case I am sadly disappointed with the commercial results of the last oratorios & for the sake of my people must not waste more time in attempting to write high "felt" music.'

On the afternoon of 7 December Carice and Elgar walked to the Porta Pia built by Michelangelo (1475-1564) at the request of Pius IV (1559-65). They then took a tram to Sant' Agnese fuori le Mura: 'we had lovely views of the country & hills. The church is very interesting, a beautiful old mosaic over the tribune.' The 7th-century mosaic has Agnes between Popes Symmachus (498-514) and Honorius (625-38) holding a model of the church. More entertaining in its way was 'the "unhappy fresco" of Pius IX, commemorating his miraculous escape from death, when the floor fell down & carried him & his cardinals through into the cellar'.

Lady Elgar wrote to 'Nimrod' on 9 December, including news he had been longing for:

> I know you will like to hear something about our surroundings & about E. especially. He loves his Rome very much & loves going for long exploring walks, one day impressed by the Palatine, going back to the wonderful days of the Caesars, another day to the wonderful Churches & *their* associations, & to gaze again & again at the wonderful Juno. The beautiful Villa in wh. the marvellous bust used to be more worthily housed has now, with its beautiful gardens, all disappeared.

The official music they had heard, quite apart from the incessantly thumping pianos, had been insufferable: 'the Church Music we have heard so far, is DREADFUL, the very tone of the organs makes you *fly*, if you can -'. Lady Elgar then mentioned work in progress: 'When Pianos &c

allow of any quiet, E. has been writing, & I TRUST you will hear the Symphony, yet, & many times.' Meanwhile the exploration of Rome continued, with Carice as indefatigable commentator. On 14 December they went to S.Paulo fuori le Mura:

> On the way there we past [*sic*] Temple of Vesta, S.Maria in Cosmedin, the supposed house of Rienzi, & under the Aventine Hill, past the Chapel of the Parting, where SS.Peter & Paul separated before their martyrdom. Before the chapel is the Porta Ostia, & the pyramid of Ca.Cestius. S.Paulo is the most magnificent building though not yet finished, we could not see the cloisters as they are being repaired. There is not one single thing that is tawdry or small in the whole church.

It would be instructive to know what guidebook or reference books they were using. There was an occasion the previous month when a visit to the Palatine was less than satisfactory because they had not realised they would go there, 'so had not read anything up about it'. Most visits were presumably well prepared. Elgar must have known that 'Temple of Vesta' was a pleasant misnomer. The real temple, scene of *La vestale* by Spontini (1774-1851), in which the sacred flame is relit by lightning from heaven and the heroine can be happily married, and of Mercadante's (1795-1870), in which heaven is unmoved and the heroine must die, had been seen by Elgar and his party in the Forum. The building they passed now may have been dedicated to Portunus, a Roman god of harbours. Elgar had quoted Virgil for both *Caractacus* and *The Dream of Gerontius*. He may well have remembered the Book V boat race organised in Sicily by the Trojan remnants, when Cloanthus came in first after proving the power of prayer. Dryden translated thus:

> The choir of nymphs, and Phorcus, from below,
> With virgin Panopea, heard his vow;
> And old Portunus, with his breadth of hand,
> Pushed on, and sped the galley to the land.
> Swift as a shaft, or winged wind, she flies,
> And, darting to the port, obtains the prize.

San Paulo was virtually a 19th-century building, dating from after a disastrous fire of 1823. The original basilica was built under Constantine over the spot where the martyred Paul was reputedly buried. A larger basilica gathered in time mosaics from that Galla Placidia (c.388-450) who had been interred amid such splendour at Ravenna. The church had strong English connections. Before the Reformation the king of England had been an *ex officio* canon, and the abbot received the Order of the Garter. Rienzi's (c.1313-54) 'supposed house' was familiar through the Bulwer

Lytton who featured in Elgar's Brinkwells reading and whom Wagner used for his first Dresden success in 1842. There were operatic links for Elgar the following day as well, when he went alone to S.Andrea della Valle, a grand and spacious church with dome second only to that of St.Peter's.

The Strozzi chapel is said to have been designed by Michelangelo and has in it reproductions of his *Pietà* from St.Peter's and his Leah and Rachel statues. It was also the church of Act 1 in Puccini's *Tosca* (1900), a work Elgar greatly admired and was indeed playing while scoring the third movement of the Symphony the following August. Angelotti takes refuge in the 'Attavanti' chapel, but the magisterial *Te Deum* that ends the Act takes place in the immense body of the church. Elgar could conjure for himself the gradually increasing crowd, expectant for the arrival of the cardinal, some already on their knees. As the cardinal advances towards the high altar, the waiting Scarpia bows to him, and the Swiss guards thrust back the surging people. Puccini took trouble with his *Te Deum* tune, even if it was to be sung under false pretences, on the assumption, as reported by the Sacristan, that Napoleon (1769-1821) had been defeated at Marengo (1800). The singing is punctuated by repeated sounds of cannon from the Castel Sant' Angelo, signal that Angelotti, an important political prisoner, has escaped. It is not easy to wander that church unaccompanied by echoes of Puccini; it is unlikely Elgar managed. That same day Elgar wrote to Littleton and mentioned progress on what was to be op.55: 'We have complained of the piano *practising* & have some mitigation - I have bought some *heavenly* M.S. paper & have scored some of the symphony! But I see little signs of its being finished.'

The 'Juno' again attracted the Elgar party on 22 December. By this time they must have been familiar with the layout of the Baths of Diocletian, home now to both the church of Santa Maria degli Angeli and the Museo Nazionale. Vitruvius (fl. late 1st century BC), writing under Augustus and responsible for much of his building work in Rome, devotes a chapter (Book V, 10) to baths in his book on architecture. He begins with eminently practical advice:

> Firstly a site must be chosen as warm as possible, that is turned away from the north and east. Now the hot and tepid baths are to be lighted from the winter west: but if the nature of the site prevents, at any rate from the south. For the time of bathing is fixed between midday and evening. We must also take care that the hot baths for men and for women are adjacent and planned with the same aspects. For in this way it will follow that the same furnace and heating system will serve for both baths and for their fittings.

Diocletian's baths indeed had the *frigidarium* open to the south-west, with massive protection from the elements on the other side. They were built about AD 305 and could accommodate some 3000 people. As supposed centres of immorality, they were less approved in a Christian empire, which had a different attitude to cleanliness. After visiting the museum, the Elgarian party went to Mass in Santa Maria degli Angeli, the church carved by Michelangelo in 1563 out of the central *tepidarium*. The dimensions of this tepid bath were remarkable, and not far from those recommended three hundred years before by Vitruvius; it was 200 feet long, eighty feet wide and ninety feet high. The cross-vaulting of Roman concrete still survives, resting on eight massive columns of Egyptian granite from Aswan. Michelangelo's huge nave was made by Luigi Vanvitelli (1700-73) into a transept in 1749, with a vaguely east-facing choir thrust into the old *frigidarium*, and a new façade incorporating part of the *caldarium*. Elgar cannot have failed to notice the vast painting by Pompeo Batoni (1708-87), originally intended for St.Peter's, *The Fall of Simon Magus*, sensational end of a character who should have appeared the previous year in *The Kingdom*, and whose music was held over to characterise the 'projector' Meercraft in Elgar's unfinished opera, *The Spanish Lady*.

Carice reported much of Elgarian interest on Boxing Day. There was not only a teasing cipher, but work by the artist who had given his name to the Elgars' first permanent Malvern home:

> In the morning Father wanted a long walk, so we went to S.Croce in Gerusalemme, very muddy walk, through the Piazza Vittorio Emmanuele, where we saw the cipher, the secret of gold-making which is carved up there, waiting to be deciphered. S.Croce is of course interesting as containing a piece of the True Cross, & the inscription, but it is too modernised to be at all beautiful.

The 'cipher' is an alchemist's prescription on the so-called 'Porta Magica'. S.Croce is said to have been founded by the empress Helena who, when divorced in 292 by Constantius Chlorus (c.250-306), is supposed to have taken all her Jerusalem treasures, including the 'True Cross' to the nearby Lateran Palace. At a lower level than the church, Baroqued by Benedict XIV, are rooms traditionally described as Helena's chapel and bedroom. Melozzo da Forli (1438-94) worked on the mosaics of the vault, depicting Christ with the evangelists, Peter, Paul, Pope Sylvester (314-35) and a cardinal.

On 12 January 1908 Carice and her father went to the Protestant Cemetery and saw the graves of Keats and Shelley. The one looked back to *Froissart* and on to the biography (1917) by Sidney Colvin who, with his wife Frances, was to receive the dedication of the Cello Concerto (1919). The other looked on to the 'Spirit of Delight' in Symphony no.2 (1911) and the proposal of *Adonais* for a Worcester Three Choirs Festival work of 1929. In his preface to *Adonais*, Shelley describes the burial place in Rome:

The romantic and lonely cemetery of the Protestants in that city, under the pyramid which is the tomb of Cestius, and the massy walls and towers, now mouldering and desolate, which formed the circuit of ancient Rome. The cemetery is an open space among the ruins, covered in winter with violets and daisies. It might make one in love with death, to think that one should be buried in so sweet a place.

Adonais (1821) is an elegy for Keats, and Colvin's *Life of John Keats* (p.518) pays eloquent tribute:

A rushing train of abstractions, such as were at all times to Shelley more inspiring and more intensely realized than persons and things, - a rushing train of beautiful and sorrowful abstractions sweeps by, in *Adonais*, to a strain of music so entrancing that at a first, on even at a twentieth, reading it is perhaps more to the music of the poem than to its imagery that the spiritual sense of the reader attends.

Colvin writes also about Sir Walter Scott's month in Rome during his last spring in 1832. Wordsworth had sent him on his way with a sonnet:

Blessings and prayers in nobler retinue
Than sceptred king or laurelled conqueror knows,
Follow this wondrous Potentate. Be true,
Ye winds of ocean, and the midland sea,
Wafting your charge to soft Parthenope!

Scott was able to do a little sight-seeing, but Colvin recalls the touching moment when Joseph Severn (1793-1879) showed him a portrait of Keats, whose poems had been savaged by his son-in-law Lockhart, and Scott remarked, 'yes, yes, the world finds out these things for itself at last'.

The Elgars were often in the Roman Forum and presumably in the Forum of Trajan (98-117), dominated by the emperor's column. At the beginning of 1915, when *Carillon* was already launched on its triumphal course, Elgar's mind went back to Rome and its wonders. Lady Elgar's diary for 15 January reports some war news but continues on another matter: 'E. to Puttick Sale & bought portfolios. Some lovely *Piranesi engravings* of Trajan's Column. Found E. so happy examining them & Alice S.W. helping him arrange them on the billiard table - nice time over them later'. The following day they seemed 'such a nice world to go back to, away from war & gales & earthquakes'. This was presumably Piranesi's volume of c.1774-5, of which the title-page reads:

The Trophy or Magnificent Spiral Column of Marble composed of large drums on which are carved the Dacian Wars of Trajan, raised in the middle

of the large Forum, erected in honour of the same Emperor on the order
of the Senate and People of Rome after his Triumphs.

Perhaps, like the Trajan basilica, it was designed by Apollodorus of
Damascus (d.c.125). The spiral band ascending the column, which was set
up in 114, has twenty-four windings. Formerly there was a statue of Trajan
at the summit; now St.Peter blesses his victories. Ascending the column are
2500 figures in some 150 scenes, less than a quarter of which deal with
fighting. The feats of the Romans are shown, but also the generosity of the
emperor, scenes of delegations to Trajan and the benefits of the *Imperium
Romanum*. Wordsworth might have the last word in his poem of 1825:

Trajan as cast for Maximilian I

Still are we present with the imperial Chief,
Nor cease to gaze upon the bold Relief
Till Rome, to silent marble unconfined,
Becomes with all her years a vision of the Mind.

Trajan's Column by Piranesi

12 - Alassio to Tintagel

From time to time Elgar's music turned to Shelley. The earliest occasion concerned *In the South*, the 1904 concert overture that begins with bulldog Dan 'triumphant (after a fight)' and concluded the Covent Garden festival. The 'Canto popolare' of the development section could be isolated for separate publication. This was Elgar's 'Shepherd singing softly' when 'the peace & the sunshine once more take the chief place in the picture'. Detached from its context, it might also become a night scene, indeed a song to Shelley words of 1822, the year he was drowned. The poem Elgar chose for the vocal arrangement, 'In Moonlight', was entitled 'To Jane: "The Keen Stars were Twinkling" '. Elgar adapted the second and fourth verses in a manner that earned strong disapproval from Ernest Newman in his 1906 Elgar book (p.123): 'It is quite true that you can sing Shelley's words to the music, but only by the same process by which Procrustes made his victims, tall or short, fit his bed of torture.' Later that year Alfred Littleton sent Elgar a copy of Shelley poems in the hope they might provide inspiration. Elgar replied on 14 November 1904: 'Many thanks also for the Shelley: I will think over the poems you name but I fear they are too lyrical for a scene painter like me but I would do anything to please you & will try anyhow.' He seems not to have tried till the following year, when he attempted a bass scena on the *Ozymandias* poem, but left it unfinished, tentatively transferring it to mezzo-soprano in 1917. At the end of 1907, with the decision for Symphony no.1 recently taken, Elgar turned to partsongs, the third of which again used Shelley words. This was the 1819 *Ode to the West Wind*, to which Shelley added a note:

> This poem was conceived and chiefly written in a wood that skirts the Arno, near Florence, and on a day when that tempestuous wind, whose temperature is at once mild and animating, was collecting the vapours which pour down the autumnal rains. They began, as I foresaw, at sunset with a violent tempest of hail and rain, attended by that magnificent thunder and lightning peculiar to the Cisalpine regions.

Elgar set only the initial words, 'O wild West Wind' and the fifth section beginning

> Make me thy lyre, even as the forest is.

Yet in the opening of the second section and the third Shelley almost foretells his fate at sea:

> Thou on whose stream, mid the steep sky's commotion,
> Loose clouds like earth's decaying leaves are shed,
> Shook from the tangled boughs of Heaven and Ocean,
>
> ***
>
> Thou who didst waken from his summer dreams
> The blue Mediterranean, where he lay,
> Lulled by the coil of his crystalline streams.

Shelley was invoked again to provide the motto for Symphony no.2, as Elgar wrote to Littleton on 2 February 1911: 'I was delighted to receive your letter about the Symphony (II) & am glad you heard a note or two - it *is* decidedly joyous 'Spirit of Delight' sort of thing - but ends sedately.' The poem was simply called *Song*, and there was a further letter to Littleton about it on 20 February: 'I will think over your idea about the

Shelley in the Baths of Caracalla by Joseph Severn

Stanzas. I proposed to put only the first two *lines* - in the score - which suggest all the rest - & let the programme makers put the whole poem.' On 13 April Elgar wrote again to Littleton, with ideas for the programme notes Rosa Newmarch (1857-1940) was to write for the first performance of the Symphony: 'To get near the mood of the Symphony the whole of Shelley's poem may be read, but the music does not illustrate the whole of the poem, neither does the poem entirely elucidate the music.' This was enigmatic enough; nor was Elgar more explicit when writing to Ernest Newman in early May: 'My attitude towards the poem, or rather to the 'Spirit of Delight' was an attempt to give the reticent Spirit a hint (with sad enough retrospections) as to what we should like to have!' The eight stanzas of the poem split into two. The first four stanzas are concerned with how to regain the elusive 'Spirit':

> Wherefore hast thou left me now?
> Many a day and night ?
>
> ***
>
> How shall ever one like me
> Win thee back again ?
>
> ***
>
> Even the sighs of grief
> Reproach thee, that thou art not near,
> And reproach thou wilt not hear.
>
> ***
>
> Let me set my mournful ditty
> To a merry measure;
> Thou wilt never come for pity,
> Thou wilt come for pleasure.

The second half of the poem makes the case for the 'Spirit's' return:

> I love all that thou lovest,
> Spirit of Delight!
> The fresh Earth in new leaves dressed,
> And the starry night;
> Autumn evening, and the morn
> When the golden mists are born.
>
> I love snow, and all the forms
> Of the radiant frost;
> I love waves, and winds, and storms,
> Everything almost

> Which is Nature's and may be
> Untainted by man's misery.
>
> I love tranquil solitude,
>   And such society
> As is quiet, wise, and good;
>   Between thee and me
> What difference? but thou dost possess
> The things I seek, not love them less.
>
> I love Love - though he has wings,
>   And like light can flee,
> But above all other things,
>   Spirit, I love thee -
> Thou art love and life! Oh, come,
> Make once more my heart thy home.

Elgar quoted more Shelley in connection with the Symphony. This was in a letter of 1 February 1911 to Frances Colvin in which he said he was 'busy with the "Spirit of Delight" Symphony'. He went on to cite:

> 'I do but hide,
> Under these notes, like embers, every spark
> *Of that which has consumed me.*
> Julian & Maddalo

Hide is hardly the right word is it for this case?' Shelley calls his piece, written in 1818 after a first visit to Venice, 'A Conversation'; he then describes the characters:

> Count Maddalo is a Venetian nobleman of ancient family and of great fortune, who, without mixing much in the society of his countrymen, resides chiefly at his magnificent palace in that city. He is a person of the most consummate genius, and capable, if he would direct his energies to such an end, of becoming the redeemer of this degraded country. But it is his weakness to be proud: he derives, from a comparison of his own extraordinary mind with the dwarfish intellects that surround him, an intense apprehension of the nothingness of human life.

If Maddalo is anyone in Shelley's circle, he is Lord Byron; and Julian is Shelley himself:

> Julian is an Englishman of good family, passionately attached to those philosophical notions which assert the power of man over his own mind,

and the immense improvements of which, by the extinction of certain moral superstitions, human society may be yet susceptible. Without concealing the evil in the world, he is for ever speculating how good may be made superior. He is a complete infidel, and a scoffer at all things reputed holy; and Maddalo takes a wicked pleasure in drawing out his taunts against religion.

And then there is the madman, from whom Elgar quotes, though substituting 'notes' for 'words'. Shelley tells so much about him:

> He seems, by his own account, to have been disappointed in love. He was evidently a very cultivated and amiable person when in his right senses. His story, told at length, might be like many other stories of the same kind: the unconnected exclamations of his agony will perhaps be found sufficient comment for the text of every heart.

Shelley introduces the poem with a translation from Pan's speech in Virgil's *Eclogue* 10:

> The meadows with fresh streams, the bees with thyme,
> The goats with the green leaves of budding Spring,
> Are saturated not - nor Love with tears.

The Elgars came to Venice on 30 May 1909 and were met in a gondola: 'Evening fairly clear. E. & A. so disappointed! the others in state of rapture. It seemed like Bank holiday Whistling launches, opera airs in Chinese lantern lit boats.' A poet could arrange things better:

> Just where we had dismounted, the Count's men
> Were waiting for us with the gondola. -
> As those who pause on some delight
> Though bent on pleasant pilgrimage, we stood
> Looking upon the evening, and the flood
> Which lay between the city and the shore,
> Paved with the image of the sky ... the hoar
> And aëry Alps towards the North appeared
> Through mist, an heaven-sustaining bulwark reared
> Between the East and West; and half the sky
> Was roofed with clouds of rich emblazonry
> Dark purple at the zenith, which still grew
> Down the steep West into a wondrous hue
> Brighter than burning gold, even to the rent
> Where the swift sun yet paused in his descent
> Among the many-folded hills.

Count Maddalo points out the island where the maniacs are detained, and they visit it the following day. The count had befriended one of them and provided him with separate accommodation. It is he who, in dislocated phrases, speaks of the woman he had loved, and addresses her:

> Then when thou speakest of me, never say
> "He could forgive not." Here I cast away
> All human passions, all revenge, all pride;
> I think, speak, act no ill; I do but hide
> Under these words, like embers, every spark
> Of that which has yet consumed me - quick and dark
> The grave is yawning.

It is idle to speculate the reason for Elgar's quotation. If Frances Colvin, a most sympathetic friend, was privy to certain confidences of Elgar's, confidences they would have remained. More important is the fact that on 6 June, Independence Day, he was twice in St.Mark's Square, 'wonderful with flags', morning and evening. This may have been the occasion he recalled to Alfred Littleton when writing about Symphony no.2 on 13 April 1911: 'The Rondo was sketched on the Piazza of S.Mark.Venice: I took down the rhythm of the opening bars from some itinerant musicians who seemed to take a grave satisfaction in the broken accent of the first four bars.'

St.Mark's, Venice by Ruskin

At the end of 1928 Elgar proposed for the next Worcester Three Choirs festival a final Shelley idea: he might set something from either *The Daemon of the World* or *Adonais*. The former was a reworking of sections from *Queen Mab*, about which Shelley wrote on 22 June 1821:

> A poem entitled *Queen Mab* was written by me at the age of eighteen, I daresay in a sufficiently intemperate spirit - but even then was not intended for publication, and a few copies only were struck off, to be distributed among my personal friends. I have not seen this production for several years. I doubt not but that it is perfectly worthless in point of literary composition; and that, in all that concerns moral and political speculation, as well as in the subtler discriminations of metaphysical and religious doctrine, it is still more crude and immature.

Nonetheless, the first appearance of the Daemon cries out for music:

> Hark! whence that rushing sound?
> 'Tis like a wondrous strain that sweeps
> Around a lonely ruin
> When west winds sigh and evening waves respond
> In whispers from the shore:
> 'Tis wilder than the unmeasured notes
> Which from the unseen lyres of dells and groves
> The genii of the breezes sweep.
> Floating on waves of music and of light,
> The chariot of the Daemon of the World
> Descends in silent power:
> Its shape reposed within: slight as some cloud
> That catches but the palest tinge of day
> When evening yields to night,
> Bright as that fibrous woof when stars indue
> Its transitory robe.

The other poem was Shelley's extended threnody on the death of Keats. He considered *Adonais* one of his most perfect works and carefully supervised its printing in Italy. His preface to the poem mentions future plans he could not fulfil:

> It is my intention to subjoin to the London edition of this poem a criticism upon the claims of its lamented object to be classed among the writers of the highest genius who have adorned our age. My known repugnance to the narrow principles of taste on which several of his earlier compositions were modelled prove at least that I am an impartial judge. I consider the

The Pyramid of Caius Cestius by Piranesi

fragment of *Hyperion* as second to nothing that was ever produced by a writer of the same years.

Did Elgar have any particular stanzas in mind, or was he simply playing a Shavian game with the dean of Worcester, knowing well that his suggestions would be rejected? The beauty of Shelley's tribute is irresistible, but it cannot make the sentiments Christian:

> He is made one with Nature: there is heard
> His voice in all her music, from the moan
> Of thunder, to the song of night's sweet bird;
> He is a presence to be felt and known
> In darkness and in light, from herb and stone,
> Spreading itself where'er that Power may move
> Which has withdrawn his being to its own;
> Which wields the world with never-wearied love,
> Sustains it from beneath, and kindles it above.
>
> ***
>
> Go thou to Rome, - at once the Paradise,
> The grave, the city, and the wilderness;
> And where its wrecks like shattered mountains rise,
> And flowering weeds, and fragrant copses dress
> The bones of Desolation's nakedness

Pass, till the spirit of the spot shall lead
Thy footsteps to a slope of green access
Where, like an infant's smile, over the dead
A light of laughing flowers along the grass is spread.

Shelley's final stanza prophetically links his own fate with that of Keats:

The breath whose might I have invoked in song
Descends on me; my spirit's bark is driven,
Far from the shore, far from the trembling throng
Whose sails were never to the tempest given;
The massy earth and spherèd skies are riven!
I am borne darkly, fearfully, afar;
Whilst, burning through the inmost veil of Heaven,
The soul of Adonais, like a star,
Beacons from the abode where the Eternal are.

On 3 December 1928 the dean responded to Ivor Atkins as he must: 'I have looked through the two poems you mentioned - 'The Demon' and 'Adonais' - As poems they are beautiful - 'Adonais' is the best, but it is frankly pagan. I have been trying to see if it can be twisted into a Christian poem. It is not possible.'

In the afterglow of the Diamond Jubilee, Elgar had sought and been granted permission to dedicate *Caractacus* to Queen Victoria. He hoped to dedicate Symphony no.2 to her successor, Edward VII from a real sense of gratitude, respect and affection. It was the arrival of an invitation to Marlborough House in January 1904 that persuaded the Elgars to leave Alassio earlier than intended. On 3 February Elgar met the King, who 'talked music to E. & took him out 1st after dinner'. At the succeeding concert the King insisted on a repeat of *Pomp and Circumstance* March no.1. The following month he attended two of the Covent Garden festival concerts, while Queen Alexandra was at the third as well. In June came tidings of Elgar's knighthood, which he received from the King's hands on 5 July. Clare Stuart Wortley reports a remark of Elgar's at dinner on some occasion: 'I shall dedicate the Symphony to Edward the Seventh, so that dear kind man will have my best music.' It seems probable Elgar said this while the King was still alive. He was very ill on 6 May 1910, as Lady Elgar noted in her diary: 'Terrible news only too true - So difficult to believe the King was really dangerously ill - So terribly sudden. 1000s round Buckingham Palace. E. walked round. Maud Warrender to tea She thought the illness was very dangerous - Oh! our own King.' He died early the following morning: 'Intense feeling of sadness. E. feeling desolate ... Nos. & nos. of people in black already - Papers with beautiful articles - &

people saying King Edward VII's loss the greatest calamity wh. cd. befall the country.' The next day Elgar wrote to Frank Schuster: 'These times are too cruel & gloomy - it is awful to be here now - that dear sweet-tempered King-Man was always so 'pleasant' to me.' He ended: 'We are dismally gay - walk like ghosts & eat like ghouls Oh! it is terribly sad.'

The Elgars stayed with Colonel and Lady Mary Trefusis near Truro from 2 to 7 July 1910. She was the former Lady Mary Lygon, subject of Variation 13 in the 'Enigma' set. The possibility of dedicating the future Symphony to the memory of Edward VII may have arisen during this visit; certainly it was Lady Mary, from 1895 a Woman of the Bedchamber to the future Queen Mary (1867-1953), who took up the matter in March 1911. She gave Arthur Bigge (1849-1931), private secretary to George V (1910-36) a résumé of a letter from Elgar:

> Encouraged by King Edward's interest & kind enquiries about his Compositions, he intended to ask permission to dedicate a recent symphony (a big orchestral work) to H.M. before his death.
> Would His Majesty sanction its dedication to the Memory of King Edward - in some such form as: Dedicated to the memory of King Edward VII by gracious permission of HM. King George V.

She added by way of conclusion: 'As Elgar is the greatest living composer in any country, the work would be worthy of such a dedication'; so permission was granted.

At the end of his scores Elgar usually named places of significance to their creation. In case of the keyboard draft for Symphony no.2, he signed it off with 'Careggi' and 'Tintagel'. The MS full score added two other names and a mis-spelling: 'Carreggi', 'The Hut', 'Tintagel' and 'Plas Gwyn'. The printed full score links 'Venice' to 'Tintagel'. Some sketching was done at Careggi near Florence in April 1909; further work had been done at 'The Hut', Frank Schuster's Maidenhead home on the Thames; Venice had provided inspiration for the two middle movements; Plas Gwyn was where concentrated work on the Symphony and its scoring had brought the task to conclusion on 28 February 1911. But what of Tintagel?

Elgar was at the rocky headland in Cornwall for two nights at the beginning of April 1910. It was part of a motor tour with Frank Schuster. Elgar kept a diary, and on 3 April they left Plymouth: 'Weather changed. drizzling rain so Frank quickly changed plans so as to get better roads for bad weather - at 11 started to Tintagel' The weather deteriorated: 'Snowstorm on crossing the moors - arrd. at Tintagel about 3.30 Sent in *wrong* names to the Wortleys - Frank's joke. Walked to cove & thro' cavern - then tea - then to Wortley's & walked with them to castle.' Alice Stuart

Wortley, Elgar's 'Windflower', had been anxious he should see Tintagel, as her daughter explained:

> It was Mrs Wortley who after much persuasion induced Sir Edward and their mutual great friend Mr.Schuster to visit Tintagel, saying that if only Sir Edward once saw it, he would write something so wonderful! Sir Edward, highly amused, used to say that she would have to be responsible for anything, however dreadful, that he might compose as a result of the visit!

Clare Stuart Wortley confirms the poor weather:

> We all walked down to the sea in the 'Cove', below the Castle ruins; and saw it all in very bad weather, at its most stern and forbidding; we three Wortleys loudly bewailing that Tintagel should so badly greet so great a guest. Sir Edward said very little, but did not complain.

He and Schuster stayed at the Wharncliffe Arms in the village, which did not impress him at all despite the presence of the Old Post Office, a delectable 14th-century survival which Pevsner describes as 'the most famous of Cornish stone cottages, low, dark, picturesque, with roofs like a cluster of hills, and of a slaty hue like elephant skin'. But much of the village had been swept away in the 19th century, due largely to Tennyson's visit in 1848, when he noted 'Black cliffs and caves and storm and wind', and the subsequent success of the *Idylls of the King*. Elgar was determined not to be impressed, as his diary of 4 April makes clear: 'Weather seems improving, some sun rose early & breakfast alone. *Awfully* dreary village. Coast fine but not so fine as Llangranog', his 1901 Welsh refuge which greatly influenced the Introduction and Allegro. In the afternoon they drove to Boscastle, and Clare Stuart Wortley reported better conditions: 'On the drive home some evening sunshine was enjoyed, and the party walked (a regular custom with Mrs.Wortley) the steep parts of the road down into, and up out of, the Rocky Valley. It was then ... that the austere yet lyrical beauty of the Tintagel country really showed itself to Sir Edward at last.' The next morning they left. What, then, was the inspiration of Tintagel for Elgar? Perhaps not more than two chords.

Elgar could not know that structures on the Lower Terrace at Tintagel went back to c.400 and that some fifty years later begins a period when Tintagel seems to be the main base for imported pottery from the eastern Mediterranean. It probably came from mainland Greece, Crete and the Greek islands where wine was produced. Some may have come from the Antioch area and formed a link between Tintagel and Elgar's Mediterranean cruise of 1905. Costly imports such as amphorae for olive oil and wine may have been exchanged for Cornish tin or lead, but they suggest a stronghold of considerable importance. The importance of the citadel may have generated the legends that cling to the wild headland. And they in turn may have been the reason why Richard, Earl of Cornwall (1209-72), brother of Henry III and his regent when the king was absent in France, decided to build a castle at Tintagel, a hardly practical site. Defence of the castle was easy enough, since there was only one narrow entrance; but by the same token siege was equally easy. The sloping contours making for the slate cliffs needed much levelling before the mainland and island courts could be laid out and the great hall built. Richard of Cornwall began his castle in 1233. By that time King Arthur's connection with the site was well established. Richard was therefore entering on a rich heritage of association. With his election as king of the Romans in 1257, he could make King Arthur serve his ends not only as Earl of Cornwall but also as a potential Holy Roman Emperor (an ambition he never achieved). By now Arthur had widespread continental fame such as would eventually establish him as a plausible ancestor for the Habsburgs in the reckoning of Maximilian I.

Richard seems to have constructed his impractical castle in the hope that he was occupying the very site of such strong Arthurian associations and would therefore be heir to the traditions of chivalry and bravery that hung about the place. He would thus become legitimate successor to Arthur and have natural claim on the loyalty of Cornwall. The castle itself was not of the most recent design, such as Richard used elsewhere. In this also Richard may have wished to give the impression he occupied an Arthurian castle on its Arthurian rock. The castle was Richard's creation, though he was probably rarely there, and future earls had little use for it. The roof of the great hall was dismantled a hundred years after it was built, and the Black Prince as Duke of Cornwall showed no interest in the place. In about 1540 John Leland (c.1503-52) reported its condition: 'the residew of the buildings of the castel be sore wetherbeten and in ruine (but it hath been a large thinge).' The site became pasturage for sheep.

If it was the legends that drew Richard of Cornwall to Tintagel, this was largely the responsibility of Geoffrey of Monmouth (c.1100-55), probably a Benedictine monk who studied at Oxford, became archdeacon of Llandaff, and bishop of St.Asaph in 1152. His *Historia Regum Britanniae* was in circulation by 1139, and it purported to translate a work given him by Walter, archdeacon of Oxford, who had brought it from Brittany. Geoffrey describes it as 'a very old book in the British tongue', which may have meant early Welsh. He covers a period of almost two thousand years, from Brutus to Cadwallader (d.689). Drawing on such sources as Nennius (fl.c.830) and Bede and a powerful imagination, Geoffrey made Brutus or Brut the ancestor of British kings that included Arthur. Brut was the great-grandson of Aeneas who had fled the destruction of Troy to found Rome. He had killed his father and gathered a Trojan following to land in Britain and found Troynovant or New Troy. The name was derived from that of the Trinovantes, a British tribe settled in the London region, and in course of time London became the name of the new stronghold. Lear and his daughters featured in Geoffrey's history, a subject suggested to Elgar in July 1913 when Chaliapine (1873-1938) was at Severn House; but Elgar was too much absorbed at the time in *Falstaff.*

Geoffrey's main achievement was to construct the picture of a Britain that gained immortal fame from the splendour of Arthur's rule. The idea of a great warrior defeating the Saxons comes from the history of Nennius. But Geoffrey, in magnificent flights of imagination, has Arthur triumphant over Scotland, Norway and France. Refusing to pay tribute to Rome, he conquers a Roman army in the east of France. That is the summit of his achievement, and it is then he must return to quell a rebellion by his nephew Mordred, who had taken possession of his kingdom and his queen. Mordred is killed, but the wounded Arthur is taken to Avalon, described in Geoffrey's Latin verse Life of Merlin as 'the island of fruits called Fortunate presided over by Morgan and her eight sisters skilled in leechcraft'.

Geoffrey is indeed the first to introduce Merlin, who has a special link with Tintagel. When Elgar accompanied the Stuart Wortleys to the cove where once ships of the late Classical period had beached, he probably entered 'Merlin's cave', where the aged wizard is said to have held the infant Arthur in his hands. But it was the castle above that was most important for Arthur's origin. Geoffrey tells how Uther Pendragon celebrated one Eastertide in London with all his nobles about him: 'Among the others there was present Gorlois, Duke of Cornwall, with his wife Ygerna, who was the most beautiful woman in Britain. When the King saw her there among the other women, he was immediately filled with desire for her, with the result that he took no notice of anything else, but devoted all his attention to her.' Gorlois was justifiably alarmed and departed with his wife without the necessary leave. Uther's wrath and lust were such that he ravaged Cornwall. Gorlois would not risk pitched battle but fortified his castle. He left Ygerna at Tintagel, as 'the safest place under his control'. In his desperation for Ygerna, Uther consulted a soldier friend. Ulfin suggested the only possible solution:

> The castle is built high above the sea, which surrounds it on all sides, and there is no other way in except that offered by a narrow isthmus of rock. Three armed soldiers could hold it against you, even if you stood there with the whole kingdom of Britain at your side. If only the prophet Merlin would give his mind to the problem.

Merlin was summoned and had the necessary drugs to transform the appearance of all of them. Uther became Gorlois and was able to sleep with Ygerna: 'That night she conceived Arthur, the most famous of men, who subsequently won great renown by his outstanding bravery.' Meanwhile Gorlois had sallied from *his* castle and been slain so that Uther could take rightful possession of Ygerna. Tradition bound Arthur ever more closely with Tintagel, making it his birthplace and ultimately his fortress.

For the Elgar of 1910, who had recently found inspiration for the two 'Windflower' themes in the Violin Concerto, was to quote so tellingly from *Julian and Maddalo* the following year, and was to send Alice Stuart Wortley materials from which he had worked up Symphony no.2, the more relevant legends of Tintagel were likely to have been those involving Tristan and Isolde. The day before departure for his last tour of America, which he disliked more than ever, Elgar wrote to the 'Windflower' on 24 March 1911: 'I have asked Alice to send you (- only a loan!) the sketches of the (your) Symphony - they may amuse you & you can let me have them again when I return - if you have a piano at Tintagel you can play them there & - well, *and* - .' While in the States he heard from her, as he wrote on 26 April: 'I loved having your letter from Tintagel & all the sea was in it.'

The association of Tintagel with Tristan and Isolde may well antedate that of Arthur. There is a memorial pillar at Castle Dore near Fowey marking a Christian burial of the early 6th century. The inscription reads, 'Drustanus hic iacit Cunomori filius', which is as near the name 'Tristan' as probability needs, and 'Eselt' occurs as a female name in a charter boundary of 967 concerning West Cornwall. It may well be, then, that theirs is an ancient Cornish tale, discovered and adapted by Béroul at the end of the 12th century. He identifies Tintajol or Tintaguel as a stronghold of King Mark. In an early version of the Tristan tale, he is son to a prince of northwest Britain and born to Blancheflor, Mark's sister, who died in childbirth. He is trained in all the arts of chivalry and the court, becoming an expert minstrel, linguist and chess player, peerless as horseman or fencer, and in hunting skills. It is after capture by pirates that he comes to Cornwall and the court of his uncle Mark at Tintagel. A first task was to protest in fight the claim that the Irish giant Morholt made against King Mark for unpaid tribute. Morholt's ship rode in the sea, as Malory has it, 'evyn by Castell of Tyntagell'. Morholt is slain and Tristan wounded. The only hope for Tristan is Ireland and its medical skill. Mark prepared a boat for Tristan without sail or oar which should take him where it would: 'sir Trystrames toke his harp with hym. And so he was putt into the see.' His landfall near the Irish royal castle could not have been more propitious: 'And at his aryvayle he sate and harped in his bedde a merry lay: suche one herde they never none in Irelonde before that tyme.'

The King of Ireland put the now named 'Tramtryste' into the hands of his daugher, 'because she was a noble surgeon'; and so she healed him. He 'learned hir to harpe and she began to have a grete fantasy unto hym'. Like many mediaeval knights, Tristan must slay a dragon. In time Isolde realises he is the killer of Morholt, and she takes the Wagnerian course of sparing him. Despite this, she is to be the wife of King Mark, with the added complication of the love potion drained with Tristan. But as in Wagner, there were watchful courtly eyes upon them: 'Than sir Andret gate unto hym twelve knyghtis, and at mydnyght he sette uppon sir Trystrames secretly and suddeynly. And there sir Trystrames was takyn naked a-bed with La Beale Isode.' He was bound in 'a chapell that stood upon the see rockys'. Thence 'he lepe oute and felle uppon the craggys in the see'. In Malory there follow many adventures which Wagner, stripping away all but essentials, omits. Tristan is exiled and marries Isolde of Brittany; but it is no love match. Returning to Cornwall, he is slain eventually by Mark himself: 'Also that traytoure kynge slew the noble knyght sir Trystram as he sate harpynge afore hys lady, La Beall Isode, with a trenchaunte glayve, for whos dethe was the most waylynge of ony knyght that ever was in kynge Arthur dayes.' King Mark was killed in his turn and Isolde did not long survive. Malory's tears and those of the mediaeval world were shed for the lovers but not for Mark.

As in so much else, Walter Scott was a Tristan pioneer. His *Minstrelsy of the Scottish Border* was published in 1802-3, and his main pastiche contribution was 'Thomas the Rhymer'. Part 3 has the bard of Ercildoune sing of Tristrem and Isolde:

> Through many a maze the winning song
>   In changeful passion led,
> Till bent at length the listening throng
>   O'er Tristrem's dying bed.
>
> His ancient wounds their scars expand,
>   With agony his heart is wrung:
> O where is Isolde's lilye hand,
>   And where her soothing tongue?
>
> ***
>
> She comes! she comes! She only came
>   To see her Tristrem die.
>
> She saw him die; her latest sigh
>   Join'd in a kiss his parting breath;
> The gentlest pair that Britain bare
>   United are in death.

In his 'Notes', Scott gives Thomas high praise:

> Few personages are so renowned in tradition as Thomas of Ercildoune, known by the appellation of *The Rhymer*. Uniting, or supposed to unite, in his person, the powers of poetical composition, and of vaticination, his memory, even after the lapse of five hundred years, is regarded with veneration by his countrymen.

Part 3 propounds Scott's view about the authorship of *Sir Tristrem*: 'Thomas the Rhymer was renowned among his contemporaries as the author of the celebrated romance of *Sir Tristrem*.' Scott and the contemporaries deserved to be right, but were wrong. *Sir Tristrem* probably originated in London and was clerk's work and not a minstrel's, dependent on the French rather than inspiring it. But Scott's publication of *Sir Tristrem* in 1804 was a rallying cry to the century which was answered with enthusiasm.

Thomas Hogg, of Scott's period and born at Kelso, preserved a strange Tintagel tradition in his *Fabulous History of the ancient Kingdom of Cornwall* (1827). He was a Truro schoolmaster, but is unlikely to have known the *Folie Tristran* fragment at Oxford, the earliest source for the legend:

> The wonderous fabric, twice a-year,
> From nature's face would disappear.
> At Christmas-eve, when blazing fires
> Illumed the halls with wreathing spires,
> Dissolved in clouds, it passed away,
> Like mist before the morning ray.
> When vernal flowers perfumed the plain,
> The pile, majestic, towered again.
>
> When vaulted rose the summer skies,
> Again, it fled from mortal eyes:
> And heaven's broad canopy of blue
> Hung bootless o'er the vanished view.
> Skilled natives of the neighbouring place,
> No vestiges, could ever trace:
> By landmarks, permanent, they told,
> Where would arise the enchanted hold.

Tales of so elusive a Tintagel may have arisen from tricks of mist and fog swirling densely round the headland.

Matthew Arnold was first of the Victorian poets to rehearse the Tristan legend. Perhaps his version, superficially cool and balanced, linked most closely to his own experience. The idea came to him at Thun in Switzerland, when he had taken his decision to break with 'Marguerite' in 1849 and was pursuing the idea of marriage to Frances Wightman. If he had two 'Iseults' in his life, these were they. It became a favourite poem of Arnold's and was originally published with *Empedocles on Etna*, his grandest achievement, in 1852. Elgar was fascinated by *Empedocles*, and the music he associated with it was eventually to find a home in Symphony no.3. The other poem he surely knew, but the subject was eternally Wagner's. Arnold adopts a partly dramatic form for *Tristram*, who is in dialogue with his page and the two Iseults; but the bulk of the poem is narrative, painfully so and resignedly. Tristram on his sick bed addresses his page:

> Is she not come? The messenger was sure.
> Prop me upon the pillows once again -
> Raise me, my Page: this cannot long endure.
> Christ! what a night! how the sleet whips the pane!
> What lights will those out to the northward be?

The page replies they are 'The lanterns of the fishing-boats at sea'. Iseult of Brittany stands by the dying fire, but it is the other Iseult for whom Tristram yearns. The narrator tells how Tristram is haunted by troubled dreams in his sickness:

> Tyntagel on its surge-beat hill,
> The pleasaunce walks, the weeping queen,
> The flying leaves, the straining blast,
> And that long, wild kiss - their last.

But then:

> What voices are these on the clear night air ?
> What lights in the court ? what steps on the stair ?

It is indeed Iseult of Ireland; but she comes too late, as Tristram knows:

> Now to sail the seas of Death I leave thee;
> One last kiss upon the living shore!

That granted, Iseult cannot long survive, and the narrator takes over:

> The air of the December night
> Steals coldly around the chamber bright,
> Where those lifeless lovers be.

Study for Iseult on the Ship by Morris

***

A year had flown, and o'er the sea away,
In Cornwall, Tristram and queen Iseult lay;
In King Marc's chapel, in Tyntagel old.

Tennyson's treatment of the Tristan story is contained within 'The Last Tournament', penultimate section of 'The Round Table', when Arthur's world is disintegrating. It was added to *The Idylls of the King* in

1871. It is framed by glimpses of Dagonet, cavorting at the outset and in tears at the end. By now adultery has struck at the roots of Arthurian chivalry:

> Dagonet, the fool, whom Gawain in his mood
> Had made mock-knight of Arthur's Table Round,
> At Camelot, high above the yellowing woods,
> Danced like a wither'd leaf before the hall.

Tristram had recently returned to Camelot and been victor in a tournament of the previous day, when there had come a message through a churl maimed by the Red Knight:

> "My tower is full of harlots, like his court,
> But mine are worthier, seeing they profess
> To be none other than themselves - and say
> My knights are all adulterers like his own,
> But mine are truer, seeing they profess
> To be none other; and say his hour is come."

Tristram makes his way to Lyonnesse and the west and attains his goal,

> Tintagil, half in sea, and high on land,
> A crown of towers.

Isolt recognises at once the footsteps are Tristram's:

> Catlike thro' his own castle steals my Mark,
> But warrior-wise thou stridest thro' his halls.

The Mark of Tennyson follows Wagner at the start of Act 2:

> But harken! have ye met him? hence he went
> To-day for three days' hunting - as he said -
> And so returns belike within an hour.
> Mark's way, my soul!

It was Mark who told Isolt about the marriage in Brittany:

> Then flash'd a levin-brand; and near me stood,
> In fuming sulphur blue and green, a fiend -
> Mark's way to steal behind one in the dark -
> For there was Mark: "He has wedded her," he said,
> Not said, but hiss'd it.

Tristram puts round Isolt's neck the ruby carcanet he won at the tournament:

> But, while he bow'd to kiss the jewell'd throat,
> Out of the dark, just as the lips had touch'd,
> Behind him rose a shadow and a shriek -
> 'Mark's way,' said Mark, and clove him thro' the brain.

That same night King Arthur returned from the north to find that Guenevere had fled to Almesbury. Dagonet clung sobbing about his feet: 'I shall never make thee smile again.'

The poetic dedication to Swinburne's *Tristram of Lyonesse* is dated April 1882, just three months before Richter conducted at Drury Lane the first complete English performance of Wagner's *Tristan*. Favourable accounts went to Bayreuth, where Wagner was preparing to launch *Parsifal*. The nine sections that make up *Tristram of Lyonesse* have many incidents more than Wagner's and also the addition of Iseult of Brittany. But it is Swinburne who approaches closest to the heady music of Wagner and his intensity. The love-draught is administered thus:

> Nor other hand there needed, nor sweet speech
> To lure their lips together; each on each
> Hung with strange eyes and hovered as a bird
> Wounded, and each mouth trembled for a word;
> Their heads neared, and their hands were drawn in one,
> And they saw dark, though still the unsunken sun
> Far through fine rain shot fire into the south;
> And their four lips became one burning mouth.

They approach Tintagel, as at the end of Wagner's Act 1:

> They heard not how the landward waters rang,
> Nor saw where high into the morning sprang,
> Riven from the shore and bastioned with the sea,
> Toward summits where the north wind's nest might be,
> A wave-walled palace with its eastern gate
> Full of the sunrise now and wide at wait,
> And on the mighty-moulded stairs that clomb
> Sheer from the fierce lip of the lapping foam
> The knights of Mark that stood before the wall.

Swinburne has his attempt at Wagner's Act 2 and its night of love:

Tintagel from the air

So fared they night and day as queen and king
Crowned of a kingdom wide as day and night.
Nor ever cloudlet swept or swam in sight
Across the darkling depths of their delight
Whose stars no skill might number, nor man's art
Sound the deep stories of its heavenly heart.
Till, even for wonder that such life should live,
Desires and dreams of what death's self might give
Would touch with tears and laughter and wild speech
The lips and eyes of passion, fain to reach,
Beyond all bourne of time or trembling sense,
The verge of love's last possible eminence.

Tristram is already dead when Iseult arrives in Brittany:

> And ere her ear might hear her heart had heard,
> Nor sought she sign for witness of the word;
> But came and stood above him newly dead,
> And felt his death upon her: and her head
> Bowed, as to reach the spring that slakes all drouth;
> And their four lips became one silent mouth.

Laurence Binyon, soon to be an Elgarian acquaintance and friend, had a 'poetry working holiday' in Cornwall during the summer of 1899; one of the results was *Tristram's End*, which won golden opinions from W.B.Yeats (1865-1939):

> Swinburne's 'Tristram' has the 'voluptuous beauty' in its heart & Matthew Arnold's has but stray beautiful passages & nothing in its heart. But in your poem is the whole shining substance & for generations & generations it will come to lovers not as literature, but as their own memories. There will never be a true lover, who shall read it without tears, I think.

Binyon's Tristram is near death in Brittany, tended by Isoult of the White Hands. A ship approaches and she declares the sail is black, but Tristram is incredulous:

> "It cannot be, it cannot, shall not be!
> I will not die until mine own eyes see."
> Despair, more strong than hope, lifts his weak limbs;
> He stands and draws deep effort from his breath,
> He trembles, his gaze swims,
> He gropes his steps in pain,
> Nigh fainting, till he gain
> Salt air and brightness from the outer door
> That opens on the cliff-built bastion floor
> And the wide ocean gleaming far beneath.

Binyon takes us towards the end of Wagner's Act 3, and now Isoult, arriving under a white sail, must climb a steep dark stair that taxes all her strength:

> But when that wasted face anew she sees,
> Despair anew subdues her knees:
> She fails, yet still she mounts by sad degrees,
> With all her soul into her gaze upcast,
> Until at last, at last . . .

With both lovers dead, there is no 'Liebestod', unless it be the steady movement of the sea:

> Calm, calm the moving waters all the night
> On to that shore roll slow,
> Fade into foam against the cliff's dim height,
> And fall in a soft thunder, and upsurge
> For ever out of unexhausted might,
> Lifting their voice below
> Tuned to no human dirge;
> Nor from their majesty of music bend
> To wail for beauty's end
> Or towering spirit's most fiery overthrow.

Elgar's admiration for and debt to Wagner has been well documented. The two works for which his veneration seems never to have wavered were *Tristan* and *Die Meistersinger*, which happens to contain in Act 3 the most moving of all *Tristan* quotations, when Hans Sachs expresses no desire to share the fate of King Mark. Elgar first heard the *Tristan* prelude and 'Liebestod' at a Crystal Palace concert in memory of Wagner on 3 March 1883. Against the programme mention of the 'Liebestod' he wrote: 'This is the finest thing of W's that I have heard up to the present. I shall never forget this.' The vocal score of *Tristan* given him by Alice Elgar for his 1893 birthday bears his inscription at the start of the prelude: 'This Book contains the Height, - the Depth, - the Breadth, - the Sweetness, - the Sorrow, - the Best and the whole of the Best of This world and the Next.' In his letter to Littleton of 13 April 1911 Elgar wrote about the Second Symphony finale: 'the whole of the sorrow is smoothed out & ennobled in the last movement, which ends in a calm &, *I hope & intend*, elevated mood.' And he added: 'The last movement speaks for itself I think: a broad sonorous, rolling movement throughout.' As so often, though, Elgar did not quite give everything away. That last *crescendo* and *fp* at the end of the movement indicate two chords that, just for a moment, in the midst of radiant diatonics, conjur the world of Wagner's *Tristan*. It is indeed Elgar's heartfelt homage to all that Tintagel meant to him.

13 - Immemorial Ind

'Severn House', Hampstead, became the Elgars' home from 1 January 1912. During the preceding months they had become increasingly metropolitan, and a move to the capital seemed the logical step. King George V's Coronation, for which Elgar had written a march and brief Offertorium, was in June 1911. Lady Elgar reported the events of 17 June: 'E. was looking at letters. He suddenly looked up & said "It is the O.M." What a thrill of joy - A. cd. see the pleasure in his face - *The* thing he wished for so much - D.G. for such happy moments ... E.'s first idea was to give a present to each servant & joy was general.' The afternoon activities were also significant: 'E. to see fancy dresses A. & C.. to Albert Hall to hear C.Butt sing The King's Way *splendid* It was another thrill to hear it.' The great success of *Pomp and Circumstance* March no.4 in 1907 had induced Lady Elgar to provide words for the trio tune celebrating 'Kingsway', the new London street that had emerged from a slum clearance scheme. Lady Elgar was again her father's daughter as she rose to the occasion in 1909:

> The noblest street in London town,
> The stir of life beats up and down;
> In serried ranks the sabres shine,
> And Art and Craft and Thought divine,
> All crowd and fill the great highway,
> The Kingsway, the Kingsway!

Less fortunate had to be considered in a new C minor section specially added by Elgar:

> On dreary roads in London town
> The sick and poor sink sadly down
> In gloom: but grace and pity meet
> When King and Queen stretch hands and greet
> The weary ones;
> 'This is,' they say, 'Our King's Way, and our Queen's way.'

Elgar himself wrote the final verse:

> England's sons across the sea;
> They too will fight to keep it free:
> Let every voice in England say, -
> 'God keep the Way by night and day,

> The King of England's Way!
> The King's Way, the King's Way!

That was surely Coronation stuff, and indeed Elgar seemed attuned to royal matters when he answered Lord Knollys's letter that same day:

> I accept with the greatest gratitude the Order of Merit which His Majesty the King has done me the honour to wish to confer upon me.
> If it should be convenient, & not unusual, I shall be much obliged if you will be so good as to convey to His Majesty an expression of my deep appreciation of the distinction and of my loyalty & devotion now & at all times.

The glow continued three days later at a Coronation rehearsal in Westminster Abbey:

> After Music rehearsal, E's Offertorium & March, most beautiful, we went into the Nave & sat in front seats & saw rehearsal of procession, peers in robes &c. - Some of them & Mary Trefusis saw E. & called out their Congratulations, very nice. We all three really enjoyed it It is a happy moment to look back on.

That evening Elgar went to a Shakespeare Ball. Friends had been impressed with his costume and 'thought he looked regal in it'. It was of the Henry V period. On 21 June Lady Elgar chose a dress for the Coronation and bought 'veil & feather in *case* of going to Westminster Abbey'. Was it not going to be too difficult 'to sit 7 hrs. in those seats'? On Coronation day it seemed so. In one of his less chivalrous acts, Elgar had decided they would stay at home: 'A. very tired & dreadfully disappointed, in bed till afternoon.' When he wrote to Ivor Atkins on 17 July, Elgar was still exultant, basking in the splendour of his new Order:

> Worcester people (save you!) seem to have small notion of the glory of the O.M. I was marshalled correctly at Court & at the Investiture *above* the G.C.M.G. & G.C.V.O. (the highest Lord Beauchamp can go!) - next G.C.B. in fact. Such things as K.C.B.'s &c are *very cheap* it seems beside O.M.

Thus were the Beauchamps of Madresfield put in their place, and so, yet more decisively, was Sir Henry Gee Roberts.

The first score to emanate from the Severn House music room in 1912 was *The Crown of India*, Elgar's bid to take over also the Major-General's territory. What of the house itself? It had been commissioned in 1887 from Norman Shaw (1831-1912) by the artist Edwin Long (1829-91). Such was his commercial success that this was the second Shaw house built for

Callista the Image Maker *by Edwin Long*

him. He had been able to fill the gap left by the death of Doré (1832-83), as explained in the *Magazine of Art* for 1891 (xl):

> When Gustave Doré died, the caterers for that devout and sentimental portion of the public who took unctuous delight in the wonders of the Doré gallery could find in England no worthier heir to his mantle than Mr.Long, who exerted himself considerably in their behalf, and produced a number of gently inspired and scriptural paintings.

Indeed in the 'Kelston' year of 1887 (Long named the house after his father's family home in Somerset) Long was engaged on a large painting to be called *Callista the Image Maker*. The subject was taken from John Henry Newman's novel of 1856, which traced the conversion and ultimate martyrdom of the sculptress Callista, a fine type of cultivated pagan. The novel was set in Carthage, and a selling point in the publicity material when the Elgars were considering the house was 'old Carthaginian mosaics' in the hall, 'believed to be 2000 years old'.

The house was twice featured in *The Architect* of 1890. The first occasion, on 7 March, showed two exterior views, plans of the house, and the extensive ground-floor corridor, usually described as a 'picture gallery'. H.H.Spielmann in his *Painters in their Studios* described it as 'the splendid corridor that has been designed it would seem, to allow of the inmates taking extensive walking exercise on a rainy day or for hanging up long rows of Elizabethan ancestors'. Edwin Long used it for paintings and much furniture; the Elgars had General Roberts's Indian weapons and trophies on a part of the wall near the porch. *The Architect* of the following week concentrated in two photographs on the front door, covered by a semicircular stone hood supported on Doric columns.

Spielmann was rightly impressed by it: 'The front door, as it glistens under the ample porch, is a marvel to look at, consisting as it does of brass plates beaten into the representation of a mediaeval knight at the wars - his departure, his victories, and his glorious return.' Perhaps so. The five bands of narrative between ornamental borders were designed by Long and are indeed concerned with mediaeval knighthood. At the top are fourteen knights with their shields and hands clasped in prayer. Beneath is an inscription in French: 'PIEUX QUOIQUE PREUX' (pious though valorous).[1] The second register shows knights in prayer before a priestly figure holding a cross aloft; and to the right knights ride up to their ladies. In the central panel the knights ride off from their ladies to the ferocious combat of the fourth register. Below are two scenes: a knight is dubbed by his lady; and a slain knight is carried to burial. At the bottom two fiercely arched snakes hiss hatred at each other. Under the three central scenes runs an English inscription more suited to Elgar the literary man and lifelong devotee of Scott than to the knight-composer and O.M. entering his latest residence:

> THEIR BONES ARE DUST THEIR GOOD SWORDS ARE RUST
> THEIR SOULS ARE WITH THE LORD I TRUST
> THEIR PEACE TO SHARE WAIT PATIENTLY WE MUST

This is Long's adaptation of Walter Scott out of Coleridge. The original is *The Knight's Tomb* by Coleridge, where the last three lines run

> The Knight's bones are dust,
> And his good sword rust; -
> His soul is with the saints, I trust.

Scott used an adaptation in both chapter 8 of *Ivanhoe* and chapter 9 of *Castle Dangerous*. He cites his source:

> These lines are part of an unpublished poem by Coleridge, whose muse so often tantalizes with fragments which indicate her powers, while the manner in which she flings them from her betrays her caprice, yet whose unfinished sketches display more talent than the laboured masterpieces of others.

---

[1] I am grateful to Brian Trowell for elucidating the two words on the front door inscription that baffled me.

Scott's version approaches that of Long:

> The knights are dust,
> And their good swords are rust,
> Their souls are with the saints, we trust.

What became Elgar's music room is described in 1891 by Sir Merton Russell-Cotes, Long's main patron, in *Home and Abroad* (Bournemouth, 1921):

> He afterwards invited me to go up with him into his studio, which was reached by a wide corridor running the whole length of one side of the house, and a grand staircase at the other end. It was one of the finest studios that I have ever entered, both for size and light. He explained to me that it extended over the whole of the house. He was at work at that time on a huge canvas depicting our Saviour preaching from a boat on the Sea of Galilee.

The Crown of India music was commissioned for a masque at the Coliseum to commemorate the Delhi durbar of 1911. It was Elgar's opportunity to sum up the various Indian influences that had been brought to bear on him during his life. Ann Elgar's scrapbook cuttings did not ignore India. There is an article on 'Indian Art', largely concerned with George Birdwood's *The Industrial Arts of India*. The point was made that Hindu religious life was the dominant influence on art, and a not altogether happy one 'assignable to the fact that all the Puranic deities are hideous monsters, as unsuitable as toads and dragons to the higher forms of artistic representation'. *Ramayana* and *Mahabharata* scenes might, however, have considerable charm. Whether General Roberts had inclination or leisure to inspect the superb Kota art collection once the Mutiny had subsided is unknown. Maharao Ram Singh (1827-66), whom Roberts had rescued, was described as 'one of Kotah's most vigorous and jovially eccentric rulers', having persuaded an elephant to walk round a lofty balustrade of the palace. He was painted more than any ruler of Kota, in a vivid series of secular scenes, a last fling before the onslaught of photography. General Roberts may have looked and admired; but there is no evidence for Indian miniatures at Hazeldine.[2]

Elgar wrote to Alfred Littleton about *The Crown of India* on 8 January 1912, a week after moving into Severn House: 'The Masque is going to be

[2] Thakur Jaswant Singh of Kota, at the age of eighty-six, not only sang local songs to me but supplied me with much information about the Maharao and Sir Henry Gee Roberts; it was enjoyable and I am grateful.

very gorgeous & patriotic - Indian Durbar - & will last only 30 mins: I shall write the music at once & it will not interfere with other things - I think you will like the idea.' The author of the text, Henry Hamilton, was a prolific and varied playwright. At one moment it was a 'Dick Whittington' pantomime, then dramas from the French or Hungarian, a *Joan of Arc*, and a *Carmen* that met with Bernard Shaw's scorn in 1896: 'The dialogue only rises, not without effort, to the point of making the bare story intelligible to those of us who know the opera by heart.' George V was to be the only King Emperor to visit India, and the climax of the durbar ceremonies was when the King and Queen, in imperial purple and on golden thrones, received the homage of the Indian princes. *The Times* thought them 'remote but beneficent, raised far above the multitude but visible to all'.

Yet not all the Indian princes had come. Maharana Fateh Singh (1853-1924) of Mewar (Udaipur) had been unable to face the 1903 durbar of Lord Curzon (1859-1925), reaching his local railway station before turning back, mindful of the fact that no Maharana had paid respect to the Moguls in Delhi. In 1911 he was offered a seat of honour beside the King and Queen as senior prince; but he stayed in Udaipur. The Maharaja of Gwalior, on the other hand, received the signal honour of an additional two guns in his salute; his reply was to request George V and Queen Mary as godparents to his children named George Jivajirao and Mary Kamlaraja. George V himself had not been quite impeccable, entering Delhi on a horse rather than on the imperial elephant. He mounted an elephant later, to receive the princes' homage. Laurence James is eloquent on how appropriate this was:

> In many ways the late-Victorian and Edwardian Raj resembled the spectacles it staged so splendidly. It was stately and moved with the firm, deliberate tread of the principle prop of Indian state pageantry, the elephant. The direction was always forwards, but the pace was unhurried, which was fortunate, for no one was certain as to the ultimate goal, or when it would be reached. There was also something distinctly elephantine about the government itself. It was a complex and ponderous organism, fundamentally good-natured, but capable of frightening tantrums when its patience was exhausted.

This was the occasion for a grand political gesture. At the time of the Mutiny, the capital had been moved from Delhi, city of the Moguls and of their last remnant, the disgraced Bahadur Shah (1837-58), to Calcutta, mercantile base of the East India Company and of the magnificent Victoria Memorial planned by the viceroy Lord Curzon as some sort of answer to the Taj Mahal, and still under construction in 1911. *A Little Tour in India* by R.Palmer (1913) casts a dubious light on the durbar:

Untold millions of rupees have been spent, which go to enrich hotel-keepers, contractors and dressmakers; and all that is got for it is three or four fine shows and the rather arrogant assertion of the British Raj. Meanwhile there is already actual famine in some districts and great distress in others. The rajahs have spent all their spare cash in this show, and have no means of relieving their subjects: indeed, they themselves are likely to be hard up, as their revenues will probably fail them. And I very much doubt whether the political effect will be good. The common people are no doubt impressed by the display: but in this respect their own rajahs far outshine the King, and they are quite as likely to get the impression that their own princes are finer than ours as to realize that their fine princes are vassals of our King.

At Severn House, however, there was a work in hand that promised some financial reward and the shift of the capital back to Delhi was occasion for a show of patriotism that might involve a deal of Elgarian swagger touched by a glint of orientalism. Delhi had been an Indian capital from time immemorial, but Calcutta, though less conveniently placed, and notably so after the opening of the Suez Canal had magnified the status of Bombay, was the power base of the East India Company, and had become the administrative centre of British India. But the great durbars of 1877, when Victoria was declared Empress of India, and 1903, took place in Delhi as homage to its ancient history. While Elgar was at work in Severn House on the *Crown of India*, Edwin Lutyens (1869-1944) was summoned to the India Office in January 1912 and taken to the Garrick Club for discussion about the new capital. His address in the visitors' book was entered by his host as 'Delhi'. Herbert Baker (1862-46), soon to be his colleague, was interested what style he would adopt:

I wonder what you will do - whether you will drop the language and classical tradition and just go for surfaces - sun and shadow. It must not be Indian, not English, nor Roman, but it must be Imperial. In 2000 years there must be an Imperial Lutyens tradition in Indian architecture.

Elgar begins the exuberant prelude to *The Crown of India* with a quotation from his 'bulldog' music dating in this case from April 1903; it describes 'The sinful youth of Dan'. Tableau I of the Masque had for scene a temple 'typifying the legends and traditions of India' with the Taj Mahal as background. A semicircular amphitheatre of white marble led by steps to seats for India and her twelve great cities, all in position at curtain-up except Calcutta and Delhi. Darkness was infiltrated gradually by a steel-blue light, turning to amethyst, rose and then a golden glow. At the final rehearsal on 10 March Lady Elgar thought the 'dresses lovely. lights rather vague'. An Indian crowd filled the front of the stage, lying and squatting, with a drummer at one side and a couple of snake-charmers at the other, while Nautch Girls performed behind. India then greets her ten cities in words multiplied with historical references that must have been a delight to assemble but caused only *ennui* to the audience. At the end of the rehearsal Lady Elgar could only say: 'Speeches & Calcutta's & Delhi's arguments much too long.' Benares (now Varanasi) was first to be welcomed, by means of somewhat doubtful history and geography:

> Benares, Welcome, Eldest-born, to thee.
> Oh, dear among my daughters unto me!
> Whom three-score centuries have set supreme,
> Immutable, where Ganges' sainted stream
> To lave thy feet and lap thy threshold pours
> Those waters which a Pilgrim-world adores.
> Tyre knew thy traffic, Carthage owned thy state,
> And Prince and Paladin and Potentate
> About thine Imperial purple flung
> When Babylon and Nineveh were young
> And Rome was yet to be. In peace and war
> Thrice famed, thrice welcome!

Lucknow is greeted as a bulwark against the Mutiny, in terms Sir Henry Gee Roberts could well have approved:

> All hail, Lucknow! who rebel rage
> Dared and defied: a living glory yet
> Thy Leaguer! England shall never forget
> But thrill to think on, to her latest day,
> Thy stirring story of her sons at bay;
> While memory wakens, sweeter than her merle,
> The far, faint echo of thy bagpipes' skirl!

Elgar knew his history too. Snatches of music accompany India's greetings in melodrama, and the 'skirl' reminded him of Sir Colin Campbell (1792-1863), Indian commander-in-chief at the time, soon to be Lord Clyde, and so there are brief hints of *The Campbells are comin'* to comfort Lucknow in her hour of need.

Agra is the last to be addressed, with reference exclusively to the Taj Mahal:

> Though last, not last in love, upon whose brow
> Thy Shah Jahan his shining coronal,

The world's white wonder of the Taj Mahal,
Hath set, or like a pearl hath laid between
Thy hands to keep the memory green
Of her he loved; and give Man's Soul a sign
Of Death made luminous by Love divine.

Benares, from her position of pre-eminence as 'eldest-born' was called on
to reply in praise of India. This she did in a speech that was eventually
omitted in its entirety:

Thy daughters bless thee and their voices blend
With that unceasing song which doth ascend
To thee, and hath: triumphant over Time;
With thousand, thousand temple bells a-chime;
From endless plains from everlasting hills,
Vales ever-verdant, ever-running rills
That swell to rivers still to sound thy praise,
From wonder-haunted heights, from hidden ways,
From forest-fastness that thy jungle wreathes,
For ever and for evermore there breathes.

Agra prefers to sing her praise, and immediately the orchestral
introduction has recourse to what was the main refrain of Elgar's 1905
piano piece, *In Smyrna*. Later comes music from the *ad lib* cadenza
section near the end. The original inspiration was indeed 'Asiatic' but
belonged to the naval cruise with the Mediterranean Fleet, of which Lord
Charles Beresford had been appointed commander-in-chief on 1 May
1905. They reached Smyrna on 29 September and Elgar was impressed:
'Colour; movement; & camels - 100s - led by a donkey through the bazaar.
(This was my first touch with Asia. & I was quite overcome. the endless
camels made the scene more *real* than in Stamboul. the extraordinary
colour & movement, light & shade were intoxicating.' Elgar ended the
day's account with reference to his mosquito bites 'too awful', and to
Smyrna as 'one of the seven churches', to which allusion might be made in
the third oratorio that was never written. Specific musical stimulus came
on 1 October at the Mosque of dancing dervishes. The goal proved to be
a 'Small mosque. Received in great style. Music by five or six people very
strange & some of it quite beautiful - incessant drums & cymbals (small)
thro' the quick movements.'

There the music waited for Agra to take it up and expatiate on it at
some length. *The Times* felt the song was 'rather hampered by the
awkward refrain "O Immemorial Ind," which does not fall easily into
music'. Nor does it lead readily into sense, though it is repeated four times

Dancing Dervishes c.1610

by a chorus of all the cities, and once more by Agra herself. That, at least, is how the libretto has it; but the printed vocal score reduces the cities' interventions, and Agra's stock of religious references is curtailed. Urged on by Agra, India paints the contemporary scene as she sees it from her vantage point of the Coliseum:

> Each man reclines in peace beneath his palm.
> Brahman and Buddhist, Hindu with Islam
> Into one nation welded by the West,
> That in the Pax Britannica is blest.

India was becoming loquacious, and her imagination was outstripping fact. So her lines were cut. But she laments the continued absence of both Calcutta and Delhi from a conclave that must prepare an event of supreme importance:

> For, know, ere long in radiance on our skies
> The Sun of India shall himself arise.

She concludes with a sigh:

> Delhi her rights of old maintains, her new
> Calcutta; would the discord we might heal
> Giving to *both* content.

Elgar's trumpets peal for the arrival of Calcutta, attended by Commerce and Statecraft. She is in no mood for apology:

> Late! Am I late? Your pardon; but the cares
> Of council and of business, state-affairs
> Have kept me: not my fault that made you wait.
> But, 'tis the fortune that attends the great
> To be thus harassed. Even at my heels
> Stalks Commerce, while my leisure Statecraft steals.

India laughs at her mounting arrogance, but bids her be seated at her right. Calcutta is complacent that Delhi will sit less honourably:

> And on thy left! At last it would appear
> She learns her place. I do not see her though.
> Hath she departed - like her glories?

Elgarian trumpets are heard again, and Delhi makes her solemn entry in C minor, attended by Tradition and Romance. Her music foreshadows also that of St.George. Now Delhi demands the seat of honour, hurling insult at Calcutta's very site:

> Of mouldering village and of muddied creek
> By streaming rice-fields neighboured, by the reek
> And roar of the primeval jungle girt,
> While brimmed thy Hooghly with diluvial dirt!
> Thy 'mandate' mist and thy Maidan a marsh!
> Thy 'councillors' the bull-frogs croaking harsh!
> And wilt thou vaunt to *me* thy mushroom pomp
> Of new-made palaces? that wast a swamp
> One hundred years ago; when I a Queen
> Enthroned for forty centuries had been!

India has to keep the peace, and her first argument is that times change: 'Upon the longest day the sun must set.' Delhi will have none of it: 'When was it known the sun should set at noon?' India now realises the contestants must fight it out, and the cities agree that is the only course. Calcutta says she will give as good as she gets.

Delhi begins her case against the background associated with 'Immemorial Ind' in Agra's song, so we know at once she will plead antiquity:

The Red Fort, Delhi by James Harding

Fifteen centuries before
The Cross outflamed upon the Syrian sky
To change the history of the world - was *I*.

The 'Cross' had later to be omitted, if only because it had changed India
so little. But Delhi had those mighty Moguls to call on, and *The Times*
approved of Elgar's music: 'The march to which Delhi's Emperors of the
Mogul Dynasty enter in glittering procession reflects the glitter of the
stage.' Delhi summons them one by one: first Akbar (1556-1605), wise in
his dealings with the proud Rajputs and his impartiality towards many
religions; Jehangir (1605-27), whose splendid court at Agra as described
by our ambassador, Sir Thomas Roe (?1581-1644), was adapted by Milton
(1603-74) for the start of *Paradise Lost* Book 2:

> High on a throne of royal state, which far
> Outshone the wealth of Ormus and of Ind,
> Or where the gorgeous East with richest hand
> Showers on her kings barbaric pearl and gold,
> Satan exalted sat.

Then Shah Jehan (1627-58), who could only gaze from afar at the Taj
Mahal when imprisoned in his later years by his son Aurangzeb within the
fort of Agra; and Aurangzeb (1658-1707) the last, fanatic warrior for his
faith and subject during his life of a London play by Dryden (1631-1700).
All four repudiated Calcutta with varying degrees of scorn.
   Calcutta founds her claim on a vibrant present:

> A strenuous Yesterday, a strong To-day
> Are better than an aeon of decay,
> Barbaric splendours and bejewelled ease
> Adorned by Despots - and by Debauchees!
> Behold *me* throned upon thy shores, O Ind,
> Where to my footstool wafted by each wind
> There come of every nation to my quays,
> Peaceful Armadas out of all the seas.

Her main witness is 'John Company', personification of the East India
Company founded (1600) by Queen Elizabeth, and introduced by Elgar in
a graceful minuet, marked originally 'Maestoso antico'. Calcutta puts the
question: 'Shall Delhi be thy Capital - or I?' John Company expresses
breeding in the manner of his choice: approving of Calcutta, he shakes her
hand, but bows gracefully to Delhi while rejecting her. His agents are then
summoned to support Calcutta, among then Clive (1725-74), Warren
Hastings (1732-1818), Cornwallis (1738-1805), and Wellesley (1760-1842).

New Government House, Calcutta after James Fraser

In answer to Calcutta's demand that she be India's capital, Delhi plays
her masterstroke:

> Calcutta hath appealed to Britain's might,
> But Delhi will a worthier witness cite.
> Illuminant of England's aim and act,
> Spirit of England's chivalry compact,
> Thou that in Cappadocia's gloomy gorge
> Did'st beat the Dragon down - Appear, St.George!

He does so, but proves ultra-chivalrous to the extent that he feels unable
to choose between the contestants and delegates the task to the King-
Emperor, who not only embodies the saint's spirit but shares his name:

> Cities of Ind, on England's Saint that call,
> Think ye the choice of Chivalry can fall
> On one of you to leave the other bare,
> Where either famous is and both are fair?
> Nay, Delhi, - Oh delight of ancient days!
> Mine to approve thy beauties, not appraise
> Nor blur: not mine, Calcutta, to control
> Nor dim thy destinies, but to extol

> Thy growing greatness. Thus St.George upsums
> Your merits mutual. But one there comes
> In whom my spirit lives - in whom my name
> Is crowned! Let him your claim and counterclaim
> Adjudge.

A herald then announces that the Emperor and his consort are indeed on their way to receive the cities' homage. Much of India's rapturous response was cut, including some lines that push her vocabulary to its limit:

> With flags a-flutter and with flowers a-flame
> Unite, O Cities mine in clear acclaim
> As one, conjoint, conjubilant!

Delhi's response is almost biblical: 'So let it be! To Caesar I appeal!' while Calcutta is more matter-of-fact: 'And I commit my claim, Come woe, come weal!' India can only applaud and extol the British Raj in terms that were doubtless gratifying at the time and contained perhaps a grain of truth:

> Oh, happy India, now at one, at last;
> Not sundered each for self as in the past!
> Happy the people blest with Monarch just!
> Happy the Monarch whom His People trust!
> And happy Britain - that above all lands
> Still where she conquers counsels not commands!
> See wide and wider yet her rule extend
> Who of a foe defeated makes a friend,
> Who spreads her Empire not to get but give
> And free herself bids others free to live.

Not surprisingly St.George now bursts into song, managing three verses in praise of England's flag:

> Wherever England flies her flag
>   O'er what her sword hath won,
> Her claim to keep, to rule, to reap
>   She rests on duty done.
> Her title strong no tyrant brag
>   Of frowning fort nor fleet,
> But Right upheld and Rancour quelled
>   And Wrong beneath her feet.
>
> Of old I trod the Dragon down,
>   And yours it is to-day

The Dragons great of Greed and Hate
    And Ignorance to slay.
So, ne'er shall England lose renown
    Nor ever love shall lack,
But Freedom stand at her right hand
    Beneath the Union Jack.

Oh, Sons of merry England born!
    Oh, Knights of good St.George,
Still may your steel from head to heel
    Be bright from Honour's forge.
Still be your blades for England worn,
    Dear Land that hath no like!
And for her fame and in her Name
    Unsheathe the sword and strike.

The chorus after each verse starts with the cry to 'Lift aloft the Flag of England!' and continues in much the same vein, thus ending the first Tableau. The *Times* correspondent was disappointed with the saint's music: 'We looked for a second "Land of Hope and Glory" in St.George's song, "Lift aloft the flag of England," ... and it seemed laboured by comparison, nor when its refrain came as the climax of the Imperial Procession did it thrill us as it ought to have done.' As if by way of apology, Elgar slipped in a two-bar reference to the trio of *Pomp and Circumstance* March no.1 at the words 'Dear Land that hath no like!' His best bet would have been to offer the trio of *Pomp and Circumstance* no.4 to St.George, requesting Hamilton to match its rhythm, as Benson had done for no.1, or urging Lady Elgar to follow up the real success of *The King's Way* with an alternative devoted to a saint temporarily holding forth in the land of her birth.

Tableau II, 'Ave, Imperator', shifts to Delhi and presents a scene symbolical of the durbar, with an imperial pavilion and its thrones to await the royal pair. The introductory music is again supplied by Dan the bulldog, young still and sinful. Trumpets on the stage herald the entrance of warriors, accompanied by persistent striking of a tamtam. This is presumably what had been noted by *The Times* on 7 March: 'The orchestra will include a new gong contrived by Sir Edward Elgar for his special purpose.' Having poured in tumultuously, the warriors execute a G minor dance. Then at last India can enter in grand procession with all her cities and the Mogul emperors. It is not explained why the East India Company has preferred to stay at home. This is India's finest hour, when she reaches far and wide (some Latin even) for words adequate to exalt the imperial pair:

> Thunder ye cannon, play your clamourous part!
> The volleyed homage of a People's heart
> Outvoices you; tumultuous it tells
> Its tribute. Hark! the note of triumph swells!
> He comes! he comes! Upon our dazzled eyes
> The Sun of Britain and of Ind doth rise.

There follows a 'fanfaronade of trumpets' and the head of the imperial procession, with functionaries, soldiers and courtiers, files on to the stage. India now excels herself in a deft adaptation of Virgil, from Book 1 of the *Aeneid* (l.405). But alas, we do not see the goddess Venus on this occasion: ' "Incessu patuit Imperator" ' -

> Slow
> And stately comes he! Blow, ye trumpets, blow!
> Blow till ye waken Fame and bid her lips
> Acclaim that day she never shall eclipse.
> Now let her fanfare to the world proclaim
> "George, by the Grace of God, of that great name
> The Fifth - of those three Kingdoms that enring
> One realm, one royalty - Great Britain - King!
> And of Dominions broader born of these,
> Of all those Greater Britains overseas
> Yet again - King! - Defender of the Faith!
> Emperor of India!" -

Elgar has here his second great opportunity for a triumphal march, with clamorous trumpets on stage, St.George's introductory music now marked 'nobilmente', and a grand cantabile tune, inducing the chorus on its second appearance again to 'Lift aloft the Flag of England'. Yet maybe *The Times* was right to be disappointed:

> the music to which the Powers of India assemble to receive the "King-Emperor" in the second scene has something of the energy and culminating power which we have known in the "Pomp and Circumstance" marches, the Coronation Ode of 1902, and the Imperial March of last year's Coronation. Yet though they reflect these things there is no number in the masque which excels or even quite equals them.

The procession has now culminated in the arrival of the King-Emperor and his Queen, robed in purple splendour and crowned, their trains carried by pages. Here was another sticking-point for *The Times*:

Though we have the Durbar and the King-Emperor and his Consort, the whole is, of course, intended to be symbolical and not realistic, and it is necessary to remember this when a smooth-faced female figure heralded as "George, by the Grace of God, of that great name the fifth," enters in triumphal procession. Any other arrangement would be likely to be a still greater shock to loyal sensibilities, but it may be suggested that it was not quite necessary to identify the "King-Emperor" of the masque so closely with his Majesty as to name him, and the symbolic character essential to a masque might have been better maintained by the omission of these lines.

India has no such doubts and advances first to salaam, prostrate herself, and then resume her unquenchable eloquence with an initial touch of her own language: 'Kaisar i-Hind!' Her speech continues as 'melodrama' with the 'Crown of India' cantabile tune as background:

> The splendour of thy light
> Our day ennobles and redeems our night.
> Goal of our hopes, Protector of the poor,
> Beneath thine aegis India rests secure.
> Thou not on one thy presence dost bestow
> But on *all* lands that fealty to thee owe.
> Wherever lifts thy standard to the breeze,

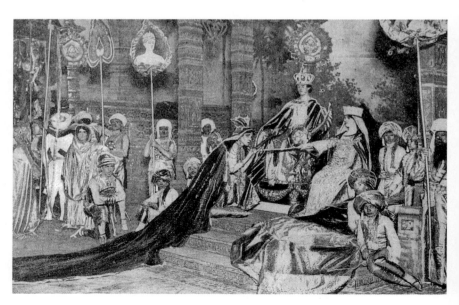

Homage before the Royal Pair in the Coliseum Masque

> Thy foot has fallen. Not by mere decrees
> The burthen of thine empire dost thou bear,
> But by desert and deed. Along the air
> Thy stirring 'Wake up, England!' lingers yet
> Dull sloth to whip and dear resolve to whet,
> Imperial pilot, still, thy Ship of State
> To safeguard, waking early, watching late;
> By thy reveille roused thine every Realm
> *Must* 'wake' and work whilst thou art at the helm!

India turns to the Empress, and to back her Elgar breathes a gentle song of the English countryside:

> And Thou, Illustrious Lady of our Love,
> Crowned with delight and Sceptred with the Dove,
> Who to our swooning Indian heats dost bring
> The fragrant freshness of a Northern Spring,
> The breath and beauty of some woodland way,
> A daisied meadow or an English - May!

Elgar resumes the march's cantabile tune, and India turns again to the King-Emperor:

> Gracious Sire,
> In whom our eyes behold our hearts' desire,
> Sum of our wealth and Chart of all our ways.

To the music of Agra's 'Hail, Immemorial Ind!' the speech continues:

> Low at thy feet thy loving India lays
> Her loyal homage.

After kneeling before the imperial thrones, she puts a hand on each royal sceptre and bows her forehead to both. She asks permission to present the Indian princes:

> Thine gracious leave accord me mine array
> Of Princes at thy footstool to present,
> That wait to do thee worship reverent;
> From out my utmost confines gathered here
> Nizam and Maharajah and Emir.

Then comes the crucial moment. Delhi and Calcutta are led before the thrones and plead their case in dumb show (at this stage in the proceedings quite a relief). The Emperor summons India and indicates his decision, which she now declares:

> The Majesty of Ind his will proclaims:
> Delhi to be his capital he names:
> And, of his Empire, further makes decree
> Calcutta shall the Premier City be.

Music has accompanied the silent action, leading to a salvo of stage trumpets before the critical announcement. More trumpets follow, and then *sff* a stroke on the gong. Against scurrying orchestral triplets there are choral cries of 'Delhi' until the singers revert *ff* to 'Hail, Immemorial Ind!' and proceed as in Agra's song to celebrate 'Him thou hast revealed'. As before, his identity remains uncertain. India resolves the question in her own way during her final speech:

> A loving people and a loyal Land
> Commend thee unto Him within Whose Hand
> Are set the shining destinies of kings.

Elgar has a last chance to let us hear some of the masque's best music played *pp* before stage trumpets remember it is time for Arne. The words with which Agra launches the National Anthem have at least the excitement of novelty:

> God save the Emperor,
> Hear now, as ne'er before,
> *One* India sing!

The verse then reverts to type as thundered out by the chorus. Elgar gives us a last reminder of *In Smyrna* and ends with the motif that has been India's ever since she first rose up to introduce her cities. *The Times* reported that the work was 'deliberately intended to be (in the best sense) popular'. The writer wondered whether Elgar's music had ever been otherwise, except in some few cases when the music was popular in not quite the best sense. *The Crown of India* was so occasional a work that the exact sense of its popularity hardly arose. Some might have questioned Elgar's judgment in allying himself to Hamilton's words, however ruthlessly cut.

Much was indeed cut from the outset, so that the complete text in the programme-book contained a proviso that: 'Much of the verse is necessarily omitted in the representation.' But not enough: it was generally agreed that India, Delhi and Calcutta had protested too much in the early performances. Elgar noted, 'N.B. There is *far too much* of this political business E.E.' The Colvins were at an early performance, and Frances wrote on 13 March:

> A line dear E.E. to tell you how much we enjoyed the Masque - your music is gorgeous & gave one just the right thrill. I longed to stop those women shrieking & just have the music, & the wonderful colours to look at, it would be superb! We did love it, & longed to see you to tell you. It ought to stir a thrill of patriotism even at this sad time & I believe it will.

Frances Colvin went on to say that her husband Sidney wanted Elgar and John Masefield (1878-1967) to meet: '*he* is a poet, & fit for your genius.' So much for Henry Hamilton. Masefield and Elgar co-operated only once, in a joint act of homage and chivalry to the mother of the King-Emperor, the memorial ode *So Many True Princesses*, performed in 1932 at the dedication of a statue by Alfred Gilbert to Queen Alexandra. Elgar replied to Frances Colvin the following day:

> So many thanks for your letter: it was understood that the thing was to be mainly pantomime & now the dialogue will be cut out - it was an inoffensive thing & some of the music is good!
>
> When I write a big serious work e.g. Gerontius we have had to starve & go without fires for twelve months as a reward: this small effort allows me to buy scientific works I have yearned for & I spend my time between the Coliseum & the old bookshops: I have found poor Haydon's autobiography - the which I have wanted for years & all Jesse's Memoirs (the nicest twaddle possible) & metallurgical works & oh! all sorts of things - also I can more easily help my poor people - so I don't care what people say about me - the real man is only a very shy student & now I can buy books - Ha! ha! I found a lovely old volume 'Tract against POPERY!' - I appeased Alice by saying I bought it to prevent other people seeing it - but it wd. make a cat laugh. Then I go to the. N Portrait Gallery & can afford lunch - now I cannot eat it. It's all very curious & interesting & the *people* behind the scenes are so good & so desperately respectable & so honest & straightforward - quite a refreshing world after Society - only don't say I said so.
>
> My labour will soon be over & then for the country lanes & the wind sighing in the reeds by Severn side again & God bless the Music Halls!

Sir Sidney Colvin was to retire from the Department of Prints and Drawings at the British Museum in 1912, and therefore leave his Museum accommodation. Hence Frances Colvin's contrast in a letter of 15 March between their situation and that of Elgar, newly at Severn House:

How sweet of you dear Edward to write us such a delightful letter it has made us both laugh & cry, & love *you* more than ever - Oh *how* glad I am you can buy the books you love - that is a joy! & more power to the Music Halls! The Masque must be a pure delight freed from that commonplace dialogue - we must go again - I loved the music. I only fear *you* will be too tired - *do* take a real *deep* rest when it's over - & listen to the winds in those reeds you love. I wish you could hear Sidney's last lecture today I know you would love that too - of course we know it's impossible. *We* are making up our minds to face going <u>OUT</u> of our dear home (in three or four months more) & having to *give up* buying books, & going to music & plays - back to the simple life in our old age - it's a little hard - but we have *had* a good time & the gods can't take that back.

Take care of your dear self - we all love you & hold you very precious & dear.

The question of cuts to Hamilton's verse was obviously urgent. *The Times* made the position clear at once: 'Moreover, the whole might have been made to move more easily by the omission of a good many other lines, though some cuts had been made; probably others will be found to be advisable in later performances.' Elgar was at the Coliseum on the morning of 13 March, two days after the première, 'busy with Mr.Schmidt about arrangements of Masque'. Perhaps these included the dialogue. Later he took the orchestra out to lunch, as Lady Elgar reported:

All so happy & so proud & pleased. E. the most sweet & charming host. Immense enthusiasm for E. & health drunk - "We are the proudest Orch. in London" - It seemed as if all cares & troubles had been forgotten. Only a beautiful influence from E. left. Then to Nat. Portrait Gallery.

On 15 March the cuts needed only the blessing of Oswald Stoll (1866-1942), owner of the Coliseum, whose idea the Masque had been. Elgar and Carice saw to the matter: 'E. & C. to Putney to see Mr.Stoll about cuts.' The next day Elgar was at the theatre rehearsing the actresses in the abbreviated script; subsequent performances were played accordingly. Elgar's niece, May Grafton, was staying at Severn House, and her copy of the libretto gives some idea how extensively Hamilton was cut. Tableau I lost half its lines: Tableau II a third. The author's reaction is missing from Elgarian literature.

Elgar's health was poor when the Masque was done, but Severn House echoed still with Indian concerns. It was indeed the most suitable setting his daughter had yet provided for General Roberts's Indian memorabilia. There was not only the lower gallery for his weaponry, but upstairs was the Oriental room with a large lantern in the roof, leading from the music room. Though later becoming Elgar's billiard room, this was presumably where Lady Elgar arranged the bulk of her father's Indian possessions, as detailed in the 1913 inventory. Included were such items as any Englishman might bring back after long residence in India. Among them were 'Indian brass snuffers'; a 'carved Bombay rosewood square footstool'; a 'marble group of two elephants fighting'; an 'elephant with howdah'; an 'elephant and ram'; a 'cow and calf'; a 'marble idol with dog'; an 'octagonal game board'; a 'brass tray'; a 'salver decorated with peacocks & foliage'; 'a brass vase'; a 'stuffed antelope head'. The arms also appeared in the inventory. Most important was Sir Henry's own 'general's sword in gilt scabbard'; there were also a 'trooper's sword in steel scabbard', a 'straight sword in sheath', and sundry 'cavalry swords'; a 'tulwar in sheath' (Indian sabre); a 'Sikh dagger'; a 'Cingalese dagger'; two more daggers, one in its sheath; a 'fire lock damascened'; and the 'Shield of hide' that was the centrepiece of the Severn House display. After Lady Elgar's death and the sale of the house, the weapons were given to the Victoria and Albert Museum. From there General Roberts's arsenal went to Monmouth, according to a letter from the Town Clerk to Carice Elgar Blake dated 11 August 1949 and now at the Birthplace Museum:

> I would now advise you that the following Indian Armour has been received from the Victoria & Albert Museum, South Kensington.
>
> 5 Indian swords and scabbards (one with knife attached)
> 1 Indian Musket
> 1 Indian dagger with sheath
> 1 Indian Katar dagger with sheath
> 1 shield of hide

There, indeed, the material evidence of the General's campaigning for his country should be available for inspection.

14 - The glory, jest and riddle of the world

Elgar had strong views about the Falstaff he had delineated in his 'symphonic study': 'As the work is based solely on the Falstaff of the historical plays (1 and 2 Henry IV. and Henry V.), in examining it or listening to it, the caricature in The Merry Wives of Windsor, which, unluckily, is better known to English playgoers than the real Falstaff, must be forgotten.' So much for Nicolai (1810-49), Verdi (1813-1901) and Vaughan Williams (1872-1958). Fortunately, though under pressure, Elgar wrote an analytical essay to anticipate the first performance, as he explained to Alice Stuart Wortley on 22 August 1913:

> I have been more than busy; as the score is behindhand I undertook to furnish the notes (analysis) *myself* for the *October* number of the Musical Times;- no outsider cd. write about Falstaff without the score. After my offer was accepted they said it was *September* they wanted the analysis for! so for two days I have done nothing else - two lovely fine days.

Elgar has an impressive list of sources in his analysis, none more impressive than the earliest, Maurice Morgann (1726-1802), who was secretary to the embassy for peace with America in 1782. Morgann wrote political pamphlets but was also a considerable Shakespearean scholar. His *Essay on the Dramatic Character of Sir John Falstaff* (1777) is a moral rehabilitation of Sir John. Falstaff's 'cowardice' is anathema to him, and he discredits those who would impute it. So Poins gets short shrift, whereas Doll Tearsheet and Sir John Colevile of the Dale are reliable witnesses. Even Justice Shallow can be taken at face value and not as Falstaff's gull. It is special pleading of the most attractive kind and chimed precisely with the music Elgar wished to write. Prince Hal was 'nobilmente' in a sketch, but not in the final score. Falstaff cannot be, but he approximates to it more than most would allow.

Morgann states his position at the outset: 'The ideas which I have formed concerning the Courage and Military Character of the Dramatic Sir *John Falstaff* are so different from those which I find generally to prevail in the world, that I shall take the liberty of stating my sentiments on the subject.' Morgann wisely starts by admitting that things look black for Falstaff from the beginning of *Henry IV* Part 1:

We see this extraordinary Character, almost in the first moment of our acquaintance with him, involved in circumstances of apparent dishonour; and we hear him familiarly called *Coward* by his most intimate companions. We see him, on occasion of the robbery at *Gads-Hill*, in the very act of running away from the Prince and *Poins*; and we behold him, on another of more honourable obligation, in open day light, in battle, and acting in his profession as a Soldier, escaping from *Douglas* even out of the world as it were; counterfeiting death, and deserting his very existence; and we find him, on the former occasion, betrayed into those *lies* and *braggadocioes* which are the usual concomitants of Cowardice in Military men and pretenders to valour.

It is as a static character that Morgann sees Falstaff, averting his gaze from his less attractive traits in Part 2:

we can scarcely forgive the ingratitude of the Prince in the new-born virtue of the King, and we curse the severity of that poetic justice which consigns our old good-natured companion to the custody of the *warden*, and the dishonours of the *Fleet*.

Morgann postulates that Falstaff's wit and alacrity of mind made him so acceptable to society as a young man that he hardly bothered to acquire other virtues: 'He found himself esteemed and beloved with all his faults; nay *for* his faults, which were all connected with humour and for the most part grew out of it.' Moreover he was a soldier: 'He had from nature, as I presume to say, a spirit of boldness and enterprise; which in a Military age, tho' employment was only occasional, kept him always above contempt.' Completely at ease in society, Falstaff had passed his life pleasantly enough:

Laughter and approbation attend his greatest excesses; and being governed visibly by no settled bad principle or ill design, fun and humour account for and cover all. By degrees, however, and thro' indulgence, he acquires bad habits, becomes an humourist, grows enormously corpulent, and falls into the infirmities of age; yet never quits, all the time, one single levity or vice of a youth, or loses any of that cheerfulness of mind, which had enabled him to pass thro' this course with ease to himself and delight to others.

Morgann relishes Falstaff's resource when faced with the Douglas:

Whilst in the battle of *Shrewsbury* he is exhorting and encouraging the Prince who is engaged with the *Spirit Percy* - 'Well said Hal, to him Hal,' - he is himself attacked by the *Fiend Douglas*. There was no match; nothing remained but death or stratagem; grinning honour, or laughing life. But an expedient offers, a mirthful one: - take your choice *Falstaff*, a point of

honour or a point of drollery. - It could not be a question: *Falstaff* falls,
Douglas is cheated, and the world laughs. But does he fall like a Coward?
No, like a buffoon only; the superior principle prevails, and *Falstaff* lives
by a stratagem growing out of his character, to prove himself *no
counterfeit*, to jest, to be employed, and to fight again.

Falstaff so enjoyed the joke, says Morgann, that he 'continues to
counterfeit after the danger is over, that he may also deceive the Prince
and improve the event into more laughter'. So he lies still and listens to
his own epitaph 'with all the waggish glee and levity of his character' . The
Prince is indeed generous:

> What old acquaintance, could not all this flesh
> Keep in a little life? poor Jack farewell,
> I could have better spar'd a better man:
> O I should have a heavy miss of thee,
> If I were much in love with vanity:
> Death hath not struck so fat a Deer today,
> Though many dearer in this bloody fray,
> Embowell'd will I see thee, by and by:
> Till then in blood by noble Percy lie.

To Morgann this is as pleasurable as it must have been to Falstaff: 'This is
wonderfully proper for the occasion; it is affectionate, it is pathetic, yet it
remembers his vanities, and, with a faint gleam of recollected mirth, even his
plumpness and corpulency; but it is a pleasantry softned and rendered even
vapid by tenderness.' Morgann does his best for Falstaff when he rises up,
spies the dead Hotspur, pierces his thigh and pretends to have killed him:

> The circumstance of his wounding *Percy* in the thigh, and carrying the
> dead body, on his back like luggage, is *indecent* but not cowardly. The
> declaring, though in jest, that he killed Percy seems to me *idle*, but it is not
> meant or calculated for *imposition*; it is spoken to the *Prince himself*, the
> man in the world who could not be, or be supposed to be, imposed on.

Morgann goes on to sum up the character of Shakespeare's Falstaff in
the terms that so appealed to Elgar, and which he quoted near the
beginning of his analysis:

> Tho' I have considered *Falstaff*'s character as relative only to one single
> quality, yet so much has been said that it cannot escape the reader's notice
> that he is a character made up by *Shakespeare* wholly of incongruities: - a
> man at once young and old, enterprising and fat, a dupe and a wit,
> harmless and wicked, weak in principle and resolute by constitution,

cowardly in appearance and brave in reality; a knave without malice, a lyar without deceit; and a knight, a gentleman, and a soldier, without either dignity, decency, or honour. This is a character which, though it may be decompounded, could not, I believe, have been formed, nor the ingredients of it duly mingled, upon any receipt whatever. It required the hand of *Shakespeare* himself to give to every particular part a relish of the whole, and of the whole to every particular part.

It is Morgann's view that Shakespeare gave Falstaff certain talents and qualities which were in the course of the action perverted or obscured so as to produce a comic character unlike any other and one impervious to any assault:

It was clearly to furnish out a Stage buffoon of a peculiar sort; a kind of Game-bull which would stand the baiting thro' a hundred Plays, and produce equal sport, whether he is pinned down occasionally by *Hal* or *Poins*, or tosses such mongrils as *Bardolph* or the Justices sprawling in the air. There is in truth no such thing as totally demolishing *Falstaff*; he has so much of the invulnerable in his frame that no ridicule can destroy him; he is safe even in defeat, and seems to rise, like another *Antaeus*, with recruited vigour from every fall.

Morgann recognises his infinite variety and infinite capacity:

And hence it is that he is made to undergo not one detection only, but a series of detections; that he is not formed for one Play only, but was intended originally at least for two; and the author, we are told, was doubtful if he should not extend him farther, and engage him in the wars with *France*. This he might well have done, for there is nothing perishable in the nature of *Falstaff*. He might have involved him, by the vicious part of his character, in new difficulties and unlucky situations, and have enabled him, by the better part, to have scrambled through, abiding and retorting the jests and laughter of every beholder.

That was the Falstaff Elgar loved and portrayed so lovingly. As Elgar, an intermittent wanderer in the world of 18th-century letters, is likely to have known, Morgann's essay inspired others to examine the character of Falstaff, so that he develops a critical life of his own by the end of the century. Henry Mackenzie (1745-1831), known as the 'Addison of the North', took up the subject in two issues of *The Lounger* that came out in May 1786. He was a novelist, wrote important critical assessments of Burns and Byron, and influenced Walter Scott towards an interest in German literature. He alludes to Morgann:

Though I will not go so far as a paradoxical critic has done, and ascribe valour to Falstaff; yet if his cowardice is fairly examined it will be found to be not so much a weakness as a principle. In his very cowardice there is much of the sagacity I have remarked in him; he has the sense of danger but not the discomposure of fear.

Mackenzie contrasts the knight of the rueful countenance with the fat knight:

> *Don Quixote*, like Falstaff, is endowed with excellent discernment, sagacity, and genius; but his good sense holds fief of his diseased imagination, or his over-ruling madness for the achievements of knighterrantry, for heroic valour and heroic love. The ridicule in the character of Don Quixote consists in raising low and vulgar incidents, through the medium of his disordered fancy, to a rank of importance, dignity, and solemnity to which in their nature they are the most opposite that can be imagined. With Falstaff it is nearly the reverse; the ridicule is produced by subjecting wisdom, honour, and other the most grave and dignified principles to the controul of grossness, buffoonery, and folly.

Don Quixote has his Dulcinea, but Falstaff is all for getting a 'wife in the stews', has 'weekly sworn to marry' old Mistress Ursula, is accused by the Hostess that he swore to marry her when she was washing his wound and Mistress Keech the butcher's wife called in for some vinegar: 'And didst thou not (when she was gone down stairs) desire me to be no more familiar with such poor people, saying, that ere long they should call me Madam? And didst thou not kiss me, and bid me fetch thee thirty shillings?' Falstaff is never happier than with Doll Tearsheet upon his knee, or with the thought of the 'dozen or fourteen honest gentlewomen' who are habituées of the Boar's Head. Elgar wondered if there was too much of them in his score, as he wrote to 'Troyte' on 2 September 1913: 'Alice is horrified I fear with my honest gentlewomen - of course they must be in - do you think I have overdone them?' When Falstaff and Shallow are waiting at Westminster in eager anticipation of the new King's arrival, and Pistol says the Hostess and Doll have both been haled to prison, Falstaff's instant reply is 'I will deliver her'. This flash of chivalry was most likely to be put in effect through Falstaff's assumed influence with Henry V, but the next speeches of 'my royal Hal' make clear it is not to be and Falstaff is deflated. Essentially Elgar is in agreement with Mackenzie, emphasising in his music the knightly origins from which Falstaff had only partly fallen away.

The 1788 *Transactions of the Royal Irish Academy*, ii (3-37) contain 'An Examination of an Essay on the Dramatic Character of Sir John Falstaff'. It was a paper read by the Rev.Richard Stack (d.1812), rector of Omagh and author of a book on chemistry, on 11 February 1788, in which

Falstaff and Mistress Quickly downstage

he examines Morgann's arguments one by one, finds them wanting, yet owns them admirably rehearsed and reaches conclusions about Falstaff's eternal worth not so different from Morgann's or Elgar's. He pays generous tribute to Morgann:

> The essay which I intend to examine must be acknowledged to be one of the most ingenious pieces of criticism any where to be found. For though its design seems to be in contradiction to the general sentiment of mankind, yet has the writer managed his subject with so much ability and address that some have been gained over to his opinion, others hesitate, and all must admire.

Stack goes to the nub of the matter at once, failing to see why the addition of 'cowardice' to Falstaff's other defects should make much difference:

> That Falstaff is vicious, a rogue, a liar, and a profligate, is allowed on all hands; yet covered with all this infamy, he entertains, surprises and charms, nay he engages our hearts. What then? Shall an infusion of cowardice reduce the character to a caput mortuum, and no spirit, no salt remain? For my part, I can see no reason for this.

Elgar could only concur with Stack's peroration:

> Genius and wit never fail to recommend themselves to the notice and admiration of mankind; and always throw a dignity round a character even above its true merit. These principles are sufficient to explain the superior pleasure and peculiar interest we feel in Falstaff above all other characters which have not half his vices. His creative fancy, playful wit, characteristic humour, admirable judgment and nice discernment of character, are so rare and excellent endowments that we lose the exceptionable matter in contemplating them. Nor is it owing to these alone that we admire and almost love Falstaff, but to another exquisite contrivance of the poet in catching occasions of mirth from his very vices. Thus, by making them the ground into which he has wrought the most entertaining fancies and delightful humour, he has made it almost impossible to separate matters thus closely interwoven, and has seduced judgment to the side of wit. These are the strange arts by which Shakespeare has drawn our liking toward so offensive an object; or to speak with more precision, has contrived to veil the offensive parts of his character. Defence is a thing of too serious a nature for Falstaff, he laughs at all vindication; *crescit sub pondere virtus*. His elastic vigour of mind repels all difficulties; his alacrity bears him above all disgust; and in the gay wit we forget the contemptible coward.

Stack has quoted the motto of the Earls of Denbigh, which maybe has a side-glance at Book II of the Statius (c.45-96) *Silvae* (iii, 65); it might be translated here as 'Virtue grows beneath a weight'.

Professor of Humanity at Glasgow University, William Richardson (1743-1814) wrote much on Shakespeare. He tackled the ever-stimulating Falstaff in *Essays on Shakespeare's Dramatic Character of Sir John Falstaff, and on his Imitation of Female Characters* (1788). He admires Falstaff's quicksilver ruses of escape:

> Another kind of ability displayed by our hero is the address with which he defies detection and extricates himself out of difficulty. He is never at a loss. His presence of mind never forsakes him. Having no sense of character he is never troubled with shame. Though frequently detected, or in danger of detection, his inventive faculty never sleeps; it is never totally overwhelmed. Or, if it be surprised into a momentary intermission of its power, it forthwith recovers, and supplies him with fresh resources. He is furnished with palliatives and excuses for every emergency. Besides other effects produced by this display of ability, it tends to amuse, and to excite laughter: for we are amused by the application of inadequate and ridiculous causes. Of the talent now mentioned we have many instances. Thus, when detected by prince Henry in his boastful pretensions to courage, he tells him that he knew him. 'Was it for me,' says he, 'to kill the heir-apparent?' So also in another scene, when he is detected in his abuse of the Prince and overheard even by the Prince himself: 'No abuse, Ned, in the world; honest Ned, none. I dispraised him before the wicked, that the wicked might not fall in love with him.'

Richardson prepares the way for the catastrophe with skill and insight:

> Falstaff, who was studious of imposing on others, imposes upon himself. He becomes the dupe of his own artifice. Confident in his versatility, command of temper, presence of mind, and unabashed invention; encouraged too by the notice of the Prince, and thus flattering himself that he shall have some sway in his counsels, he lays the foundation of his disappointment.

But the Prince is not deceived. For the sake of present amusement he suffers himself to seem so, and Falstaff is led to imagine himself more successful in his wiles than is the case. Elgar ends his account of the first *Falstaff* scene, a conversation piece between the fat knight and the Prince, with the following comment: 'the persuasive Falstaff has triumphed, the dominating Sir John is in the ascendant.' Hal has apparently agreed to the Gadshill robbery: 'once in my days I'll be a madcap.' Then follows the coda to Shakespeare's scene, with the Prince alone on stage revealing his true thoughts, such thoughts as may have withheld from him the Elgarian *nobilmente*:

> I know you all, and will a while uphold
> The unyok'd humour of your idleness,
> Yet herein will I imitate the sun,
> Who doth permit the base contagious clouds
> To smother up his beauty from the world,
> That when he please again to be himself,
> Being wanted he may be more wonder'd at
> By breaking through the foul and ugly mists
> Of vapours that did seem to strangle him.

Richardson makes his case: 'Thus in the self-deceit of Falstaff, and in the discernment of Henry, held out to us on all occasions, we have a natural foundation for the catastrophe.' The scene is set:

> Falstaff brings Shallow to London to see and profit by his influence at court. He places himself in King Henry's way as he returns from the coronation. He addresses him with familiarity; is neglected; persists, and is repulsed with sternness. His hopes are unexpectedly baffled, his vanity blasted; he sees his importance with those he had deceived completely ruined. He is for a moment unmasked.

King Henry V does indeed now 'imitate the sun':

> I know thee not, old man: fall to thy prayers:
> How ill white hairs become a fool, and jester!
> I have long dream'd of such a kind of man,
> So surfeit-swell'd, so old, and so profane:
> But being awake, I do despise my dream.

Falstaff is of course not so easily put down, and has ready reason to convince Master Shallow: this is a rebuke only for the public ear: 'I shall be sent for in private to him: look you, he must seem thus to the world: fear not your advancement: I will be the man yet, that shall make you great.' But the professor also has hardened his heart: 'Thus Shakespeare, whose morality is no less sublime than his skill in the display of character is masterly and unrivalled, represents Falstaff not only as a voluptuous and base sycophant but totally incorrigible.' Richardson is aware he has emphasised Falstaff's just deserts, but realises the punishment may seem too harsh:

> I may be thought perhaps to have treated Falstaff with too much severity. I am aware of his being a favourite. Persons of eminent worth feel for him some attachment, and think him hardly used by the King. But if they will allow themselves to examine the character in all its parts they will perhaps agree with me that such feeling is delusive, and arises from partial views.

They will not take it amiss, if I say that they are deluded in the same manner with Prince Henry.

A series of Shakespeare essays was written by Richard Cumberland (1732-1811), caricatured by Sheridan (1751-1816) in *The Critic* as Sir Fretful Plagiary, and published in *The Observer: being a Collection of Moral, Literary and Familiar Essays* (1785-91). One section is devoted to 'Remarks upon the characters of Falstaff and his group'. He imagines Shakespeare first pondering the subject of the Falstaff plays:

When it had entered into the mind of Shakespeare to form an historical play upon certain events in the reign of Henry the fourth of England, the character of the Prince of Wales recommended itself to his fancy as likely to supply him with a fund of dramatic incidents. For what could invention have more happily suggested than this character, which history presented ready to his hands? a riotous disorderly young libertine, in whose nature lay hidden those seeds of heroism and ambition which were to burst forth at once to the astonishment of the world and to atchieve the conquest of France.

Shakespeare then needed a worthy foil to the Prince, a leader of the disorderly rabble with which it pleases him to revel a while:

His lies, his vanity and his cowardice, too gross to deceive, were to be so ingenious as to give delight; his cunning evasions, his witty resources, his mock solemnity, his vapouring self-consequence, were to furnish a continual feast of laughter to his royal companion. He was not only to be witty himself, but the cause of wit in other people; a whetstone for raillery; a buffoon, whose very person was a jest. Compounded of these humours, Shakespeare produced the character of *Sir John Falstaff*; a character which neither ancient nor modern comedy has ever equalled, which was so much the favourite of its author as to be introduced in three several plays, and which is likely to be the idol of the English stage as long as it shall speak the language of Shakespeare.

The epilogue to *Henry IV* Part 2 foretells further adventures for Falstaff:

One word more, I beseech you; if you be not too much cloyed with fat meat, our humble Author will continue the story (with Sir John in it) and make you merry, with fair Katharine of France: where (for any thing I know) Falstaff shall die of a sweat, unless already he be kill'd with your hard opinions.

Cumberland can readily conceive of Falstaff flourishing even in the Fleet prison and emerging once again for battle:

I cannot doubt but there were resources in Shakespeare's genius, and a latitude of humour in the character of Falstaff, which might have furnished scenes of admirable comedy by exhibiting him in his disgrace, and both Shallow and Silence would have been accessories to his pleasantry. Even the field of Agincourt, and the distress of the king's army before the action, had the poet thought proper to have produced Falstaff on the scene, might have been as fruitful in comic incidents as the battle of Shrewsbury. This we can readily believe from the humours of Fluellen and Pistol which he has woven into his drama; the former of whom is made to remind us of Falstaff in his dialogue with Captain Gower.

There is much discussion between the two captains of the similarities between King Henry and Fluellen's Alexander the Pig. Gower corrects to 'Alexander the Great'. Fluellen plays Welsh variations on the name: 'Why I pray you, is not pig, great? the pig, or the great, or the mighty, or the huge, or the magnanimous, are all one reckonings, save the phrase is a little variations.' Henry was born at Monmouth, custodian of General Roberts's weaponry, and Alexander in Macedon. Fluellen sees the happiest parallels between Macedon and Monmouth, parallels that could only have delighted Elgar, with his love of the 'sweet border country':

> There is a river in Macedon, and there is also moreover a river at Monmouth, it is call'd Wye at Monmouth: but it is out of my prains, what is the name of the other river: but 'tis all one, 'tis alike as my fingers is to my fingers, and there is salmons in both.

Fluellen has another similarity to hand:

> Alexander God knows, and you know, in his rages, and his furies, and his wraths, and his cholers, and his moods, and his displeasures, and his indignations, and also being a little intoxicated in his prains, did in his ales and his angers (look you) kill his best friend Cleitus.

Gower objects that King Henry is not at all like that. 'Don't interrupt', continues Fluellen:

> as Alexander killed his friend Cleitus, being in his ales and his cups; so also Harry Monmouth being in his right wits, and his good judgements, turn'd away the fat Knight with the great-belly doublet: he was full of jests, and gipes, and knaveries, and mocks, I have forgot his name.

Gower supplies it, and Fluellen concludes: 'I'll tell you, there is good men porn at Monmouth.' It is an exchange Cumberland greatly approves: 'This passage has ever given me a pleasing sensation, as it marks a regret in the poet to part with a favourite character, and is a tender farewell to his memory.'

The death of Falstaff in *Henry V* Act 2 scenes i and iii is a matter primarily for Mistress Quickly, Nym, Bardolph, Pistol and the Boy; but it was also to involve Elgar and Bernard Shaw in Shakespearean debate. The Hostess, now become Mistress Pistol, bids his old confederates visit the stricken knight: 'As ever you came of women, come in quickly to Sir John: Ah, poor heart, he is so shak'd of a burning quotidian tertian, that it is most lamentable to behold. Sweet men, come to him.' Nym knows the real reason: 'The King hath run bad humours on the Knight, that's the even of it'; and Pistol understands the result: 'Nym, thou hast spoke the right, his heart is fracted and corroborate.'

It is Pistol who announces the melancholy news: 'Bardolph, be blithe: Nym, rouse thy vaunting veins: Boy, bristle thy courage up: for Falstaff he is dead, and we must earn therefore.' Bardolph, hardly made for the French wars, is both loyal and lonesome: 'Would I were with him, wheresome'er he is, either in Heaven, or in Hell.' It is left to the Hostess to recount Falstaff's deathbed confession; perhaps she recalls the moment when, in happier days, Falstaff entered singing 'When Arthur first in court' in expectation of a satisfactory evening with Doll. 'Abraham' does not form part of her vocabulary:

> Nay sure, he's not in Hell: he's in Arthur's bosom, if ever man went to Arthur's bosom: a' made a fine end, and went away and it had been any christom child: a' parted ev'n just between twelve and one, ev'n at the turning o' the tide: for after I saw him fumble with the sheets, and play with flowers, and smile upon his fingers' end, I knew there was but one way: for his nose was as sharp as a pen, and a' babbled of green fields. How now, Sir John ? (quoth I) what man? be o' good cheer. So a' cried out, God, God, God, three or four times: now I, to comfort him, bid him a' should not think of God; I hop'd there was no need to trouble himself with any such thoughts yet: so a' bad me lay more clothes on his feet: I put my hand into the bed, and felt them, and they were as cold as any stone: then I felt to his knees, and so uppear'd, and upward, and all was as cold as any stone.

He cried out for sack, and women too (Elgar's gentlewomen make a last ghostly appearance). The Boy is more candid than all of them and quotes Falstaff saying 'the Devil would have him about women'. The Hostess excuses him: 'but then he was rheumatic, and talked of the Whore of Babylon', whatever that might mean. But Morgann and Elgar were right, the one in his spirited defence, the other in his incomparable music, to agree with the Hostess in placing Falstaff where he belonged, in Arthur's bosom, a place earned through his half-forgotten chivalry.

Bernard Shaw communicated to Elgar his delight at a first hearing of *Falstaff* in a letter of 26 September 1921: 'I never heard Falstaff before. It's magnificent, and perfectly graphic to anyone who knows his Shakespear. All the other geniuses whom I venture to admire let me down one time or another; but you never fail.' He felt the Elgar should be played thrice to every single performance of Strauss's *Till Eulenspiegel* or *Don Quixote*, and that Elgar had demonstrated the right way of setting drama to music. Elgar sent Shaw a copy of the *Falstaff* analysis that had appeared in the *Musical Times*, which Shaw acknowledged on 29 September:

> I agree that Theobald's variation on 'His nose was sharp as a pen on a table of green frieze' is as irresistible as Mozart's variations on The People who Walked in Darkness; but I have seen a man's nose look so exactly like that that I am sure Shakespear is correctly represented in the folio.

Elgar had adopted the suggestion of Lewis Theobald (1688-1744) in his analysis, 'now beyond cavil if not beyond criticism'. It was Shaw's view that Falstaff 'suddenly grew out of a piece of mere streetboyishness' and had run away with Shakespeare as various characters had run away with Shaw. He asked Elgar: 'Have you ever had a symphony transfigured by a mere bridge passage suddenly insisting on being the first subject?'

Francis Gentleman (1728-84) made a judicious assessment of Theobald in 1774:

> *Theobald*, in our opinion, is the only ingenious liberal Critic. He evidently wished to do the Author justice; and though he often went conjecturally too far, yet in the main he illustrated *Shakespeare* better than any other commentator, neither the laborious Bishop of *Gloster*, nor the tremendous Dr.*Johnson* excepted.

Elgar might well have enjoyed some of the Bishop's notes to Theobald's edition (1733-4). He was William Warburton (1698-1779), author of controversial writings on religion, philosophy and literature. His own edition of Shakespeare (1747) was criticised for poor scholarship. He became Bishop of Gloucester in 1760 and opposed the 'enthusiastic' preaching of John Wesley (1703-91). The Bishop is at his most perceptive on the rejection of Falstaff by the young King; he quotes part of Henry's speech:

> -*Know, the grave doth Gape*
> *For Thee, thrice wider than for other Men.*

He then comments:

I cannot help observing on this Passage as one of *Shakespeare*'s grand Touches of Nature. The *King*, having shaken off his Vanities, in this Scene reproves his old Companion Sir *John* for his Follies with great Severity. He assumes the Air of a Preacher; bids him fall to his Prayers, and consider how ill grey Hairs become a Buffoon; bids him seek after Grace, &c. and leave gourmandizing. But that Word, unluckily presenting him with a pleasant Idea, he can't forbear pursuing it in these words, - *Know, the Grave doth gape for thee thrice wider*, &c. and is just falling back into *Hal* by an humourous Allusion to *Falstaff*'s Bulk when He perceives it at once, is afraid Sir *John* should take the Advantage of it, so checks both himself and the Knight with

> *Reply not to me with a Fool-born jest*,

and resumes the Thread of his Discourse, and moralizes on to the End of the Chapter. This, I think, is copying Nature with greet Exactness, by shewing how apt Men are to fall back into old Customs when the Change is not made by degrees, as the Habit itself was, but determined of all at once, on the Motives of Honour, Interest, or Reason.

The Bishop is rather surprisingly on home ground with a note on the episode in *Henry IV* Part 2, Act 5 scene iv, where the Hostess and Doll Tearsheet are in dire trouble with the Beadles. Doll feigns pregnancy with a cushion and has rare abuse for the officers who would hale her off to 'whipping-cheer' in Bridewell. One of her oddest phrases, '*Thou thin man in a* Censer!', has nonplussed many, but not the future Bishop:

A *Censer*, 'tis well known, is a Vessel for burning Incense, a Perfume-pan. But what is this *thin Man* in it? I have seen several antique *Censers* exactly in the Shape of our Dishes for the Table, which, being of Brass, were beat out exceeding thin. In the Middle of the Bottom was rais'd up in imboss'd Work, with the Hammer, the Figure of some *Saint* in a kind of barbarous hollow *Bass-relief*, the whole Diameter of the Bottom. The Saint was generally He to whom the Church in which the Censer was us'd was dedicated (tho' I once saw one with an *Adam* and *Eve* at the Bottom.) Now this *thin Beadle* is compar'd, for his Substance, to one of these *thin* hammer'd *Figures*.

At the end of his score, Elgar dismisses Falstaff tenderly, as he explains in his analysis: 'Softly, as intelligence fades, we hear the complete theme of the gracious Prince Hal, and then the nerveless final struggle and collapse; the brass holds *pianissimo* a full chord of C major, and Falstaff is dead.' At the outset of the work the 'persuasive Falstaff' triumphed, but Elgar knows the future lies elsewhere so that his final thoughts acknowledge political reality:

In the distance we hear the veiled sound of a military drum; the King's stern theme is curtly thrown across the picture, the shrill drum roll again asserts itself momentarily, and with one *pizzicato* chord the work ends; the man of stern reality has triumphed.

William Richardson had emphasised Shakespeare's skill in portraying both the Prince's enjoyment of Falstaff but his essential detachment. John Stow (1525-1605) gives evidence enough in his *Chronicles of England* (1580) for Shakespeare's description of the rakish Prince Hal:

> He liued somewhat insolently, insomuch that, whilest his father liued, being accompanied with some of his yong Lords and gentlemen, he would waite in disguised aray for his owne receiuers, and distresse them of their money; and sometimes at such enterprises both he and his company were surely beaten.

King Henry IV has been enlarging in Part 1, Act 3 scene ii on the military prowess of young Harry Hotspur of the north, and contrasting him with the wastrel behaviour of his own Hal. Shakespeare as expert historian, dramatist and psychologist, knows the Prince must show his mettle at the real threat of danger to the realm:

> And that shall be the day whene'er it lights,
> That this same child of honour and renown,
> This gallant Hotspur, this all praised knight,
> And your unthought of Harry chance to meet,
> For every honour sitting on his helm
> Would they were multitudes, and on my head
> My shames redoubled. For the time will come
> That I shall make this Northern youth exchange
> His glorious deeds for my indignities.

In Act 4 scene i Hotspur can still refer to the 'nimble footed madcap Prince of Wales'; but Vernon issues a note of warning:

> I saw young Harry with his beaver on,
> His cuisses on his thighs gallantly arm'd,
> Rise from the ground like feather'd Mercury,
> And vaulted with such ease into his seat,
> As if an Angel dropp'd down from the clouds,
> To turn and wind a fiery Pegasus,
> And witch the world with noble horsemanship.

The Prince declares before the Earl of Worcester his admiration for Hotspur's valour but his willingness to meet him in combat:

Henry IV in Canterbury Cathedral

> The Prince of Wales doth join with all the world
> In praise of Henry Percy, by my hopes
> This present enterprise set off his head,
> I do not think a braver Gentleman,
> More active, valiant, or more valiant young,
> More daring, or more bold is now alive
> To grace this latter age with noble deeds.
> For my part I may speak it to my shame,
> I have a truant been to Chivalry,
> And so I hear he doth account me too;
> Yet this before my father's majesty,
> I am content that he shall take the odds
> Of his great name and estimation,
> And will to save the blood on either side
> Try fortune with him in a single fight.

In 1403 the battle of Shrewsbury, a town looped by Elgar's river Severn, to which Falstaff led his 'scarecrow army', proved a royal victory against the Percys. At the age of 16, Prince Henry had proved himself.

After his warfare, Falstaff will to Gloucestershire and Justice Shallow's orchard; but so much of the politics in the Henry plays is centred on Elgar country, fished and cycled over and later driven round. As evidence of Mortimer's loyalty, Hotspur cites to Henry IV his ferocious combat with Glendower (Part 1, Act 1 scene iii):

> When on the gentle Severn's sedgy bank,
> In single opposition hand to hand,
> He did confound the best part of an hour,
> In changing hardiment with great Glendower:
> Three times they breath'd and three times did they drink
> Upon agreement of swift Severn's flood,
> Who then affrighted with their bloody looks,
> Ran fearfully among the trembling reeds,
> And hid his crisp head in the hollow bank,
> Bloodstained with these valiant combatants.

In Act 3 scene i Glendower himself relates how he has prevailed repeatedly against Henry IV:

> Three times hath Henry Bolingbroke made head
> Against my power, thrice from the banks of Wye,
> And sandy-bottom'd Severn have I sent him
> Bootless home, and weatherbeaten back.

If Falstaff did not cross to France, his Hal, now king,did so with utmost success in 1415. Shakespeare makes his Archbishop of Canterbury bid Henry V take war across the Channel and seek inspiration at the tomb in Westminster Abbey of Edward III (Act 1 scene ii):

> Stand for your own, unwind your bloody flag,
> Look back into your mighty ancestors:
> Go my dread lord, to your great-grandsire's tomb,
> From whom you claim; invoke his warlike spirit,
> And your great-uncle's, Edward the Black Prince,
> Who on the French ground play'd a tragedy,
> Making defeat on the full power of France:
> Whiles his most mighty father on a hill
> Stood smiling, to behold his lion's whelp
> Forage in blood of French nobility.

Shakespeare, master of his 'wooden O', somehow packs it with opposing armies, battle siege, and bids his Act 2 Chorus gather the English forces:

> Now all the youth of England are on fire,
> And silken dalliance in the wardrobe lies:
> Now thrive the armourers, and Honour's thought
> Reigns solely in the breast of every man.
> They sell the pasture now, to buy the horse;
> Following the Mirror of all Christian Kings,
> With winged heels, as English Mercuries.

The Chorus of Act 3 has Henry's force embarked for France:

> Suppose, that you have seen
> The well-appointed King at Hampton pier,
> Embark his royalty: and his brave fleet,
> With silken streamers, the young Phoebus fanning.

The fleet is 'Holding due course to Harfleur', where the King stands by the scaling ladders and urges his men aloft: 'Cry, God for Harry, England, and Saint George.' Agincourt crowns the campaign on 25 October 1415, and Raphael Holinshed (d.?1580) describes the aftermath:

And so, about foure of the clocke in the after noone, the king, when he saw no apperance of enimies, caused the retreit to be blowen; and, gathering his armie togither, gaue thanks to almightie God for so happie a victorie; causing his prelates and chapleins to sing this psalme: "In exitu Israel de

Henry V

Aegypto;" and commanded euerie man to kneele downe on the ground at
this verse: *'Non nobis,* Domine, non nobis, sed nomini tuo da gloriam.'
Which doone, he Caused *Te Deum,* with certaine anthems to be soong;
giuing laud and praise to God, without boasting of his owne force or anie
humane power.

Henry V showed himself not only a consummate commander but a
notable diplomat. Sigismund, the future Holy Roman Emperor and
Garter Knight from 1417, collaborated with Henry in bringing to an end
the Schism in the Church and securing the election that same year of
Martin V (1417-31) as Pope. For dramatic purposes Shakespeare concentrates on France, and the Chorus to Act V admits that the play has had
to omit

> All the occurrences, whatever chanc'd,
> Till Harry's back return again to France:
> There must we bring him; and myself have play'd
> The interim, by remembering you 'tis past.
> Then brook abridgement, and your eyes advance,
> After your thought, straight back again to France.

Henry's French successes were spectacular, culminating in the capture of
Rouen and conquest of Normandy in 1419. The Treaty of Troyes (1420)
was the summit of his achievement, resulting in the disinheritance of the
Dauphin in favour of the House of Lancaster. Shakespeare assembles his
cast for the last scene of the play and, after the formal greetings, it is the
Duke of Burgundy who makes the case for a treaty between the royal
houses. Since John the Fearless (1404-19) had been assassinated the
previous year, it is Philip the Good, one of Maximilian's statues, who now
advances the cause of peace:

> Great Kings of France and England: that I have labour'd
> With all my wits, my pains, and strong endeavours,
> To bring your most Imperial Majesties
> Unto this bar, and royal interview;
> Your Mightiness on both parts best can witness.
> Since then my office hath so far prevail'd,
> That face to face, and royal eye to eye,
> You have congreeted: let it not disgrace me,
> If I demand before this royal view,
> What rub, or what impediment there is,
> Why that the naked, poor, and mangled Peace,
> Dear nurse of arts, plenties, and joyful births,

> Should not in this best garden of the World,
> Our fertile France, put up her lovely visage?

Henry V made formal entry into Paris on 1 December 1420 as regent of France and heir to the throne. Charles VI, whose madness is so vividly described by Froissart, was beside him, and Philip the Good just behind. The clergy of Notre Dame were less than welcoming, as Henry and Philip had tried to impose their own man as bishop. French divisions between the Armagnacs and Burgundians had allowed Henry's military triumphs, and it now seemed possible he would become King of France. Eight months of tortuous negotiation had led to the Treaty of Troyes, signed on 21 May 1420, by which time Henry was to marry Catherine of Valois and succeed Charles VI, in precarious health and the elder by eight years. When Queen Catherine returned to Paris on 30 May 1422, two ermine cloaks were carried in front of her, perhaps symbolising the two kingdoms. The Parisians claimed to have great confidence in the government of Henry V, as his fiscal measures tended towards a strong coinage. Henry had to drive back supporters of the Dauphin, who was eventually to succeed as Charles VII (1422-61), through the early deaths of both Henry and his father and the mystical prowess of Joan of Arc (1412-31). Henry decided to demolish various fortresses in the Paris region that had sheltered the enemy, and was much concerned with the armoury and gunpowder stocks in Paris. A list of eighteen arms dealers was compiled. It proved a political error to give the captaincy of Paris to an Englishman, but the main English presence was at the Bastille, under command of Sir John Fastolf (1380-1459), who was later stripped of the Garter but left money towards the foundation of Magdalen College, Oxford. Henry stayed at the palace of the Louvre in 1420 and 1422. The language problem was increased by the fact that English was supplanting French even among the upper classes, so that Henry V could claim that his ambassadors did not and need not understand French. Parisian French was the 'doulce tongue' the English were far from speaking. Shakespeare takes happy advantage of the language difficulties in the scene between Henry and Kate, when he presents the King as a rough wooer and a warrior.

Conflict in France meant that in the case of both Edward III and Henry V, many foreign knights joined the royal household. A result was an increase in the number of stranger knights elected to the Garter. Distinguished service in France on the part of Englishmen qualified them for the Garter, as in the case of the Lords Willoughby, Stafford and Clifford, and the war united the peerage behind the King. The Garter fraternity was once more pre-eminent in the world of chivalry. Some members had indeed been Henry's supporters when Prince of Wales, and

The marriage of Henry V and Catherine of Valois

he was careful also to enlist representatives of families who had been formerly disaffected, following his father's shrewd policy. Stranger knights were important because of Henry's diplomatic manoeuvres on the Continent; such well-placed knights might smooth the making of crucial alliances.

Under Henry V, the Garter became the most prestigious chivalric order in Christendom. Henry had a keen sense of the Order's potential significance, made certain changes to its constitution, and also encouraged research into chivalric learning and the lore of heraldry. The creation of Garter King of Arms in 1417 was Henry's initiative. He became the Order's own herald, known as 'Jartier, Roy d'armes des Angloys'. Traditionally the annual festival began on the eve of St.George's day, 'Vigilia Sancti Georgii', as described by Hugh Collins (p.195):

> The solemnities commenced at terce (around 3.00 p.m.), with the Garter knights, habited in the livery of the previous year, awaiting the sovereign in his privy lodgings with the officers of the fraternity. In formal procession, the companionship then progressed from the great chamber towards the chapter house, walking in pairs and ranked according to seniority. They were accompanied by the officers of the order, the prebends of Windsor, the officers of arms, and possibly the alms-knights ... The procession moved through the cloister and great gate of the king's lodgings to the upper ward of the castle, and thence to the middle and part of the lower ward, before passing on to the chapel, and then to the chapter house itself.

It is possible that the seating of the companion knights in the chapel, with the King at the head of one group and the Prince of Wales heading the other may have represented symbolically two teams assembled for the tourney.

Henry's new statutes for the Order were promulgated in 1421, some eight of them. Garter knights should bow first to the altar and then to the king or to his stall if the sovereign was absent. Provision was made for installation *in absentia*, not only for the convenience of foreign candidates but also because of the risks involved in military service and the desire to ensure the saying of Masses for any Garter knight who was killed. The sovereign was now allowed, because the future suggested Henry would be frequently in France, to hold a chapter abroad if he could muster a quorum. Garter companions were obliged to wear the insignia when appearing in public, unless on horseback, when a blue silk ribbon should be tied around the leg.

Holinshed sums up the virtues of a king who had married 'la plus belle Katharine du monde' (she became in 1421 the only new female recipient of Garter robes) and died only two years later on 3 August 1422:

> Knowen be it therefore, of person and forme was this prince rightlie representing his heroicall effects; of a stature and proportion tall and manlie, rather leane than grose, somewhat long necked, and blacke haired, of countenance amiable; eloquent and graue was his speech, and of great grace and power to persuade: for conclusion, a maiestie was he that both liued & died a paterne in princehood, & a lode-starre in honour, and mirrour of magnificence; the more highlie exalted in his life, the more deepelie lamented at his death, and famous to the world alwaie.

William Bruges, first Garter King of Arms,
observed by St.George

Henry's last words were a desire to rebuild the walls of Jerusalem. As national leader he had tried to emulate King Arthur; his other hero for action in the Middle East was Godfrey of Bouillon, both of them to be eternal sentinels for Maximilian I. Charles VI of France died on 21 October 1422, and the possibility of an Anglo-French kingdom became increasingly remote.

Shakespeare must have the last word, as King Henry wanders about the camp incognito in Act 4 scene i to test the temper of his soldiers, and Michael Williams speaks not just for what may befall at Agincourt, but in other fields of France or in warfare at any time:

> But if the cause be not good, the King himself hath a heavy reckoning to make, when all those legs, and arms, and heads, chopped off in a battle, shall join together at the latter day, and cry all, We died at such a place, some swearing, some crying for a surgeon; some upon their wives, left poor behind them; some upon the debts they owe, some upon their children rawly left: I am afear'd, there are few die well, that die in a battle: for how can they charitably dispose of any thing, when blood is their argument ?

15 - This is the way the world ends?

The Elgars' 1914-18 war was charted mainly by Lady Elgar, who recorded triumphs and disasters with characteristic vigour. At the outset Elgar was as anxious to serve his country as any man of 57. Gradually, though, as weary month followed weary month, he disengaged more and more from the horror of the conflict, wanting less of London and more of the countryside where he grew up, less of London society and more of companionship with his sister Pollie Grafton and her growing family. Musically Elgar did his duty, writing three works in support of the crushed Belgians, now under the jackboot: *Polonia* for a nation that had not known freedom for a century and a quarter; *The Spirit of England* as a setting (1915-17) of Binyon poems written within six weeks of the outbreak of hostilities, and all published by 21 September 1914, far too early for the full horror of the war to have made its impact; *The Fringes of the Fleet* and *Big Steamers* as final tribute to his pleasant naval connection that at the same time brought Elgar into awkward contact with a Rudyard Kipling devastated by loss of his only son and embarked on a heartbroken search for his missing body. Then there are such escapist works as *The Starlight Express* (1915), with all its whimsical trappings, and *The Sanguine Fan* (1917), which perhaps turned out less escapist than Elgar intended; in it Elgar could give some expression to his pent-up wrath against not only the gods of ancient Greece but against God himself, wherever he might now be found; and finally there was the chamber music, product of Brinkwells and the English countryside that had been Elgar's solace throughout the war.

What does it all add up to? Not much in the sum of Elgar's creative achievements. *Une voix dans le désert* is the only Belgian recitation that hints at the pity of war and its desolation. There is a stark numbness in the opening section and its brief recapitulation that can still sear the mind, and Elgar's tune for the central song is one of his simplest and yet most moving inspirations. For the rest, the Belgians and Poles had to make do with effective pieces for an occasion, bombastic and dated. In *The Spirit of England*, 'To women' has some of the eloquence the subject so richly deserved, but it is the spectral passing of the death-devoted troops in the last movement that remains in the memory, again a grimmer picture perhaps than Elgar intended to paint, though the introduction touchingly includes a 'wistful' Dan '(outside the Cathedral)'. Yet maybe the most telling Elgar war music was near the end of the Cello Concerto, the agonised passage that bridges the finale's essential matter to the reminiscence of the Adagio. It is a passage in no way integral to the concerto's themes or structure. Was this the passage Elgar wrote on 22 July 1919? Lady Elgar's diary describes an early morning at Brinkwells: 'E. went to the music room before breakfast & wrote wonderful passage - most haunting.' Some of Elgar's most inspired ideas in major works were almost afterthoughts, and perhaps it was that summer morning that he felt again the pain of what they had all gone through.

At the beginning of the war the Elgars were in Scotland. The major-general's daughter dreaded dishonour on 1 August 1914: 'Most anxious - Feared the government wd. not take action & feared betrayal of Belgium & treaty &c.' But all was well, and on 5 August she could write:

> May God preserve us Our conscience is clear that we tried all means for peace & waited at our own disadvantage in patience and forbearance. So we can go on with a brave heart. Glorious spirit seems to pervade all. Saw the Territorials start on the old Char-a-Banc. Splendid spirits. All flocked out to see them - shaking hands & waving. Very thrilling.

The high spirits seemed universal. Departure for the front in Paris was a joyous occasion:

> At six in the morning, without any signal, the train slowly steamed out of the station. At that moment, quite spontaneously, like a smouldering fire suddenly erupting into roaring flame, an immense clamour arose as the *Marseillaise* rose from a thousand throats. All the men were standing at the train's windows, waving their képis.

There was further exhilaration along the line:

> Crowds gathered at every station, behind every barrier, and at every window along the road. Cries of 'Vive la France! Vive l'armée' could be heard everywhere, while people waved handkerchiefs and hats. The women were throwing kisses and heaped flowers on our convoy. The young men were shouting: 'Au revoir! A bientôt!'

The situation in St.Petersburg was described by the French ambassador:

> an enormous crowd had congregated with flags, banners, icons and portraits of the Tsar. The entire crowd at once knelt and sang the Russian national anthem. To those thousands of men on their knees at that moment the Tsar was really the autocrat appointed of God, the military, political and religious leader of his people, the absolute master of their bodies and souls.

Kaiser Wilhelm II held forth on the palace balcony in Berlin: 'A fateful hour has fallen upon Germany. Envious people, on all sides are compelling us to resort to a just defence. The sword is being forced into our hands.' He bade the Berliners turn to God: 'And now I command you all to go to church, kneel before God and pray to him to help our gallant army.' And in the cathedral was sung Psalm 130: 'Out of the depths have I cried unto thee, O Lord.' Meanwhile Adolf Hitler (1889-1945) was in Munich: '[I am] not ashamed to acknowledge that I was carried away by the enthusiasm of the moment and . . . sank down upon my knees and thanked Heaven out of the fullness of my heart for the favour of having been permitted to live in such times.' The Oranienstrasse synagogue resounded likewise with pleas for victory.

Elgar was far from exultant, as he wrote on 6 August to Alice Stuart Wortley: 'I am quite ill with the awful business - but that is nothing - the confusion is terrible & reduces me to a sort of comic despair.' Before the end of the month he was writing to Frank Schuster on a matter that exercised him cruelly. The background was the great mustering of horses in the first week of August, 165,000 on the British side as cavalry mounts, and draught animals for artillery and transport. The Russians commandeered more than a million. The Austrians mobilised 600,000, and the Germans 715,000. A German officer-candidate, who was a reservist, explained the German position: 'The horses were reservists, too. Owners of horses - sportsmen, businessmen and farmers - had to register them regularly and the army knew at all times where the horses were.' Elgar's letter to Schuster is dated 25 August::

> Concerning the war I say nothing - the only thing that wrings my heart & soul is the thought of the horses - oh! my beloved animals - the men - and women can go to hell - but my horses; - I walk round & round this room cursing God for allowing dumb brutes to be tortured - let Him kill his human beings but - how CAN HE? Oh, my horses.

Meanwhile Elgar was in correspondence with Benson about new words for 'Land of Hope and Glory'. Initially, Benson got the metre wrong. Elgar then sent a poem by John Hay (1838-1905), a former American ambassador, remembering in a postscript that 'wider still & wider' might now be inappropriate. For Benson there was too much 'vengeance in it', as he was uncertain what there was to revenge. Elgar retreated on 'vengeance' but greatly wanted 'The sons of braggart scorn'. Benson had a fit of pedantry and wouldn't allow it; but the public refused to abandon the old 'Coronation' words, and attempts at revision proved abortive.

Perhaps the coolest head at the beginning of the war was Bernard Shaw's. Already an Elgarian, he was soon to be a friend. His *Common Sense*

Dead horses in France

about the War came out on 14 November 1914 as a supplement to *The New Statesman* and caused increasing outrage. He begins movingly enough:

> The time has now come to pluck up courage and begin to talk and write soberly about the war. At first the mere horror of it stunned the more thoughtful of us; and even now only those who are not in actual contact with or bereaved relation to its heartbreaking wreckage can think sanely about it, or endure to hear others discuss it coolly.

He went on to speculate about the eventual peace:

> The European settlement at the end of the war will be effected, let us hope, not by a regimental mess of fire-eaters sitting round an up-ended drum in a vanquished Berlin or Vienna, but by some sort of Congress in which all the Powers (including, very importantly, the United States of America) will be represented.

Shaw spelt out his vision for England:

> In future we must fight, not alone for England, but for the welfare of the world. But for all that, the lion is a noble old beast; and his past is a splendid past and his breed more valiant than ever: too valiant nowadays, indeed, to be merely English *contra mundum*. I take off my hat to him as he makes his last spring, and shall not cease to wave it because of the squealing of the terrified chickens.

On the last day of August Mrs.Wedgwood came to tea at Severn House: '*Very nice* - Much cheered & greatly impressed at E's "How martial he is" splendid - "If our first musician is like that" &c.' Marie Joshua wrote to Lady Elgar on 14 August: 'My sympathies are entirely with England & France. The despotic German ruler & his horrid influence arouse my greatest indignation, & I am glad that my dear Mother's family were all french, and I love this great England which has sheltered me so long & which has a conscience even in Politics.'

Count von Schlieffen (1833-1913) had proposed a lightning defeat of France, rounding Paris and taking her army in the rear; then it would be Russia's turn. Little account had been taken of initial formidable resistance by Belgium and the speed with which the Russians mobilised. The French policy was 'attack to the limit', whatever the cost. Lieutenant Spears describes their insensate bravery:

> The sense of the tragic futility of it will never quite fade from the minds of those who saw these brave men, dashing across the open to the sound of drums and bugles . . . The gallant officers who led them were entirely ignorant of the stopping power of modern firearms, and many of them thought it chic to die in white gloves.

The Boers had taught the British the deadly effectiveness of judicious musketry, and they now shot with exemplary accuracy. Field-Marshal Lord Kitchener had been appointed Secretary of State for War on 5 August, and the British Expeditionary Force was under Sir John French (1852-1925). A British sergeant describes an early encounter: '[The Germans advanced] in solid square blocks, standing out sharply against the skyline, and you couldn't help hitting them.' The marksmanship was further noted by a private: '[the first company of Germans] were simply blasted away to Heaven by a volley at seven hundred yards, and in their insane formation every bullet was almost sure to find two billets.' Benson had transposed Boer tactics into the *Coronation Ode*: 'When the hillside hisses with death - and never a foe in sight.' It was now the German turn to report an enemy 'Well entrenched and completely hidden' and opening 'a murderous fire'. The allies, however, were short of artillery, and in Germany the Krupp and Skoda works had produced the 'Big Bertha' howitzers with unheard of range and power.

Helmuth von Moltke (1848-1916), the German commander, admitted there had been no holds barred in Belgium: 'Our advance in Belgium is certainly brutal, but we are fighting for our lives and all who get in the way must take the consequences.' Many cities got in the way, but it was the burning of Louvain ostensibly because of untoward civilian resistance, that caused most outrage. Lady Elgar began her war as she meant to continue, writing on 28 August: 'Heard of destruction of Louvain - utter barbarians. Heard of losses to our beloved army Anxious to do something for Belgian refugees.' Next day she was in the same vein: 'Lovely hot day, & harvest moon, looking down on what a death Harvest through one nation's depravity.'

As the war went on, even certain lines in Binyon's 'For the Fallen' seemed inadequate. The third stanza, for instance,

> They went with songs to the battle, they were young,
> Straight of limb, true of eye, steady and aglow.
> They were staunch to the end against odds uncounted,
> They fell with their faces to the foe.

The additional verse requested by Elgar belonged almost to the world of 'The Happy Warrior' conjured by Wordsworth and Watts, a world of chivalry rather than machine guns and poison gas. Elgar included neither verse in his reworking of 'For the Fallen' into the post-war *With proud Thanksgiving*. In 'To Women' Binyon had written of

> those hawks of war,
> Those threatening wings that pulse the air,

annotated in a sketch by Elgar, 'aeroplanes stanza III'. Churchill in France pondered aerial warfare and foresaw the future: 'I saw for the first time what then seemed the prodigy of a British aeroplane threading its way among the smoke-puffs of searching shells.' He contrasts the plane with the airship:

> I rated the Zeppelin much lower as a weapon of war than almost any one else. I believed that this enormous bladder of combustible and explosive gas would prove to be easily destructible. I was sure the fighting aeroplane, rising lightly laden from its own base, armed with incendiary bullets, would harry, rout and burn these gaseous monsters.

Binyon meanwhile wrote a poem, *The Zeppelin*:

> Guns! far and near,
> Quick, sudden, angry,
> They startle the still street.
> Upturned faces appear,
> Doors open on darkness,
> There is a hurrying of feet,

And whirled athwart gloom
White fingers of alarm
Point at last there
Where illumined and dumb
A shape suspended
Hovers, a demon of the starry air!

Strange and cold as a dream
Of sinister fancy,
It charms like a snake,
Poised deadly in the gleam,
While bright explosions
Leap up to it and break.

Alice Elgar noted the destruction of Reims Cathedral on 21 September 1914: 'Much upset. Felt must go & see Westminster Abbey was there so E. & A. went - Saw the Bath Chapel & Banners & Crests.' Shaw commented pertinently in *Common Sense* : 'The injury to the cathedral must therefore be suffered as a strong hint from Providence that though we can have glorious wars or glorious cathedrals we cannot have both.' Yet war might still have its glamour. *Letters from a Lost Generation* tells of Vera Brittan's brother, fiancé and two friends who were all to be killed. Her fiancé Richard Leighton writes to her on 29 September: 'I feel, however, that I am meant to take some active part in this war. It is to me a very fascinating thing - something, if often horrible, yet very ennobling and very beautiful, something whose elemental reality raises it above the reach of all cold theorising.' He was a 2nd Lieutenant in the 4th Norfolk and 7th Worcestershire regiments.

Violet Asquith (1887-1969), the future Violet Bonham-Carter, explained a bizarre situation to Venetia Stanley in a letter of 29 August:

Lord Elcho has just issued an abrupt ultimatum to all his employees servants etc. - to join the Army or leave his service - & then gone off to London leaving poor Lady Elcho to cope with the situation - which he created without consulting her in any sort of way. It is too cruel as the people here have hardly heard of the war.

On 18 October Violet Asquith went to France, writing to her Prime Minister father:

Soldiers everywhere - the French ones just like toys - in their red trousers - ours in khaki about two feet taller - gaga-looking doddering old French generals covered with stars.

A day later she wrote again:

> Streams of refugees came by with their pathetic bundles on their backs. I cross-examined one old woman in hopes of atrocities 'Les Allemands se sont mal conduits dans votre village?' '*Très* mal - ils ont tout ravagé etc.' - 'Ils étaient cruels?' - '*Très* cruels - ils ont tué un cochon'! - I felt relieved at the death of a pig having loomed so large in the category of horrors!

Meanwhile Elgar was both heraldic and nostalgic. On 3 October he was 'busy painting his shields'. These were for the billiard room, and are likely to have included the coats of arms of the Three Choirs cities, if nothing more. Then he wrote to Ivor Atkins on 26 October:

> Have you read Masefield's poem in the *English Review*? *That* is the best thing written yet, & here I feel as if you in the country were doing something but altho' I am busy from morning till night the *houses* seem to choke it all off - we are fighting for the *country* & I wish I could *see* it.

The poem Elgar admired was *August, 1914*, and the central section must have stirred him deeply:

> These homes, this valley spread below me here,
> The rooks, the tilted stacks, the beasts in pen,
> Have been the heartfelt things, past-speaking dear
> To unknown generations of dead men,
>
> Who, century after century, held these farms,
> And, looking out to watch the changing sky,
> Heard, as we hear, the rumours and alarms
> Of war at hand and dangers pressing nigh.
>
> And knew, as we know, that the message meant
> The breaking off of ties, the loss of friends,
> Death, like a miser getting to his rent,
> And no new stones laid where the trackway ends.
>
> The harvest not yet won, the empty bin,
> The friendly horses taken from the stalls,
> The fallow on the hill not yet brought in,
> The cracks unplastered in the leaking walls.
>
> Yet heard the news, and went discouraged home,
> And brooded by the fire with heavy mind,
> With such dumb loving of the Berkshire loam
> As breaks the dumb hearts of the English kind,

Masefield inscribed for Sassoon

Then sadly rose and left the well-loved Downs
And so by ship to sea, and knew no more
The fields of home, the byres, the market towns,
Nor the dear outline of the English shore,

But knew the misery of the soaking trench,
The freezing in the rigging, the despair
In the revolting second of the wrench
When the blind soul is flung upon the air,

And died (uncouthly, most) in foreign lands
For some idea but dimly understood
Of an English city never built by hands
Which love of England prompted and made good.

Elgar ends his letter by referring to Worcester Cathedral:

If it is sunshiny just go round to the W. end & look over the valley towards Malvern - bless my beloved country for me - & send me a p.c. saying you have done so.

It was exactly the time the 2nd Worcestershires were showing outstanding gallantry at Ypres. Elgar expressed further his feeling for Worcester and his home country in a letter of 13 November to the Windflower:

Yesterday I went to Worcester & had the joy of sitting in the old Library in the Cathedral amongst the M.S.S. I have often told you of - the view down the river across to the hills just as the monks saw it & as I have seen it for so many years - it seems so curious, dear, to feel that I played about among the tombs & in the Cloisters when I cd scarcely walk & now the Deans & Canons are so polite & shew me everything new - alterations discoveries &c.&c. It is a sweet old place   especially, to me, the library into which so few go. I will take you in one day.

Shaw felt the war was already over but for four more years of needless butchery and maiming. The crucial days had been 3-6 September:

The battle of the Marne was as decisive as the battle of Waterloo; and we now know that the German commanders felt this, and yet had to go on slaughtering and being slaughtered for four years more because the German people, like the other people concerned, were so thoroughly humbugged all through the war (they were not told about the Marne) that they would not have believed in the conclusiveness of the defeat even had their military advisors dared to let them know that it had happened.

The zeal to continue, however, did not depend only on misinformation. As Mark Girouard makes clear, there was in England at any rate a seemingly limitless reservoir of chivalrous ambition:

> In thousands of nurseries and schoolrooms children had been brought up on the exploits in battle of heroes new and old: Hector and Achilles, Horatius holding the bridge, Arthur and his knights, Roland blowing his horn, Richard Coeur de Lion charging the Saracens, the Black Prince at Crécy, Henry V at Agincourt, Sir Philip Sidney at Zutphen, Richard Grenville on the *Revenge*, Prince Rupert charging with his cavaliers, Sir John Moore at Corunna, Nelson at Trafalgar, Wellington at Waterloo, the charge of the Light Brigade, Nicholson falling at the gates of Delhi, Gordon proudly facing the screaming Dervishes, the heroes of Rorke's Drift, the gallant little garrison at Mafeking playing cricket in the jaws of the enemy.

Sir Walter Scott, Kenelm Digby, Charles Kingsley (1819-75), and Henry Newbolt (1862-1938) had not written in vain. If Tennyson had formed the Victorian gentleman from the lineaments of the mediaeval knight, the new generation imagined they were reversing the process.

The forces unleashed, though, were beyond human control. A.J.P.Taylor could look back with ironic detachment:

> The statesmen where overwhelmed by the magnitude of events. The generals were overwhelmed also. Mass, they believed was the secret of victory. The mass they evoked was beyond their control. All fumbled more or less helplessly. They were pilots without a chart, blown before the storm and not knowing where to seek harbour. The unknown soldier was the hero of the First World War.

On the sea, where it had been British policy to have a naval force capable of outmatching any two foreign fleets in combination, the situation had changed. In the end the German fleet was routed without any decisive battle; but there was anxiety along the way. Admiral Christopher Cradock (1862-1914), for instance, a society man as accomplished as Lord Charles Beresford, had written his *Whispers from the Fleet* (1907), in which he outlines his future fate: a 'naval officer should never let his boat go faster than his brain - the headstrong unthinking "dasher" is bound to come to grief before long'. He did so through the skill and daring of the German Graf von Spee (1861-1914), who started from Chinese waters, crossed the Pacific, and had as his aim destruction of the British wireless station on the Falklands. Cradock was hopelessly outgunned and went down on his flagship, fulfilling his desire to 'be killed in battle or break his neck in the hunting field'. Winston Churchill as First Lord of the Admiralty and John Fisher as First Sea Lord sent battle cruisers sufficient to eliminate Graf Spee's threat.

Admiral Jellicoe (1859-1935), Commander-in-Chief of the Grand Fleet, felt that Scapa Flow in the Orkney Islands was insufficiently secure and, on the false alarm of a German periscope being sighted, despatched the fleet to the west coast of Scotland and then even more remotely to the west of Ireland. Nonetheless, it could be said and sung that Britannia still ruled the waves. The main menace and threat came from what was underneath the waves, the mines and submarines. On 10 January 1915 the Kaiser emphasised caution in the use of German surface strength:

> As far as possible the Commander-in-Chief is to avoid encounters with superior enemy forces, as in the present circumstances the High Seas Fleet has the added importance of being a valuable political instrument in the hands of the All Highest War Lord: an unfavourable outcome of a naval action would therefore be a particularly serious matter.

Kitchener saw the western front situation with perfect clarity, writing to Sir John French on 2 January 1915:

> I suppose we must now recognise that the French army cannot make a sufficient break through the German lines of defence to bring about the retreat of the German forces from northern France. If that is so, then the German lines in France may be looked upon as a fortress that cannot be carried by assault, and also cannot be completely invested.

Churchill and Lloyd George therefore wondered whether France should be the main sphere of British activity. In France the advance on both sides could be measured in yards, with the churned land and endless mire providing only the solace of a less vile trench from time to time. The diaries of Gerald Burgoyne (1874-1936), descendant of the 'Gentleman Johnny' Shaw had dramatised in *The Devil's Disciple*, give a sombre picture of the situation at the start of 1915. On 3 January he wrote: 'A man in another Company, coming off parade, deliberately, it is said, put a bullet through his instep, in order to get sent home wounded. There's a good deal of self-mutilation out here.' A couple of days later he added: 'About 50 yards in front of us are some old French rifle pits full of dead, and I can see the red breeches of one poor fellow; yesterday, when the sun came out for an hour, the men opposite them said they commenced to smell.' He noted that no staff or brigade officer had been to the trenches, which to them was *terra incognita*. On 7 January he paints a grim picture:

We slosh on our way, my men, sullen, patient, spiritless, I cursing, urging, imploring, threatening, exhorting, in every endeavour to get my poor sheep safely and quickly across 300 yards of high, open, shell pitted, slippery, waterlogged clay plough into which 'strays' are thudding, most unpleasantly and frequently. I fell full length over a telephone wire, and my leading men, missing me, at once go astray.

Three days later he mentions Elgar's regiment: 'The Worcesters, on the right, last week rushed an advanced German trench and bayoneted the 20 men in it, and clubbed the officer to death.'

Meanwhile Churchill's plan for the Dardanelles was taking shape. He had wanted such an expedition at the beginning of the war, even with Turkey neutral, and indeed with the idea of her remaining so. For the moment Fisher backed him, quoting Napoleon: 'CELERITY' - without it - 'FAILURE'. On 3 January Churchill had written to Vice-Admiral Carden (1857-1930): 'Do you consider the forcing of the Dardanelles by ships alone a practicable operation?' It was attempted, but poor weather and the loss through a mine of an old battleship caused naval hesitation. Ultimately a landing on the least hospitable coast imaginable was to supplement the attempted breakthrough to Constantinople. Rupert Brooke (1887-1915) was excited by the idea, as he wrote to Violet Asquith on 22 February 1915: 'Do you think *perhaps* the fort on the Asiatic corner will want quelling, & we'll land & come at it from behind & they'll make a sortie & meet us on the plains of Troy?' He went on to wonder whether the sea would be 'polyphloisbic & wine dark & unvintageable', anticipating in the first adjective an Elgarian letter of August 1923 to the *Times Literary Supplement* . Brooke, however, was not to land on Gallipoli. He died of septicaemia at the island of Lemnos on St.George's day, and Shakespeare's day, 23 April.

Elgar's setting of Binyon's 'For the Fallen' suffered a check when he heard that Cyril Rootham (1875-1938) of St.John's College, Cambridge, was also attempting it. When Novello agreed to publish both versions and he had yielded to pressure from a number of friends, Elgar continued, completing the work by the end of June 1915 and dedicating it 'to the memory of our glorious men, with a special thought for the Worcesters'. The following month Binyon took his annual British Museum leave in France, arriving on 25 July. He was a Red Cross volunteer ambulance man posted to a military hospital in Haute Marne. Masefield had been there three months previously. It was a château in a spacious park, with guns audible in the distance. Night jobs involved meeting Red Cross trains with more and more wounded. His most bitter task was the burning of amputated limbs. *Fetching the Wounded* sprang from his experiences:

Each hurries on his errand; lanterns swing;
Dark shapes cross and re-cross the rails; we bring
Stretchers, and pile and number them; and heap
The blankets ready. Then we wait and keep
A listening ear. Nothing comes yet; all's still.
Only soft gusts upon the wires blow shrill
Fitfully, with a gentle spot of rain.
Then, ere one knows it, the long gradual train
Creeps quietly in and slowly stops. No sound
But a few voices' interchange. Around
Is the immense night-stillness, the expanse
Of faint stars over all the wounds of France.

Now stale odour of blood mingles with keen
Pure smell of grass and dew. Now lantern-sheen
Falls on brown faces opening patient eyes
And lips of gentle answers, where each lies
Supine upon his stretcher, black of beard
Or with young cheeks; on caps and tunics smeared
And stained, white bandages round foot or head
Or arm, discoloured here and there with red.

The Gallipoli expedition ended in disaster. Churchill took full blame: the plan was his, the mistakes were not. On the Turkish side Enver Pasha (1881-1922) reinforced Fisher's and Napoleon's point: 'If the English had only had the courage to rush more ships through the Dardanelles, they could have got to Constantinople; but their delay enabled us thoroughly to fortify the Peninsula.' Churchill's notes to cabinet were characteristically trenchant. On 15 October he was particularly concerned for the imperial contingent, the Australians and New Zealanders who represented their first army sent to Europe against Germany: 'Anzac is the greatest word in the history of Australasia. Is it for ever to carry to future generations of Australians and New Zealanders memories of forlorn heroism and of sacrifices made in vain?' In November 1915 Kitchener decided to evacuate, and in January 1916 it was done. The failure left an indelible mark on the Australasian consciousness, with a sense of betrayal uppermost. Kitchener's reputation was also tarnished.

The battle of Jutland took place on the day after Elgar's 59th birthday. He was at Stoke, and wrote to the Windflower on 3 June 1916: 'I am here & *much* better - so far: it is lovely and - lo*n*ely. I rest & play with the dog & cut down thistles . . . but this *awful* navy news! it's killing to the spirit.' Lady Elgar was at the Navarros' home and was equally upset by the news:

'Terrible shock hearing of naval battle & loss of English ships - but it seems as if nos. of Germans had been sunk & they had fled - but still.' The next day things were better: 'As news came, it seemed we had a great naval Victory so thankful & might have been spared the horrid first shock.' A.J.P.Taylor asked pertinently: 'Who won?' The British lost more ships: 'But, at the decisive moment, the German fleet fled from the British; and in Jellicoe's eyes this was all that mattered.' Taylor argues that the German conviction they had lost at Jutland turned their attention the more completely to the submarine as the weapon which might cripple Britain; and it nearly did.

On 6 June Lady Elgar was still with Mary de Navarro at Broadway: 'In evening the dreadful shock of hearing K. of K. and his Staff were lost with the Hampshire. Expect some horrible treason & German murder. Stormy sea so fear few rescued. D.G. that the great man had finished his work - & that his great Army was made.' Kitchener's proposed visit to Russia was the result of an official invitation from the Tsar. C.E.Callwell (1859-1928), director of intelligence, described Kitchener's attitude to the trip: 'the Field Marshal was in rare spirits, looking forward eagerly to his time in Russia, merry as a schoolboy starting for his holidays, only anxious to be off.' Kitchener stopped in Orkney to hear from Jellicoe about the battle of Jutland, and was advised to postpone sailing because of poor weather. He decided to leave as scheduled, but Jellicoe changed the *Hampshire*'s route so as to avoid the worst of the storm at the outset. But the wind veered and the *Hampshire* struck a mine. A leading seaman reported that the captain urged Lord Kitchener to make for a lifeboat. Perhaps he did not hear him; perhaps he took no notice. He had appeared entirely composed when emerging after the explosion and remained so at the order to abandon ship. Jellicoe held himself to some extent responsible. Asquith announced that after the war a memorial to Kitchener would be erected. It did not happen, and the 'pointing finger' that rallied a nation to form Lady Elgar's 'great Army' became an object of satire. Elgar would doubtless have remembered that it was Kitchener's Nile expedition that urged him towards a 'Gordon' symphony and was the ultimate inspiration for the glowing 'Committal' theme in *The Dream of Gerontius.*

Elgar was not to meet Siegfried Sassoon (1886-1967) until after the war; Schuster was a mutual friend. But Sassoon had long been an admirer of Elgar's music. He had enlisted on 1 August 1914, even before war was officially declared. On 17 November of the following year he left for France, and poetry that had been largely conventional began to reflect more and more the horror of his war experience. His poem of 10 February 1916, *In the Pink*, was refused by the *Westminster Gazette* on the grounds that it would discourage Kitchener's recruiting drive:

Siegfried Sassoon c.1916

And then he thought: tomorrow night we trudge
Up to the trenches, and my boots are rotten.
Five miles of stodgy clay and freezing sludge,
And everything but wretchedness forgotten.
Tonight he's in the pink; but soon he'll die.
And still the war goes on - *he* don't know why.

At the battle of the Somme he could keep an eye on Henry V's road to Agincourt in 1415. This time there were more casualties. Sassoon developed lung trouble and was sent to Oxford for convalescence in August 1916. The following January he wrote one of the strangest poems that Elgar can ever have inspired. He had been to a concert that included the Violin Concerto and 'Enigma' Variations. He told Edward Dent at Cambridge that they had given him 'as much pleasure as usual, which is a lot'. His diary entry for 23 January 1917 pinpoints cue 94 in the concerto finale and leads on to the poem: '*pp nobilmente* etc made me glorious with dreams tonight. Elgar always moves me deeply, because his is the melody of an average Englishman (and I suppose I am more or less the same).'

In all the noblest passages and the noblest strains of horns and violins I shut my eyes seeing on the darkness a shape always the same - in spite of myself - the suffering mortal figure on a cross, but the face is my own. And again there are hosts of shadowy forms with uplifted arms - souls of men, agonised and aspiring, hungry for what they seek as God in vastness.

THE ELGAR VIOLIN CONCERTO

I have seen Christ, when music wove
Exulting vision; storms of prayer
Deep-voiced within me marched and strove.
The sorrows of the world were there.

A God for beauty shamed and wronged?
A sign where faith and ruin meet,
In glooms of vanquished glory thronged
By spirits blinded with defeat?

His head forever bowed with pain,
In all my dreams he looms above
The violin that speaks in vain -
The crowned humility of love.

O music undeterred by death,
And darkness closing on your flame,

Christ whispers in your dying breath,
And haunts you with his tragic name.

When he returned to the front, Sassoon's poems emphasised more and
more the sheer ugliness of the war, and he was himself wounded at the
battle of Arras on 16 April 1917. By now he had seen enough. Invalided
home and appalled more by what he heard about the politicians than by
such military incompetence he might have experienced, he was ready to
make his 'statement' dated 15 June 1917:

> I have seen and endured the sufferings of the troops, and I can no longer
> be a party to prolonging those sufferings for ends which I believe to be evil
> and unjust.
>
> I am not protesting against the military conduct of the War, but against
> the political errors and insincerities for which the fighting men are being
> sacrificed.
>
> On behalf of those who are suffering now, I make this protest against
> the deception which is being practised on them. Also I believe that it may
> help to destroy the callous complacence with which the majority of those at
> home regard the continuance of agonies which they do not share and
> which they have not sufficient imagination to realise.

It was an act of astonishing courage; but publication of the 'statement' and
its mention in the House of Commons would have involved inevitable
court martial but for the prompt action of Robert Graves (1895-1985),
fellow officer and poet, who was able to achieve a judgment of
'neurasthemia' for Sassoon and his transfer to Craiglockhart Hospital
near Edinburgh, what Sassoon called 'a live museum of neuroses'.

Meanwhile Bernard Shaw had been 'Joy Riding at the Front'. His
account, satisfactorily censored by himself, appeared in the *Daily
Chronicle* of 5, 7 and 8 March 1917. Nonetheless, he was able to mention
later matters he could not publish at the time:

> The appallingly slaughterous British offensives that just stopped short of
> getting there; the bombarded coast towns about which our authorities lied
> so heroically; the holocausts of British youth sacrificed in holding the
> ground for French offensives that never came off; the air raided cities and
> torpedoed ships; the Red Cross vans, with their loads of mutilated men;
> the 'combing out' of the civilians as the need for more cannon fodder made
> the medical examinations for fitness less and less fastidious and the
> tribunals more and more inflexible: above all, the reaction of unreasoning
> patriotic enthusiasm into equally unreasoning disillusion: all this could
> easily have been exploited to rub in Pacifist and anti-Imperialist morals, or

Let the bugles sound the truce of God
To the whole world for ever. *Summer*

Bugles sound the truce of God

conversely, to harden the public temper in the opposite direction. Neither of these opportunities appealed to me.

That same month there was the first of the 1917 Russian revolutions. For the allied war effort it seemed hopeful, and on 16 March Lady Elgar greeted it with enthusiasm: 'Revolution in Russia & Czar deposed - May it have all success!' The Russian royal family had discredited itself by court corruption circling round the sinister figure of Rasputin (1871-1916), and Nicholas II (1894-1917) had proved himself little wiser in the field than in politics. For the moment Lenin (1870-1924) was fuming in the wings, but on 16 April he arrived in Petrograd within a sealed train shrewdly provided by the Germans. The October revolution pleased Lady Elgar less, as the Russians had ceased to fight. On 16 November she could report only topsy-turvydom: 'from Russia wildly confused & conflicting statements.' In his chapter headed 'Cataclysm', Shaw elaborated on the situation:

> To us it seemed nothing but an infamous backing out of our war by an Ally on whom we had depended to steamroller our enemies on their eastern front. When the steamroller went over our own toes our fury was unbounded. We cared nothing for Marxian ideology: all we knew was that the Russians had stopped fighting and intended to make peace with Germany. We could not stand that at any price.

On 15 February 1918 Elgar had his first lunch with the Shaws, taken there by Lalla Vandervelde. In January 1917 she had taken part in Shaw's *Augustus does his Bit*, an occasion noted with disdain by Lady Elgar: 'E. to Sloane Square to see Lalla in B.Shaw's horrid little play.' But the officials who had to clear Shaw for his visit to the western front had greatly appreciated the fun poked at Augustus Highcastle's officious and obstructive bumbledom, telling Shaw: 'We are up against Augustus all day.' An additional pleasure at that first lunch was the presence of Harley Granville Barker, whose Shakespeare productions Elgar had greatly enjoyed. Elgar was an admirer of Shaw's music criticism, as he had confessed in a Birmingham lecture. Whether Shaw also mentioned his youthful efforts as a composer is not recorded. In one respect he anticipated Elgar, sketching a Shelley setting as early as 23 June 1883, the year of Elgar's engagement to Helen Weaver.[1] Shaw's poem began,

> When the lamp is shattered
> The light in the dust lies dead -
> When the cloud is scattered
> The rainbow's glory is shed.

[1] See *Shaw's Music*, vol.1, p.205

> When the lute is broken,
> Sweet tones are remembered not;
> When the lips have spoken,
> Loved accents are soon forgot.

Elgar found Shavian conversation increasingly enjoyable; but the lifelong Conservative had little sympathy for Shaw's Socialism, increasingly unFabian and authoritarian as the years went by. In this he was at one with Sidney Colvin, who had expressed forcible views about Shaw. Elgar replied on 13 December 1921:

> Your explosion was quite in order &, as it brings a letter from you, really divine ire. I don't think we shd. have 'liked' Aristophanes personally or Voltaire (perhaps) but I cannot do without their work. GBS's politics are, to me, appalling, but he is the kindest-hearted, gentlest man I have met outside the charmed circle which includes you.

At the end of the letter he added. 'About the brains & the enormous Churchillian satire I do not speak now - but they have my deepest admiration.' Elgar is referring to Charles Churchill (1732-64), who made verse onslaughts on many notables of his time.

Elgar's wartime excursions to Stoke and Worcester were superseded from May 1917 by prolonged stays at Brinkwells in Sussex, which from the beginning he found 'too lovely for words'. There he was not only woodman and carpenter, but he became again a significant composer, first with the three chamber works, but above all with the Cello Concerto. An added attraction was the proximity of Sidney and Frances Colvin. He had been knighted in 1911 and retired from the keepership of Prints and Drawings at the British Museum the following year. He shared with Alice Elgar an Indian background. His father was a partner in a leading firm of Eastern merchants and had Indian connections going back several generations. His uncle John was lieutenant-governor of the North-West provinces. Colvin reported an incident in the Mutiny, which in general caused his father much anxiety:

> Sometimes the strain would end in relief, as in the case of my cousin James Colvin, cooped up almost without stores in a hurriedly half-fortified bungalow at Arrah, with seven or eight English and fifty-odd faithful Sikhs, by a whole horde of Sepoy mutineers well armed and provided. 'There is much in common,' writes Sir George Trevelyan, 'between Leonidas dressing his hair before he went forth to his last fight, and young Colvin laughing over his rice and salt, while the bullets spattered on the wall like hail'.

His mother knew and idolised Ruskin; hence her feeling for 'hill or mountain majesty'. Like Elgar, Colvin remained much in debt to his mother: 'I cannot be grateful enough for one thing: she set me reading *Rob Roy* aloud to her when I was eight years old; the other Waverleys followed; and subsequent years have only confirmed and deepened my delight in the imaginary world of which I was thus early made free.' He was taken to visit the Ruskins on Denmark Hill and by 15 was a devoted Ruskinian: 'I had become intensely sensitive both to the magnetism of Ruskin's personality and to the power and beauty of his writings. No man had about him more - few can ever have had so much - of the atmosphere and effluence of genius.' Colvin's ambition was to be a combination of Ruskin 'without his extravagances and lack of balance' and Matthew Arnold 'without his superior airs and graces'. As a Suffolk boy, he would often pass Edward FitzGerald:

> I was used constantly to encounter and, I fear, unknowing all he was, inwardly to deride that eccentric, ineffectual recluse of genius (remember his own name for himself, Ballyblunder), as he strolled or rather vaguely drifted, an odd, rumpled, melancholy-looking figure in grey plaid, green eye-shade, and shabby back-tilted hat, along the lanes and highways of the Woodbridge neighbourhood.

Ruskin was not ready to recommend him to the Slade professorship at Cambridge because he was not a draughtsman. He secured the post, however (1873). Burne-Jones was among his best hopes for English art, and Colvin was fascinated by the contrast between the melancholy of his painted figures and his own 'rich laughter-loving gaiety'. He admired Burne-Jones's literary taste: 'his two chief favourites being (as they are the favourites of every wise reader) Walter Scott and Dickens'. Colvin admired also Rossetti, perhaps more for his verse translations (Elgar's superb *Go, Song of Mine* was a Rossetti version of Cavalcanti (c.1255-1300)) than his painting. Robert Louis Stevenson (1850-94) became a particular friend, and in *Memories and Notes of Persons and Places* (1921) Colvin gives his impressions of him in August 1873 as an unearthly sprite or Ariel: 'And imagine that, as you got to know him, this sprite, this visitant from another sphere, turned out to differ from mankind in general not by being less human but by being a great deal more human than they; richer-blooded, greater-hearted; more human in all senses of the word.' He later edited Stevenson's works and letters. It is not difficult to understand the appeal Colvin had for Elgar. His easy familiarity with the intellectual giants of the day was instantly attractive, and the breadth of his scholarship, perhaps even more literary than artistic, stimulated Elgar into the oddest byways of research in the British Museum.

Lady Colvin was born Frances Fetherstonhaugh (1839-1924) and spent some of her early years in Frankfurt, where the young Frederic Leighton was a family acquaintance. A disastrous marriage at 16 to the Rev. Albert Sitwell took her to Calcutta. A cholera epidemic drove them back to the London East End, but at the death of her second son she left her husband and became secretary of the Working Men's College, the movement to which Ruskin, Rossetti, Burne-Jones and Morris gave much time. She has left an interesting description of Robert Browning (1812-89):

> The stimulating geniality of his presence, the warm grasp of the hand that sent us on our way rejoicing if we met him but for a moment in a London crush, made a difference in the day. And those who had heard his somewhat strident voice grow tender even to tears in reading out his own *Andrea del Sarto* have a memory of him that will remain with them for life.

Bertie Sitwell, her elder son, was ordered to Davos in Switzerland for the sake of his lungs but died in January 1881 aged 18. Philip Burne-Jones (1861-1926), who was later to paint the portrait of Elgar now, despite the sitter's protests, in the Worcester Guildhall, wrote to her:

> But that you should in any way love me for being a young creature - for having known Bertie & been at school with him - is an honour which I should consider most sacred - & should try with all my might to make myself - the shadow of the reality that is gone - worthy of the affection I still marvel you can bestow.

The Colvins did not marry till 1903, and their friendship with the Elgars dates from some three years later. It was Frances Colvin's ready sympathy that made Elgar write to her on 3 May 1910, almost as soon as he heard of Peter Rabbit's death: 'You are always so very lenient to me in my foolishness so I write to tell you how very sad we are to-day.' In the last summer of the war the Colvins were near neighbours to Brinkwells, if established rather more grandly. Ideas for the Cello Concerto were already simmering in Elgar's mind and on 26 June 1919 he offered the dedication of the completed work to the Colvins: 'Your friendship is such a real & precious thing that I should like to leave some record of it.'

16 - But in his ways with men I find him not

The Elgars were at Severn House when they heard on 11 November 1918 that the armistice had been signed: 'E. put up our Flag, it looked gorgeous - Crowds out & all rejoicing. DG. for preservation & Victory.' They then left for Brinkwells, where barley was being threshed. Carice had meant to come too but went instead to the Coliseum: ' "Land of Hope & Glory" was sung twice   the 2nd time the words of refrain were thrown on the screen & people stood & joined in - Very exciting & moving.' An Elgarian flag flew at Brinkwells too. Laurence Binyon had recently sent Elgar a draft of a 'Peace' ode, wondering if he might consider setting it. Elgar had replied on 5 November:

> I think your poem beautiful exceedingly - but - I do not feel drawn to write peace music somehow - I thought long months ago that I could feel that way & if anything could draw me your poem would, but the whole atmosphere is too full of complexities for me to feel music to it: not the atmosphere of the poem but of the time I mean. The last two divisions VI & VII are splendid altho' I regret the appeal to the Heavenly Spirit which is cruelly obtuse to the individual sorrow & sacrifice - a cruelty I resent bitterly & disappointedly.

As published, the poem has no mention of the 'Heavenly Spirit', and the sections Elgar admired run as follows:

VI
Not with folding of the hands,
Not with evening fallen wide
Over waste and weary lands,
Peace is come; but as a bride.
It is the trumpets of the dawn that ring;
It is the sunrise that is challenging.

VII
Lovely word, flying like a light across the happy Land,
When the buds break and all the earth is changed,
Bringing back the sailor from his watch, upon the perilled seas,
Rejoining shores long severed and estranged,
Peace, like the Spring, that makes the torrent dance afresh
And bursts the bough with sap of beauty pent,

Laurence Binyon without a wounded French soldier

Memorial to the Cavalry of the Empire

> Flower from our hearts into passionate recovery
> Of all the mind lost in that banishment.
> Come to us mighty as a young and glad deliverer
> From wrong's old canker and out-dated lease,
> Then will we sing thee in thy triumph and thy majesty,
> Then from our throes shall be prepared our peace.

Elgar was right: it would not do. Binyon had done much better before, and was to do so again. The fourth section of the poem has echoes in it of *The Happy Warrior* as imagined by English Wordsworth and the Watts now held in Bavarian Munich:

> Now let us praise the dead that are with us to-day
> Who fought and fell before the morning shone,
> Happy and brave, an innumerable company;
> This day is theirs, the day their deeds have won
> Glory to them, and from our hearts a thanksgiving
> In humbleness and awe and joy and pride.

The young Herbert Read (1893-1968), a captain in the Green Howards who survived the war towards eminence as poet and wide-ranging critic of art and literature, made his own version of *The Happy Warrior*:

> His wild heart beats with painful sobs
> his strain'd hands clench an ice-cold rifle
> his aching jaws grip a hot parch'd tongue
> his wide eyes search unconsciously.
>
> He cannot shriek.
>
> Bloody saliva
> dribbles down his shapeless jacket.
>
> I saw him stab
> and stab again
> a well-killed Boche.
>
> This is the happy warrior,
> this is he . . .

Chivalry had taken a severe knock but was able to lift up a lance or two on high in the countless war memorials dotted over the British Isles. Typical in Hyde Park, London, for instance, is the 'Cavalry of the Empire' monument by Adrian Jones (1845-1938), displaying an armed and mounted St.George, with horse bestriding the scaly body of a monstrous dragon, and sword held proudly aloft. Different, and tenderly vulnerable, is the naked youth leaning on his spear by the Wellington Arch (Derwent Wood, 1871-1926), in memory of the Machine Gun Corps. More in keeping with the brute facts of the war was the massive stone gun nearby on its raised plinth, behind which lies the body of a slain soldier covered but for the visible foot and hand with the decency of a blanket; this is the Royal Artillery monument by Sargeant Jagger (1885-1934). When unveiling a memorial at Doune, Perthshire, Sir Ian Hamilton (1853-1947) spoke about the generous peace Kitchener had achieved in South Africa: 'What has been the result? The war lasted three years; South Africa was more completely ruined than Central Europe; hate was stronger than it is in Germany: - and yet, within one year South Africa was smiling and so were we.' The politicians had wanted a vindictive peace against the Boers; the Treaty of Versailles was the disastrous sequel.

What remained for Elgar after the unsatisfactory première of the Cello Concerto on 27 October 1919? Any musical schemes he had in mind were shattered by the death of Lady Elgar on 7 April 1920. It seemed indeed as if the rest might be silence. What stirred Elgar initially was the music of Bach and Handel. It might have been thought for a moment that Elgar was hitching himself to the neo-classical bandwaggon. Nothing could be farther from the truth. His Bach and Handel orchestrations, and particularly the former, deck the mighty Baroque composers in the utmost splendour of Elgar's late-Romantic orchestra. He had never scored more daringly than in the Bach C minor fugue. It was almost an act of defiance to the world of contemporary music, which tended to equate the opulence of the pre-war orchestra with the over-weening pride that had just destroyed four empires and sent countless millions to their death. In earlier times Elgar fugues had often been associated with devilment or devilry. There is the C minor fugue in *The Light of Life* to the words 'The wisdom of their wise men shall perish', thus cocking a snook at the professors of music at whose feet he never sat; *Gerontius* has its snarling fugal demons; the Introduction and Allegro includes its 'devil of a fugue' by way of development. But now, after the hideous carnage of the war and the agony of his private grief, Elgar turned to Bach and Handel fugues as a source of strength and almost benediction. And a new C minor fugue, originally written for piano in June 1923 and virtually his first original music since taking Napleton Grange and returning to the West Midlands with housekeeping nieces around him, was eventually to evoke the atmosphere of his beloved Worcester Cathedral in the *Severn Suite*.

Just before abandoning London as main base, Elgar had written incidental music to Binyon's *Arthur*. The project for such a play went back to 1912, when John Martin Harvey (1863-1944) had played a formidable Oedipus opposite the Jocasta of Lillah McCarthy (1875-1960) at Covent Garden. Harvey, brought up in the tradition of Henry Irving (1838-1905), now wanted a grandiose play based on Malory's *Morte d'Arthur*. 'What could be more glorious', he wrote in his autobiography, 'than to produce a play on the great British theme of Arthur, written by a British poet, in settings by a British artist, in the foremost British theatre? Laurence Binyon for the poet, my old friend Professor Robert Anning Bell for the designer, and Covent Garden Opera House for the production!' Binyon wondered about attempting 'so pawed over & "stock" a subject'; but already he had offered Elgar a libretto on Merlin's madness, and the idea of investigating again the mythological heritage of the land had its appeal. The war intervened, but Binyon worked on *Arthur*, discussing progress and future possibilities with Harvey, whose original plan had been to play Launcelot. As the play shaped, he decided to be the king, which involved Binyon in some rewriting. Nevertheless, *Arthur* was scheduled to open in December 1919 with lavish costumes and elaborate staging. Disaster then struck the Launcelot. Robert Loraine (1876-1935), Shaw's 1907 Don Juan in Act 3 of *Man and Superman*, had been a flying ace during the war and was wounded in the leg. Shaw foretold for him an eternity of Richard III unless he wrote him a Lord Byron play; meanwhile he had been Cyrano de Bergerac for much of 1919. Towards the end of the year his doctor ordered rest. *Arthur* was again postponed, and Harvey now abandoned the play despite his admiration for it. The grandiose production he had in mind hardly suited the spareness of Binyon's dialogue and a leanness of language that owed much to Matthew Arnold. Nor did Binyon forget his war experience when Guenevere and the First Novice converse at the convent of Amesbury. The Queen says:

> Still rumour.
> And never the one certain thing. Two hours
> Since any word came how the battle goes.
> Yet all night long
> Have our replenished torches flamed to guide
> The bearers of the wounded to our gates.

The Novice replies:

> Cloister and ante-chapel both are filled;
> And still they bring them in, dying and dead.
> Never was seen such slaughter in the world.

Covent Garden was now out of the question; there was a chance of New

York; but ultimately it was to be the Old Vic Theatre in the Waterloo Road. Once the production date was fixed, Binyon felt able to approach Elgar with a project that interested him at once and kindled the smouldering embers. If the war had maimed chivalry and all but killed off the gentleman, Arthur had always been the once and future king. A potent presence in Victorian and Edwardian days, he might yet act as antidote to postwar superficiality and giddiness. Lady Elgar would have approved the subject and always liked the author. Just as Binyon's language was taut and disciplined, so Elgar's music, even when conjuring the warmth of knightly courtesies, eschews all luxury of harmony and counterpoint. So often does the bass-line seem to follow a pattern subtly different from Elgarian norms. The result is spare and strangely austere.

Binyon's play was avowedly based on Malory, who had shaped into some sort of order the mass of material that had gathered round the name of Arthur by the 15th century. Binyon pared Malory to produce a workable drama. The play that might have celebrated the high tide of imperial chivalry in 1912 had become by 1923 profoundly elegiac, dealing with the collapse of Arthur's realm and the Round Table ideals. Its mood was consonant with Elgar's at the time. Perhaps the situation was not so different from that of Caxton himself, who was lamenting a decayed chivalry in his printing of Malory. Elgar undoubtedly knew his Caxton, and indeed he and Ivor Atkins played around in their correspondence with the language of Caxton's 1481 version of the *History of Reynard the Fox*, taken from the Flemish. Caxton was not only a printing pioneer but also a successful merchant in the Low Countries, engaged in the wool trade and becoming in 1463 governor of the English Nation of Merchant Adventurers there. In 1470 he entered the service of Margaret of York (1446-1503), sister to Edward IV; in 1468 she had married as his third wife Charles the Bold of Burgundy, who so fascinated Walter Scott in *Quentin Durward* and *Anne of Geierstein*, and who still maintains his vigil beside the mausoleum of Maximilian I. Caxton was probably her financial advisor in the Burgundian capital. It was she who urged him to complete his translation of the *Recuyell of the Historyes of Troye*.

Caxton's preface to Malory is a moving document. He mentions such earlier productions as 'dyvers hystoryes as wel of contemplacyon as of other hystoryal and worldly actes of grete conquerours and prynces, and also certeyn bookes of ensaumples and doctryne' and goes on to say that 'many noble and dyvers gentylmen' urged him to the subject of King Arthur and the Holy Grail. Caxton had initially demurred, uncertain whether Arthur had ever existed. After a careful review of all the evidence he was convinced: 'Thenne, al these thynges forsayd aledged, I coude not wel denye but that there was suche a noble kyng named Arthur, and reputed one of the nine worthy, and fyrst and chyef of the Cristen men.'

Caxton's aim is that 'noble men may see and lerne the noble actes of chyvalrye, the jentyl and vertuous dedes that somme knyghtes used in tho dayes, by whyche they came to honour'.

Malory divides his book into eight parts, of which Binyon uses mainly the last two, 'The Book of Sir Launcelot and Queen Guinevere' and 'The most Piteous Tale of the Morte Arthur saunz Guerdon'. Binyon's nine scenes concentrate on the decline and fall of Arthur's fellowship. He begins in 'Sir Bernard's castle at Astolat'. Malory affirms 'that is in Englysh Gylforde' and is equally clear about Camelot, which is 'otherwyse called Wynchester'. Binyon follows Malory closely in the Elaine drama, sometimes quoting him almost verbatim; but he stretches it over three scenes, so that the wistful 'Windflowerish' music Elgar wrote for Elaine features early in the 'overture', recurs often in melodrama to accompany Binyon's dialogue, and closes Scene IV as the last music heard before the interval. Though much of the *Arthur* score was eventually subsumed into the sketches for Symphony no.3 and some for *The Spanish Lady*, Elaine's music found no other home and remained as eloquent tribute to a doomed love. Like Guenevere herself, she was victim to the knightly code of courtesy that bound members of the Round Table exclusively to their ladies.

Binyon demands a cast of 28 speaking parts, but he does not attempt Malory's tournament or other interruptions to the Elaine story. He has his own manner of pacing the episodes. At the outset of Scene I Lavaine is in terse conversation with his father, reporting that the king has returned to London after victory in the north, but that now trouble brews in the west. He wonders, too, why a herald has been despatched in search of Launcelot:

> Father, have you ever thought
> Perhaps our guest, this knight my sister found
> Pierced by an arrow among the forest leaves,
> Who will not tell his name, might be none other
> Than Launcelot himself?

Binyon has brought Launcelot a wounded Tristan to the castle, where only Elaine has tended him. Torre, the elder son has recognised Launcelot by a scar the herald mentioned. For Torre, appalled by Elaine's obvious love, Launcelot is 'the Queen's paramour', 'A traitor!' Sir Bernard mislikes Torre's suspicions:

> You read him backward, as the witches do
> The holy writ.

Launcelot does not suspect how totally Elaine has surrendered her affection to him:

> If - if there be some fondness, some young spring
> Of fondness in her heart, Time soon amends
> Such wounds. She is a child. If this be gone
> More deep than tenderness and pity's tears,
> I have means to cure it. Let me speak with her.

It does not help when he describes the scars on his shield that Elaine has guarded and cherished: one came from preserving Arthur's life; another by a mistaken blow from Gawaine, and a third:

> By the black winter waves
> Under Tintagel towers, that blow was dealt.

Launcelot agrees to the wearing of Elaine's favour, and she declares her passion. Malory's offer of an annual thousand pounds to Elaine becomes more seemly as 'A dowry of my treasure and my lands'. At the end of Scene I Torre knows his sister will die.

Elgar's music for Scene II is based mainly on a 'Chivalry' theme from the overture and its augmentation into a majestic 'Arthur' motif, both awaiting further development in Symphony no.3. The scene is mainly political, though it sows the seed of the Guenevere disaster. It is 'A room in the Palace at London. At the back a colonnade, through which is seen a rose hedge.' Arthur and Bedivere discuss the recent northern victory. Arthur feels it had been not far from defeat. 'There was some treason', hints Bedivere; 'Like fog on a sour wind', comments Arthur. The talk is so earnest Arthur does not notice Guenevere at first. In sadness she says 'I am but an idle corner of your kingdom'. Now Launcelot returns, but the king chides his absence when he most had need of him. Launcelot half says he had been trying to escape his love for Guenevere, yet affirms undying loyalty to the king. When he is alone with the queen, she expresses fear of Mordred, but Guenevere assumes Launcelot's delayed return was because of Elaine and departs in anger.

In Scene III, again at Astolat, 'Sir Bernard and Torre stand watching Elaine, who sleeps by the window'. Her music is as before, at the start of the scene and briefly at the end. She wakes and thinks she hears a rider. Torre replies: 'I hear nothing but the blackbird in the sycamore. See, sister Elaine, it is May. The thorn-boughs are white. Shall we go a-maying in the woods? Just as we used?' Elaine now wants a letter written to 'Most noble Launcelot', and Torre complies with a bitter reluctance. Binyon follows Malory almost word for word, but subtly includes also Queen Guenevere in the 'lament to all fair ladies'. Her steersman on the Thames is to be 'old Simon, dumb Simon'. That is how she will come to Launcelot.

At the start of Scene IV Lavaine is pensive on the river steps before the great banqueting hall at Westminster. Gareth and Gaheris are pitted against the sullen plotting of Mordred and Agravaine to trap Guenevere, whose radiant tune was to have done duty later in the overture to *The Spanish Lady*. There is talk of the red sleeve Launcelot wore at the jousts. The banquet music that pervades much of the scene and was to be main theme in the second movement of Symphony no.3 summons them to dine. With disquiet in the west, Launcelot is in consultation with the king. At the Round Table are hints of dissent, which Guenevere seeks to quell:

> A woman has no armour, has no sword;
> And absent, how shall she defend herself?
> If tongues be sharp with malice,
> A woman must be silent.

Mordred then raises the matter of the red sleeve, and assumes it was the queen's. Guenevere arises in proud wrath and the meeting breaks up. Binyon has handled the sleeve differently from Malory. For Binyon's Launcelot it is a symbol that he must forget his guilty love for Guenevere; or it was so till he saw her again. Now he is summoned to a denunciation from the queen until the barge appears with dumb Simon and dead Elaine. Guenevere hears the content of the letter and is stricken. Launcelot knows he must now leave the kingdom, and the Scene ends with the sad lament of Elaine 's 'Windflowerish' music.

Malory's first paragraph in 'The most piteous Tale' is a masterpiece of art. He seems to celebrate the flowering of the year as spring slides towards summer; but by the end the flower of chivalry is withered:

> In May, whan every harte floryshyth and burgenyth (for, as the season ys lusty to beholde and comfortable, so man and woman rejoysyth and gladith of somer commynge with his freyshe floures, for wynter wyth hys rowghe wyndis and blastis causyth lusty men and women to cowre and to syt by fyres), so thys season hit befelle in the moneth of May a grete angur and unhapp that stynted nat tylle the floure of chyvalry of the worlde was destroyed and slayne.

Malory refers to his French source as he draws tighter the strings of the action. He is not quite sure how physical was the love Launcelot and Guenevere were exploring in the night they were taken. Such conventions change with time, to say nothing of the geographical leap across the Channel. Malory has Arthur away hunting, and Launcelot is determined to speak with the queen. Sir Bors, his nephew, counsels against it, urging the ever-watchful Agravaine. Launcelot, however, will have none of it:

Elaine in the death barge by Gustave Doré

So sir Launcelot departed and toke hys swerde undir hys arme, and so he walked in hys mantell, that noble knyght, and put hymselff in grete jouparté. And so he past on tylle he cam to the quenys chambir, and so lyghtly he was had into the chambir.

Then the French book must come to Malory's aid:

> For, as the Freynshhe booke seyth, the quene and sir Launcelot were
> togydirs. And whether they were abed other at other maner of disportis,
> me lyste nat thereof make no mencion, for love that tyme was nat as love
> ys nowadayes.

Malory raises the alarm at once, and there ensues such carnage that
Launcelot knows he will have incurred the everlasting enmity of Arthur.

Binyon covers Malory's ground in two scenes. The first, Scene V, is set
in the Queen's tower: 'Night. At the back a bolted door. At one side a prie-
dieu, with a footstool before it. A single lamp burning on a tripod.
Guenevere stands by a window, holding the curtain and peering out.'
Elgar sets the scene again with music he did not plan to use elsewhere.
The queen's sorrow and anxiety are portrayed in doleful muted strings
watched over with a ray of hope on solo violin. Her anxiety motif recurs
as she looks on to the darkness full of foreboding:

> It's nothing; fancy's fever,
> That shapes the shadows into forms of fear!
> And yet there is a shadow among those shadows,
> And I could swear that shadow had human eyes,
> Watching. It stirs not. Is it a tree-stem
> Gives body to the dark? No tree was there.

Binyon brings in Shakespeare's owl from *Macbeth* Act 2:

> There's the owl again, crying, and there again!
> As if it knew the secret of the night
> And called me warning notes.

It proved indeed a 'fatal bellman'. Launcelot has come by a secret way,
determined on exile:

> Look on me, Guenevere, for the last time.
> The hard hour's here, the bitter moment's come;
> To-morrow I hoist for Brittany.

Almost at once, whatever the implications of the French book, they are
interrupted: 'As they gaze silent on one another, voices are heard without.
A knocking at the door; then the voice of Agravaine calling aloud.'

> Launcelot! Traitor knight!

Binyon now follows Malory closely, though heaping insults on Guenevere from the intruders. Launcelot has not even a sword, but by opening the door a little he admits Colegrevance, who sees nothing in the darkened room but is felled by Launcelot, who acquires both weaponry and armour. Binyon has Mordred with only four accomplices, to keep cast numbers under some control, reduce on-stage bloodshed at the Old Vic, and make Launcelot a more credible warrior than Malory would have him against fourteen or indeed Shakespeare has Falstaff in combat with his 'eleven buckram men'. Guenevere understands the situation clearly:

> Launcelot, from this hour all's war and ruin.
> I foresee it, I that made it.

Launcelot is determined to go to Arthur and explain all, despite Guenevere's conviction that Mordred will have anticipated him.

No music introduces Binyon's Scene VI, which is in the king's tower the same night. Arthur quizzes Gawaine about the silence that descended upon his knights when he came among them as the Scene IV banquet broke up. Had there been insult to Guenevere? Gawaine is reluctant to answer and protests the innocence of Launcelot:

> Think not of Launcelot ill. Who sought your good,
> Who fought for you, who toiled, who suffered, who
> Gave of his marrow and heart's faith for you?
> Launcelot! Has Mordred? Not a jot. If ever
> There is dissension, rancour, envy, strife,
> Seek Mordred: you will find him under it
> Like a snake. Mordred loves you not.

Yet suspicion of Launcelot's relations with the queen haunts Arthur despite the arguments of Gawaine. Entry of the bloodstained Mordred himself, as in Malory, hastens the catastrophe. Having heard Mordred out, Arthur turns to Gawaine:

> Arm you now, Gawaine, arm! Arrest the Queen.
> Seek Launcelot out, and take him.

This Gawaine refuses to do:

> It would be said Gawaine abetted what
> To him is shame and an unreason both.
> It may be Mordred lured him to the Queen
> With some feigned message.

Gawaine's refusal becomes the turning-point. Arthur bids him send his
brothers, Gareth and Gaheris and then soliloquises in deep gloom, aching
for night, not day:

> Dawn. Is it dawn so soon?
> The birds sang soft so when I wooed her, soft
> And thrilling with low pipe. Smell of the grass,
> Dew, and her face, wonderful, coming towards me . . .
> Ah, God, that it were night again, the night,
> The dark, where I knew nothing, where I loved
> And trusted, where I had a wife, a friend.

Gareth and Gaheris are as unwilling for the errand as was Gawaine, but
they insist they will go unarmed on the king's business. Arthur knows as
clearly as did Guenevere that the end is upon him:

> The graves are dug
> For all mortality; our woes have been
> Wept for from the beginning of the world.
> I feel the creeping of the rust that dims
> Excalibur, and those lamenting Queens
> That come to take me draw like shadows near.

A man who had accompanied Gareth and Gaheris now reports:

> We came to the Queen's door, and it was open.
> The Queen stood there, like one that waited us.
> There was a lamp burning above her head;
> Oh, very pale she seemed and very calm.

As she moved among them, a rumour arose amid those watching that she
was going to her death:

> It was dark
> In the shadow by the walls. There was a mist,
> A summer mist. The dawn was far above.

Suddenly Launcelot raged upon them, hacking with his sword in all
directions. Gareth and Gaheris fell, and Gawaine at once denounces
Launcelot:

> I will believe all evil of him now.
> I am with you now, my King, and he shall die.

A messenger announces that Mordred has made common cause with the rebels in the west. Gawaine remains implacable:

> Who recks of Mordred? Drop him down the wind
> To his own hell. But Launcelot that I loved
> Has slain my brothers. Death to Launcelot!

Arthur is at last the man of decisive action:

> Northward now!
> Summon my knights about me in the hall.
> Send a strong force on Mordred's heels to hold
> The traitor back. Ourselves will swiftly ride
> To take the Queen from Launcelot. Day is come,
> And friends are friends and foes are foes at last.

Malory begins his account of 'The Vengeance of Sir Gawain' with a stricken Arthur:

> Now turne we agayne unto kynge Arthure, that whan hit was tolde hym how and in what maner the quene was taken away frome the fyre, and whan he harde of the deth of his noble knyghtes, and in especiall sir Gaherys and sir Gareth, than he sowned for verry pure sorow. And whan he awooke of hys swoughe, than he sayde,
> 'Alas, that ever I bare crowne uppon my hede! For now have I loste the fayryst felyshyp of noble knyghtes that ever hylde Crystyn kynge togydirs.'

Gawaine hears of his brothers' end, but Malory in his tenderness refuses to let him believe Launcelot was the agent:

> 'That may I nat beleve,' seyde sir Gawayne, 'that ever he slew my good brother sir Gareth, for I dare say my brothir loved hym bettir than me and all hys brethirn and the kynge bothe.'

Once Gawaine realised the facts, he swore vengeance before the king. He urged Arthur to summon forces for battle against Joyous Gard. Launcelot on his side could make an impressive display of knights, supporters of himself or the queen:

> Thus they were on bothe partyes well furnysshed and garnysshed of all maner of thynge that longed unto the warre. But kynge Arthurs oste was so grete that sir Launcelottis oste wolde nat abyde hym in the fylde.

Nor would Launcelot emerge from Joyous Gard to fight the man who had made him knight At a moment of such crisis Malory refers to his source:

But the Freynsh booke seyth kynge Arthure wolde have takyn hys quene agayn and to have bene accorded with sir Launcelot, but sir Gawayne wolde nat suffir hym by no maner of meane.

After fruitless parley, there was an engagement, in which Sir Bors unhorsed the king and might have slain him.[1] But Launcelot forbade him and set Arthur on his horse again:

So whan kynge Arthur was on horsebak he loked on sir Launcelot; than the teerys braste oute of hys yen, thynkyng of the grete curtesy that was in sir Launcelot more than in ony other man. And therewith the kynge rod hys way and myght no lenger beholde hym, saiyng to hymselff, 'Alas, alas, that ever yet thys warre began!'

The kingdom was so grievously torn apart that news of the warfare reached as far as Rome and the ears of the Pope, says Malory.

Binyon sets his Scene VII in the king's camp before Joyous Gard: 'Stormy weather. Black skies against which the earth shows up white and livid. The towers of the Castle appear above rising ground.' Elgar responds with the most powerful of his Introductions, depicting both the inclement weather and the bitterness of the knightly quarrel, now sustained mainly by Gawaine. He includes references to the anxiety of Guenevere before the night of slaughter in her tower and the Elaine motif last heard after the barge brought her to the palace of Westminster. The brothers Lucan and Bedivere discuss the situation after Elgar has introduced once more the 'Chivalry' theme:

This quarrel fills all Christendom. Men say the noise of it goes over the seas even to Rome. Were it not for Gawaine, the King, I think, would make his peace, and Launcelot deliver up his Queen to him.

Not while the King is fixed to bring the Queen to judgment. To that Launcelot will never yield. So stands our wrestle in a deadlock; meanwhile this dear realm splits in two.

A maiden messenger from Joyous Gard is prelude to a parley that achieves nothing except to stir further Gawaine's hatred. The heavens crash noisily as battle is rejoined, and at last Launcelot and Arthur face each other. The favoured knight makes confession to his king:

But now, since we are met as naked souls
Beneath dark heaven, I will confess me. I

---

[1] As painted by Dyce in the Queen's Robing Room at the House of Lords to exemplify 'Generosity'.

> Have done you wrong that nothing can undo,
> Not though this thunder cracked the frame of things
> And spilled the molten world. Since first my eyes
> Saw Guenevere, I loved her.

The king cannot bring himself to slay Launcelot as he requests; nor can he take back a freely pardoned Guenevere:

> A man may pardon, but the King may not.
> The King is justice, or no more a King.

Already 'distant chanting is heard' and Elgar sets the 'Ecce sacerdos magnus' text traditional to the welcome of a bishop to its 'Antiphonale Romanum' tune.
  Malory explains the concern felt at Rome:

> And than the Pope toke a consideracion of the grete goodnes of kynge Arthur and of the hyghe proues off sir Launcelot, that was called the moste nobelyst knyght of the worlde.

The Pope decided to send an emissary: 'the Freynsh boke seyth hit was the Bysshop of Rochester.' Arthur was to take Guenevere again and make peace with Launcelot on pain of excommunication: 'So whan thys Bysshop was com unto Carlyle he shewed the kynge hys bullys, and whan the kynge undirstode them he wyste nat what to do.' Gawaine was willing that Guenevere should return, but he was implacable against Launcelot. The bishop then went to Joyous Gard, and persuaded Launcelot he would be at no risk, for the Pope must be obeyed:

> So the Bysshop departed and cam to the kynge to Carlehyll, and tolde hym all how sir Launcelot answerd hym; so that made the teares falle oute at the kyngis yen.

Then Launcelot took Guenevere to Carlisle and returned her to King Arthur. But Gawaine insisted on Launcelot's banishment, which caused him great grief:

> Moste nobelyst Crysten realme, whom I have loved aboven all othir realmys! And in the I have gotyn a grete parte of my worshyp, and now that I shall departe in thys wyse, truly me repentis that ever I cam in thys realme, that I shulde be thus shamefully banysshyd, undeserved and causeles!

As in Malory, Binyon's play produces its *episcopus ex machina* : 'Certain knights of either party return on the scene, and in their midst a white banner preceding a Bishop, with a train of priests chanting. With a last remote peal of thunder the storm passes away.' The Bishop gives Malory's message of reconciliation from 'Our Holy Father on the seat of St.Peter'; but he adds a word of stern advice to the recalcitrant Gawaine:

> Man of blood, your hour is past. Exorcise from you this vain rage and lust of vengeance. Bethink you of your sins, and of God's peace. The King receives his Queen again and is accorded with Sir Launcelot.

Gawaine cannot forgive, Launcelot accepts his banishment in words that echo Malory, and Guenevere wishes only a religious peace:

> There is no absolution among men:
> Give me leave, therefore, to renounce the world
> And choose the cloister.

She specifies what she has in mind:

> There is a nunnery at Amesbury: once
> I entered there, and found strange peace within.
> I did not know such peace could be on earth.
> Suffer me, my lord, to go to Amesbury.

Bedivere is deputed to escort her there with a company of knights. Elgar had written additional music after the start of the play's run for the departure of Launcelot and his company. It was based on Launcelot's battle fanfare in slow chromatic descent. It was now repeated as Guenevere leaves the stage and Arthur is left to cry out the names of the two people he had loved best, his queen and his friend.

In despatching Guenevere to her convent before Arthur's final battle Binyon departs from Malory and relieves Elgar of the need to find more war music. Instead he can be Gregorian as he prepares for the play's Scene VIII and a final visit of the king to Guenevere. She is still racked with her memories, but a companion nun tells her that Arthur has arrived to see her. Guenevere's instant reaction is to shrink from the encounter, but Lynned tells of a moment in her own life:

> Sister, I, too, once denied
> One who had loved me, when he sought me out
> For my forgiveness. Gawaine was his name.

She explains to Guenevere that this same Gawaine is now dead of wounds received at Joyous Gard. The queen asks about the appearance of the king and is told:

> I saw him in the ghostly morning mist
> Clad in his armour, sitting on his horse.
> He rides to battle. Almost like a spirit
> He seemed, and greater than himself.

Before Guenevere can comment, Arthur appears 'as a shadow among the shadows'. He is much changed. Guenevere takes upon herself the responsibility of the realm's collapse:

> I did the wrong.
> Through me the young have perished, the young men
> Have fallen in their blood.
> From me a woe goes welling through the world
> Like waves in the black night.

But Arthur in the access of his wisdom realises his own shortcoming:

> In the beginning was my fault. I feel
> The end upon me, like the air of dawn,
> And see in light that is not of the earth
> What we have done to each other, and left undone.
> I in my far dream of that perfect realm,
> Clouded in cares of policy and state,
> Saw not what burning soul was at my side,
> Wanting the love that sees through human eyes
> And by love understands. I was blind. Now
> I am borne beyond Time's wisdom and that fear
> Which moulds men's justice.

That is far from the language and thought of Malory. Arthur is now anxious to be away:

> I feel the wizard sword Excalibur
> Like an impatient spirit within my hand,
> As if he heard voices recalling me
> Out of this ended world. But I am freed;
> I am forgiven; the dark load is off.
> Say me farewell, Guenevere.

Arthur does not end in despair, nor can Binyon quite accept that the young he saw die in France did so in vain:

> The day goes to the night,
> And I to darkness, with my toil undone.

Yet something, surely, something shall remain.
A seed is sown in Britain, Guenevere;
And whether men wait for a hundred years
Or for a thousand, they shall find it flower
In youth unborn. The young have gone before me,
The maid Elaine, Gareth, and Gaheris - hearts
Without a price, poured out. But now I know
The tender and passionate spirit that burned in them
To dare all and endure all, lives and moves,
And though the dark comes down upon our waste,
Lives ever, like the sun above all storms.

Malory grieves to recount the result of Mordred's treachery in the west. After much fighting and countless deaths, Mordred and the king come face to face:

And whan sir Mordred saw kynge Arthur he ran untyll hym with hys swerde drawyn in hys honde, and there kyng Arthur smote sir Mordred undir the shylde, with a foyne of hys speare, thorowoute the body more than a fadom.

Mordred had received his death wound, but not before he gave Arthur a mortal blow. There follows the episode in Malory of Bedivere and the despatch of Excalibur, then the departure of Arthur in 'a lytyll barge with many fayre ladyes in hit, and amonge hem all was a quene, and all they had blak hoodis. And all they wepte and shryked whan they saw kynge Arthur.' It is then that Malory finally sends Guenevere to the convent, when her royal life is at an end:

And whan quene Gwenyver undirstood that kynge Arthure was dede and all the noble knyghtes, sir Mordred and all the reamnaunte, than she stale away with fyve ladyes with her, and so she wente to Amysbyry. And there she lete make herselff a nunne, and wered whyght clothys and blak, and grete penaunce she toke uppon her, as ever ded synfull woman in thys londe. And never creature coude make her myry, but ever she lyved in fastynge, prayers, and almes-dedis, that all maner of people mervayled how vertuously she was chaunged.

Elgar's Gregorian music was to have introduced Binyon's final Scene IX, but it seems that the Old Vic production played the last two scenes without a break so that no linking music was required. It is now some hours since battle was joined in the west, and the convent clock has struck six in the early morning. Guenevere is restless for news. A novice describes the convent now as hospital and mortuary. A second novice reports the arrival of one bearing tidings:

Arthur's way to Avalon by Daniel Maclise

> There came a rider spurring from the West;
> His head was badged with blood. He implored speech
> Passionately, as heavy with his news,
> Of the Sister Lynned. She has quit the task
> That keeps her with those wounded ones, and gone
> To the gate to meet him. He is named, they say,
> Sir Bedivere.

Guenevere knows the message Lynned will bring: 'The King is dead. The flower of Kings is fallen.' She urges her to continue:

> The rebel power is broken, and he that raised it
> Dead. Woe on us that the King died with him!
> Upon a field all mounded with the slain,
> The bloodiest harvest Time did ever reap,
> He and the traitor Mordred met their last
> And smote each other, even to the death.

And yet that may not have been the end, as Lynned continues to relay the account given by Bedivere:

> Not there he died, though hurt to death: in his arms
> Sir Bedivere upbore him to a mere
> Deep in the hills. There the King bade him ride
> To Amesbury - ride swift and tell the Queen,
> How, ere he died, he had sent words of love
> Of old, long love to Launcelot overseas;
> With his life's blood his secret heart gushed out
> In love for Launcelot and his Queen. With that
> Sir Bedivere departed; but so loth
> That soon he came again, and lo! the King
> Was no more there, but in the place was sound
> He knew not whether of water or in the air,
> A music new to mortals, and the smell
> As of flowers floating through the dark, as if
> The passing of that spirit sweetened earth.
> And he remembered how it was foretold
> That three sad Queens should fetch King Arthur home
> Across the water of Avalon to his rest.

As the Gregorian music begins to be heard once more faintly in the distance, Guenevere gives way to an agony of remorse:

> I am the cost. They are fallen, those famous ones
> Who made this kingdom glorious, they are fallen
> About their King; they have yielded up their strength
> And beauty and valour.

In the tolling of the convent bell Binyon recalls the wartime horrors of France:

> The grieving bell begins,
> As if it were the mouth and voice of Death
> Emptying the earth of honour and renown.

The flower of England had indeed fallen, and whether Arthur should ever again be future king seemed improbable in 1923. Lynned can offer only the consolation of prayer, which by that time Elgar suspected was ineffective and irrelevant.

Reviews were respectful rather than enthusiastic. *The Times* made its comments on 14 March:

> The production of a play in verse by a living poet is an event so rare that it is secure of its welcome. This play of Mr.Binyon's is a direct telling of the story of Launcelot, Guinevere and Elaine. There can be no complaint on the ground that it is slow or disorderly in its action or that it is work for the library rather than the stage. It has none of these faults so common in poets who write for the theatre - the faults which spring from having forgotten both player and audience in the course of a subtle and personal intellectual adventure. Yet *Arthur* falls short of success. Perhaps it is because Mr.Binyon, with Sir John Martin Harvey at his elbow, has allowed his thought to be too often and too sharply interrupted by fear of the errors into which other men have fallen; perhaps because, in a laudable determination to pursue simplicity, he has stripped the Arthurian legend of the imagining with which he might otherwise have given it life.

The critic sums up:

> Whatever the reason, the result is bare, nor is it the bareness of austerity. There is romance enough, high colour, phrasing that is always rich and sometimes beautiful, yet always a sense that, though he felt the glamour of the story, Mr.Binyon's intellect found it a little tedious before it was done.

Edgell Rickword (1898-1982) was published in *The New Statesman* on 24 March:

It is this aftermath of passion which falls in best with Mr.Binyon's rather faintly-coloured verse, this and the despair of Arthur, when he knows himself betrayed by his friend and champion knight. In the language of actual passion he is a little formal, but never vulgar and never prosaic; perhaps this meticulousness cost too dear, but at least it has given us a noble and dignified study of the conflict between love and duty. The character of Arthur is invested with a lofty idealism which breaks at last in the humility that knows itself incompetent to pardon or condemn. But every writer yet (except Malory), by imagining Arthur first and foremost as a lover, has placed him in the position of the cuckold, which to our barbaric instincts is still ridiculous. Perhaps for this reason Arthur has so far failed to touch the popular heart.

Elgar gave Binyon his impressions on 18 March:

> Very many thanks for the copy of '*Arthur*' & your inscription which includes more than I deserve. It was the greatest pleasure to be associated with you in the matter of production & I hope you are pleased with the reception of your work. This is not the day I fear for big things but there are some still left amongst theatre people who can see & feel great stuff.
>
> The end of a play which depends upon two persons or one only is always risky: for *theatrical* purposes I shd have liked Arthur & *all* his train to march mistily past, seen through a window on the stage R. - however you know best.

How the producer actually managed the end of the play is unclear, but Binyon's printed stage direction presumably contains his considered intention:

> The chant is heard nearer, and rises louder as the scene closes in darkness. After a pause the gloom melts, gradually revealing a wide distance of moonlit water, over which glides a barge, bearing KING ARTHUR, and the three Queens sorrowing over him, to the island of Avalon.

17 - Many a tale his music tells

Elgar's *Severn Suite*, originally conceived for brass band in 1930, was dedicated to Bernard Shaw. They had become increasingly close friends since the publication in the first number of *Music and Letters* (January 1920) of an article that followed on the heels of the initial Cello Concerto fiasco, and since the death of Lady Elgar. Shaw always had two qualities: he took care to know what he was talking about; and he expressed his views with conviction. He began the article with splendid assurance: 'Edward Elgar, the figurehead of music in England, is a composer whose rank it is neither prudent nor indeed possible to determine. Either it is one so high that only time and posterity can confer it, or else he is one of the Seven Humbugs of Christendom.' For Shaw, Elgar's greatness was instinctive:

> Elgar has not left us any room to hedge. From the beginning, quite naturally and as a matter of course, he has played the great game and professed the Best. He has taken up the work of a great man so spontaneously that it is impossible to believe that he ever gave any consideration to the enormity of the assumption, or was ever conscious of it. But there it is, unmistakable. To the north countryman who, on hearing of Wordsworth's death, said 'I suppose his son will carry on the business', it would be plain today that Elgar is carrying on Beethoven's business.

Shaw goes on to write about the fashionable moderns:

> This, it will be seen, is a very different challenge from that of, say, Debussy and Stravinsky. You can rave about Stravinsky without the slightest risk of being classed as a lunatic by the next generation. You can declare the Après-midi d'un Faune the most delightful and enchanting orchestral piece ever written without really compromising yourself. But if you say that Elgar's Cockaigne overture combines every classic quality of a concert overture with every lyric and dramatic quality of the overture to Die Meistersinger, you are either uttering a platitude as safe as a compliment to Handel on the majesty of the Hallelujah chorus, or else damning yourself to all critical posterity by a *gaffe* that will make your grandson blush for you.

Shaw maintains that the current musical 'isms' would be childsplay to Elgar:

Certain things one can say without hesitation. For example, that Elgar could turn out Debussy and Stravinsky music by the thousand bars for fun in his spare time. That to him such standbys as the whole-tone-scale of Debussy, the Helmholtzian chords of Scriabin, the exciting modulations of the operatic school, the zylophone and celesta orchestration by which country dances steal into classical concerts, are what farthings are to a millionaire. That his range is so Handelian that he can give the people a universal melody or march with as sure a hand as he can give the Philharmonic Society a symphonic adagio, such as has not been given since Beethoven died.

It was the orchestration, Shaw maintained, that initially made everybody sit up:

> When Gerontius made Elgar widely known, there was a good deal of fine writing about it; but what every genuine connoisseur in orchestration must have said at the first hearing (among other things) was 'What a devil of a *fortissimo!*'

This was the result of expert knowledge and uncanny mastery:

> Elgar is no mere effect monger: he takes the whole orchestra in his hand and raises every separate instrument in it to its highest efficiency until its strength is as the strength of ten. One was not surprised to learn that he could play them all, and was actually something of a *virtuoso* on instruments as different as the violin and trombone.

Shaw emphasises Elgar's ability to innovate within a strong sense of tradition:

> Elgar, neither an imitator nor a voluptuary, went his own way without bothering to invent a new language, and by sheer personal originality produced symphonies that are really symphonies in the Beethovenian sense, a feat in which neither Schumann, Mendelssohn, nor Brahms, often as they tried, ever succeeded convincingly. If I were king, or Minister of Fine Arts, I would give Elgar an annuity of a thousand a year on condition that he produce a symphony every eighteen months.

Shaw writes at some length about the musical establishment Elgar had to outmanoeuvre:

> He pitied them, and was quite willing to shew them how a really handy man (they were the unhandiest of mortals) should write for the trombones, tune the organ, flyfish, or groom and harness and drive a horse. He could talk

Shaw working in his summer-house

about every unmusical subject on earth, from pigs to Elizabethan literature.

A certain unmistakably royal pride and temper was getatable on occasion; but normally a less pretentious person than Elgar could not be found. To this day you may meet him and talk to him for a week without suspecting that he is anything more than a very typical English country gentleman who does not know a fugue from a fandango.

Shaw remained the staunchest of champions. He was at a badly attended performance of *The Apostles* on 8 June 1922. Next day he wrote to *The Daily News* : 'I have just heard at Queen's Hall the finest performance of Sir Edward Elgar's masterpiece, The Apostles, that our present executive resources at their choral best in the North, and their solo and orchestral best in London, can achieve.' He considered the work 'one of the glories of British music' and that it placed 'British music once more definitely in the first European rank, after two centuries of leather and prunella'. He continued in scornful irony:

> It would be an exaggeration to say that I was the only person present, like Ludwig of Bavaria, at Wagner's *premières*. My wife was there. Other couples were visible at intervals. One of the couples consisted of the Princess Mary and Viscount Lascelles, who just saved the situation as far as the credit of the Crown is concerned, as it very deeply is.

Shaw noticed besides 'six people in the stalls, probably with complimentary tickets'; and in 'the cheaper seats a faithful band stood for England's culture'. He considered that the event 'was infinitely more important than the Derby, than Goodwood, than the Cup Finals' and went on to apologise to the performers 'for London society, and for all the other recreants in England's culture, who will, I fear, not have the grace to apologize for themselves'. He ended by 'apologising to posterity for living in a country where the capacity and taste of schoolboys and sporting costermongers are the measure of metropolitan culture'. He signed off 'Disgustedly yours'.

Frank Schuster died on 27 December 1927, and a fortnight later his sister Adela wrote about a bequest:

> The sum Frank left you in his Will is £7000 - (but there are death duties to come off this.) and the words in which he makes the bequest are there: 'To my friend, Sir Edward Elgar O.M. who has saved my country from the reproach of having produced no composer worthy to rank with the Great masters.

In April Elgar was to move to Tiddington House on the Avon at Stratford. Shaw wrote on 4 April from Conway in North Wales about a possible visit and admiration for Schuster: 'If we return via Stratford, and are later than the 20th., we shall turn up at Tiddington after due warning.' He continued: 'Schuster really deserves to be buried in the Abbey, though he overlooked ME.' A conclusion mentioned the Chancellor of the Exchequer and death duties: 'I grudge Churchill his share. Why don't they make us duty-free instead of giving us O.Ms and the like long after we have conferred them on ourselves?' The result was joint attendance at two Shakespeare plays, *The Merry Wives of Windsor* and *Richard III*. The Elgar household followed these with two performances of *Henry IV* Part 1, reminder of the teeming *Falstaff*, and *Julius Caesar*.

Elgar received an advance copy of Shaw's *The Intelligent Woman's Guide to Socialism and Capitalism*, published in June 1928. Perhaps he did not read all its 500 pages. In his note for the 1929 popular edition, Shaw admitted there had previously been errors, 'one of which was a mistake in the number of one of the Articles of the Church of England. It passed entirely unnoticed in this country, but was detected and very kindly pointed out to me by a well-known French atheist.' The note ends with a sensible post-war comment: 'Well, I take refuge with the intelligent women. As for the front bench male politicians, I can point out the moon in the heavens to them; but I cannot persuade them that it is anything more than a piece of green cheese.' Of course he touches on the war, as he had done so tellingly in *Back to Methuselah* (1921):

> It is absurd to pretend that the young men of Europe ever wanted to hunt each other into holes in the ground and throw bombs into the holes to disembowel one another, or to have to hide in those holes themselves, eaten with lice and sickened by the decay of the unburied, in unutterable discomfort, boredom, and occasionally acute terror, or that any woman ever wanted to put on her best Sunday clothes and be gratified at the honor done to her son for killing some other woman's babies.

Shaw deals in the *Guide* with a composer Elgar admired as much as he did:

> Mozart could have made much more money as a valet than he did as the greatest composer of his time, and indeed one of the greatest composers of all time; nevertheless he chose to be a composer and not a valet. He knew that he would be a bad valet, and believed that he could be a good composer; and this outweighed all money considerations with him.

Shaw claimed to have made the book transparently lucid, with the result that it seemed Albert Einstein (1879-1955) was the only man in the civilised world to have understood it. Certainly Elgar had a question, and

Shaw replied on 30 May 1928 to a letter no longer extant: '*Your* products have the extraordinary quality of being *infinitely consumable* without diminution or deterioration. I should have done a chapter on the Economics of Art; but it would have been too long.'

Next came tidings on 2 January 1929 of major Shavian activity: 'Lazy! I've not only begun a new play but finished it. Not since The Messiah has a work hurled itself on paper more precipitously.' It was hardly in the mould of his last play: 'But after St.Joan it will outrage the world as a hideous anti-climax. It is a scandalous Aristophanic burlesque of democratic politics, with a brief but shocking sex interlude.' Where was it to be performed?: 'It is to figure at the Bayreuth Festival which Barry Jackson is projecting at Malvern for next August.' Shaw concluded with an exhortation: 'Your turn now. Clap it with a symphony.' Shaw had foretold ruin for Jackson (1879-1961) when he produced *Back to Methuselah* at his Birmingham Repertory Theatre in the autumn of 1923. It would have ruined a man of less wealth. *Methuselah* was the tenth Shaw play his theatre had produced, but Jackson was becoming dissatisfied with an exclusively urban centre. Elgar's Malvern seemed ideal, though Shaw claimed a glassful of the waters that delighted the hypochondriacs would destroy his digestion for a week. The hills could be roamed over in giant strides by the sprightly septuagenarian, and there was to be much adulation for the basking.

Elgar was informed about plans for the new work in a card dated 13 April 1929: 'The Apple Cart (or Tart, as the papers announced it) will be rehearsed mainly in London; so I shall probably not reach Malvern until the middle of August.' The programme for the first Malvern festival could not have been more ambitious. Though other dramatists were represented at later festivals, Shaw was initially the presiding genius. But he wanted Elgar there, writing to him on 12 August 1929 from Lawnside, the Malvern girls' school Jackson had taken over for the festival: 'We are up to the neck in rehearsals here, after long preliminary immersions in London at the Old Vic, and in Birmingham last week.' Then came details about Malvern:

> I have hesitated to bother you about coming over; but the excitement on the subject can no longer be ignored. Barry Jackson has taken this house, which you know well, for entertaining, and has reserved the front row in the theatre for distinguished guests, which really means you. In his first enthusiasm he was bent on getting from you an overture for The Apple Cart; but on obtaining from Boult a rough estimate of the cost of an Elgar orchestra, and letting his imagination play on the composer's fee, he went mournfully to his accountants, who informed him decisively that he could not afford a band at all and would be lucky if he came out of the affair with a shirt on his back.

Shaw felt that any Elgar music would immediately make it an Elgar festival:

> My own view was that six bars of yours would extinguish (or upset) the A.C. and turn the Shaw festival into an Elgar one; but that it would be a jolly good thing so. I demanded overtures to Caesar, to Methuselah (five preludes), and a symphonic poem to Heartbreak House, which is by far the most musical of the lot.

It was indeed a magnificent Shavian banquet. Whether Elgar savoured every course is not clear. Perhaps he could enjoy Shaw's kitten of an Egyptian queen, ready to show her claws on the subject of learning the harp: 'You shall give me a lesson every day for a fortnight. After that, whenever I strike a false note you shall be flogged; and if I strike so many that there is not time to flog you, you shall be thrown into the Nile to feed the crocodiles.' There was then the apotheosis of Falstaff in Part IV of *Back to Methuselah*, when Zoo gives expression to Shaw's loathing for war in describing a fat man's statue:

> All I can tell you about it is that a thousand years ago, when the whole world was given over to you shortlived people, there was a war called the War to end War. In the war which followed it about ten years later, hardly any soldiers were killed; but seven of the capital cities of Europe were wiped out of existence. It seems to have been a great joke; for the statesmen who thought they had sent ten million common men to their deaths were themselves blown into fragments with their houses and families, while the ten million men lay snugly in the caves they had dug for themselves. Later on even the houses escaped; but their inhabitants were poisoned by gas that spared no living soul. Of course the soldiers starved and ran wild; and that was the end of pseudo-Christian civilization. The last civilized thing that happened was that the statesmen discovered that cowardice was a great patriotic virtue; and a public monument was erected to its first preacher, an ancient and very fat sage called Sir John Falstaff.

In *Heartbreak House* there were the aged cadences of Captain Shotover, a character based on the father of Lena Ashwell (1872-1957), who had persuaded Elgar towards *The Starlight Express* in 1915:

> I see my daughters and their men living foolish lives of romance and sentiment and snobbery. I see you, the younger generation, turning from their romance and sentiment and snobbery to money and comfort and hard common sense. I was ten times happier on the bridge in the typhoon, or frozen into Arctic ice for months in darkness, than you or they have ever

been. You are looking for a rich husband. At your age I looked for hardship, danger, horror, and death, that I might feel the life in me more intensely. I did not let the fear of death govern my life; and my reward was, I had my life. You are going to let the fear of poverty govern your life; and your reward will be that you will eat, but you will not live.

Elgar was in his element sitting next to Shaw for the first night of *The Apple Cart*, as he wrote to Carice on 21 August 1929: 'It *is splendid* fun satire & wisdom. Of course the press cannot understand it but I wd. give anything for you to be here amongst things, alas!' Shaw's preface sums up the play in a couple of sentences:

I had written a comedy in which a King defeats an attempt by his popularly elected Prime Minister to deprive him of the right to influence public opinion through the press and the platform: in short, to reduce him to a cipher. The King's reply is that rather than be a cipher he will abandon his throne and take his obviously very rosy chance of becoming a popularly elected Prime Minister himself.

Shaw saw that democracy might tend towards the election of increasingly plausible humbugs, to be superseded by the sort of strong men who captured Europe in the next decade. Shaw endows *The Apple Cart* with three queens: the comfortable married Jemima; the boudoir mistress, Orinthia; and the cheery Postmistress General, Amanda. This last has a music-hall way of dealing with the chairman of Breakages Ltd., a troublesome multinational with ubiquitous tentacles. She explains her method:

I'll tell you. He opened his campaign with a great Saturday night speech against me in the Home Lovers' Hall to five thousand people. In that same hall a week later, I faced a meeting of the very same people. I didn't argue. I mimicked him. I took all the highfalutin passages in his speech, and repeated them in his best manner until I had the whole five thousand laughing at him. Then I asked them would they like me to sing; and their Yes nearly lifted the roof off. I had two songs. They both had choruses.

On 17 August 1929 Elgar opened a Shaw Exhibition at the Malvern Public Library, making a lengthy and affectionate speech. He would not dilate on the wonder of the plays; such a succession of masterpieces had been shattering to the nerves of some, but the British public was now alive to what it owed Shaw. The title of *The Apple Cart* seemed peculiarly apt for production in a cider county. Elgar said:

Bernard Shaw knows more about music than I do. We won't grumble at that. He was a musical critic, and a good one, in those dull days when the two Universities and the Colleges of Music used to do nothing but sit around and accused one another of the cardinal virtues. I am going to quote Swift. Shaw 'drenched a desperate quill'. That's good. He wrote for our enlightenment much in favour of what I call elastic and natural music, to the destruction of the pedant.

Elgar left to last his tribute to Shaw as a friend: he was the best friend a man could have, the best friend to young artists, the kindest and possibly the dearest fellow on earth.

In reply Shaw put in a word for the musicianship of literary men. Shakespeare was not only a word-musician but it was clear from the plays how much he loved music. H.G.Wells (1866-1946) was making progress on the pianola, and Arnold Bennett (1867-1931) could at least manage half a duet. Shaw felt he had had a comparatively easy start as dramatist, since at that time the theatre had no ideas and felt it ought not to have any. Sir Edward, on the other hand, had to come in on top of Beethoven and Wagner, and he got away with it, becoming one of the greatest composers in the world. He continued:

> That is something for England to be proud of. But I do not think England is proud; that is the disgraceful thing about it. But the fact remains that in comparison with Sir Edward Elgar - although I am rather a conceited man, and in comparison with any other artist in England feel that I can carry my head high - I am sincerely and genuinely humble in the presence of Sir Edward Elgar. I recognise a greater art than mine and a greater man than I can ever hope to be.

An Elgar friend of much longer standing than Shaw, Hubert Leicester (1855-1939) was a Worcester man through and through. Five times mayor of the 'Faithful City', he was asked to write a pamphlet for the centenary of St.George's, Worcester, where he was choirmaster already for forty years, and where Elgar and his father had both been organist. On 22 May 1928 Leicester wrote to Elgar about the memoir and enclosed a copy of his section on the choir. St.George's was opened on 16 July 1829, and there were lofty musical ambitions from the outset. The Mass setting that Thursday was mainly by Haydn, though the Benedictus was from the Mozart Requiem. The *London and Dublin Orthodox Journal* of October 1829 was impressed:

> The *Credo* was sung in admirable style, and the solo *Et incarnatus est* was given by Miss Heaton with great effect; but the powers of this lady were

more effectually called into action at the Offertory *Deus, Deus mei* from
the 62nd. Psalm; here her tones were bold and sonorous, and fully justified
the opinion which had been formed of her vocal powers.

Ten years later the same journal had equal praise: 'The Catholic Choir of
Worcester is justly allowed to be one of the most distinguished and
talented in the West of England. Every individual musician sung and
played without a farthing's remuneration.' The succession of organists,
Beresford, Baldwyn, W.H.Elgar, culminated in Edward Elgar's four-year
tenure from 1885. His largest-scale work for the church had been the *Ecce
sacerdos magnus* of 1888, written for the visit of Bishop Ilsley. This was
sung again on 27 October 1929 to welcome Archbishop Leighton Williams
for the celebration of two centenaries, that of the Catholic Emancipation
Act and the opening of St.George's.

Leicester had asked Elgar for comments on and corrections to his
memoir. He now embarked on a more wide-ranging local subject,
requesting Elgar for a foreword to his *Forgotten Worcester* of 1930. Elgar
had himself become once more a Worcester man, such as he had not been
during the whole of his marriage. He had rented Marl Bank for the 1929
Worcester festival, and was able to buy it as his final home by the end of
the year. The river he had known as a boy was again to hand, and Elgar
remembered their frequent crossing of it when writing for Leicester: 'Sixty
years ago nothing escaped our notice; everything was discussed and
adjudicated upon; I trust fairly, but we dealt, with some unnecessary
philosophic weight, on the shortcomings of such things as mayors,
corporations, lord-lieutenants and clergy.' Elgar contrasts his own
wayward intelligence with Leicester's: 'I know that while my own
flibbertigibbet mind was concerned with the humorous possibilities of
such a word as Newdix, my school-fellow's more sedate intellect was busy
with the seriousness of derivation and signification; that he has pursued
this mood for our advantage this book will show.' Elgar ends with an
affectionate glance at his schoolboy encounters with the Severn:

> It is pleasant to date these lines from an eminence distantly overlooking
> the way to school; our walk was always to the brightly-lit west. Before
> starting, our finances were rigidly inspected, - naturally not by me, being,
> as I am, in nothing rigid, but quite naturally by my companion, who
> tackled the situation with prophetic skill and with the gravity now bestowed
> on the affairs of great corporations whose accounts are harrowed by him to
> this day. The report being favourable, two pence were 'allowed' for the
> ferry. Descending the steps, past the door behind which the figure of the
> mythical salmon is incised, we embarked; at our backs 'the unthrift sun
> shot vital gold', filling Payne's meadows with glory and illuminating for two

small boys a world to conquer and to love. In our old age, with our undimmed affection, the sun still seems to show us a golden 'beyond'.

The *Severn Suite* in its brass band version was complete on 16 April 1930, and Shaw accepted the dedication on 25 May:

> Naturally I shall be enormously honoured: it will secure my immortality when all my plays are dead and damned and forgotten. I am really not worthy of a symphony; but a Serenade, say: - A Serenade for Brass Band to the Author of Captain Brassbound's Conversion - that would be about my size. The cockney sailor calls him Brarsbahnd.

Elgar was not fit enough to be at the Crystal Palace for the competitive première of the Suite on 27 September; but Shaw was there and dashed off a splendid 'Corno di Bassetto' account the following day:

> I heard the Severn Suite yesterday only eight times, as extreme hunger and the need for catching the 5.10 train at King's Cross forced me to surrender before I had ceased finding new things in it.
>
> If there is a new edition of the score I think it would be well to drop the old Italian indications and use the language of the bandsmen: For instance
>
> > *Remember that a minuet is a dance and not a bloody hymn*;
>
> or
>
> > *Steady up for artillery attack*;
>
> or
>
> > *NOW - like Hell.*
>
> I think that would help some of the modest beginners who dont yet aspire to the Crystal Palace.
>
> It is a pity you did not hear them. They had all worked like Trojans at the suite; and there was not a single slovenly or vulgar bar, not a note muffed or missed.

At the beginning of 1931 Shaw proposed a revision to verse 2 of the National Anthem, and wrote to Elgar about it on 2 January:

> Somebody who couldnt stand the grotesque contrast of your gorgeous new orchestral garment for the National Anthem, with its disgraceful old literary rags has written to the Dean - your dean - Moore Ede - proposing the following amendment to the second verse.

O Lord our God arise
All our salvation lies
   In! Thy! Great! Hand! (à la Elgar)
Centre $^{his}_{her}$ thoughts on Thee
Let him God's captain be (Let her God's handmaid be)
Thine to Eternity
God save the $^{King}_{Queen}$

Shaw added his view on the dean and deans:

> Moore Ede is not enthusiastic because he feels very strongly on the Indian
> question and finds his views exactly expressed by 'Con Found Their
> Poll itticks' and also perhaps because Deans acquire the habit of ordering
> God about, and care no more for the cathedral after the first fortnight than
> if it were a fried fish shop; but on reflection he will see that the war killed
> Muscular Christianity.

When writing about the matter to Moore Ede on 12 January 1931 Elgar
seemed to feel that the war had killed Christianity altogether:

> I have no views: - the old 'Confound their politics' in this National address
> to the Almighty would have the effect - if the Almighty ever took any notice
> of anything, which of course he never did, does, or will do - of putting the
> whole Government in Hell with MacDonald in the lowest place - so from my
> point of view it does not matter what is said, sung or otherwise delivered.

Moore Ede wrote to Shaw on 15 January that the Three Choirs deans felt
that any change, if desirable, should be postponed till the Worcester
festival of 1932. Meanwhile he enrolled Elgar among the new society for
Friends of the Cathedral: 'You love the Cathedral it has been the scene
of many of your triumphs - What I am proposing has to do with preserving
the building & not with any ecclesiastical doctrine.' Just as well.

Inevitably Elgar became more and more concerned with local matters.
In June 1931 he wrote a piece about the 'College Hall', the ancient
monastic refectory, now used regularly by the King's School:

> I often speculate as to the effect on my fellow townsmen of the old
> buildings with which they are brought into contact daily. The College Hall
> is a favourite subject for meditation with me, carrying, as it does, the
> happiest memories of great music, with a halo of the middle ages
> combined with an odour of sanctity which even the sacrilege of the
> reformers has not wholly destroyed.

Elgar does not mention the Christ in Majesty at the east end, nor which reformers so severely mutilated it; but the sculpture must have sufficiently impressed the mediaeval authorities for it to be given its place of honour in a building constructed a hundred years later than the original carving.

There was then the question of the Worcester bridge over the Severn, a subject of negotiation during some months for both Hubert Leicester and Elgar. By 7 April 1932 the matter had been settled, as W.H.Reed recounted in *Elgar as I knew him* (pp.102-3):

> One day when I arrived at Marl Bank I was rushed off to see what they were doing at Worcester, widening the bridge over his beloved Severn: the old familiar bridge he had known all his life. I was taken there so often that I guessed he had something in his head about it. At last it came out. He could not bear to part with the old iron balustrades - or whatever they are called - that were being removed; so he bought two lengths of them and had them brought up on lorries to Marl Bank and set up there on a concrete bed.

The Severn had been much in Elgar's mind. He decided to orchestrate Shaw's suite and recorded it on 14 April. Shaw's postcard of 11 July expresses his delight: 'What a transfiguration! Nobody will ever believe that it began as a cornet corobbery. It's extraordinarily beautiful.' He also mentioned his 'Music in London' reprints: 'I have three volumes of musical criticism to send you when I return to London on Thursday: Resurrection pie from the nineties.' Elgar had now anchored the *Severn Suite* more firmly in his homeland by naming the movements after places or events that recalled the mediaeval splendour of Worcester. He could turn the pages of Hubert Leicester's book to refresh his own historical memories of the city and indeed recall the many prints of Worcester he had sifted through and gathered round him during his lifetime.

'Castle' now began the Suite. Leicester links his 'castle' references to the Edgar Tower near the east end of the Cathedral: '[It] has an interesting history, being originally the entrance to the Roman Camp, and later to the Castle, which so many of our kings visited. King John being particularly partial to Worcester, thoroughly restored this Tower about 1214.' Elgar had doubtless also browsed in the four Worcestershire volumes of the *Victoria County History* (1901-24) and knew much about the castle, from its beginning in 1069 to the start of its waning fortunes at the accession of Henry III (1216). The county sheriff, Urse d'Abitot, made his castle south-west of the priory, enclosing for his moat part of the monks' burial ground and bringing upon his head the wrath of Aldred, a former bishop. There had been an earthen mound along the Severn bank. John Leland was there in the 16th century and remarked: 'the dungeon

17 - Many a tale his music tells

wood.' East of the mound was the inner bailey; the outer bailey was on
what is now College Green. In 1217 the Earl of Pembroke in the king's
name compensated the priory for its initial loss. A century later the castle
was completely dismantled, stones from the walls being used in 1459
against a possible attack from the Duke of York. The castle's function as a
prison continued when a house of correction was built on the site during
the Commonwealth. John Howard (1726-90), the prison reformer,
condemned its condition in 1788, but the magistrates spent a large sum
on new cells, a room with an oven for 'purifying' prisoners and their
clothes, courts for exercise, and a decent water supply.

The site of Elgar's 'Tournament' cannot be pinpointed. There is likely
to have been a tiltyard in the area of the castle's outer bailey, under the
noses of the monks. Tournaments were little approved by the church, and
indeed had been condemned at ecclesiastical councils held in the Lateran
Palace of Rome. In England Henry II (1154-89) looked askance at the
practice of gathering in one place so many barons and knights under arms
and forbade the sport. The result was that those enamoured of the
tournament crossed the Channel for satisfaction. Richard I issued licences
for tournaments and Jocelin de Brakelond, chronicler of Carlyle's Abbot
Samson in *Past and Present*, tells of a numerous gathering devising a
tournament between Thetford and Bury St.Edmunds, despite the abbot's
veto. At Worcester Bishop William de Blois, just embarked on rebuilding
the east end of the Cathedral, threatened with excommunication all those
taking part in a 1225 tournament, and twice later Henry III, who had been
crowned in the Cathedral, forbade such events in 1249 and 1254. Many a
tournament had its fatality. Elgar's does not, and his instrumental tilting
is devised 'but for practice, and display of prowess'.

For Elgar's 'Cathedral' movement Hubert Leicester takes his history
back to the 7th century: 'In 680 the first Bishop of Worcester (Tatfrith) was
appointed.' He died before he was consecrated, but a church was built for
Bosel his successor. This was 'near the spot where the original Roman
camp and station stood, and not far from the site of the present
Cathedral'. It was dedicated to St.Peter. Ethelburga founded a minster
nearby for religious women, and both establishments existed when
Oswald, one of Worcester's two saints, became bishop (961-92). Leicester
describes him as 'A great organiser and reformer, a famous church
builder, a saintly Bishop with a fascinating personality. He formed the
priests of the Cathedral into a monastery, and built for it the Church of
St.Mary.' A lease given by Oswald to a kinsman touches on his joy in the
matter: 'our Lord and Redeemer . . . has granted so great a boon of his
loving kindness that beyond all expectation I have been able to bring to
completion the basilica in honour of Mary which I have established in my

A Tournament before King Arthur

episcopal see, namely in the monastery of Worcester.' Oswald began
St.Mary's in 966, but even c.991 he had to admit that the episcopal throne
was still in the ancient St.Peter's. Of particular interest to Elgar was the
library at the Cathedral, and the outstanding nature of the Worcester
10th-century scriptorium probably owes much to Oswald's time at Fleury
or St-Benoît-sur-Loire, where the bones of St.Benedict had been brought
in 673 and are still venerated. The Worcester library still contains two
books Oswald might have obtained from Fleury, Gregory's *Homiliae in
euangelia* and the *Historia ecclesiastica* of Eusebius. Oswald's community
at Worcester was rarely above 30 and often below 20. At Fleury it was the
custom that every member should read a book a year, and it may have
been thus at Worcester. Oswald granted a lease to a priest called Goding
on condition that he became a scribe for the monastery. A scribe called
Sistan of Oswald's time produced an *Expositio libri comitis* by Smaragdus
still in the library.

Before the death of Oswald there was little interest at Worcester in the
making of saints or collecting of relics. Byrhtferth's biography of Oswald
mentions miraculous signs at his funeral and describes the splendid shrine
where he lay. He had died at York, where from 972 he combined the
archbishopric with the see of Worcester. On 15 April 1002 he was
translated to Worcester. The body had crumbled to dust, but the bones
were washed and placed in a feretrum made for the purpose by Oswald
himself. He was enshrined in St.Mary's on the south side of the altar.
Miracles were effected, even by the water that had washed his bones. The
man responsible for the translation was Oswald's successor, Ealdwulf (992-
1002), whose enthusiasm for the monastic community increased the
importance of St.Mary's over that of St.Peter's.

Worcester has had two bishops called Wulfstan. Only the second was
canonised and mentioned by Leicester. The first, however, was a scholar
and preacher of great consequence. As bishop (1002-16) he declared it his
duty to read and correct books, but during his episcopate the Cathedral
lost many treasures, including some from the library, to pay Danish
tribute. Before coming to Worcester, Wulfstan was Bishop of London
(996-1002) and may have been scribe to King Ethelred (978-1016),
assisting in the drafting of his charters. Wulfstan gained early a reputation
for eloquence and was noted for his homilies, many of which have
survived. He wrote little on theological controversy, but much on the 'last
days'. His style shows him to have studied treatises on rhetoric; his model
was Cicero as filtered through Augustine. The *Book of Ely* equates his
words with the wisdom of God himself. His sermons are mainly in the
vernacular of contemporary English rather than Latin; this sets him apart
from Continental practice. He enjoys the use of irony and puns, signing
himself always 'Lupus' (Wolf). His sermons remained popular, and many

were compiled for the later St.Wulfstan.

He subscribed to ideas about Antichrist and the Last Judgment long current. The church fathers estimated that the world would last 6000 years. Jerome (c.347-c.420) argued by means of Psalm 90 that, since the world was created in six days and 'a thousand years in thy sight are but as yesterday', the figure was correct. There was a superstitious awe and dread about the year 1000. To Wulfstan the Danish wars seemed to realise Christ's prediction in *Matthew* 24 verse 7: 'For nation shall rise against nation, and kingdom against kingdom; and there shall be famines, and pestilences, and earthquakes, in divers places.' Wulfstan's third homily warns the people that the national calamities are a punishment for sin and that the day of judgment is near. For Wulfstan the Antichrist was the child of Satan and a virgin. Whether Elgar had any acquaintance with Wulfstan's apocalyptic ideas is not of great moment, since the third part of the 'Apostles' project never took shape. Elgar would have known, however, that English missionaries accompanied his King Olaf in 995, or joined him soon after, when he determined to make Norway a Christian country. A result was that Norwegian ecclesiastical law was based partly on Ethelred's code. William of Malmesbury mislikes the fact that, like Oswald, he held York as well as Worcester and dubs him 'Wulfstanus reprobus' for robbing Worcester to pay York. 'Reprobus' or not, he continued Oswald's support for the Worcester scriptorium, and some seven books with direct Worcester connection preserve annotations by him and other examples of his hand. Elgar is likely to have known this, if only because Ivor Atkins was so sedulous a devotee of the library, eventually producing in 1944 with N.R.Ker the *Catalogus Librorum MSS Bibliothecae Wigorniensis made in 1622-1623 by Patrick Young*, royal librarian and biblical writer (1584-1652).

Leicester investigates St.Wulfstan at some length, initially as founder of the Cathedral. Oswald's 'noble stone church' with its twenty-eight altars lasted until 1084, when the new Bishop Wulfstan (1062-95) decided a little reluctantly to replace it with 'a larger and grander Cathedral'. Leicester considers his achievement: 'Wulstan was the last of the Saxon Bishops of the diocese. A persuasive and powerful preacher, and a man of marked humility and great devotion. It was during his reign that the missionary spirit first took real hold throughout the diocese.' In 1072 Wulfstan brought a case against Archbishop Thomas of York for the recovery of Worcester property. During the trial he claimed to see both Dunstan and Oswald beside him and was sure they had come 'to help in his lawsuit'. The outcome was certain. The monastic community steadily expanded. Danish settlers began to send sons, and then Normans came. In Wulfstan's time English names predominated, but the use of 'religious' names gradually obscured national origins. It was the increase in monastic

numbers that necessitated the new church as well as the proximity of the
castle, and Wulfstan was determined to preserve the territorial integrity of
the lands left by Oswald. The monks saw his success as evidence not only
of saintly assistance but of his own sanctity. The Worcester Chronicle sums
up: 'By God's help and the king's assent, Wulfstan regained for the church
of Worcester all the immunities and privileges freely granted to it by its
first founders.'

It is an indication of Wulfstan's stature that he was consulted towards
the end of his life by Anselm (1033-1109), the new archbishop of
Canterbury consecrated in December 1093. Eadmer (d.?1124) gives
Wulfstan's reply in his *Historia novorum in Anglia*, a reply that reveals the
measure of the man:

> Your Wisdom is well aware of the hardships and oppressions to which day
> after day the holy Church is subjected, while evil men oppress her and the
> very persons who should have guarded her are themselves instigators of
> such evils. To repel these adversaries and against all such to defend the
> holy Church has your Holiness been set in the highest place. Therefore do
> not hesitate, do not be abashed by any fear of the secular power, nor
> turned aside by any favour but undertake boldly and what you have
> undertaken with God's help bring to completion; withstand opponents,
> restrain the oppressors and against all such defend our holy Mother.

Worcester Cathedral from across the Severn

Eadmer mentions that Wulfstan was too frail to attend Anselm's consecration, but he writes of him in the warmest terms: 'the one sole survivor of the old Fathers of the English people, a man eminent in all the religious life and unrivalled in his knowledge of the ancient customs of England'. Local sentiment demanded Wulfstan's canonisation, and

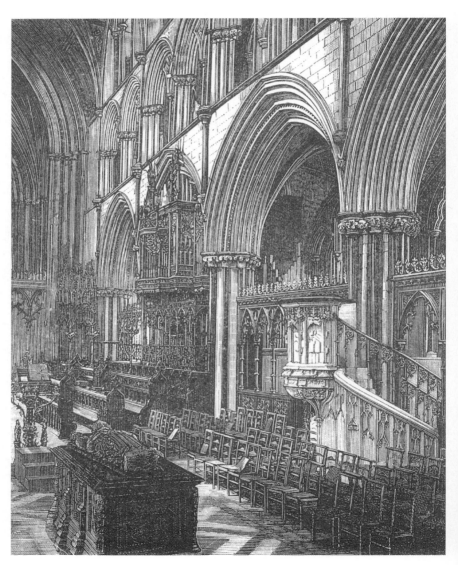

Worcester Cathedral choir and King John's tomb

Innocent III (1198-1216) allowed it. King John, eventually to die in the same year as Innocent and be buried in Worcester Cathedral, was excommunicated by the Pope in 1209. Innocent revoked the provisions of Magna Carta (1215), but presided also over the diversion to Constantinople of the Fourth Crusade in 1204, for which John Paul II has seen fit to apologise.

In *Forgotten Worcester*, Hubert Leicester continues his account of St.Wulfstan's Cathedral:

> The building was completed in 1088, and dedicated to the service of Almighty God under the patronage of The Blessed Virgin Mary. This church suffered many vicissitudes. In 1113 it was severely damaged by fire. In 1175 the new tower fell. In 1188 and 1202 it was again much damaged by fire. In 1216 it was plundered. Later the two lesser towers were destroyed by a violent storm.

The Cathedral was rededicated in 1218 with the high altar in honour of St.Mary and St.Oswald, and the lower altar in the name of St.Peter and St.Wulfstan. Bishop Silvester performed the ceremony in the presence of Henry III, then aged 11. St.Wulfstan was given a magnificent shrine to match Oswald's, and the increase in pilgrims and Cathedral finances encouraged Bishop William of Blois to commence with the east end an ambitious rebuilding programme. But beneath the whole of Wulfstan's eastern church lay the early Norman crypt that still survives with its apse of seven divisions and forest of low slender columns. There are traces of Norman work east of the west transepts, but the main impression is of the graceful Early English work, with Purbeck marble shafts, inspired by de Blois.

King John died in 1216, and a codicil to his will directed that he should be buried in the Cathedral. He was placed between the shrines of Sts.Oswald and Wulfstan, probably represented as the two small bishops either side of the king's head. The Purbeck marble effigy rests on the lid of the original stone coffin. The elaborate folds of the drapery and the sword held in the left hand reflect the reality of what was seen when the tomb was opened in July 1797. At the king's feet is a standing lion biting the end of his sword. Whether the sombre but strong features of the effigy represent an attempt at portraiture cannot be said. The 20th-century gilding of the figure was not considered a total success; nor indeed, as Elgar would have appreciated at once, was the painting of the eight surrounding shields with the arms of England and France modern.

History has not been generous to the monarch, nor was Walter Scott in *Ivanhoe* to John as prince:

His own character being light, profligate, and perfidious, John easily attached to his person and faction, not only all who had reason to dread the resentment of Richard for criminal proceedings during his absence, but also the numerous class of 'lawless resolutes,' whom the crusades had turned back on their country, accomplished in the vices of the East, impoverished in substance, and hardened in character, and who placed their hopes of harvest in civil commotion.

Jocelin of Brakelond in Carlyle's *Past and Present* saw King John face to face for two weeks. He emphasises only his meanness in a 'slight subacidity' of manner:

> *Dominus Rex*, did leave, as gift for our St.Edmund shrine, a handsome enough silk cloak, - or rather pretended to leave, for one of his retinue borrowed it of us, and we never got sight of it again; and, on the whole, that the *Dominus Rex*, at departing, gave us '*thirteen sterlingii*', one shilling and one penny, to say a mass for him; and so departed, - like a shabby Lackland as he was!

In April 1916 Elgar staked a claim on King John. He had bought at auction some fragments said to be from the tomb in Worcester Cathedral. Alice Stuart Wortley brought the stone fragments to Severn House on 14 April, and he wrote to Ivor Atkins about them on 26 May; 'I sent, instead of carrying, the K.John relics to the Dean - I wonder what you think? I *rescued* them on the chance of their being genuine & Canon Wilson & the Dean accept them.' On Elgar's 1916 birthday Lady Elgar was in Worcester: 'went to Cathedral & saw the relics of King John badly put in'. On 15 June they both saw the tomb.

The other royal burial in the Cathedral was that of Prince Arthur, eldest son of Henry VII. Born in the Arthurian city of Winchester on 20 September 1486, he had received the name of the chivalrous but shadowy king from the remote past. He had been married on 14 November 1501 to Catherine of Aragon (1485-1536), his senior by almost a year, at St.Paul's in London. Soon after he went to Ludlow to preside over a council of ten to hear cases from Wales and the Marches; there he died on the following 2 April. The prince's chantry has within its open traceried sides many small statues that point towards those in his father's chapel at Westminster with their heavy folds of drapery. The prince's monument is in the middle with the inscription: 'Here lyeth buried prince Arthur the fyrst begotten sonne of the righte renowned Kinge Henry the Seventhe whiche noble Prince departed oute of this transitory life att the Castle of Ludlowe in the seaventeenth yeare of our Lorde God one thowsand fyve hundred and two.' Within the airy openwork shrine, while gazing on figures of St.George and St.Katharine, it is impossible not to wonder whether English history might not have been very different had the young Arthur lived to be content in his marriage and to treat sympathetically the major monastic establishments of the realm. Instead there was debate whether the marriage had been consummated, and it was not till March 1505 that the Bishop of Worcester could announce that Julius II had sent with him from Rome *bullas originales dispensationis matrimonialis*. As early as June 1505 Prince Henry, not yet 14, was voicing secret doubts about his proposed marriage to Catherine. Defender of the Faith in 1521, Henry VIII (1509-47) launched the Reformation that sealed the fate of Worcester's main monastic buildings in 1534.

There was another, much simpler, monument in the Cathedral cloisters that had claimed Elgar's attention as a boy. It was a stone slab in the paving of the north-west corner inscribed with just one word, 'Miserrimus'. He mentioned it in a letter to Ivor Atkins of 28 August 1908, when he was so busy finishing the First Symphony that he missed a Three Choirs rehearsal in the Cathedral and regretted it:

> Music in the fane pleaseth me & the disturbed dust of ancestors is good to my nostrils also.
>
> Then there is Miserrimus & other things of my Xtreme youth's awe.

Wordsworth also had been struck by that one word, probably in 1828, and wrote a poem about it:

> *Who* chose his epitaph? - himself alone
> Could thus have dared the grave to agitate,
> And claim, among the dead, this awful crown;
> Nor doubt that He marked also for his own
> Close to these cloistral steps a burial-place,
> That every foot might fall with heavier tread,
> Trampling upon his vileness. Stranger, pass
> Softly! - To save the contrite, Jesus bled.

Wordsworth was right to urge respect and gentleness when descending from the south aisle into the cloister; but he was wrong to suggest any 'vileness'. The memorial marks the burial-place of Thomas Morris, a minor canon of the Cathedral, and vicar of Claines, a church with Elgarian associations. His loyalty to the Stuarts was such that he could not take an oath to the House of Orange. He died in 1748 at the age of 88, stripped of all benefice, and 'most wretched' in his poverty.

The last movement of Elgar's *Severn Suite* is named 'Commandery'. Hubert Leicester accounts thus for the institution: 'Immediately outside the Wall is The "Commandery," originally erected by St.Wulstan in the eleventh Century as an Augustinian Friary, for the purpose of providing hospitality for travellers who were unfortunate in arriving at the Gate after the hour of closing.' The name may come from the position of one of the preceptors, Walter de Wredens (1260-70), who had been a 'commander' in the Holy Land. There was sometimes friction between the prior and the commander. A prized possession for seeking 'Charities from well-disposed persons' was the pastoral staff of St.Wulfstan. The commander complained to the bishop in 1312 that this had been removed by the prior. At the Dissolution the house gained a reprieve by subscribing to the royal supremacy, and it seemed as if its charitable work might continue; but in 1545 the hospital and its lands were transferred to the endowment of Christ Church, Oxford. The present building dates from some 300 years after Wulfstan's foundation (c.1085). In the garden are some remains of the chapel, but the great hall still survives on an impressive scale, with fine oriel window. An Elizabethan staircase leads to an upper floor where one room has a series of religious wall paintings with such subjects as the martyrdom of St.Erasmus and St.Thomas Becket, the Crucifixion, and the Weighing of Souls at the Last Judgment. A representation of the Trinity looks down from the ceiling. Hubert Leicester closes his remarks on the Commandery by recalling its part in the Civil War:

> The grounds attached to the house were extensive, and included a large tract of land and the high hill known as 'Fort Royal'.
>
> When the Battle of Worcester was imminent King Charles II. selected the Commandery as his headquarters, fixing his guns on the Fort Royal.

So Worcester, even in the defeat of 1652, became the 'Faithful City'.

18 - Progress of an Antichrist to Avalon

There are many reasons why we do not have Elgar's Third Symphony precisely as he may have planned it. The most fundamental one was his psychological make-up. If Lady Elgar could marshal his moods sufficiently to produce an international composer among the greatest then alive, her death largely dissipated his forces. He had in him something of his father's indolence, and the prodigious gifts needed constant encouragement to deliver the masterpieces that flowed from him for the golden twenty years. Fred Gaisberg (1873-1951) of the Gramophone Company made pertinent comment about the symphony in his diary for 27 August 1933:

> He pretends he does not want to complete it and surrender his baby. His secretary Miss Clifford says he has not done much recently on the Sym. and seems to prefer to work on his opera. I think he misses the inspiration and driving force of Lady Elgar. Some sympathetic person, lady or man, of strong character should take him in hand and drive him on. Some exciter is needed to inflame him. He complains of the drudgery of scoring.

This last is hardly an excuse. One might shed a sympathetic tear for Wagner in his task of kindling again and again the flickering sparks of magic fire or simulating the endless waters of the Rhine. But Elgar had shown throughout his career that perhaps the most effective scoring ever heard was child's play to him. Works as recent as *Pomp and Circumstance* no.5, the *Nursery Suite* and the orchestral *Severn Suite* had shown the old wizardry at top voltage. Elgar's return to the West Midlands removed him from the various Egerias who had so effectively functioned within Lady Elgar's orbit; indeed some were dead. Vera Hockman was married and in distant Croydon. Reed was fully occupied with his LSO work or teaching and could only make flying visits. Ivor Atkins at the Cathedral did his best to relight the fires. Otherwise, there was the ready succession of homely nieces backed by a domestic staff whose function was solely to do Sir Edward's bidding.

There was in the background the towering figure of Bernard Shaw, just past his peak as a dramatist but continuing with undimmed vigour to produce reams of musical prose that coruscated with the brilliance of Elgar's orchestration. Charlotte Shaw watched over his volcanic activity, and had somehow persuaded him towards holiday breaks and cruises that took him out of England for considerable periods. Elgar missed them, as is clear from his letter to Shaw of 18 April 1933:

This is merely to welcome Mrs.Shaw & you back - the world seems a cold place to me when you are both away. I have read with increasing interest the scraps of information vouchsafed to be printable by the press here. I gather that you have had a wide sight of the world & hope you both have had a real change if not exactly a rest.

Shaw's cruise technique was gradually perfected, as he told William Rothenstein:

[I search for an] unprotected lady who is ripe for a friendship with a celebrity. I plant my deck chair beside hers and ask her whether she minds my working at a new play instead of talking. She is so delighted at being given the role of protector of G.B.S. that whenever anyone comes near she makes agitated signs to warn him off, whispering that *Mr Shaw is at work on a new play*. So I make a new friend and get perfect peace during the entire voyage.

No one, though, was more aware that Elgar's health was not as it should be. At the end of his letter about the 1930 competition première of the *Severn Suite*, Shaw referred to Elgar's indisposition: 'Now as to your health, of which I had to give heart-breaking news to console them for

Shaw at his music

your absence', Shaw recommended an osteopath. The first recommendation was 'a bull moose American; but he is a goodnatured chap and very clever and experienced with his hands'. Carice suggested writing a 'Sciatica' for orchestra. Shaw returned to the attack at the end of his 'National Anthem' letter of 2 January 1931: 'The lumbago is deplorable: Charlotte weeps over it. Are you *quite* sure that your haunch bone (*alias* The Innominate) is not out of place? Did you try Pheils? he is a virtuoso on the bones; and his personal resemblance to an ophicleide would please you.' Later in the month Shaw pleaded: '*Do* consult an osteopath.' He didn't; but Shaw persisted on 2 July 1931: 'What a damnable nuisance! The regular doctors are no use; but it might be worth while to try homeopathy.' He went on:

> Charlotte is brokenhearted, and is still convinced that her beloved osteopath would have found out all about it and traced it to a spinal lesion.
>
> It is an extraordinarily puzzling, capricious, and unexplained condition; but your vital powers are still obviously very vigorous.
>
> Damn the thing, anyhow. If only one's friends would curse these aberrations instead of praying for one!

The last letter was dated 5 December 1933 when Elgar was in the South Bank nursing home: 'I have had several impulses to rush down to see you and rescue you from the doctors.' He ended with a typical Shavian exhortation: 'Meanwhile trust to your mighty Life Force and damn the doctors unless you can find a really vitalist one.'

Perhaps it is unfair to blame dogs and horses for an incomplete symphony. Elgar's move to Napleton Grange coincided with the creation of a canine establishment such as would have been impossible while Lady Elgar was alive. There was to be no Roswal or Bevis of Sir Walter Scott's imagination; nor indeed a rumbustious recreation of Aesculapius or the heavy-jowled Dan. There had been some attempts at a 'wow' in Severn House days; but Lady Elgar seemed to cause trying irregularities among them or even total disappearance. From *The Elms*, his sister Pollie's house, where Lady Elgar never visited, there were wartime letters to the Windflower about the dog Juno. Then on 3 November 1919 there was a particularly affectionate reference: 'Juno, bless her, has six babies four days old, but when she heard my voice (after two whole years) she left her family (for the first time) & came & laid down at my feet - too, too touching.' At Kempsey, Elgar was 'to have Juno's *sister* & a spaniel', the increasingly famous Marco. Then there was 'one of Beatrice Harrison's Aberdeens whom I named *Brenda* - she sleeps in my room & rides in the car'. Within a month there was another name: 'The dogs have both been ill! etc. etc. Marco is the loveliest spaniel I have ever seen - quite a silly baby & cries for nothing; He loves riding in the car. Mina - the little cairn - is a love & so sharp.' Is it possible the cairn was named after Mina, Lady Beresford, who had died on 26 May 1922? One hopes so. The fortunes of the dogs were lovingly reported in sickness or in health. From Tiddington House, there was a letter to Carice on 8 May 1928:

> No news: garden going on: dogs well & very *opinionated*
>   I took Dick's besom down to the river, dipped it in several times & washed the mud off the bottom step: when I looked round there were three solemn folk sitting on the top step.

Elgar then drew the three dogs, with spaniel to the left and two terriers to the right. He commented: 'They are *awful*(ly nice).' At the end of the concert broadcast to celebrate Elgar's 70th birthday on 2 June 1927, he sent nocturnal greetings over the air: 'Good *night*, everybody. *Good* night, Marco.' When Gaisberg visited Marl Bank in August 1933, Elgar met him at the station with Marco and Mina. The dogs had their appointed places for meals: 'Dinner at 8.30 attended by Marco on Sir E's right & Mina on his left - properly seated on chairs. They behaved very well, patiently waiting for morsels they would receive, from Sir E.'s hand.'

As *The Apple Cart* year of 1929 drew to a close, Elgar chose for his Christmas and New Year greeting part of section 32 from Walt Whitman's *Song of Myself* (1855). Characteristically Elgar omitted a line and changed a word (Whitman is in square brackets):

> I think I could turn and live with animals,
>   they are [they're] so placid and self-contain'd,
> [I stand and look at them long and long.]

> They do not sweat and whine about their condition;
> They do not lie awake in the dark and weep for their sins;
> They do not make me sick discussing their duty to God;
> Not one is dissatisfied - not one is demented
>   with the mania of owning things;
> Not one kneels to another, nor to his kind
>   that lived thousands of years ago;
> Not one is respectable or industrious [unhappy] over the whole earth.

Whitman has also two fine stanzas on the horse:

> A gigantic beauty of a stallion, fresh and responsive to my caresses,
> Head high in the forehead, wide between the ears,
> Limbs glossy and supple, tail dusting the ground,
> Eyes full of sparkling wickedness, ears finely cut, flexibly moving.

His nostrils dilate as my heels embrace him,
His well-built limbs tremble with pleasure as we race around and return.
I but use you a minute, then I resign you, stallion,
Why do I need your paces when I myself out-gallop them?
Even as I stand or sit passing faster than you.

The day of the *Apostles* première, 14 October 1903, Elgar made a diary note, that Grey Tick won the Cesarewitch. The Worcester Races became an absorbing interest in his latter years, an interest shared with Lady Atkins. Before flying to Paris at the end of May 1933, Elgar conducted *The Apostles* in Croydon and went on to Newmarket. He had a series of code names for the placing of bets, including 'Elhamboy', 'Alectryon', 'Elmusic', 'Elbow', 'Elshie' and his palindromic 'Siromoris'. He had little success with his bets; nor was he any more fortunate in advising friends. Ernest Newman had stayed at Marl Bank, and Elgar wrote on 19 January 1932:

> I am sorry your horse behaved badly - you chose well: with this is the epic, classic history of the race - do not send any cash as I shall carry the transaction on to the next meeting: my pencil calculations, at which you smiled at breakfast, brought me £11. rather more or less.

For Christmas and the New Year at the end of 1932, Elgar wrote a fable: 'In a gorgeous, illimitable, golden corridor, several of the Higher-Beings were in waiting.' There was some dissatisfaction among them about the progress of the 'new-created world'. They inspected a trumpet. 'Have you to play that thing?' asked Raphael.

'Some day,' Uriel answered. Lucifer appeared as a vast Purple Shadow and was not depressed about the world: 'I shall like it: there will be much to amuse besides the religions.' He was looking forward to Shakespeare, but Milton . . . 'Michael fingered a sword and saw his effigy as the everlasting maître d'armes.' But then: 'From somewhere near came a curiously pleasant sound; pleasant and not unmirthful.' Michael drew back the curtain: 'HE is pleased, - HE laughs, - HE has made, (Michael whispered) - a Puppy!' The Purple Shade sensed defeat: 'Lucifer knew that through the ages Man could be serenely happy with his DOG.' The porter at Brooks's could corroborate this when he heard a telephone exchange between Elgar and his dogs. At one end barks; at the other 'Don't bite the cushions.'

In the midst of it all Shaw could not let the matter of a Third Symphony rest. Writing on 7 January 1932 from the *Carnarvon Castle* headed for South Africa, he ended on a note of drama: 'Yah! the ship has pitched fearsomely, and all but shot Charlotte into the fireplace.' Just before, he had asked: 'Why dont you make the B.B.C. order a new symphony? It can afford it.' Elgar was sufficiently fired with the idea to discuss the matter with Wayne Daley of Keith Prowse and then write on 10 June: 'I was very glad to see you again & to have your views about the third Symphony.' In view of the parlous state of the nation's exchequer, Shaw had a topical proposal on 29 June: 'Why not a Financial Symphony? Allegro: Impending Disaster. Lento mesto: Stony Broke. Scherzo: Light Heart and Empty Pocket. All° con brio: Clouds Clearing.' Elgar sent the postcard on to Gaisberg, as it had the address for despatch of the recent *Severn Suite* records. Now Elgar wondered in his turn: 'perhaps H.M.V. would like to commission (say £5,000) for such a symphony as *G.B.S.* suggests: the p.c. is worth more than my music!'

Now there was a new Shaw play. It was to open at Malvern on 6 August 1932, and Elgar wrote about it on 13 July: 'Can't you engineer that I sit *with you* for the first performance of *Too true to be good* my last chance.' Shaw explained the play in the *Malvern Festival Book*: 'The moral of my play, or rather the position illustrated by it, is simple enough.' He pointed out that previous wars had been professional affairs and 'the reversal of morality which they involved was kept in a conscience-tight compartment'. World War 1 was quite different:

> But a war like that of 1914-18, in which the whole male population of military age was forced to serve, hosts of women volunteered for work under fire, and the new feature of aerial bombardment brought the bloody part of the business crash into the civilians' bedrooms, was quite another matter.

Shaw considered the present situation:

> Our difficulty now is that what the bright young things after the war tried to do, and what their wretched survivors are still trying to do, is to get the reaction without the terror, to go on eating cocaine and drinking cocktails as if they had only a few hours' expectation of life instead of forty years.

In the play Aubrey has the last words:

> What am I? A soldier who has lost his nerve, a thief who at his first great theft has found honesty the best policy and restored his booty to its owner. Nature never intended me for soldiering or thieving: I am by nature and destiny a preacher. I am the new Ecclesiastes. But I have no Bible, no creed: the war has shot both out of my hands. The war has been a fiery forcing house in which we have grown with a rush like flowers in a late spring following a terrible winter. And with what result? This: that we have outgrown our religion, outgrown our political system, outgrown our own strength of mind and character. The fatal word NOT has been miraculously inserted into all our creeds.

Elgar's late correspondence has many hints of Aubrey's views; but after the festival Shaw reverted to the Symphony; and so perforce did Elgar, as Shaw had written on 30 September 1932 to Sir John Reith (1889-1971), director general of the B.B.C.:

> In 1823 the London Philharmonic Society passed a resolution to offer Beethoven £50 for the MS of a symphony. He accepted, and sent the Society the MS of the Ninth Symphony. In 1827 the Society sent him £100. He was dying; and he said: 'God bless the Philharmonic Society and the whole English nation.'
>
> This is by far the most creditable incident in English history.
>
> Now the only composer today who is comparable to Beethoven is Elgar. Everybody seems to assume either that Elgar can live on air, or that he is so rich and successful that he can afford to write symphonies and conduct festivals for nothing. As a matter of fact his financial position is a very difficult one, making it impossible for him to give time enough to such heavy jobs as the completion of a symphony; and consequently here we have the case of a British composer who has written two great symphonies, which place England at the head of the world in this top department of instrumental music, unable to complete and score a third. I know that he has the material for the first movement ready, because he has played it to me on his piano.
>
> Well, why should not the BBC, with its millions, do for Elgar what the old Philharmonic did for Beethoven. You could bring the Third Symphony into existence and obtain the performing right for the BBC for, say, ten years, for a few thousand pounds. The kudos would be stupendous and the value for the money ample; in fact if Elgar were a good man of business instead of a great artist, who throws his commercial opportunities about en *grand seigneur*, he would open his mouth much wider.

Shaw's advocacy was effective, and the plan to commission the Third Symphony for £1000 was laid before Elgar in London on 11 November by a member of the BBC'S Music Advisory Committee. Fourteen years ago, that date had seen national flags flying at Severn House and Brinkwells. The BBC might have felt the occasion worthy of a flag; Elgar's feelings were probably too ambivalent; but he wrote to Shaw at once: 'Landon Ronald has unfolded to-day the wonderful plan which you invented - I am overwhelmed by the loftiness of the idea & can only say *thank you* at this moment.' The plan was publicly announced at the end of a three-concert BBC tribute to mark Elgar's 75th birthday.

It was now a matter of urgency to plan the Symphony. As always, Elgar consulted his sketchbooks, where was still much unused material. Indeed there were three significant projects from the past that had stimulated

Elgar to some strong musical ideas. The plan to complete the 'Apostles' project was not finally abandoned till the mid-1920s. It is impossible to say how early some *Last Judgement* ideas may have originated; but as always with Elgar, they may have simmered in his mind, played a part in extemporisation, waiting with more or less expectation for a right context. Then there was the planned scena for the last song of Callicles, the young harp-player in Matthew Arnold's masterpiece, *Empedocles on Etna.* Ideas for this go back at least to 17 August 1905, when Lady Elgar noted in her diary: 'E. wrote beautiful melodic passage for Empedocles.' They persisted until August 1926, when Elgar sketched an important thematic germ on a scrap of MS paper that had a message for Madge Grafton on the other side. Of equal significance was the discarded idea for a pendant to the *Cockaigne* overture of 1901, which would take its inspiration from the nightmarish poem of James Thomson (1834-82), *The City of Dreadful Night* (1874). Then there was the special case of the 1923 *Arthur* music. Ivor Atkins had wanted an *Arthur* suite for the 1926 Worcester Festival and suggested it on the provisional programme. Elgar deleted it; but on 26 June 1928 he seemed to revive the idea in a letter to William Elkin: 'wd a sort of short 'Suite' (Arthur) be worth considering?' Henceforth silence, since much of the *Arthur* music was destined for the Third Symphony. The silence was such that Basil Maine, busy on his life-works account of Elgar (1933) was allowed no mention of *Arthur* and its music. At the same time Elgar was fired to much original music of considerable power.

Though Elgar had not finally settled the position of every thematic idea within the four movements, and had not fixed the order of the two central movements, many sketches had been assigned their place. *Last Judgement* material should start the work and be integral to the Adagio. As always when meditating one of his biblical oratorios, Elgar read voraciously. The Symphony was to begin with an 'Antichrist' theme, and it is interesting to consider books that went to its making. A seminal influence was the *Antichrist* of Ernest Renan (1823-92), which appeared in 1873 as volume 4 of *Les origines de la Christianisme.* The introduction to the English translation by William G.Hutchison is dated 1899. The crucial moment for Renan was the Franco-Prussian war of 1870, which coloured much of his subsequent thought; he had indeed faced hostility when advising the besieged Parisians to seek peace. Before writing the *Antichrist* he went to Rome to inspect sites connected with the primitive church and the Neronian persecution. He regarded Paul and Nero as the second founders of Christianity. Renan's admiration for Christ was boundless; Paul he regarded with suspicion. Hutchison ascribes Roman toleration and indeed admiration for Nero not so much to the democratic temper of the time as to the extraordinary mix of the city's population. He likens it to late 19th-century New York; parallels nearer home suggest

Nero as cast for Maximilian I

themselves. Nero had been fascinated since boyhood with legends about the burning of Troy; a favourite play was the *Incendium* of Lucius Afranius (fl.c.160-120 BC): his manic desire to construct a new Rome was inhibited only by the venerable survivals of buildings from old Rome. Suetonius (c.70-c.140) and Tacitus (c.55-after 115), no friends to Nero, ascribe the fire of 64 to him. Jewish sycophants, in Renan's view, may have advised the Emperor to fasten blame on the Christians. He considers that the Jews around him, always dangerous when in positions of power, may have inculcated in the Emperor's mind the idea that he was the Messiah, and that the upstart Jesus must be suppressed. The Christians who survived the hideous persecutions regarded Nero as the Antichrist, who might indeed herald the Second Coming. A paradoxical result of Nero's actions was to make the teachings of Peter and Paul known to the pagan world and to inspire the searing visions of the book of *Revelation*. Hutchison makes the point that the prophecies that came out of Patmos appeared midway between the 64 persecutions and the fall of Jerusalem in 70, both events appalling yet beneficial to the young church. Were the living torches in Rome's nocturnal gardens a response to the Christian claim of Jesus as light of the world?

Renan describes Nero's reaction to the fire:

> The sublime horror of the spectacle transported him with delight. Later, it was asserted that he had gazed on the conflagration from the summit of a tower and there, in theatrical costume, a lyre in his hand, had sung, in the touching harmonies of the ancient elegy, the destruction of Ilium.

The Christians could not doubt that Nero was the Antichrist, and Renan suspects that John of Patmos was a witness of the brutal tortures to follow: 'If the Gospel is the book of Jesus, the Apocalypse is the book of Nero.' How far the Antichrist, the logical development as Elgar saw him, of Judas and then Simon Magus, was to feature in *The Last Judgement* cannot be said; but he was to have made his mark on the Third Symphony, as were other passages from *Revelation*. The main theme of what was to become the slow movement incorporated the call of the shofar, the 'last trumpet' that Uriel so despised in Elgar's 1932 fable, written when the Symphony was already commissioned.

The Reformation produced an Antichrist alternative to Nero, as Elgar knew well. Richard Baxter (1615-91), who turned down the bishopric of Hereford in 1660, expressed himself forcibly: 'If the Pope was not Antichrist, he had bad luck to be so like.' While still a priest in the Church of England, John Henry Newman dealt with the charge in an essay entitled 'The Protestant Idea of Antichrist'. Newman's arguments were always subtle, if expressed with exemplary clarity: 'Not "bad luck;" but sheer necessity. Since Antichrist simulates Christ, and bishops are images of Christ, Antichrist is like a bishop, and a bishop is like Antichrist.' The important point for Newman is 'that the prophecies concerning Antichrist are as yet unfulfilled, and that the predicted enemy of the Church is yet to come'. He deals with the possibility that Nero might rise again as the Antichrist and, after much examination of scripture, sums up:

> And so in that judgement, or in connection with it, we have learnt that the following events are to occur: Elijah the Tishbite will come; the Jews will

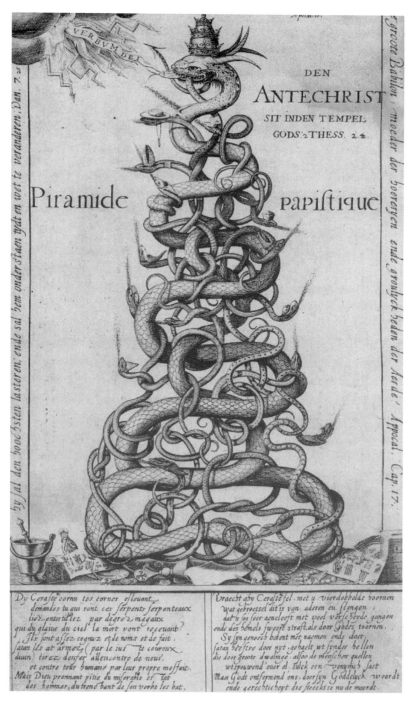

Antichrist sits in the Temple of God *by Hendrick Hondius*

believe; Antichrist will persecute; Christ will judge; the dead will rise again; the good and the wicked will be sorted out; the world will be burned in flames and will be renewed.

It is no wonder, perhaps, that Elgar felt daunted or even a little incredulous, and considered his *Last Judgement* material might be better placed in a symphony.

Newman could count Matthew Arnold among the admirers of his poetry, as he made clear at the beginning of 1868, when acknowledging the volume that included as centrepiece *The Dream of Gerontius*. His feeling for Newman had begun in Oxford days: 'Who could resist the charm of that spiritual apparition, gliding in the dim afternoon light through the aisles of St.Mary's, rising into the pulpit, and then, in the most entrancing of voices, breaking the silence with words and thoughts which were a religious music?' But when Arnold attended a splendid reception in London for Newman, now a cardinal, he could not quite bring himself to bend the knee as the Catholic admirers did. It is less likely that Newman had read Arnold's poetry, and perhaps least of all *Empedocles on Etna*, as outstanding in its author's production as *Gerontius* was in Newman's.

Empedocles appeared in 1852, but the following year Arnold withdrew it. He gives his reasons in the 1853 preface. It was not the remote antiquity of the subject, nor any suggestion that he had failed to express the feelings of 'one of the last of the Greek religious philosophers'; it was because he now understood that his treatment in the poem had little charm and nothing that could offer delight. The subject itself was at fault:

> What then are the situations, from the representation of which, though accurate, no poetical enjoyment can be derived? They are those in which the suffering finds no vent in action; in which a continual state of mental distress is prolonged, unrelieved by incident, hope, or resistance; in which there is everything to be endured, nothing to be done. In such situations there is inevitably something morbid, in the description of them something monotonous.

Arnold prepared himself for the poem by reading Diogenes Laertius, as we know from his 1851 diary. Laertius (fl.220) wrote *The Lives and Opinions of Eminent Philosophers*, and has much on Empedocles (484-424 BC). In his 'Problems XXX' Laertius asks 'Why is it that all men who have become outstanding in philosophy, statesmanship, poetry or the arts are melancholic?' Among the number he includes Empedocles. Arnold found also his Pausanias the physician, who with Empedocles and Callicles, make up the cast of the dramatic poem, in Laertius: 'Pausanias was the bosom friend of Empedocles, who dedicated to him his poem On Nature and wrote an epigram praising his medical skill as successor to Aesculapius and ability to rescue those in torment from the realms of Hades and Persephone.' The most eloquent praise of Empedocles himself is found in Book I of Lucretius (712 ff.), where he describes him as foremost of 'those who think that all can grow forth out of four things, from fire, earth, air and water'. He came from Acragas in Sicily:

> Here is waste Charybdis, and here Aetna's rumblings threaten that the angry flames are gathering again, that once more its violence may belch fires bursting forth from its throat, and once more shoot to the sky the lightnings of its flame: which mighty region, while it seems wonderful in many ways to the nations of mankind and is famed as a place to see, fat with good things, fortified with mighty store of men, yet it seems to have in it nothing more illustrious than this man, nor more sacred and wonderful and dear. Moreover, the poems of his divine mind utter a loud voice and declare illustrious discoveries, so that he seems hardly to be born of mortal stock.

The Yale Manuscript of Arnold's writings has a passage on Empedocles's balancing of life and death:

> He has not the religious consolations of other men, facile because adapted to their weaknesses, or because shared by all around and charging the atmosphere they breathe. He sees things as they are - the world as it is - God as he is: in their stern simplicity.
> The sight is a severe and mind-taxing one: to know the mysteries which are communicated to others by fragments, in parables.

His initial philosophical discoveries filled him with joy, but they have led to an intense loneliness, in which he must hold fast the truth in solitude, while his fellows are incredulous:

> Before he becomes the victim of depression & overtension of mind, to the utter deadness to joy, grandeur, spirit, and animated life, he desires to die; to be reunited with the universe, before by exaggerating his human side he has become utterly estranged from it.

Arnold's Act 1 scene i is 'A Pass in the forest region of Etna. Morning'. Callicles is enchanted with the scene but wonders about Empedocles:

> Here will I stay till the slow litter comes.
> I have my harp too - that is well. - Apollo!
> What mortal could be sick or sorry here?
> I know not in what mind Empedocles,

Whose mules I follow'd, may be coming up,
But if, as most men say, he is half mad
With exile, and with brooding on his wrongs,
Pausanias, his sage friend, who mounts with him,
Could scarce have lighted on a lovelier cure.

Matthew Arnold by Millais

Pausanias hints that Empedocles is now weary of music, but perhaps
Callicles's art might lift his settled gloom:

> Play when we halt, and when the evening comes,
> And I must leave him (for his pleasure is
> To be left musing these soft nights alone
> In the high unfrequented mountain spots),
> Then watch him, for he ranges swift and far,
> Sometimes to Etna's top, and to the cone;
> But hide thee in the rocks a great way down,
> And try thy noblest strains, my Callicles.

Scene ii is at Noon. A Glen on the highest skirts of the woody region
of Etna. Empedocles is in converse with Pausanias and Callicles sings from
below. Empedocles muses on the human condition:

> What were the wise man's plan? -
> Through this sharp, toil-set life,
> To fight as best he can,
> And win what's won by strife.
> But we an easier way to cheat our pains have found.

***

> So, loath to suffer mute,
> We, peopling the void air,
> Make Gods to whom to impute
> The ills we ought to bear;
> With God and Fate to rail at, suffering easily.

Act 2 is Evening. The summit of Etna, with Empedocles alone:

> On this charr'd, blacken'd, melancholy waste,
> Crown'd by the awful peak, Etna's great mouth,
> Round which the sullen vapour rolls - alone!

***

> Thou canst not live with men nor with thyself -
> Oh sage! oh sage! - Take then the one way left;
> And turn thee to the elements, thy friends,
> Thy well-tried friends, thy willing ministers,
> And say: - Ye servants, hear Empedocles,
> Who asks this final service at your hands!

***

> Before the soul lose all her solemn joys,
> And awe be dead, and hope impossible,
> And the soul's deep eternal night come on,
> Receive me, hide me, quench me, take me home!

He advances to the edge of the crater. Smoke and fire break forth with a loud noise, and Callicles is heard singing below:

> The lyre's voice is lovely everwhere!
> In the court of Gods, in the city of men,
> And in the lonely rock-strewn mountain glen,
> In the still mountain air.

Empedocles hears the music but is moved only to cast away his golden circlet, purple robe and laurel bough:

> But he, whose youth fell on a different world
> From that on which his exiled age is thrown,
> Whose mind was fed on other food, was train'd
> By other rules than are in vogue to-day,
> Whose habit of thought is fix'd, who will not change,
> But in a world he loves not must subsist
>
> ***
>
> Joy and the outward world must die to him,
> As they are dead to me!

A long pause, during which Empedocles remains motionless, plunged in thought. The night deepens. He moves forward and gazes round him, and proceeds:

> Ah! boil up, ye vapours!
> Leap and roar, thou sea of fire!
> My soul glows to meet you.
> Ere it flag, ere the mists
> Of despondency and gloom
> Rush over it again,
> Receive me! Save me!

He plunges into the crater.

From time to time in his life Elgar mentioned suicide as a way out of black depression; but a more fundamental attitude was his feeling about the suicide of Judas in *The Apostles*. His crime or sin, Elgar felt, was despair, as explained to Canon Gorton in a letter of July 1903: 'not only the betrayal, which was done for a worldly purpose. In these days, where every "modern" person (Ibsen &c. &c.) seems to think "suicide" is the natural way out of everything my plan, if explained, may do some good.' Callicles's final song, at a setting of which Elgar made a number of attempts, immediately follows Empedocles's suicide:

> Through the black, rushing smoke-bursts,
> Thick breaks the red flame;
> All Etna heaves fiercely
> Her forest-cloth'd frame.

Yet at once, and almost too soon, the young musician returns to the Apollo he addressed near the start of the poem and whose ensigns Empedocles had so forcibly rejected. Some of Elgar's ideas for the latter stanzas had been absorbed into *The Music Makers*; but one striking theme for the work, with no words attached, was destined for the Third Symphony. An Elgarian note suggested it might feature in the recapitulation of the first movement; but why should it not, with a muttered reference to 'Antichrist' in the bass, do equally well for the start of the development and then appear also in the coda?

The start of the Symphony's slow movement had assumed symbolic significance for Elgar, as he wrote to Ernest Newman from the nursing home on 22 December 1933: 'I am fond enough to believe that the first two bars (with the F# in the bass) open some vast bronze doors into something strangely unfamiliar.' There may have been some such function for the theme when it was being considered for *The Last Judgement*. Yet it was planned originally for the sequel to *Cockaigne*, an overture to be based on James Thomson's poem, *The City of Dreadful Night*. An edition of the poem appeared in 1930 with introduction by Edmund Blunden (1896-1974), lifelong friend of Siegfried Sassoon. He feels that a spectral London is the ghostly presence that haunts the poem: 'There is surely the element of London in his dream, London after sunset with her Embankment, her Cathedral, her monuments, her river, her vitiated children, her slaves bringing their vanloads to her sleepless markets, her northern heights.' Blunden sums up the prophetic power of Thomson's masterpiece, claiming that he

> wrote the most anticipative poem of his time, and that his poem, even if its reasoning and speculation were to be overthrown (which does not seem their imminent fate), would stand as an illustrative example of the Orphic transmutation of severe thought, and psychological discernment, into a harmony of fascinating visions.

Those visions clearly gripped Elgar, as they must anyone who makes his hallucinatory way through the cavernous spaces of Thomson's city, a

Piranesian recreation. Thomson died the day after Elgar's 25th birthday, but it is unlikely he noted the event. At some point in the next twenty years, however, he must have been so deeply affected by the poem that he was preparing to base a major composition on its content. As epigraph to the work Thomson quotes initially the first line in Canto 3 of Dante's *Inferno*: 'Per me si va nella città dolente.' Dantesque echoes are obvious throughout. In the 'Proem' Thomson defines his audience:

> Surely I write not for the hopeful young,
> > Or those who deem their happiness of worth,
> Or such as pasture and grow fat among
> > The shows of life and feel nor doubt nor dearth,
> Or pious spirits with a God above them
> To sanctify and glorify and love them,
> > Or sages who foresee a heaven on earth.

It is relevant to recall that *The City of Dreadful Night* was published in 1880 by Charles Bradlaugh (1833-91), about whom Shaw makes the essential point in *The Intelligent Woman's Guide* when discussing admission to parliament:

> The line was still drawn at Jews and Atheists; but the Jews soon made their way in; and finally a famous Atheist, Charles Bradlaugh, broke down the last barrier to the House of Commons by forcing the House to accept, instead of the Deist oath, a form of affirmation which relieved Atheists from the necessity of perjuring themselves before taking their seats.

That was in 1886.

Two of Thomson's stanzas in the first of the 21 sections describe the City and its inhabitants:

> The street-lamps burn amidst the baleful glooms,
> > Amidst the soundless solitudes immense
> Of rangèd mansions dark and still as tombs.
> > The silence which benumbs or strains the sense
> Fulfils with awe the soul's despair unweeping:
> Myriads of habitants are ever sleeping,
> > Or dead, or fled from nameless pestilence!
>
> Yet as in some necropolis you find
> > Perchance one mourner to a thousand dead,
> So there; worn faces that look deaf and blind
> > Like tragic masks of stone. With weary tread,
> Each wrapt in his own doom, they wander, wander,

> Or sit foredone and desolately ponder
>> Through sleepless hours with heavy drooping head.

Thomson persists with his terrible definition:

> The City is of Night, but not of Sleep;
>> There sweet sleep is not for the weary brain;
> The pitiless hours like years and ages creep,
>> A night seems termless hell. This dreadful strain
> Of thought and consciousness which never ceases,
> Or which some moments' stupor but increases,
>> This, worse than woe, makes wretches there insane.

In the second section the narrator finds a human form to trail:

> Because he seemed to walk with an intent
>> I followed him; who, shadowlike and frail,
> Unswervingly though slowly onward went,
>> Regardless, wrapt in thought as in a veil:
> Thus step for step with lonely sounding feet
> We travelled many a long dim silent street.

Before a gloomy tower he pronounced the death of Faith; turning always to the right, he named a villa beyond a low wall as scene of Love's end; then a squalid house at the other side of a narrow arch was where Hope died. 'How could life continue?' the narrator wondered. The reply was chilling:

> As whom his one intense thought overpowers,
>> He answered coldly, Take a watch, erase
> The signs and figures of the circling hours,
>> Detach the hands, remove the dial-face;
> The works proceed until run down; although
> Bereft of purpose, void of use, still go.

The narrator sees a line of people approach the great Cathedral in the cloistered square at the start of Section XII:

> Then I would follow in among the last:
>> And in the porch a shrouded figure stood,
> Who challenged each one pausing ere he passed,
>> With deep eyes burning through a blank white hood:
> Whence come you in the world of life and light
> To this our City of Tremendous Night? -

At the end of the section the narrator makes his way in:

> Thus, challenged by that warder sad and stern,
>   Each one responded with his countersign,
> Then entered the cathedral; and in turn
>   I entered also, having given mine;
> But lingered near until I heard no more,
> And marked the closing of the massive door.

Maybe the 'vast bronze doors' of the Symphony had originally belonged in the overture to Thomson's Cathedral. The preacher began to utter from the dark pulpit in Section XIV, and there came his essential message:

> And now at last authentic word I bring,
> Witnessed by every dead and living thing;
>   Good tidings of great joy for you, for all:
> There is no God; no Fiend with names divine
> Made us and tortures us; if we must pine,
>   It is to satiate no Being's gall.

In Section XX the narrator is by the west front of the Cathedral looking at a sphinx and opposing angel leaning on a sword; he sinks towards the sleep of stupor till a crash arouses him:

> The angel's wings had fallen, stone on stone,
>   And lay there shattered; hence the sudden sound:
> A warrior leaning on his sword alone
>   Now watched the sphinx with that regard profound;
> The sphinx unchanged looked forthright, as aware
> Of nothing in the vast abyss of air.
>
> Again I sank in that repose unsweet,
>   Again a crashing noise my slumber rent;
> The warrior's sword lay broken at his feet:
>   An unarmed man with raised hands impotent
> Now stood before the sphinx, which ever kept
> Such mien as if with open eyes it slept.
>
> My eyelids sank in spite of wonder grown;
>   A louder crash upstartled me in dread:
> The man had fallen forward, stone on stone,
>   And lay there shattered, with his trunkless head
> Between the monster's large quiescent paws,
> Between its grand front changeless as life's laws.

Melencolia *by Dürer*

In the last Section the scene shifts to the heights above the City, where broods a mighty statue of Dürer's Melencolia:

> Anear the centre of that northern crest
>   Stands out a level upland bleak and bare,
> From which the city east and south and west
>   Sinks gently in long waves; and thronèd there
> An Image sits, stupendous, superhuman,
> The bronze colossus of wingèd Woman,
>   Upon a graded granite base foursquare.

***

Words cannot picture her; but all men know
    That solemn sketch the pure sad artist wrought
Three centuries and threescore years ago,
    With phantasies of his peculiar thought:
The instruments of carpentry and science
Scattered about her feet, in strange alliance
    With the keen wolf-hound sleeping undistraught;

***

The sense that every struggle brings defeat
    Because Fate holds no prize to crown success;
That all the oracles are dumb or cheat
    Because they have no secret to express;
That none can pierce the vast black veil uncertain
Because there is no light beyond the curtain;
    That all is vanity and nothingness.

Titanic from her high throne in the north,
    That City's sombre Patroness and Queen,
In bronze sublimity she gazes forth
    Over her capital of teen and threne,
Over the river with its isles and bridges,
The marsh and moorland, to the stern rock-ridges,
    Confronting them with a coëval mien.

Thomson goes further than the preacher in *Ecclesiastes*, further than Shaw's new Ecclesiastes in *Too true to be good*, who 'must preach and preach and preach no matter how late the hour and how short the day, no matter whether I have nothing to say'. Elgar may well have felt the uncompromising poem was too nihilistic for any music, but that discarded thematic material was conveniently to hand for the Symphony. In the midst of such weighty associations for the Third Symphony, Elgar had not forgotten the chivalrous impulses that had produced *Froissart* in 1890, had been apparent in so much of his grandest music since, and had shone forth undimmed after the war in much of the *Arthur* music, the 'Castle' and 'Tournament' movements of the *Severn Suite*, and in *Pomp and Circumstance* March no.5.

Elgar's plan now was to take the main theme of his Allegretto in the Symphony from the 'banquet' music in Scene IV of Binyon's *Arthur*. Gareth first comments on it: 'Hark! There's the music'; what Gaisberg called on 27 August 1933 'a delicate, feathery short section' had appeared in many guises during the play. For the Symphony Elgar had dovetailed the motif to the end of a trio section and devised also by means of it a wistful conclusion for the movement. *Arthur* was also to provide a considerable slice of the finale. This was mainly the 'Chivalry' theme heard at the end of the overture to the play and developed at some length for the introduction to Scene II, where it achieves apotheosis first with a 'Nobilmente' marking and then with psychological insight is transferred into the minor and notated at half speed for the King himself. In the Third Symphony folder left behind by Elgar there is also a passage that happily combines the falling 3rds of the *Callicles* motif assigned to the Symphony with the dactyl rhythm of 'Chivalry'. Originally intended for *The Last Judgement*, it carried words only slightly altered from the start of *Revelation* 19: 'Alleluia, Salvation and glory, and power belong to our God.' Why should it not act as a natural pendant to the 'King Arthur' idea? Conceivably this juxtaposition was already in Elgar's mind and had indeed been played to those privileged to hear the Third Symphony in the making.

The day before an exploratory operation that proved Elgar's sciatica and lumbago had developed into a fatal cancer, he wrote on 7 October 1933 to Sir John Reith at the BBC explaining the situation: 'I am not at all sure how things will turn out and have made arrangements that in case the Symphony does not materialise the sums you have paid on account will be returned.' Again Bernard Shaw intervened, had a word with Reith, and relieved Elgar of financial anxiety over the Symphony, as he explained in a letter of 5 December. He added that he was sending a copy of *On the Rocks*, his latest play, which had had its première on 25 November; also coming was 'a set of proofs of its terrific preface'. Shaw instructed: 'Do not bother about the first half; but read, or get Carice to read you the part about Socrates, Jesus, Joan and Galileo, because it ends with a dialogue between Christ and Pilate which you will have to orchestrate and vocalize for the Gloucester Festival. It ends with a quotation written expressly for you.' Elgar dictated a reply the next day:

> Nothing could possibly give me greater pleasure than the receipt of your play *and* preface - (Kolossal!) & your wonderful letter. I fear it will be long before I can say I have read the whole of the printed matter, but I look at it with pride all day and dip into it occasionally. I am still in the depths of pain.

He then referred to Shaw's concern for him:

> It was good of you to speak to Sir John Reith about the Symphony. The very pleasant arrangement made by you in the goodness of your heart for my peace of mind & betterment last year was turning out to be my greatest worry & disappointment. At present I can only wait and see & hope for the best, but I am low in mind.

Shaw's dialogue between Christ and Pilate is a characteristic filling-out, by a born dramatist second only to Shakespeare, of the Gospel narrative. Jesus enlarges on his view that 'The greatness of Rome, as you call it, is nothing but fear'. Pilate considers Christ 'a more dangerous fellow than I thought', not for his 'blasphemy against the god of the high priests,' but he has blasphemed against Caesar and the Empire: 'you mean it, and have the power to turn men's hearts against it as you have half turned mine.' Shaw's Christ has more than a thought for Elgar on his deathbed: 'Slay me and you go blind to your damnation. The greatest of God's names is Counsellor; and when your Empire is dust and your name a byword among the nations the temples of the living God shall still ring with his praise as Wonderful! Counsellor! the Everlasting Father, the Prince of Peace.'

Elgar was in no state to take up Shaw's Handelian challenge or to finish the Symphony; but Shaw, incomparable critic though he was, thought the Symphony could not be completed. He was wrong.

Bibliography

Elgar

Anderson, Robert, *Elgar in Manuscript* (London, 1990)

Anderson, Robert, *Elgar* (London, 1993)

Atkins, E.Wulstan, *The Elgar-Atkins Friendship* (Newton Abbot, 1984)

—— *1890-1990: The Centenary of the Birth of a Friendship: Edward Elgar and Ivor Atkins* (Worcester, 1990)

Buckley, Robert J., *Sir Edward Elgar* (London, 1904; 2nd ed., 1912)

Burley, Rosa and Carruthers, Frank C., *Edward Elgar: The Record of a Friendship* (London, 1972)

Collett, Barry, *Elgar Country* (London, 1981)

Collett, Pauline, *Elgar Lived Here* (London, 1981)

—— *An Elgar Travelogue* (London, 1983)

Dennison, Peter, 'Elgar and Wagner', *ML* lxvii (1985), p.93

Dent, Edward J., 'Modern English Music', in G.Adler, *Handbuch der Musikgeschichte* (Frankfurt am Main, 1924; 2nd.ed., 1930; repr.1961)

Foreman, Lewis, ed., *Oh, My Horses! Elgar and the Great War* (Rickmansworth, 2001)

Greaves, Peter, *In the Bavarian Highlands: Edward Elgar's German Holidays in the 1890s* (Rickmansworth, 2000)

Hodgkins, Geoffrey, ed., *The Best of Me: A Gerontius Centenary Companion* (Rickmansworth, 1999)

Hunt, Donald, *Elgar and the Three Choirs Festivals* (Worcester, 1999)

Kennedy, Michael, *Portrait of Elgar* (London, 1968; 2nd ed., 1973; rev., 1983; 3rd ed., 1987)

—— ' Elgar and the Festivals', *Two Hundred and Fifty Years of the Three Choirs Festivals*, ed. B.Still (Gloucester, 1977)

—— *Elgar Orchestral Music* (London, 1970)

Kent, Christopher, 'A View of Elgar's Methods of Composition through the Sketches of the Symphony no.2 in E flat (op.63)', *PRMA*, ciii (1976-7)

—— 'Elgar's Third Symphony: the Sketches Reconsidered', *MT*, cxxvii (1979), p.224

McVeagh, Diana, *Edward Elgar: his Life and Music* (London, 1955)

Maine, Basil, *Elgar, his Life and Works* (London, 1933; repr., 1973)

Moore, Jerrold Northrop, *Elgar: a Life in Photographs* (London, 1972)

—— *Elgar on Record: the Composer and the Gramophone* (London, 1974)

—— *Edward Elgar, a Creative Life* (Oxford, 1984)

—— *Spirit of England: Edward Elgar in his World* (London, 1984)

—— *Elgar and his Publishers: Letters of a Creative Life* (Oxford, 1987)

—— *Edward Elgar: The Windflower Letters* (Oxford, 1989)

—— *Edward Elgar: Letters of a Lifetime* (Oxford, 1990)

Newman, Ernest, *Elgar* (London, 1906; repr., 1977; 2nd ed., 1922)
—— 'Elgar's Second Symphony', *MT*, lii (1911) p.295
—— 'Elgar's Third Symphony', *Sunday Times* (22 Sept., 20 and 27 Oct. 1935)
Newmarch, Rosa, *The Concert-goer's Library of Descriptive Notes*, articles on the Symphonies, Violin Concerto, *Cockaigne, Pomp and Circumstance* Marches nos.1-4, *Coronation* and *Mogul Emperor* marches, *Wand of Youth, Bavarian Dances*, vols1-4 (Oxford, 1928-31)
Parrott, Ian, *Elgar* (London, 1971)
Payne, Anthony, *Elgar's Third Symphony: The Story of the Reconstruction* (London, 1998)
Powell, D.M., *Edward Elgar: Memories of a Variation* (London, 1937, 4/1994)
Reed, William H., *Elgar as I knew him* (London, 1936, repr., 1973)
—— *Elgar* (London, 1939; rev.: 3rd edn, 1949)
—— 'Elgar's Third Symphony', *The Listener* (28 Aug.1935)
Shaw, Watkins, *The Three Choirs Festival* (London, 1954)
Shaw, George Bernard, 'Sir Edward Elgar', *ML*, i (1920), p.7
Simmons, Kenneth E.L. and Marion, *The Elgars of Worcester* (London, 1984)
Tovey, Donald F., 'Elgar, Master of Music', *ML*, xvi (1935), p.1
—— *Essays in Musical Analysis* (Oxford, 1935-9)
Trowell, Brian, 'Elgar's Marginalia', *MT*, cxxv (1984), p.139
Whittall, Arnold, 'Elgar's Last Judgement', *MR*, xxvi (1965), p.23
Willetts, Pamela, 'The Elgar Sketch-books', *British Library Journal*, xi/1 (1985)
Young, Percy M., *Elgar O.M.: a Study of a Musician* (London, 1955; rev.2/1973)
—— ed., *Letters of Edward Elgar and Other Writings* (London, 1956)
—— *A Future for English Music and Other Lectures by Edward Elgar* (London, 1968)

Art and Architecture

Aslet, Clive and Moore, Derry, *Inside the House of Lords* (London, 1998)
Bond, Maurice, *Works of Art in the House of Lords* (London, 1980)
Bridges, Tim, *Churches of Worcestershire* (Logaston, 2000)
Casteras, Susan P. and Denney, Colleen, *The Grosvenor Gallery: A Palace of Art in Victorian England* (Yale UP, 1996)
Dakers, Caroline, *The Holland Park Circle: Artists and Victorian Society* (Yale UP, 1999)
Dorment, Richard, *Alfred Gilbert* (Yale UP, 1985)
Egg, Erich, *The Tomb of Emperor Maximilian I* (Innsbruck, 1993)
Engen, Rodney, *Pre-Raphaelite Prints* (London, 1995)
Ficacci, Luigi, *Piranesi: The Complete Etchings* (Cologne, 2000)
Fleming, G.H., *John Everett Millais: A Biography* (London, 1998)
Funnell, Peter and Warner, Malcolm, eds., *Millais: Portraits* (London, 1999)
Gully, Anne, ed., *John Ruskin and the Victorian Eye* (New York, 1993)
Hager, June, *Pilgrimage: a Chronicle of Christianity through the Churches of Rome* (London, 1999)
Hawksley, Lucinda, *Essential Pre-Raphaelites* (Bath, 1999)
Honer, Julian, ed., *C.R.W. Nevinson: the Twentieth Century* (London, 1999)

Marsh, Jan, *The Pre-Raphaelites: Their Lives in Letters and Diaries* (London, 1996)
Kilmurray, Elaine and Ormond, Richard, *Sargent* (Tate Gallery, l998)
Melville, Jennifer, ed., *A Scottish Collection: Treasures from Aberdeen Art Gallery* (Aberdeen, 2000)
Murray, Peter, *Piranesi and the Grandeur of Ancient Rome* (London, 1971)
Naylor, Gillian, ed., *William Morris by Himself: Designs and Writings* (London, 2000)
Parris, Leslie, ed., *The Pre-Raphaelites* (Tate Gallery, 1984)
——— ed., *Pre-Raphaelite Papers* (Tate Gallery, l984)
Pevsner, Nikolaus, *The Buildings of England: Herefordshire* (Harmondsworth, 1963)
——— and Wedgwood, Alexandra, *The Buildings of England: Warwickshire* (Harmondsworth, 1966)
——— *The Buildings of England: Worcestershire* (Harmondsworth, 1968)
Scheicher, Elisabeth, *Das Grabmal Kaiser Maximilians I.* (Vienna, 1986)
Thirlwell, Angela, ed., *The Pre-Raphaelites and their World from Writings of W.M. Rossetti* (London, 1995)
Verey, David, *The Buildings of England: Gloucestershire: The Vale and the Forest of Dean* (Harmondsworth, 1970, 2/1976)
Victoria County History of Worcestershire, four vols. (1901-24)
Wildman, Stephen and Christian, John, *Edward Burne-Jones: Victorian Artist-Dreamer* (New York, 1998)
Wilton, Andrew and Upstone, Robert, eds., *The Age of Rossetti, Burne-Jones and Watts: Symbolism in Britain 1860-1910* (Tate Gallery, 1997)

Chivalry

Applebaum, Stanley, ed., *The Triumph of Maximilian I* (London, 1964)
Biddle, Martin, ed., *King Arthur's Round Table: An Archaeological Investigation* (Woodbridge, 2000)
Chmelarz, Eduard, ed., *Maximilian's Triumphal Arch* (Vienna, 1885-6, London, 1972)
Collins, Hugh E.L., *The Order of the Garter 1348-1461* (Oxford, 2000)
Girouard, Mark, *The Return to Camelot: Chivalry and the English Gentleman* (Yale UP, 1981)
Johnes, Thomas, trans. and ed., *Sir John Froissart's Chronicles of England, France, Spain and the Adjoining Countries* (London, 1839)
Kaeuper, Richard W. and Kennedy, Elspeth, eds., *The Book of Chivalry of Geoffroi de Charny* (Pennsylvania UP, 1996)
Mancoff, Debra N., *The Return of King Arthur* (London, 1995)
Nicholson, Helen, *Templars, Hospitallers and Teutonic Knights: Images of the Military Orders 1128-1291* (Leicester UP, 1993)
Squibb, G.D., *The High Court of Chivalry: a Study of the Civil Law in England* (Oxford, 1959)
Strickland, Matthew, *War and Chivalry: The Conduct and Perception of War in England and Normandy, 1066-1217* (Cambridge UP, 1996)
Thomas, Charles, *Tintagel: Arthur and Archaeology* (London, 1993)

Thompson, Guy Llewelyn, *Paris and its People under English Rule: The Anglo-Burgundian Regime 1420-1436* (Oxford, 1991)
White, Richard, ed., *King Arthur in Legend and History* (London, 1997)

Friends

Bliss, Arthur, *As I Remember* (London, 1970)
Brewer, A. Herbert, *Memories of Choirs and Cloisters* (London, 1931)
De Navarro, Mary Anderson, *A Few More Memories* (London, 1936)
Gaisberg, Frederick W., *Music on Record* (London, 1946)
Leicester, Hubert, *Forgotten Worcester* (Worcester, 1930)
Lucas, E.V., *The Colvins and their Friends* (London, 1928)
Sassoon, Siegfried, *Diaries 1920-1922* and *1923-1925* (London, 1981, 1985)
Speyer, Edward, *My Life and Friends* (London, 1937)
Stockley, William C., *Fifty Years of Music in Birmingham 1850-1900* (Birmingham, 1900)
Vandervelde, Lalla, *Monarchs and Millionaires* (London, 1925)
Williams, Dorothy E., *The Lygons of Madresfield Court* (Logaston, 2001)
Wood, Henry J., *My Life of Music* (London, 1946)

Literature

Bellasis, Edward, *Coram Cardinali* (London, 1916)
Binyon, Laurence, *Collected Poems*, two vols. (London, 1931)
—— *Arthur: a Tragedy* (London, 1923)
—— *The Madness of Merlin* (London, 1947)
Birch, Dinah, *Ruskin and the Dawn of the Modern* (Oxford, 1999)
Burd, Van Akin, ed., *The Ruskin Family Letters: Correspondence of John James Ruskin, his Wife, and their Son John, 1801-43* (Ithaca and London, 1973)
—— ed., *The Winnington Letters: John Ruskin's Correspondence with Margaret Alexis Bell and the Children at Winnington Hall* (London, 1969)
Brock, M.G. and Curthoys, M.C., eds., *The History of the University of Oxford* VI (Oxford, 1997)
Dearden, James S., *John Ruskin: a Life in Pictures* (Sheffield, 1999)
Dessain, Charles, Ker, Ian, Gornall Thomas and Tracey, Gerald, eds., *The Letters and Diaries of John Henry Newman*, thirty-one vols. (Oxford, 1963-2003)
Froissart, Sir John trans. Johnes, Thomas, *Chronicles* (London, 1939)
Hamilton, Ian, *A Gift Imprisoned: The Poetic Life of Matthew Arnold* (London, 1998)
Heffer, Simon, *Moral Desperado: A Life of Thomas Carlyle* (London, 1995)
Hewison, Robert, *Ruskin and Oxford: the Art of Education* (Oxford, 1996)
Holroyd, Michael, *Bernard Shaw*, five vols. (1988-92)
Holt, Tonie and Valmai, *My Boy Jack? : The Search for Kipling's Only Son* (Barnsley, 1998)
Laurence, Dan H., *Bernard Shaw: Collected Letters*, four vols. (London, 1965-88)
—— ed., *Shaw's Music*, three vols. (London, 1981)
Longfellow, Samuel, *Life of Henry Wadsworth Longfellow with Extracts from his Journals and Correspondence* (London, 1886)

Lycett, Andrew, *Rudyard Kipling* (London, 1999)
MacCarthy, Fiona, *William Morris* (London, 1994)
Monk, Raymond, ed., *Edward Elgar: Music and Literature* (Aldershot, 1993)
Monk, Raymond, ed., *Elgar Studies* (Aldershot, 1990)
Newman, J.H., *Essays Critical and Historical*, two vols. (London, 1871)
―――― *The Dream of Gerontius with facsimiles of fair copy and some rough drafts* (London, 1909)
Pottle, Mark, ed., *Champion Redoubtable: The Diaries and Letters of Violet Bonham Carter 1914-45* (London, 1998)
Roberts, John Stuart, *Siegfried Sassoon* (London, 1999)
Rosenberg, John D., *Carlyle and the Burden of History* (Oxford, 1985)
Rowse, A.L., *Matthew Arnold: Poet and Prophet* (London, 1976)
Shaw, Bernard, nine volumes from the Standard Edition (London, 1930-34)
―――― *What I really Wrote about the War* (London, 1930)
―――― *Pen Portraits and Reviews* (London, 1931)
Sutherland, John, *The Life of Walter Scott* (Oxford, 1995)
Ullman, S.O.A., ed., *The Yale Manuscript of Matthew Arnold* (Michigan UP, 1989)
Vickers, Brian, ed., *Shakespeare: the Critical Heritage*, six vols, (London, 1971-81)
Wilson, Jean Moorcroft, *Siegfried Sassoon: The Making of a War Poet: A Biography 1886-1918* (London, 1998)

Warfare

Bishop, Alan and Bostridge, Mark, eds., *Letters from a Lost Generation: First World War Letters of Vera Brittain and Four Friends* (London, 1998)
Brown, Malcolm, *The Imperial War Museum Book of the Somme* (London, 1996)
―――― *The Imperial War Museum Book of 1918: Year of Victory* (London, 1998)
Churchill, W.S., *The Boer War* (London, 1900)
―――― *The World Crisis*, five vols. (London, 1923-31)
Davison, Claudia, *The Burgoyne Diaries* (London, 1985)
Doyle, Arthur Conan, *The Great Boer War* (London, 1901)
Gordon, Andrew, *The Rules of the Game: Jutland and British Naval Command* (London, 1996)
Keegan, John, *The First World War* (London, 1998)
Kochanski, Halik, *Sir Garnet Wolseley: Victorian Hero* (London, 1999)
Moorehead, Alan, *Gallipoli* (London, 1956)
Macdonald, Lyn, *To the Last Man: Spring 1918* (London, 1998)
Pakenham, Thomas, *The Boer War* (London, 1979)
Pollock, John, *Gordon: The Man* (London, 19**)
―――― *Kitchener: The Road to Omdurman* (London, 1998)
Shermer, David, *World War I* (London, 1975)
Sibbald, Raymond, ed, *The War Correspondents: The Boer War* (Stroud, 1993)
Simkins, Peter, *Chronicles of the Great War: The Western Front 1914-1918* (Godalming,1997)
Strachan, Hew, ed, *The Oxford Illustrated History of the First World War* (Oxford UP, 1998)

Index

References to photographs are shown in *italics* following references to text entries. All musical and literary works are listed under the name of their composer or author, and buildings are listed under the town or city in which they are located.

The Elgar Society was formed in 1951 with the objective of promoting interest in the composer and his music. With a number of significant achievements to its credit, the Society is now the largest UK-based composer appreciation society with ten regional branches in Britain and about 10% of its membership resident outside the UK. In 1997 the Society launched its own Internet website (http://www.elgar.org) with the aim of spreading knowledge of Elgar around the world and, in the process, attracting a greater international membership. This was followed in 1999 by Elgar Enterprises, the trading arm of the Society, whose purpose is to raise funds for the Society's charitable projects through the publication and sale of books, CDs, CD-ROMs and other material about the composer and his music, and in October 2001 by the launch of the Elgar Society Edition, a scheme to continue the uniform edition of all the composer's music.

All enquiries about membership should be addressed to :

David Morris, 2 Marriotts Close, Haddenham, Aylesbury,
Bucks, England HP17 8BT
telephone : +44 1844 299239; fax : +44 870 734 6772
e-mail : membership@elgar.org

On-line and postal membership application forms
can be found on the website at:

'http://www.elgar.org/5memform.htm'

The Elgar Foundation was established in 1973. Its objectives include supporting the Elgar Birthplace, the cottage in which Elgar was born in Lower Broadheath, some three miles west of the city of Worcester. The Birthplace now houses a collection of memorabilia associated with the composer, while the adjacent Elgar Centre provides an introduction to the composer's life and music and a meeting place for Elgarian events. They are open to the public daily throughout most of the year.

To check opening times or for further information:
telephone +44 1905 333224; fax +44 1905 333426;
e-mail: birthplace@elgar.org